MONICA ATTARD

RUSSIA

WHICH WAY PARADISE?

To Dad and Paul

MONICA ATTARD

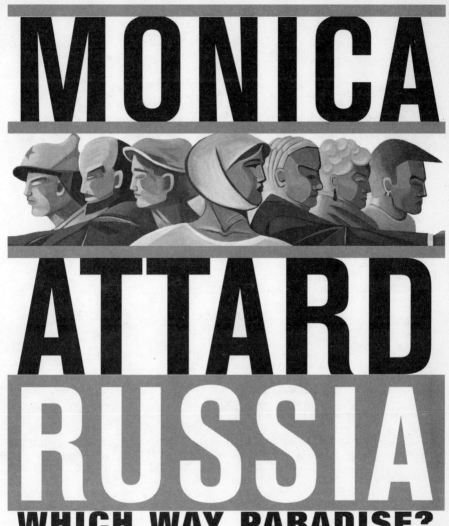

RUSSIA

WHICH WAY PARADISE?

DOUBLEDAY
SYDNEY • AUCKLAND • TORONTO • NEW YORK • LONDON

RUSSIA: WHICH WAY PARADISE?
AN ANCHOR BOOK

First published in hardback in Australia and New Zealand
in 1997 by Doubleday.
First published in paperback in Australia and New Zealand in 1998 by
Anchor.

National Library of Australia.
Cataloguing-in-Publication Entry
Attard, Monica.
  Russia: which way paradise?

  Bibliography,
  Includes index.
  ISBN 0 86824742 1.

  1. Russia (Federation) – Social conditions – 1991– .
  2. Russia (Federation) – History – 1991– . 3. Russia
  (Federation) – Politics and government – 1991– . 4. Soviet
  Union – Politics and government – 1985–1991. 5. Soviet
  Union – History – 1985–1991. I. Title.

947.086

Anchor books are published by

Transworld Publishers (Aust) Pty Limited
15–25 Helles Ave, Moorebank, NSW 2170

Transworld Publishers (NZ) Limited
3 William Pickering Drive, Albany, Auckland

Transworld Publishers (UK) Limited
61–63 Uxbridge Road, Ealing, London W5 5SA

Bantam Doubleday Dell Publishing Group Inc
1540 Broadway, New York, New York 10036

Edited by Amanda O'Connell
Cover design by Liz Nicholson–Design Bite
Cover illustration by Nick Stewart–Design Bite
Text design by Liz Nicholson–Design Bite
Typeset in 11.5pt Weiss by Midland Typesetters
Printed by McPherson's Printing Group

10 9 8 7 6 5 4 3 2 1

Talking about Russia one always imagines that one is talking about a country like the others; in reality this is not so at all. Russia is a whole separate world, submissive to the will, caprice, fantasy of a single man, whether his name be Peter or Ivan, no matter—in all instances the common element is the embodiment of arbitrariness. Contrary to all the laws of the human community, Russia moves only in the direction of her own enslavement and the enslavement of all the neighbouring peoples. For this reason it would be in the interest not only of other peoples but also in that of her own that she be compelled to take a new path.

PETER CHAADAEV, RUSSIAN PHILOSOPHER, 1836

CONTENTS

ACKNOWLEDGMENTS

There are many people without whom this book might not and could not have been written. Natasha Yakovleva, and Masha and Rob Stubblebine were among my closest friends and teachers. Max showed me Moscow's underbelly, the part of it which might otherwise have been hidden from me as a foreigner, and what it was to live like an average Russian. Zhenya, who couldn't cope with life in the new Russia and who died in 1996, always placed a human perspective on otherwise brutal situations. Sasha, my KGB friend, added doses of Soviet reality. Lena Nestegina and Irina Stelliferovskaya provided me with instant translations—literal and otherwise—of everything that happened in Russia's turbulent political life between 1992 and 1994. They all, in different ways, taught me a lot.

Many correspondents who served in Moscow during the dying days of the Soviet empire have expressed the sentiment that we were truly lucky. We were. We were able to speak with the players, often with those just a few steps away from Gorbachev and Yeltsin. I was especially lucky as I had access to Nikolai Shishlin, an *apparatchik*-turned-reformer who was a member of the outer layer of Gorbachev's perestroika circle. Throughout the years of turmoil, he was completely unselfish with his time and ever willing to explain the inner workings of the men who were attempting to change life in the former Soviet Union. Others too, like Georgi Shakhnazarov, gave me their time, as did Boris Kagarlitsky, Yevgeny Kisilev, Oleg Kalugin, Sasha Lubimov, Andrannik Migranyan, Sergei Stankevich, Galina Staravoitova and Alexander Pumpyanski. There are many more, too many to thank here, for their insight and their willingness to surrender their time to speak to me.

I am grateful, too, to fellow correspondents whose journalism and books on the Soviet implosion are impossible to emulate. Jonathan Steele and David Remnick are but two of them. I have acknowledged their work extensively throughout my Notes on Sources, along with the work of others that has contributed to mine and is evident in it.

Professor Graham Gill, of Sydney University, was extremely generous with his time, both during the writing of the book and as he read the completed manuscript for factual accuracy. I thank him for this. And Kirill Nourzhanov, a research scholar at the Australian National University, a close friend and one of my husband's oldest mates, often selflessly put aside his own work to search for facts and material for me. Without Kirill's superb research skills and fine academic mind, I might well have floundered.

Special thanks also to the former publisher of Transworld, Judith Curr, its current publisher, Shona Martin, and commissioning editor, Fiona Henderson, all of whom have been encouraging and unbelievably patient. They were wise, too, in their choice of editor for in Amanda O'Connell I found someone whose empathy with the plight of the Russians and grip on the material added immeasurably to this book.

And, of course, there's the ABC, which posted me to Moscow to begin with. Thanks to the producers of radio current affairs which daily broadcasts 'AM', 'The World Today' and 'PM', and to the former managing director of the corporation, David Hill, for making the decision to open the Moscow Bureau in 1988.

Special thanks also to my family—my mother, my sister, Vivienne—for their patience and support while I was posted to Moscow and when I was writing this book. It wasn't easy for them to accept that I wanted to be so far from home. To Rebecca for ploughing through the early parts of the manuscript and making helpful suggestions. To Matthew for his endless cynicism and wit. To Stefie for her enthusiasm.

When my husband Grisha entered my life late in 1992, a whole new dimension opened in my understanding of Russia. He, of course, deserves special thanks not only for the long hours he spent explaining all things Russian to me and the hours he spent reading the manuscript, but for the incredible and unstinting encouragement and love he showered me with during the writing process and beyond. He is truly my best mate.

NOTE ON RUSSIAN NAMES

Russians have a first name, a patronymic and a family name. The patronymic is generally the father's first name. So Boris Nikolaevich Yeltsin is Boris, son of Nikolai Yeltsin. Maria Vladimirovna Korotich is Maria, daughter of Vladimir Korotich.

Formally, Boris Yeltsin would be referred to as Boris Nikolaevich and Maria Korotich as Maria Vladimirovna. Informally, most Russian names have a diminutive form used by family and close friends. So Mikhail would be Misha, Grigori would be Grisha, Tatyana would be Tanya, Natalia would be Natasha.

Throughout this book, when I have referred to people in official positions of authority, I have tried to use the rough English equivalent of their names without the patronymic. Sometimes, in direct speech, I have retained the patronymic as Russians would. My friends are mostly referred to by their diminutive names.

CHRONOLOGY

1917

In the face of mass discontent, Tsar Nicholas II abdicates and a Provisional Government is established. Effective power, however, lies with the Petrograd Soviet created by St Petersburg's workers and supported by the city's garrison.

Following the decision of the Provisional Government to close down Bolshevik newspapers, the Military Revolutionary Committee established by the Petrograd Soviet orders its troops to occupy strategic installations. Vladimir Ilych Lenin emerges from hiding and the Provisional Government is arrested.

On 25 October Lenin proclaims that power has passed from the Provisional Government to the Soviets.

1918

A civil war between the Bolsheviks (the Reds) and the anti-Bolsheviks (the Whites) begins, ending only in 1920.

1921

Lenin introduces the New Economic Policy (NEP).

1922

Joseph Stalin is elected General Secretary of the Communist Party and several months later the Union of Soviet Socialist Republics is formed.

1924
Vladimir Lenin dies after a long struggle with a neurological disease.

1928
Stalin becomes the nation's leader and establishes the first Five Year Plan.

Agricultural holdings begin to be collectivised under a decree of the Fifteenth Party Congress.

1939
The Molotov–Ribbentrop Pact is signed which includes a secret protocol allowing the violent annexation by the Soviet Union of the three Baltic states—Estonia, Latvia and Lithuania.

1941
Germany invades the Soviet Union, beginning the Great Patriotic War.

1945
Germany surrenders unconditionally.

1953
Joseph Stalin dies. Nikita Khrushchev becomes First Secretary of the Communist Party.

1956
Khrushchev delivers a 'secret speech' to the Twentieth Party Congress in which he details the extent of Stalin's genocide and condemns the Cult of Personality.

Hungary is invaded by Soviet troops.

1961
Khrushchev announces a Twenty Year Plan, during which time communism will be achieved.

1964

Khrushchev is dismissed as First Secretary and Leonid Brezhnev is appointed.

1968

Soviet troops invade Czechoslovakia.

1970

Alexander Solzhenitsyn, the exiled author, wins the Nobel Prize for Literature.

1971

Mikhail Gorbachev becomes a member of the Central Committee of the Communist Party.

1975

Andrei Sakharov, the dissident scientist, is awarded the Nobel Peace Prize.

1979

Gorbachev is elected a candidate member of the Politburo (the decision-making body of the communist party).

A month later, Soviet troops invade Afghanistan.

1980

Gorbachev becomes a full member of the Politburo.

1982

Brezhnev dies and Yuri Andropov is elected General Secretary of the Communist Party.

1984

Andropov dies and Konstantin Chernenko is elected General Secretary of the Communist Party.

1985

Chernenko dies and Mikhail Gorbachev is elected General Secretary of the Communist Party.

Boris Yeltsin is appointed to the Central Committee secretariat and succeeds a Soviet hardliner as first secretary of the Moscow city party committee.

1986

Gorbachev calls for radical economic and social reform. He introduces *perestroika* (economic restructuring) and *glasnost* (openness) aimed at reviving the economy and society.

There is an explosion at the Chernobyl Nuclear Reactor in Ukraine.

Gorbachev announces that Soviet troops will be withdrawn from Afghanistan.

Andrei Sakharov and his wife Yelena Bonner are returned from exile in Gorky to Moscow.

1987

Gorbachev agrees with President Ronald Reagan of the United States to a reduction in offensive arms.

State enterprises are given more freedom, private co-operatives are expanded and the elimination of intermediate-range nuclear missiles is acheived.

Yeltsin criticises the slow pace of reform and singles out hardliners as obstructing the reform processes. He is removed from the Politburo and replaced as Moscow party boss.

1988

President Reagan visits Moscow.

Gorbachev announces a new parliament to be called the Congress of People's Deputies.

Gorbachev announces the withdrawal of a large proportion of Soviet troops from Eastern Europe.

Latvia demands sovereignty.

1989

The Baltic nationalist movement begins in earnest.

Boris Yeltsin wins a seat in the Congress of People's Deputies.

Gorbachev's visit to Beijing triggers the Tiananmen Square democracy protests.

Poland elects Solidarity to government and the communist regimes fall in Hungary, Czechoslovakia and Romania. In East Germany, Erich Honecker is replaced as head of state and flees to Moscow.

At its second sitting, the Congress refuses to discuss the repeal of Article Six of the Soviet Constitution under which the Communist Party is guaranteed power to rule.

The Communist Party admits the secret protocols of the 1939 Molotov–Ribbentrop pact.

Andrei Sakharov dies.

1990

Lithuanians elect a pro-independence parliament and begin protesting for independence.

In Moscow mass protests call for the abandonment of Article Six. A few days later, the Communist Party agrees to repeal it.

The Congress votes to create a 'strong presidency' to replace the previous head of state. Gorbachev becomes President of the Soviet Union.

Local elections are held throughout the USSR and democratic candidates are overwhelmingly successful.

The traditional May Day Parade turns into a protest against Gorbachev and the Communist Party.

Boris Yeltsin is elected to the Russian Supreme Soviet and becomes its chairman. Under his chairmanship the parliament declares Russian laws take precedence over Soviet laws.

Yeltsin resigns from the Communist Party.

A 500-Day Plan to Move to a Market Economy is adopted by the Russian parliament but rejected by Gorbachev. Private trading, however, has become the norm.

Ukraine declares sovereignty but remains within the Soviet fold.

Gorbachev is awarded the Nobel Peace Prize. Thousands of people gather outside KGB headquarters to commemorate the victims of totalitarianism.

Eduard Shevardnadze, the Soviet Foreign Minister, resigns citing an imminent dictatorship as his reason.

1991
Gorbachev removes the remaining reformers from cabinet and appoints hardliners.

In January Soviet forces attempt to seize Vilnius, the Lithuanian capital. Gorbachev is suspected of knowing of the assault in advance. He proposes the temporary suspension of media freedom but backs down. Yeltsin calls for his resignation.

Gorbachev holds a referendum on the future of the USSR. A majority vote to retain the Union and hold elections for a new position of Russian president.

Gorbachev declares a ban on all protests in Moscow. The ban is defied by pro-Yeltsin supporters.

In June, the first democratic election for a Russian president is won by Boris Yeltsin who receives 57 per cent of the vote. The nationalist Vladimir Zhirinovsky receives 8 per cent.

Yeltsin issues a decree banning the Communist Party from all state organisations on Russian soil.

Gorbachev announces that the leaders of ten republics have agreed on a new Union treaty.

In August, an Emergency Committee is formed under the KGB chief and attempts to oust Gorbachev, who is holidaying in the Crimea. It is defeated by its own incompetence and staunch resistance mounted by Boris Yeltsin. Gorbachev returns to Moscow where he attempts to reassert his authority.

The Soviet republics one by one declare independence and Boris Yeltsin bans the Communist Party on Russian territory, though this decree is later reversed by the Russian Constitutional Court.

Gorbachev resigns as General Secretary of the Communist Party and disbands the Central Committee. The Supreme Soviet votes to ban the activities of the Communist Party.

Gorbachev forms a State Council as he plans a new confederation of republics. The State Council recognises the independence of the Baltic states.

Leningrad renames itself St Petersburg.

The leaders of seven former Soviet republics agree to a new treaty but refuse to sign it.

Ukraine declares independence. The leaders of Ukraine, Russia and Belorussia meet to form a Commonwealth of Independent States (CIS) which they invite the other Soviet republics to join.

Gorbachev protests against the formation of the CIS. He meets military leaders and asks for their support. The next day Yeltsin promises the military corps a 90 per cent pay rise.

The Russian parliament ratifies the CIS and seizes control of the Kremlin, the Foreign and Interior Ministries and the KGB.

On Christmas Day, Gorbachev resigns as President of the USSR and disolves the Union. The Soviet flag is lowered for the last time.

The KGB on Russian territory becomes the Federal Security Bureau (FSB).

1992
The Russian government unleashes economic shock therapy on the country. Price liberalisation is the first step. Inflation skyrockets.

A split emerges in the parliament over the nature and pace of reform. Protests against the reforms begin.

The process of privatisation begins with the distribution of 10 000 rouble vouchers to all citizens, in order to give them a stake in the new capitalist economy. People become angry as the process is corrupted by Soviet-era *nomenklatura*.

After a prolonged battle with the parliament, Yeltsin is forced to sack the architect of economic reform, Yigor Gaidar, who is replaced as prime minister by Victor Chernomyrdin.

Mass demonstrations throughout Russia call for the resurrection of the Soviet Union.

The Constitutional Court hearing into Boris Yeltsin's banning of the Soviet Communist Party begins. Later in the year the court upholds the ban on the party's top organs but allows it to regroup at a local level.

Yeltsin issues a decree resuming the premises allocated to Gorbachev for his Gorbachev Foundation.

Crime rates soar throughout Russia as mafia clans battle for the wealth released by privatisation and the unemployed turn to petty crime.

1993

Yeltsin announces his intention to rule by special decree. A vote of no confidence against the Russian president fails.

A referendum on the economic reforms is held and a slim majority of Russians vote to continue with them. A new constitution giving the president almost dictatorial powers is proposed.

The government announces the withdrawal of all Soviet bank-notes and its unpopularity grows.

Yigor Gaidar is returned to government.

Parliament refuses to pass the government's budget. Yeltsin dissolves parliament. A stand-off between pro and anti-Yeltsin forces unfolds in violence and the president turns his tanks on his opponents. More than 150 people die.

Elections to the Russian parliament are held and the democrats fail to achieve the level of support they had hoped for. Instead, the nationalist, Vladimir Zhirinovsky, rises to prominence.

1994

Economic reforms continue but are largely unsuccessful. Most Russians believe the privatisation process has been corrupted. The mafia consolidates its wealth and power.

Boris Yeltsin is rumoured to be seriously ill. The 'Party of War', made up of men trusted by the president, launches a military offensive against the Russian province of Chechnya which had three years earlier declared independence.

1995

The war in Chechnya is not won in three days as promised by the Russian Defence Minister. It continues.

Elections to the Russian parliament, now renamed the Duma, are held and the Russian Communist Party is successful.

1996

The second democratic election for the Russian presidency is held and Boris Yeltsin is forced into a second round of voting. With the help of a popular general, Alexander Lebed, he succeeds. He rules for ten days before being hospitalised for a heart bypass operation.

As head of the Russian Security Council, Lebed negotiates an end to the Chechen war. In practice, fighting continues.

1997

After months out of office recuperating from his heart bypass operation, Boris Yeltsin is hospitalised for acute pneumonia. His leadership seems precarious.

Yeltsin's entourage attempts to find ways to alter the constitution so that in the event of the president's death, he can be replaced by the prime minister without the need for an election.

Yeltsin returns to the Kremlin and reasserts his authority by sacking much of the cabinet and reappointing Anatoly Chubais, responsible for the privatisation process widely criticised for its inequality. Also appointed to cabinet is Boris Nemstov, the president's Governor in Nizhni Novgorod. Boris Yeltsin annoints Nemstov as his successor.

INTRODUCTION

When my parents were young and living in Malta, their homeland, the world was dominated by tyrants. My father was fascinated by Benito Mussolini, Adolf Hitler and Joseph Stalin. Many years later, and half a world away in Australia, it wasn't the slightest bit unusual for my family's breakfast conversation to be overtaken by them— their thirst for power, the way they manipulated it, the dangers of its unfettered accumulation combined with fanaticism and popular support, the gross and unseemly manner in which the world's workers had been duped into following men who promised a better way of life. The workers, my father would say to me when I was child, have been historically the scapegoats for tyrants who adopt political philosophies as a cloak for their personal ambition.

Needless to say it made little sense to me then. I had no personal experience of dictatorship. I'd stare blankly at him as he pondered out loud the maniacal deviations of Hitler's mind. But over the years, listening to him, I learnt about the appalling misery created by the three autocrats who had changed the face of the world before my birth. And when I was old enough to understand these things, I thought my father must be right.

'But capitalism is no better than the dictatorships of Hitler or Stalin!' he would tell me. 'Money is the root of all evil. It's a means of suppressing the working class. That's us.' Humanity, he believed, had been left with very few choices. But of the political systems which had led to genocide this century, he would say communism was the one which at least held out some hope of a better future for the working class. With Stalin gone, he thought there was every chance the Soviet communists could put things right.

When, in 1983, I first decided to see communism in action for myself, I was expecting the Soviet Union to be a workers' paradise. It's not that I hadn't heard about the repression, the food shortages, the KGB, corruption, laziness, collective irresponsibility. But this I put down to western propaganda. I went to the USSR thinking that the communists were right and we were wrong.

But it was no paradise. Old *babushkas* chipped away at the packed ice on the streets while others sat at the tills in the state bread shops as shoppers screamed their frustrations at them. The shops were mostly bare. Once I managed to buy some *pelmeni* (Russian dumplings) but they were inedible. I thought myself lucky to have been able to venture into a shop at all, because I was told that as a tourist I could go nowhere without an Intourist guide provided by the state. Only once did I venture away from the tourist beat, and then only to be escorted back to the hotel by the *militsiya*.

Still I thought the place was fantastic. Grand and mystical. The soldiers on duty at the door of Lenin's Mausoleum refused to crack a smile even when I could see they wanted to laugh. Fat *militsiya* sat in their cars watching black marketeers ply watches and caviar to tourists. Restaurants offered menus even though nothing on them was available. Moscow even smelled different. Nothing was familiar. The country was like a clock working anti-clockwise. And I understood absolutely nothing. But I was sure—in the pit of my belly— I'd end up spending a lot of time there. I still believed the Russians were somehow right.

It was lucky for me, even on this first foray into the communist netherworld, that a friend in Paris had given me a phone number for a woman she said would explain the place. Natasha Yakovleva, she said, was a communist but an honest one who understood all that was wrong with her country. I rang the number I was given and met Natasha in a subway.

She was then in her mid-thirties. Slight and agile, Natasha had classic Russian beauty. Born on the Volga, she had huge eyes, high cheekbones and flawless skin. She was a graduate of the Russian Film School and, since her early twenties, a member of the Soviet Communist Party for which she was an organiser collecting dues in the village just outside Moscow where she lived. She'd met lots of foreigners and was used to our ways and so, unlike most Russians I came across on my first visit, she wasn't judgmental about how different I looked, ignoring my clothes, my haircut, my earrings—all of which seemed to attract undue attention on the streets of Moscow. Natasha unashamedly accepted me. And we got on like the proverbial house on fire, scheming, even on that first trip, about how I might organise to live in Moscow for a while. It had to be possible. There were media correspondents based in the Russian capital, ploughing through *Pravda* every day for clues about what was going on in the Kremlin. I was still at university, working as a casual journalist in the ABC radio newsroom, a long way off being considered for a posting. Indeed, the ABC was a long way off opening a Moscow Bureau. But perhaps I could push the point!

I didn't need to. In 1985 Mikhail Sergeyevich Gorbachev was elected the General Secretary of the Soviet Communist Party and began to change the world. The Soviet Union was creaking open. For the first time since the 1917 Bolshevik revolution, the west had a chance to observe the Russians and the people of the fourteen other republics which made up the USSR. They could listen in as Gorbachev told his people they'd been lied to for a long time, that they lived in a society which was far from democratic and a long way from functioning as a productive economy.

New Soviet films—along with some old ones which had been banned by the censors—were being shown around the world. In 1987 every film shown at the Soviet Film Festival in Sydney—which I attended from beginning to end—utterly condemned the exploitation of workers in the workers' paradise. I was genuinely shocked. How could the Russians themselves believe all that western rubbish about the Communist Party? I'd been travelling to Moscow regularly since my first trip in 1983, and it was obvious to me that the system needed a bit of fixing. But beyond that, I believed that the Communist Party was on the right track, that socialism was the only way forward for the Soviet Union, that the Soviet Union would always *be*. Natasha agreed.

But a year later, in 1986, I began to change my mind. It was December, I was in Moscow and it was cold. Natasha and I had met at one of the subway entrances in the centre of the city and walked the streets for more than an hour searching for a cafe. None were open. I suggested we go back to the Cosmos Hotel where I was staying and where there always seemed to be a plentiful supply of coffee and food for dollar-fisted western tourists. In the front lobby of the hotel, a KGB officer stopped Natasha, demanding her internal passport. After he glanced through it, he turned her away, literally throwing her documents back at her. I argued that his behaviour went against the spirit of *glasnost*. The Russians were now free I said, waving my finger before his face; Natasha could go wherever she wanted. The officer was unmoved. Natasha wasn't going to be allowed inside.

Leaving Moscow a few weeks later, I was stopped by passport control at the airport—for no apparent reason—and thoroughly searched. So thoroughly, I missed my flight home. At the time, I thought the two incidents must be linked. The KGB officer at the hotel must have reported me to his comrades at the airport. Only years later did I realise that the system was too inefficient by the mid-1980s for anything of the sort to have taken place. In any event, rather than turn me off the place for good, the experience only served to heighten my fascination with the country.

It was the one place in the world which defied my reasoning. It didn't work the way I thought it should. People were treated like a herd of cattle, pushed and prodded then penned up without any degree of personal freedom. Yet they could still speak well of communism. Their fate, Natasha would tell me, was not to work to pay bills. It was to continue the battle for a new society—the one Lenin promised. That it was a long way from realisation and that those leading the people to it were corrupt hypocrites made the task all the more critical to her.

More determined than ever that I would one day be in a position to understand what made the place tick, I returned to Australia and started seriously studying Russian. Until then, I'd managed only to master the alphabet and a few words which I could string together in badly structured sentences.

By 1987, Gorbachev's reforms were going mad. Groups of young people hauled their musical equipment out of the basements and onto street corners where they sent the old *babushkas* crazy. A small degree of private trading became legal. Democratic movements were sprouting all over the country—from eastern Siberia to western Ukraine. People condemned the party openly but were still afraid of it even though Gorbachev promised there was nothing to fear and Soviet communism was looking very shaky. And it became clear to the ABC that the time had come. In 1988, it opened a bureau in the Russian capital.

I was disappointed when I didn't get the first correspondent's job in Moscow. It didn't seem fair to me. By then I'd come on board as a full-time ABC employee, working in radio current affairs for 'AM',

'The World Today' and 'PM', and I knew Moscow reasonably well having travelled there several times over the years. I was learning Russian and had even written a few papers on the social changes I'd witnessed on my visits. In my own head, I was eminently well equipped for the job. But I'd have to wait until 1990 when I was thirty and the tide of change began swamping the Soviet Union. When the ABC created a second position, I won it relatively easily. My mother blamed my father for the obsession which was taking me so far away from home and family.

It was an extraordinary time to be in the Soviet Union, 1990–1994. I witnessed Gorbachev's final year of power. His moves to the left, then the right in a crazed attempt to save the reforms, the party and his own position. Then the coup of August 1991 when the reactionaries of the party struck back, deeply insecure about where the economic and social reforms were heading. And as if this wasn't enough, the Communist Party would then collapse and leave Russia to Boris Yeltsin and capitalism. I had a front row seat at one of the most dramatic pieces of real-life theatre this century.

We were privileged journalists, those of us who covered the collapse of what was one of the mightiest empires the world has ever known. We could talk freely to average people and politicians about the Soviet earthquake which was changing the world. Some were so immersed in the pathos of the story that it hurt. Others preferred the sanctity of their foreign compounds. They didn't think it was possible to report objectively if they were too involved with the Russians. I couldn't have agreed less and after a few months I decided that if objectivity required reporting strictly from media conferences and the wire services, then it was time to jump ship. I wanted to report the changes the Russians were experiencing through *their* eyes. That meant I'd have to improve the schoolgirl Russian I'd learnt in Australia and learn to speak the way the Russians spoke. I'd also have to accept that I'd be ostracised by the ex-pat social club which held insular moveable feasts every weekend during which the regular topics of discussion would include how much the office driver was being paid and what the maid had cooked for lunch the day before. It wasn't such a huge sacrifice. In any event, the decision to move into the Russian community was the best I could have made. By the time I left Russia, I could communicate freely and I felt I understood the Russians, even if some of them might disagree.

I don't remember a day when I didn't wake and thank God I was alive. I had the best job in the world, reporting the biggest story in the world back to my own people. And they weren't dispassionate observers of a decaying system. Australians were intensely interested in Russia. At times, their appetite for all things Russian was insatiable. Almost hourly news reports and extended stories on 'AM', 'The World Today' and 'PM' didn't seem enough for them. People often wrote to me in Moscow, sending their letters via the ABC or the Australian embassy. Sometimes mail arrived through Australians who were visiting. And they would ask all sorts of questions. People wanted to know how the Russians felt about the changes which were turning their lives inside out, whether I'd ever spoken to Gorbachev, why the Russians didn't like him, whether they wanted capitalism, could capitalism work, was communism perhaps not a better way to go, how did the average worker manage to eat during the food shortages. They wanted to know about my friends who I sometimes mentioned in my dispatches—Natasha, Masha, Sasha (not his real name) and, in the last two years, about Grisha, my husband, whom I met, ironically, through some Australian friends in 1992 and married in Moscow in 1993.

Often I felt that the people who listened to our programs on ABC Radio felt they were part of the upheaval which made the lives of my friends so difficult, so exciting. All contact our listeners made with me seemed to indicate that they could understand what it was like to live in a sprawling metropolis of 11 million people. What they didn't understand because it was not their experience was that the inhabitants of this exotic city had been bred to feel fear instinctively. They were enemies in their own country with a KGB still looking for anyone who might disagree with the party, while at the same time a sort of deep-rooted anarchy reigned. What wasn't easy to take in was that even though there seemed to be consensus that the old system was evil, most agreed that communism was as bad as it was good. Many didn't want to travel the road to communism anymore. But they didn't want to be thrown into the unknown either.

Natasha told me when I arrived to take up my posting that I'd be shocked. The place had changed, she said. People didn't care about each other as they had in the dark years when they were all in the same boat. And the official line was that the west wasn't to be feared. Russia had turned into a bizarre version of a mad hatter's tea party. It was a political wonderland where everyone thought the bad days were over. But no-one was really sure. And, in any event, there was an even bigger question to be answered—whether anyone wanted them to be!

All that was certain was that the fairytale on which Lenin's children—among them Natasha—had been weaned had turned itself inside out. The workers' paradise was anything but. Out of communist conformity and the ever-present fear of the state emerged a nation which was now being told to embrace capitalism in order to remake itself as a copy of the west where, the workers were told, people without exception lived well. The anti-communists figured that under capitalism the place might begin to function as a normal civil society—despite the past.

'It won't be that easy,' said Natasha. And it wasn't. Stalinism had bequeathed the people some appalling characteristics—chief among them a fatalistic torpor and disinclination to take or accept any responsibility for most aspects of daily living. And recognition of these faults seemed only to make the less able in Soviet society love their chains even more—for the security they offered. By 1995, ten years after Gorbachev's experiment with his people began, the more able—the party thieves and the black marketeers the communist

economy had created—had declared themselves and made off with
the booty, leaving behind a sad shell of a Tolstoy epic. Only the
ending remains unwritten.

When I first contemplated writing a book, I wanted to avoid anything based strictly on my experiences as a correspondent in
Moscow. I wanted to portray and explain the lives of the Russians
I'd met and come to treasure as friends. Yet it was inevitable that
my experiences as a journalist would form the background of any
book I would write on the years of change—after all had I not been
a Moscow correspondent I might not have met so many of the
people whose experiences inspired me to write. And, of course, I
wouldn't have had access to the political and community leaders
whose thoughts and actions could profoundly affect ordinary Russians' lives. In so far as it's possible, I have attempted to write about
those ordinary people, about *their* reactions to what many western
scholars now call the second Russian revolution.

The book is written in three broad sections. In the first I deal
with aspects of Soviet life before the collapse of the Communist
Party—corruption, a Soviet version of communal welfare known as
'*blat*', Lenin, the party and the politics of dissent. In the second I
recount the details of the period of change—1989 to 1991—when
the Soviet Union finally collapsed. Part 3 looks at the new Russia,
independent, free of the shackles of communism, boldly capitalist.
The story is complex, the people complicated. There are many
threads in the story of the demise of the Soviet empire and the
disillusionment the Russians still face. I hope this book unravels some
of them.

THE SOVIET UNION

PART ONE

CHAPTER 1

AN EMPIRE CRUMBLING

It is a sower of crosses in graveyards ... it is an exploitation of human beings by all forms of oppression and ecological vandalism. It is a paradox unknown in history—the creation of riches in the name of poverty ...

Bolshevism's ideological monopolism guaranteed universal control of everything and everyone. Minds and hearts were in the same category as things. Society was politicised ... those who disagreed were destroyed or isolated.

ALEXANDER YAKOVLEV, *THE FATE OF MARXISM IN RUSSIA*, 1993

By the time I arrived in Moscow in 1990 to take up my posting as the ABC's radio correspondent, open anarchy had taken hold of the place and it was clear that if communism was going to survive in the Soviet Union, it would take a miracle.

Mikhail Gorbachev could try as hard as was humanly possible, but it would be an enormous task to breathe life into a system which had proven itself to be corrupt, inept and unworthy of loyalty. Sure, the communists had provided the Soviet people with cradle to grave certainty. And they'd built an urbanised, industrialised superpower which had the United States quivering throughout the Cold War.

But long before 1985 when Gorbachev was elected General Secretary of the Soviet Communist Party, it was clear the nirvana on earth promised by Lenin had fled to another planet. The communist experiment was clearly staggering to its death. Marxist–Leninist ideology was dying for lack of affirmation.

And the evidence was everywhere. The people were angry. Fear of the party—the Communist Party of the Soviet Union (CPSU)—was waning. 'Biznez' was the buzz word. Most people I knew had reduced their thoughts on the party to jokes. The *anekdot*, long before Gorbachev came along, had kept people sane and laughing at the system as though they were somehow living outside it. They sent up every aspect of it—the shortages, the lack of choice, the corruption, the farce of elections for leaders who rarely changed and were always clearly communists. Just a few years after Gorbachev was elected General Secretary of the party, people were sitting in poorly stocked restaurants and on rickety old buses, telling their party jokes openly. They wouldn't have dared five years earlier.

My friend Natasha, a committed though clear-eyed communist, was on the metro one day, on her way to Moscow, when the young man sitting next to her burst into laughter. She glanced towards him.

'Hey, listen to this!' he said, demanding her attention with his elbow as he read from one of the dozens of independent newspapers which had blossomed since 1985.

'An Azerbaijani fruit seller is standing on Red Square trying to sell his one watermelon. Leonid Brezhnev is strolling to his office in the Kremlin. He stops and offers to buy it.

"Which one do you want?" says the seller.

"What do you mean," says Brezhnev, "You have only one."

"There's only one Brezhnev," replies the seller, "but we still go to the polls to choose you!"' Natasha was still a card-carrying member of the party. She still believed the communists were right and that all the country needed was Gorbachev to tinker with the system a little. Tweak it back to some sort of morality. As the young man next to her chuckled, Natasha smiled and looked away. She was amused. Sort of. But Natasha was in the minority—people who knew the system was evil even though they believed the dogma was correct.

The political system—its roots firmly planted in lies, terror and moral poverty—was utterly incapable of winning the loyalty of the middle-aged and their children who had experienced only its darker side. Gorbachev was for the Soviet people a breath of fresh air. He was prepared to admit that there were problems, prepared to force change upon the party so that the way people lived would improve. When he was elected General Secretary, he said to his wife Raisa, *'Tak j'itz n'ilzbya!'* ['We can't live like this!'] and he was right. But in order to change people's lives, the old certainties would have to be sacrificed. And for all their faults, the communists had provided certainty.

People knew they couldn't speak freely. They knew they couldn't leave the country and that generally they couldn't rise above their given station in life. But they had been assured of jobs and income, of subsidised food without inflation, of holiday homes provided by their workplace and ultimately a small plot of land to dig and sow and call their own.

They could, for a small gift to the right person, be treated in polyclinics and hospitals even if they were run-down and staffed by people who no longer cared. They could send their children to child-care centres for an insignificant bribe, then on to school and university. And even though every demand they made of the state was likely to cost them a bribe of some sort, it all took place within a well-oiled, highly refined system with which they were familiar. That the state thought the production of weapons had priority over new housing and better schools could be reasoned away by the security of knowing that from the cradle to the grave, they would never go hungry.

So in the hope of keeping what was good about the place and reforming what was bad, Gorbachev gave new meaning to the words *perestroika* (economic restructuring) and *glasnost* (openness)—principles which he convinced the party to adopt in order to stop the rot which was eating away at the economy and Soviet society. Gorbachev figured that unless he changed things, the party which had nurtured him would come perilously close to imploding. And the old men in grey suits who made up the CPSU's ruling bodies believed him.

I'd heard all about *Homo Sovieticus*. Western scholars had decided that there was a Soviet character which stood in stark contrast to the Russian character. I thought it was gross propaganda to claim that communism had moulded a new species which, generally speaking, was lazy, dependent, jealous, corrupt and incapable of taking responsibility for anything—especially in the workplace. And it was indeed an inaccurate generalisation. But I soon discovered there *was* something very different about the Soviet people. They were very unlike westerners and very unlike the model worker Soviet propaganda had mythologised. Lenin's Bolshevik revolution had created something truly revolutionary.

Homo Sovieticus believed in an egalitarianism different to that which Lenin claimed to have intended for the people he led through revolution. Soviet egalitarianism was a willingness, indeed a deep desire, to make sure everyone lived at the same level of poverty. People rightly felt cheated by the communist system. They were told they couldn't strive to be better than their neighbour. Everyone would be equal in this new society. Equally poor. Except of course for those who worked for the party. The proletariat revolution had evolved into a hideous, all-consuming, multi-layered bureaucracy whose members, known as *apparatchiks*, enjoyed the party's trust and lived well, featherbedding themselves and their superiors, the ruling elite (the *nomenklatura*). Average people who didn't work directly for the party but who seemed to be doing better than their neighbours were assumed to have done so courtesy of bought privilege or favour, which in the west we would call corruption and which was always in abundant supply in the Soviet era.

'They pretend to pay us. We pretend to work,' is the Russian workers' proverb. Workers had been duped into accepting low wages to honour an ideal they mostly knew their leaders were betraying. So it was reasonable that workers in the workers' paradise felt bitter about their impoverishment. They were also helpless. Those who bothered to think about the matter knew they would probably never become masters of their own fate as they'd been promised. The party was too powerful to be overpowered. So it was every man for himself. The Russians themselves satirised the flaw in their joke about one neighbour 'complimenting' another about his new *dacha* (country house). He burns it down.

Helpless and poor, *Homo Sovieticus* was dependent on the state for his livelihood. He had no other option. Private enterprise was illegal. Incentive was rarely given and on occasions when initiative was displayed it was almost always punished. Worse still, one's personal labour was worthless because no amount of hard work seemed to produce choice or even, at times, what a person needed to live. Soviet workers waited for the state to do what it promised it would do—provide—and in the meantime they refused to make decisions, sending the system creaking a little faster to its death. But who could blame them? Making a decision could be punished regardless of whether it was correct.

As the economy tailspinned into oblivion, people began to help themselves. Corruption and theft had become so great a problem that they produced yet another characteristic of *Homo Sovieticus* which would prove to be more problematic and enduring than any of the others—a belief that because property didn't belong to individuals, it was there to be stolen.

'The Soviet Communist Party is a mafia. Once you understand this, everything else will make sense,' said Masha, her huge dark Armenian eyes insisting that I pay attention. I'd met Masha in 1990 through a young Australian woman who had lived in Moscow for several years and who worked for a time as a translator for the ABC television correspondent. Masha was the fastest speaker I'd ever met. The words tumbled out of her mouth, painting such vivid pictures that, despite the early shortcomings in my comprehension of Russian, I understood her.

Masha's attitude towards the Soviet Union made sense. It was, for her, an entity, huge and imposing. She recognised that almost all relations in the country were corrupt so she felt free to create her own rules of morality, ones she felt more comfortable with. Life in Soviet Russia, she would say, is all about taking yourself outside reality. It's a matter of being enterprising when no-one around you is. Of believing in something, anything, when no-one around you does. And of rejecting what the party says are absolute truths.

'Most people have just surrendered to the propaganda,' she would say of the common fear of foreigners. 'And the party won't ever let that change. It's in their interests to have us all believing fervently in their power and their superiority. That way they can continue to live well while we scurry around, corrupting each other and them to get by,' she told me.

But the CPSU was there to stay as far as Masha was concerned. She, like most others I knew, couldn't conceive of a time when they'd have any other choice. 'Life is a matter of beating the party mafia at its own game,' she said.

And indeed, it was obvious, even after five years of Mikhail Gorbachev's campaign to reform his country, that the Communist Party he led was still a mafia. It guarded its own turf, operated protection rackets to ensure that its members profited while everyone else floundered, and poured its money into bank accounts and enterprises overseas while at home it had created a new breed of owners and workers, nothing like the society Lenin and his revolutionaries promised.

The new owners were the bureaucrats and party secretaries in whose care the state's property and property owned by individuals before the revolution was placed. These people had been appointed by the Communist Party to get on with the job of building communism. And in the process they indulged any number of scams at all levels against all classes. There was no rule of law to keep them in check other than laws created by corrupt bodies within the party. And so the vast majority of people whose lives were difficult, sometimes impossible, were simply forced to live corruptly.

'How can you live like this?' I asked Masha. 'It's demoralising, dehumanising.'

'It's a matter of knowing the system. You see everything is capable of being bought, if not with money then with connections. Visas. Passports. Food when there's none on the shop shelves. Everything. Actually, in some ways we have a perfect market operating here, only it's underground,' she said.

And indeed, nothing was impossible to do or get hold of, primarily because the ruling culture was 'vzyatki', from the verb 'to take'. Anyone with power was on the take. This made life somewhat simpler for average Muscovites than it might have been if they'd been forced to make do with what was officially available to them. It made my life a lot easier as well. I might not have received the magical card authorising me to operate as a foreign correspondent in Moscow had I not paid the bureaucrat who supervised my life in the Soviet Union. And this, despite the fact that the government had already issued me with a visa! I might not have had an apartment to live in had not the officials who granted foreigners apartments been given something to allow me to rent a state flat in a foreigners', compound. And this, despite the fact that having been given a visa and authorisation to live in Moscow, it was assumed I would need an apartment! And, once ensconced, I would have lost my driving licence on average once a week had I not been willing to hand over the odd American five or even ten dollar bill, and sometimes much more, to Moscow's greedy *militsiya*. And to dispel the thought that I might have been bribing myself out of situations where, in fact, I had committed some wrong, let me say that wrong plays no part in the process which causes the Moscow *militsiya* to stop cars and extract 'donations' from drivers.

Much of the time, being a foreigner was enough to attract the *militsiya's* attention. In fact one might have been forgiven for thinking in the Soviet era that everyone in a police uniform was actually a thief (many were) or that most foreigners couldn't drive properly. The party had struck a system to identify those of us who weren't locals. Our car registration number plates were yellow and coded. Australian journalists drove around in cars marked K 016 followed by a three digit number. The K was for correspondent. The 16 was the number which designated the car owner as Australian. D 004 would be an American diplomat, T 007 a French businessperson.

Of course I'd heard dozens of stories about the corrupt Moscow *militsiya* but I didn't think my first experience of them would come the first time I drove my new red Lada. And I certainly didn't think they would stop me almost every time I drove the car.

I was cautiously driving home from the city, unsure of the roads, frightened of being pulled over. There at the side of the Rublevskoye Highway which links the city centre to the new Gorbachev-style suburb of Krylatskoe which the ABC called home, was a rotund, fur-headed officer in knee-high felt boots, white traffic stick waving me to the kerb.

'Do you know you were exceeding the speed limit by ten kilometres an hour?' he asked. I was baffled. He didn't appear to have any sort of speed monitor. I hadn't exceeded the speed limit and I knew he was about to extract a bribe from me. And I knew I had to pay. If I refused, he'd take away my driver's licence and I'd spend weeks paying people in an effort to find the bureaucrat who had it. Worse still, I'd be reported to my supervisor in the Foreign Ministry and be given a warning. And I would be harassed by police who would happen, always, to be posted on roads I'd be most likely to use, until they lost interest in me. So I quickly shook off all pretensions to moral indignation.

'Can we settle this matter in a businesslike manner?' I asked sheepishly.

'*Noou,*' ['Well'] he replied, nose nodding towards me, urging me to make an offer. I started with a packet of cigarettes which I'd been warned to keep in my glovebox for just such an occasion. He looked unimpressed. What about five American dollars? He again declined even though, at the time, this was roughly about a day's pay. The bribe hit twenty dollars before he seemed satisfied that I had no more to offer.

Of course corruption wasn't ushered in by Gorbachev's *perestroika*. Nicolai Gogol wrote of the corruption of the provincial bureaucrats in Tsarist times. And Soviet-style corruption was already an accepted fact of life in 1917, the year of the revolution. The propagandist poet Vladimir Mayakovsky who wholly supported the Bolsheviks wrote to his lover about the demands Lenin's Red Guard made of the managers of the Poets Cafe in Moscow where the city's artistic community would crowd around a small stage to listen as the Futurist poets beat the revolutionary drum. It was a place to talk over new ideas which would help create the new society. The place was a refuge, Mayakovsky wrote, for artists who believed in the revolution and wanted to help lay the foundation stones for a new order. On the streets, the Red Guard enthusiastically shot anyone they thought didn't support the revolution. And then one day they turned to the cafe, 'demanding money from its co-operative owners. We closed the Poets Cafe's doors because of corruption.'

On my earlier visits, I'd seen corruption at work on all levels—from the hotel chambermaid who wouldn't clean your room until you gave her a few dollars to the customs agent at the airport who wouldn't let you take in a Walkman unless you offered a bribe. But it had always seemed to me to be discreet. And from everything I'd heard bribes weren't openly offered across the table of the local council, let alone in the central government departments. More often, it was a bunch of flowers or a box of chocolates which would convince a functionary to do his or her job. Even the police disguised their avarice by confining their bribe-taking to the theft of official fines for slight misdemeanours. But all this seemed to have changed by 1990.

In fact corruption and its cohort theft were a social phenomenon, their scale almost impossible for a westerner to imagine and their effect on the economy devastating. Everyone stole with greater or lesser degrees of recognition of what they were doing. Not long after I arrived in Moscow, I was hitching a ride into the city while my car was being repaired. As an old white ambulance pulled up beside me, I wondered what the driver wanted. Directions perhaps?

'Where are you going?' asked the driver.

'Are you offering a ride?' I asked.

'Why else would I stop?' he said. Lying in the back of the ambulance was an old woman, a *babushka*, who was being taken to a polyclinic.

'But what about the *babushka*?' I protested. 'You have a patient in the ambulance!'

'Ah! She's not that sick. She can wait,' he said, not at all embarrassed. The old woman shrugged her shoulders and beckoned me to jump in.

'It's harmless commerce,' the driver said as I handed over five dollars for the ride. 'Everyone does it!'

And they did. The ambulance driver was being 'soviet', a characteristic of which was a willingness to steal public property because it belonged to no-one. In fact, according to the statistics, until the early 1990s more than a third of privately owned cars used stolen, state-owned petrol pilfered from workplaces.

By 1986 when Gorbachev added *perestroika* and *glasnost* to the ingredients of socialism, people seemed to think the words meant that they could help themselves more openly to the state's spoils.

Rorting by workers paled in comparison with the various shades of corruption the *nomenklatura* inflicted upon their own people. If not the diversion of limited consumer goods to their own homes or to the black market, then it was the corrupt manipulation of their positions to ensure subservience, loyalty and, of course, a bribe. As the joke goes: the director of a Soviet plant is interviewing a young man for a job as plant manager. The director asks the candidate: 'How much is one plus one?' The young man answers: 'How much do you need, Comrade?' It was a rare moment to be savoured if you managed to complete a legitimate business exchange without offering a *vzyatki* [bribe].

And in a country so heavily laden with rules and regulations, written and overseen by the bureaucracy, there was barely an aspect of life which didn't require a little gift, and sometimes cold hard cash, to be resolved satisfactorily.

'You have to understand,' explained Natasha, 'most of the time, the way the communists controlled life here was through the bureaucracy. If they didn't want you to do something, they just made it impossible by inventing all sorts of little rules which sometimes we would break, and sometimes we would be too scared to break. But a lot of the time the rules were so silly, we just bribed the bureaucrats. And they were happy to be bribed.'

Not long after I arrived in Moscow, I got to see for myself the way the system worked for Russians. I met a woman named Svetlana, a model who wanted to travel to Europe to try her hand on the catwalks of Milan and Paris. But getting a passport and then a visa to leave the Soviet Union needed Herculean effort and staying power, not to mention good contacts.

In the old Soviet Union, the system of governance and the rule of law, despite what Gorbachev was trying to tell his people, was still skewed against individuals and against individual rights. As Lenin had preached, there was no place for the individual in his new society. 'The individual is nothing against the society.' And so the situation largely remained.

Leaving the country was considered to be the greatest act of individual treachery that one could contemplate, although those the party trusted or thought would return—its *apparatchiks* or the *nomenklatura* and their families—were allowed out. To leave for personal enhancement, education or even folly was the mark of a self-seeking individualist.

Svetlana was also an artist and therefore considered to have a mind of her own which could act independently of the state's imposed thought processes. The reason for her deviation was attributed to her penchant for consorting with foreigners who brought to the Soviet Union not just prostitution and HIV but worse, their evil thoughts about individual freedom. At least this is what Svetlana had been told when she was unceremoniously booted out of the Moscow College of the Arts in 1988 for having an English boyfriend.

Svetlana was considered especially risky because officialdom thought she was unlikely to return to the Soviet Union if granted permission to leave. They figured—rightly so—that the reason she wanted to travel abroad was to escape the oppressive attitude of the regime to pursuits such as hers. Modelling was considered a mild form of prostitution not to be countenanced under any circumstances, even though in every corner of any of the big cities across the Soviet Union you could find nightclubs where women worked as striptease dancers. They were sleazy, grubby basement bars where *apparatchiks* would drool and pick up women they would then order to be arrested or otherwise punished for their activities. In reality, Svetlana had no choice but to try to escape.

The biggest obstacle was getting a passport. She, like every Soviet citizen, had an internal passport which was to be carried at all times as proof of the fact that you actually existed and that you had permission to live where you said you lived. An international passport was an elite document of proven privilege not granted to just anyone.

But assuming you weren't a dissident, a scientist, a poet or playwright, if you really wanted to travel there were ways and means.

Chief among them was finding a bribable bureaucrat in the Ministry of Foreign Affairs, better known by its Russian acronym of MID. Smouldering over the Smolyenskaya district of central Moscow was a gothic skyscraper Joseph Stalin had built—one of seven—which housed MID and literally hundreds of the bribable species.

The task was simply to find one with whom you resonated so that when you posed the all important question of whether you could get an international passport, the answer wouldn't be 'nyet'.

Svetlana's uncle was a clerk in the Department for the Security of Socialist Property which was attached to the Department of Internal Security. The agency against corruption was not only a notable failure, it was a notable contributor to the problem, as Svetlana's uncle well knew. He gave her the name of a bribable Foreign Ministry clerk who was in a position to create the necessary documents which could then be signed by the appropriate official who would also require payment in order to get Svetlana her passport. Her birth certificate was magically found in the Registry of Births, Deaths and Marriages in Kiev where she was born, a process which might otherwise have taken months. Her clearance of internal crime was summonsed from the Police Department without effort or delay. Her certificate of no impediment proving she had never been married was handed over by the ZAGS—the Register of the Status of Citizens—without question. She had documents. Svetlana was suddenly a person.

The bribe was US$500 which in 1987 was a hefty amount. Its equivalent, 3000 roubles, was enough to buy a second-hand car. It was roughly half a year's salary. Certainly nothing any self-respecting bribable bureaucrat would scoff at, even though it was at the bottom of the scale of fees. Five hundred dollars was the price of a passport which wasn't needed in a hurry. This particular process could take up to six months. If you needed your passport rather more quickly, then it could cost anything up to US$2000.

But the official with whom Svetlana was 'doing business' conducted herself with complete professionalism. Not once did she display embarrassment at her behaviour, nor fear of being caught. Her colleagues were no doubt aware of her activities and the money was handed to her over her desk at the Foreign Ministry.

'It's creeping capitalism,' said Svetlana. And she was right.

But obtaining a passport wasn't the end of the story. It wasn't as simple as going to the local travel agent to buy a ticket before heading off to Sheremetyevo Airport for a pleasant trip overseas. The next step was to get OVIR—the Department of Visas and Registration, another organ of state control—to stamp the passport with an exit visa, a move this particular agency was generally loath to make without some incentive.

OVIR was an arm of the Department for Internal Affairs which made it especially formidable. It opened just twice weekly in central Moscow—an open declaration that it intended dealing with as few people as possible. Indeed the queue to get to one of the OVIR clerks could be days long. Svetlana would go to the central branch whenever it opened to check the queue's progress, asking, as was generally acceptable in Soviet Russia, for the person in front to keep her place in the line while she went off to buy whatever was available in the shops on the day. Of course, she would offer to buy the person helping her some of whatever she came across, or, the next time they met at OVIR, would offer to queue while he or she went shopping.

Nearly a month passed before Svetlana's number was called. But her passport was rejected because its serial number, without notice or reason, was rescinded by the Foreign Ministry despite the fact that it had only recently been issued. There was no point bribing the OVIR officials into turning a blind eye because customs officials and passport control at the airport would also be notified of the change and would also need to be bribed.

A phone call to the Foreign Ministry clerk who'd issued the passport was all that was needed, however, and within days the problem was fixed. Svetlana had thought ahead and paid the OVIR official to see her immediately the problem was rectified. With passport and exit visa in hand, it seemed she would soon be on her way to the catwalks.

Now for a ticket.

The Aeroflot office on Oktyabrskaya Square in Moscow was a hellish place. It still is. I tried to get some co-operation out of it when two young Australian girls turned up on the ABC's doorstep in 1991 having had their passports and Aeroflot tickets stolen on the train to Moscow from Leningrad. The Australian embassy took care of the passports. And it seemed to me an easy task to get Aeroflot in Sydney to cable Aeroflot in Moscow with confirmation of the purchase of the tickets in order for the Moscow office to reissue them. But no! Day after day, the cable, I was told, hadn't arrived. Finally, in a fit of frustration, I demanded to know where the cables from Aeroflot's overseas offices were kept. Servile to the end, a portly woman with teased blonde hair pointed me towards a desk where mounds of paperwork lay, presumably unchecked. And there it was, buried deep in a file, beneath a pile of files. The cable had arrived days before—a few lines which might have ended my misery before it caused me to feel physical symptoms of anxiety and stress.

Aeroflot treated Russian citizens with a somewhat greater degree of contempt.

Svetlana queued for days and when finally she was allowed to enter Aeroflot's main office, she was told there was a one-year waiting list for tickets to Paris. The problem, according to the clerk, was that the government was unable to supply Aeroflot with enough fuel to service the extra flights which were needed by 1990 when Soviet citizens were being told they were free to leave the country— the borders having finally opened. There seemed little point wondering why the government would bother to grant such a freedom if it wasn't prepared to facilitate the easy production of passports and put on extra flights to cope with the traffic. But ours was not to question!

So there would be no extra flights scheduled. But, of course, if

Svetlana was in a position to try to hurry things along then ...

She was and she did. For a small bribe of US$100 she was granted the pleasure of queuing on the street outside Aeroflot for just five days, midwinter, after which she finally received a two-way ticket to Paris.

Natasha told me when I first arrived in Moscow that I was now living in the richest country in the world, a comment that struck me as rather odd given the sad-looking shop shelves, the run-down buildings and poorly dressed people I was seeing.

'How can this be the richest country in the world?' I asked her.

'Well, as we say in Russia, people have been stealing for seventy years and there's still something left to steal.'

Few in the old Soviet Union would have disagreed that the most profound corruption problem the country faced was in production and retail trading. It was big enough to have endowed the country with a counter economy (or black market) which provided what the official economy couldn't and, from the Soviet Union's grave, still undermines it.

The central problem was the Five Year Plan, introduced by Joseph Stalin in 1928. It caused mayhem. Conjured up by the country's economists to answer the leader's call to speed up industrialisation, the Five Year Plan was skewed towards the production of cement and steel for an industrial base which churned out seven times more military hardware than consumer goods. Until the 1960s people seemed prepared to accept that industrial growth and a mighty military were more important than refrigerators, furniture and cars. For a long time, it seemed that if the system produced 'economic growth', it commanded loyalty. But by the 1970s and '80s loyalty had all but disappeared. People wanted computers and modern cars, electronics and baby baskets, only the system couldn't adapt.

In any event, even though the Five Year Plans had achieved

phenomenal industrial and military growth in the first four decades of totalitarianism, no-one would have argued, even at the moment of their inception that they produced anything remotely resembling an orderly economy capable of providing everything people needed, let alone wanted. The Russian verdict on the Five Year Plans was neatly summed up in a joke which started doing the rounds in the 1950s and has persisted in one form or another ever since: Ivan needs a zipper for his trousers so he goes down to the zipper shop.

'We're out of zippers,' says the store director.

'Do you know where I can get one?' asks Ivan.

'The nearest shop would be in Helsinki!' comes the answer.

Consumer goods were produced to meet targets which were set by *apparatchiks* sitting in the offices of the mighty *Gosplan*—the state planning commission, housed in a Stalinesque grey building opposite the Kremlin—which ensured that only products which the masses needed (rather than wanted) were produced. The targets were set for the entire nation, all fifteen republics, regardless of local needs, let alone desires. The *apparatchiks* who dreamt up the quotas—along with the many factory and enterprise managers below them with whom they were largely in informal business partnerships—devoted much of their work time to rorting the Plan so that they could hide its inefficiencies and in the process earn money and privileges on the side. Of course, when the quotas they set were fulfilled, even if they had only cooked the books, they would receive a pat on the back, which could often turn into something more tangible like an extra week at a holiday resort or access to another of the special shops especially stocked for the *apparatchiks* and the *nomenklatura*. But there were many ways to earn a little on the side.

It wasn't unusual for an *apparatchik* sitting in Moscow to under-state the amount of rubber being sent from Azerbaijan to Ukraine to produce tyres so that the factory manager in Ukraine could produce more than his quota. The extra tyres, needless to say, would be sold on the black market. Of course to achieve this the bureaucrats and the manager often needed a little help. The system was so inefficient that often it couldn't provide the materials needed to actually produce. So black marketeers were engaged to steal materials from other state enterprises to ensure that factories received what they needed. In turn, the black marketeers would have to be paid.

The opportunities for theft and corruption were limitless, largely because the entire system of production and distribution was circular and depended on a degree of efficiency beyond the capacity of the system. The Five Year Plan could operate successfully only under optimal conditions, when all the equipment worked properly, when workers were diligent, when supplies arrived on time.

Gos is the Russian abbreviation for state. So *Gosplan* needed *Gossten*—state-listed prices which were rigid and rarely increased. *Goszakaz* ordered goods on behalf of every republic, every region. *Gosnab* distributed goods produced by the state (and all were). *Gostrud* decided labour and wages policy, while *Gostekhnika* oversaw technology and research. To ensure that everyone abided by the determinations of the various 'gos' agencies and, of course, by the diktat of the party, there was *Gosbezapasnost*—better known in the west as the KGB—which among its various functions was charged with devising means to ensure against corruption. But it failed. Much of the time, *Gosplan* issued directives for goods to be manufactured from materials which were either not produced or diverted to factory managers beholden to it. Finding the corrupt link in the chain must have been like trying to find a needle in a haystack, if only because the Plan could rarely be fulfilled. It produced shortages right down the line. The problem was more than mere corruption.

'Nothing, not even heavy industry, works normally because no-one fulfils the plan,' explained Igor, a factory worker I met at an anti-Gorbachev rally near Red Square in 1990. 'They can't. Officially, we wait for supplies at the beginning of each month. They don't arrive. That means we work with what material we have left over from the previous month's delivery, so things are slow. This is sleep time. But then suddenly the supplies arrive. This is hot time, even though what's been delivered is rarely enough to fulfil the quota *Gosplan* has set us. So we wait and when more supplies arrive— usually towards the very end of the month—we work hard to get the job done.'

Often, the factory manager would call on one of the hundreds of black-market ringleaders, known as the *zory v'zakone*. They would provide the materials the factory manager needed (but which had been stolen from or not delivered by *Gosnab*) by doing deals with the supplier (itself state-owned) or by stealing. This way the factory manager could usually get materials to either fulfil the quota or over-produce in order to supply the black market. Either way, as Igor said, the system didn't work according to the Plan.

So the Five Year Plans created compounding deficits that could be years long. The waiting list for cars was ten years. For washing machines, twelve years. For building materials, five years or more. Televisions, radios, washing machines, these were but pipedreams in the workers' paradise unless one had enough money or access to goods with which to bribe the *apparatchiks* in control of the waiting list. One could always be sure, however, that the smaller items could be bought easily, simply by taking a trip down to the nearest taxi rank where the black marketeers usually operated in full view of the police from whom they bribed silence.

In the boots of their cars, the illegal traders would store bottles of vodka and beer, bras, underpants, ties, shirts, cans of caviar and pots and pans. When I first arrived in Moscow to live, I searched for Russian-made kitchenware in the shops but there was none. There were dusters and kitchen tidy-bins, but never any pots and pans. Masha suggested we try the local 'taxi park', the equivalent of an Australian taxi rank. There, Russian men would pretend they were waiting for passengers, but in reality they were waiting for customers to inspect their bootloads of consumer goods. Just two blocks away from the Kremlin, I found my pots and pans, a whole set of them, shiny and new. If you needed tyres for your car, a radiator or even a new bumper bar, you could simply place an order and be assured that the trader would find it. Masha was right. The black market was the only market which worked.

And that, of course, accounted for the outright theft by factory and shop managers who systematically stole cash, goods and raw materials and spent much of their work time moonlighting. If it was produced, it was available. If it was available, it could be stolen. If it was stolen, it could be sold. During the petrol shortages of 1991 and 1992, I would go to the outer ring road around Moscow in search of a tanker which hadn't quite made it to its allocated stations. Drivers openly stole not only the petrol to sell for personal profit, but the whole tanker, the parts of which would be disassembled and sold off to state factories producing petrol tankers. Everyone profited. The driver who stole the tanker, his factory manager who would be cut in on the deal and, of course, the manager to whom the parts were on-sold, who would be able to produce trucks using parts the state couldn't supply.

Not once did I see a police officer enquire what the tanker driver was doing as cars lined up for their fill on a major arterial road, sometimes causing traffic jams. Nor do I remember being able to buy caviar, which one could almost call a Russian staple, across the counter in central Moscow until 1993. It may have been different in other regions of Russia, but in Moscow it was a case of knowing someone who knew the factory manager, a well-connected worker or a black marketeer who'd stolen a case of the stuff before it ever had a chance of making it into the back of a truck for delivery.

The degree of theft was obvious. Blindingly so. I wondered whether the problems were so deep the authorities simply didn't know how to fix them. And though this might have played some part in their reasoning, pragmatism was the real culprit. Small-time black-market operators (the *tolkachi*) who managed to swindle or buy state goods to sell privately, and their brothers in crime, the *vory v'zakone* who moved goods from one factory to another to grease the production cycle, were actually essential. By distributing goods to the public and to factories when the state couldn't or wouldn't, they kept the command system afloat and, as a result, the *nomenklatura* who benefited more than anyone else from the system lived well. Some even became rouble millionaires, receiving much of the profit from the illegal over-production of some goods and a slice of the action from the sale of scarce consumer goods stolen for or mysteriously diverted to the black market. It was not uncommon for *nomenklatura* to go into business with the black-market traders, thousands of whom set up entire industries on pilfered machinery and materials. For the country's leadership, the political rationale was 'better to let them steal than think of changing the system'.

At the retail level, the problem might have been funny had it not been so damaging.

There were few exceptions to the habit of theft. Shop assistants the country over would put away part, sometimes even most, of what came in for sale. Then they'd on-sell it to family, friends or even black marketeers either for money or in exchange for something they needed or could barter with others. More often than not, the goods were diverted as they left the factory, long before they made it to the shops. Even so, shop workers were privileged. They had something to sell or barter for goods they needed. And their ingenuity was remarkable. I'm not sure if the story is true but Masha told me that the KGB had been called to a shop in Sverdlovsk in the 1970s to check for a bomb. The shoppers refused to leave their places in the queues on the shop floor so the KGB decided to turn the place upside down and inside out regardless of the shoppers as they looked for a ticking parcel. They found nothing in the storage depot, nothing underneath the counters and nothing on the shelves. Tapping away at the wall separating the retail space from the staff room, they detected a hollowness which they decided to investigate. And there in the wall cavity they discovered enough jumpers, shoes and belts to fill one floor of a medium-sized western department store.

The shop attendants would no doubt have shrugged their shoulders and pleaded innocence. Signs of commitment, professionalism or job satisfaction were rarely evident in their behaviour towards the paying customer. I remember shopping for sheet music in a small shop in the Moscow suburb of Kuntsevo where an unhelpful shop assistant told me the store didn't have what I could see lying on a shelf behind her.

'But it's right behind you,' I protested.

'No it isn't,' she said, staring me down across the counter.

I was dumbfounded but Natasha flew into a rage and hurled one of the worst curses possible: 'May you be doomed to live off your wages'.

But the perversity of the system was best described by the once banned satirist Mikhail Zhvanetsky: 'Incompetence caused shortages. Shortages caused theft. Theft caused impudence. Impudence caused incompetence which, in turn, caused shortages. One assumes that if there's a vicious cycle, there's an exit. It's just that no-one has found it as yet.'

When goods weren't in deficit, they were mostly second-rate, badly made. Igor's theory was that the goods produced in the slow period of production, when workers had more time to pay attention to their work, went to the *nomenklatura* while those produced in the frenzied part of the cycle went to the masses. I didn't doubt he was right. Never will I forget the television pictures of the old Leningrad Hotel on the banks of the Neva River disappearing in a raging fire caused when one of the Soviet-made television sets in a guest's room exploded when it was turned on. Soviet production came down to the simple rule of *Homo Sovieticus*: 'It belongs to no-one so no-one cares'.

Natasha's 85-year-old father thought that the Soviet people—like people the world over—wanted to express themselves through their personal endeavour, not the party's diktat. They were capable of good work, even long hours if they were paid well and with their earnings could buy what they needed. But neither the party nor its economic system allowed this. So people were not only forced to live corruptly, they cared little about their work.

Natasha agreed. Russian work habits, she would say, began to decline during the 1950s by which time, when they bothered to work at all, people realised that money was worth very little, or even nothing.

'What's the point of a factory worker or a nurse working hard and proving his or her efficiency?' she'd say. 'If they do that, they'll be given more work, more responsibility. There's almost no chance they'll earn more money and even if they do, what could they spend it on?'

But discipline, or lack of it, was also a problem. When I went to Russia to live, I found Russian workers seemed to do whatever they wanted. It wasn't unusual for people I knew to arrive at work at 10 a.m. and leave at 1 p.m. citing as their reason the need to go searching for sugar or meat. When they worked, they were mostly disorganised, as one would be in jobs which paid so little. The simplest task would be made so complicated by the ruling bureaucrats that exasperated office workers would give up and leave it to someone else or no-one at all. It took me months to cotton on to a favourite trick of the Russian bureaucracy from which, thankfully, I was largely shielded by our Russian staff.

I'd decided to see for myself why it took the ABC office driver weeks of devoted attention to pay an electricity bill which brought the state roughly thirty cents. I went to the *Sberegatelnaya Kassa* (the local branch of the state bank) to pay my own bill. Queue 1 would proffer Ivan Ivanovich to tick a piece of paper confirming the price for the quarter's electricity. This was taken to Queue 2 where Maria Ivanovna would accept your money. Queue 3 ticked you off the list as having paid and provided a receipt. But the process could consume several days, sometimes weeks, because if one of the queue attendants wasn't there, no-one else would perform their duties. You'd be told that Ivan Ivanovich had *'vyshel'* (stepped out for a moment) and, as proof, you'd be directed to lay eyes on his jacket slung over the back of his chair. For weeks, I believed my apparent bad luck in arriving at the office when Ivan was out 'for a moment'. The office secretary finally put me out of my misery and suggested that Ivan probably had two jackets. One to hang on his office chair, another which he wore as he drank himself into oblivion at the local bar, or queued for something which had suddenly become available. 'Or maybe he's just gone to his *dacha* for a few months,' she added.

When I moved to Moscow in 1990, I quickly learnt the real meaning of the Russian word *'seichas'* (now) which was the usual reply to any request, especially urgent ones. But I discovered the hard way that *seichas* could mean hours, days, even months. The ABC-ordered refurbishment of my apartment was almost complete, but not quite, when I arrived. A small group of workers still had to glue the tiles to the bathroom walls, lay the parquet floors in two rooms and install a new, secure front door. They were waiting for the floor panelling to arrive from a local producer but the tiles were there as was the door, so they confidently told me, 'In a week, it'll all be done'.

A month later they were still there. I'd pop up to the apartment at lunchtime to have a peek only to find them propped up against the walls, smoking and telling tales. At 2 p.m. they'd leave. In the end I offered the three workers US$100 each to speed up the process. It worked. After three months, a job which should have taken two weeks was done. Throughout the ordeal, the ABC was paying rent on the incomplete apartment which was twenty, perhaps even thirty times what a Muscovite would have paid, and not in roubles which could then still be bought cheaply on the black market.

The special bonus could work magic. Even the most highly placed *apparatchiks* in *Gosplan* saw that bonuses could be used to great effect to get the bigger, more important projects completed. Massive gold mines in Siberia are linked together across thousands of kilometres by trains and phone lines. Nuclear power stations, albeit rather dilapidated and in need of billions of dollars of western finance to repair, continue to supply millions of homes with heat and light. And factories churn out the most sophisticated military tanks in the world, even if, these days, they're driven out of the factory and across the road to another where they're melted down. In the winter of 1983, long before it was razed by fire, I sat in a room at the Hotel Leningrad looking out over the Neva River as a huge atomic icebreaker ploughed its way at incredible speed through metres of ice, making way for smaller merchant ships to pass.

Soviet workers could build giant aluminium plants in remote parts of the country in a matter of months. Even if they were poorly constructed, they worked. But there would have to be an incentive. For workers, there would need to be special rates of pay. For the regime, there would need to be a question of honour. It was concerned only with proving the Soviet Union was as advanced and industrialised as any capitalist country. In 1917, when Lenin seized power, 90 per cent of Russia was rural and uneducated. By 1990, 70 per cent of the population was not only educated, they were living in heavily industrialised cities in which one factory might employ up to 130 000 workers, all of them receiving subsidised housing, food, education and health care. This, according to the regime, was the best reason to keep communism on track.

But success was not defined by how well the workers lived, for everyone understood the subsidies were no more than a means of keeping the lid on discontent. Or as Alexander Yakovlev, Gorbachev's propagandist, would put it, a means of turning workers into a lumpen mass of the equally impoverished. Success was defined by military and strategic strength. It was not by chance that 70 per cent of realised production occurred in the military sector of the economy which received the best of everything—materials, managers and funding. Security was etched deep in the national psyche. It had been for centuries.

Russia had suffered from an overwhelming inferiority complex since the Middle Ages. Its geographical isolation, comparative underdevelopment and its climate made it extremely difficult for it to keep up with Western Europe. At least industrially. Militarily too, Russia seemed always vulnerable to attack. And over the centuries, this vulnerability turned into a paranoic need to protect itself. Lenin's Bolsheviks merely picked up where the tsars left off. The military–industrial complex into which was poured an inestimable amount of human and financial resources was really little more than an expression of national feeling. Given the historic obsession with security, it's not strange that Soviet workers accepted for as long as they did that the defence sector should be more important than the people, their lives, their human dignity. In any event, those who didn't accept this knew better than to question the regime.

To the average Russian there was nothing abnormal in the fact that Soviet military industry could produce sophisticated nuclear devices as big as your fist, yet it was impossible to find briefcases produced in the USSR which could carry them. Nor that Soviet medical science could create chemicals capable of killing off the continent, yet was unable to produce some of the more basic requirements like sanitary pads for women.

As the atomic icebreakers inched their way across the Neva, the barges they made way for were probably empty. Almost certainly, they would have borne none of the little luxuries like briefcases, torches, calculators, reliable television sets, well-made clothes and phones which worked. If they were produced at all, the chances were they'd been pilfered long before they could make it to the point of distribution. In any event, the chance of getting hold of anything remotely useful, let alone luxurious, depended largely upon how much time you could take off work to scour the shops, who you knew, or what you could pay for the right connections.

CHAPTER 2

KINGDOM OF CONNECTIONS

The purpose of one hand is to wash another hand.

RUSSIAN PROVERB

Blat was a given in the Soviet Union. It was as necessary to life as air itself. Without it, one could starve, or go cold. Its existence was secretly acknowledged by everyone but publically denied by all. It made careers and created a class system which was the workers' response to the egalitarianism the Bolsheviks thought they'd successfully imposed. *Blat* was influence, connections and protection, a sort of informal understanding between people that whatever they needed could be obtained by barter if not with money.

I have to admit that for the entire time I lived in Russia, *blat* confused and confounded me—no doubt because I'm not Russian and therefore wasn't able to completely comprehend its rites of entry, the web of obligation and intrigue it encompassed, the utterly fundamental role it played in allowing people to actually survive. At first I thought the phenomenon I was observing was some primitive form of communal welfare. In a sense it was. But it was more complex, more ingrained and more political.

While I would wonder how my friends managed to find food to cover the table, especially during the dire food shortages of the late

1980s and early 1990s, they understood the train of people and favours which got it there. I could only guess at how they managed to keep themselves so well dressed with just about everything in official 'deficit'. They knew what it took.

To understand *blat*, you really have to hark back to another time— to that frightening moment in the Soviet Union's history when all hope of the new world the communists said they could create began to give way to greed, envy and a very different world of privilege.

Russians referred to it as the birth of the communist nobility, the *nomenklatura*—people who worked for the party and accordingly were paid more (in money and privilege) than anyone else in the egalitarian society Lenin had mapped out.

Nomenklatura privilege, to be fair, was not entirely Lenin's creation. Its formation had begun during Lenin's leadership but this new social strata only started to assume its own set of rules in Stalin's years of terror. Adulation of his leadership and the replacement of the old specialists who'd run the country since the revolution by people absolutely loyal to him were among the mechanisms the Georgian dictator used to ensure his successful, unchallenged rule.

And so he appointed Communist Party members to positions of power and authority in industry, academia, government and almost every other walk of life in which the party's grip had been less than total. They were beholden not only to Stalin, the great leader, but to the myths he created of the need for continued struggle against enemies of the people who wanted the country to abandon Leninism and, with it, the 'truth' that communism was better than capitalism. As they assumed authority, the *nomenklatura* didn't appear to live by any of the Marxist principles their positions were meant to sustain and administer—like fairness and non-materialistic living. As the *nomenklatura* grew and became more pervasive, it became more closed, corrupt and self-serving. Its members took it for granted, as a matter of right, that as the country's new economic managers, they were its main beneficiaries.

The Soviet *nomenklatura* were relying on what Stalin himself had said in 1934: 'that every Leninist knows that equalisation in the sphere of requirements and individual life is a piece of reactionary petty bourgeois absurdity'. The *nomenklatura* embraced the leader's sentiments wholeheartedly.

As any Russian will tell you, the basic principle of *blat* is *'ty mne, ya tebe'* ['you for me and me for you'].

In Stalin's day it was a political tool to protect the system of patronage and privilege which allowed the *nomenklatura* and those they favoured down the line to live as though they were the chosen people, while the workers were given the bare minimum and told to plough on for the glory of the state. *Blat* turned privilege into a class system.

The working classes knew little about the privileges of the *nomenklatura*, and no doubt they cared even less during the dark years under Joseph Stalin when to question or speak out could cost you your life. In any event, life was ordered enough and for many, that's all that mattered. Virtually free housing, free health care, free education for the children, it all seemed reasonable payment for turning a blind eye to a system which rewarded only one large group of people. Listen to the old people who protest now in Russia at the new economic order and you'll hear their cry that with Stalin there was food in the shops, transport ran on time, factories produced. The advantages which were making the lives of the new ruling class comfortable, even profitable, were hidden in Stalin's day. In any case, many would have thought them deserved for the *nomenklatura* were managing the Soviet Union's industrialisation, hauling it into the modern world and at the same time preparing for war. And war was always imminent.

Never mind that when the factory director wanted a holiday, he'd go to one of the party's marble castles on the Black Sea or a well-equipped health sanatorium, while workers considered themselves lucky to have a wooden *dacha* to go to. So long as roads were being built, processing plants were being established, storage depots were under construction, privilege was acceptable. Soon, of course, when communism arrived the wealth would be shared by all!

What's more, in the early years when the *nomenklatura* was still in its formative stages, it was recruiting so average workers hadn't as yet been locked out of the system. If they grovelled to the right people, mouthed the mantra of Leninism, said nice things about Stalin, informed on their colleagues and friends, they had a chance to rise and become *nomenklatura* themselves.

It was only when privilege turned into *blat* that it was clear the *nomenklatura* had become self-perpetuating and closed. Positions which brought privilege and material benefit would be distributed by the *nomenklatura* system. If one failed to please a superior, or questioned Leninist dogma, promotion would be effectively barred. Toadyism became normal. When a ministry head wanted his son admitted to a scientific faculty at university, he would use *blat* and call the head of the faculty who would ensure a place, no matter what the child's ability. Perhaps somewhere down the line, the *apparatchik* or one of his underlings would organise scarce consumer goods for the scientist. If a highly ranked party member working in the diplomatic corps wanted his offspring enrolled at a prestigious foreign languages school, a phone call would be enough to secure success. They were scornfully called the 'Zolotaya molodezh' (Golden Youth) and they had automatic entry to the good life. They were the second generation in a class closed to outsiders, but ever-increasing as privilege was passed from parents to children.

In time, special shops were created to service their needs. By the end of the 1940s, there were special tailors, watchmakers, dry-cleaners and food stores to cater to the *nomenklatura* and their families. They operated behind closed doors, beyond the reach and the sight of the workers. Indeed, secrecy soon became vital to the survival of the new class. And not only because knowledge of what the *nomenklatura* had access to might have given rise to mass discontent. A favour asked of the wrong person could be fatal, providing a reason otherwise absent to be taken by the NKVD (the KGB of the 1930s and '40s).

University professors would keep secret lists holding the names of the children of the *nomenklatura*, scientists, artists, anyone upon whom the party had bestowed the right of privilege. Without fail and without so much as a phone call the *Zolotaya molodezh* would receive not just places at the university but good grades. When they graduated they got prestigious jobs in the institutes, embassies and ministries where their parents had either worked or had connections.

They travelled freely, albeit much of the time within Eastern Europe and they lived a well-heeled life in good apartments. But there were, of course, drawbacks.

Sometimes with, but more often without, reason Stalin would take what he had given. Stalin's terror was indiscriminate. Millions of ordinary people disappeared, were tortured and killed, but so too were millions of the *nomenklatura*. Alexander Yakovlev, Gorbachev's propagandist, better known in Moscow as Mr Glasnost for his attempts to rip away the veil of deception and self-deceit in which the party robed itself, summed it up succinctly though tragically when decades later he recounted the toll of Bolshevism. The revolution, he said, had proved not to be a festival of justice as Lenin promised but a bacchanalia of revenge, envy and reprisal.

A knock at the door in the middle of the night would mean that, often without reason, someone would be hauled off for questioning, imprisonment, or to the Gulag, the concentration camps where the party and its executioners turned human beings into dehumanised fodder for a system which served only the elite. Millions were interrogated and tortured for no reason other than the flimsy claims of party men whose lives were dependent on quotas of the dead. Paranoia was understandably at a frenzied peak. So those who managed to escape the purges and hold onto their positions and the privileges which went with them operated quietly, gratefully, trusting very few.

They called it the Fraternal Grave or the House on the Embankment. It still stands, an ugly grey building on the banks of the Moscow River, built on prime land just across the road from the Kremlin.

It was built on Stalin's order in 1929, so that all of Lenin's closest comrades could live together in luxury and fear. After many of the old Bolsheviks had been killed, the House became Stalin's *blat*. Those who Stalin wanted to reward were given apartments, sometimes entire floors, in the Fraternal Grave. The privileged would be spared the degradation of living the way the rest of Moscow lived. But in return, they would write poems, prose, novels, policies and scientific theories which supported the ideology and showered communism with praise.

The Fraternal Grave was a self-contained city. The five hundred and five apartments had their own post office, telegraph office, laundry, pharmacy and polyclinic, and their own devoted cleaners and tradesmen who vowed not to reveal how their bosses lived in return for access to special shops and extra food. The apartments were unimaginably spacious and beautifully furnished. Their mahogany desks and cupboards were the stuff of dreams in the Soviet Union.

It took me months to organise a tour of the building. Either no-one answered the central office telephone, or Tamara Ter-Egiazaryan, the unofficial concierge, wasn't available to take my call. Eventually she organised a meeting.

Tamara had come to live in the Fraternal Grave in 1931. Her brother was a pre-revolutionary Bolshevik student leader in the southern Soviet republic of Azerbaijan who was brought to Moscow to refine the Soviet Union's education system.

Eighty-two when I met her, Tamara lived in one of only a

dozen or so apartments in the House on the Embankment still being used by the remaining elderly descendants of the first Bolsheviks.

The CheKa, the NKVD (the predecessors of the KGB) and then the KGB itself had destroyed most of the documents which showed who had lived in the House and who'd been taken in the purges. But Tamara had hoarded letters and documents found in the apartments of the hundreds who'd disappeared from the House over the years, collating them with the help of a group of long-standing residents.

In the basement of the building, she had plastered the walls of a room she called her office with old photographs and charts detailing the horrors which enveloped Stalin's inner circle.

'Everyone lived here,' Tamara told me. 'All of Stalin's Politburo: Lavrenti Pavlovich Beria, the head of the NKVD, and Lazar Moiseyevich Kaganovich, you know about him don't you? He's the one who destroyed all the churches.'

My interpreter, Tanya, shuddered when Tamara mentioned his name. Kaganovich was Stalin's commissar for transport, heavy industry and oil but he was still talked about, still hated. Indeed he was so hated that when Russians refer to him now, they don't mention the fact that he built Moscow's famous metro. He's remembered for his cruelty, his role in the extermination of the *kulaks* (those who resisted joining the collective farms) and the fact that his sister was Stalin's third wife. He was still alive when I went to live in Moscow but was old and sick and spoke to no-one except his daughter who kept an apartment at the Fraternal Grave.

'You know, in this house, there were different floors for different strata of *nomenklatura*,' said Tamara. 'Kaganovich and Beria lived on the top floor. Everyone who lived here, even tiny children, always knew that they were very dangerous men. Their apartments had double walls and secret corridors.'

Among the descendents of the old Bolsheviks was Victoria Volina, the daughter of the founding father of *Pravda*, the Communist Party newspaper, who lived in a huge apartment in the House on the Embankment.

Somewhere in her late eighties—she didn't want to reveal her age—Victoria Volina looked preserved, her skin pale and smooth as though she'd been sheltered from the harshness of Soviet life. But she hadn't been.

'We lived fear. Not just *with* fear. We lived it. I don't like to remember the past, but it's impossible to forget it and I have clear memories, like the 1930s were yesterday. I remember we would come home from school and we never caught the lift to the floor on which we lived. We would go to the floor above and look down the stairwell to see whether there were NKVD behind the door. One day I came home and looked down the stairwell and all the doors on our floor were sealed. I was so frightened. I thought they'd taken my mother. But they'd come to take Malinovsky. He was a Marshal.'

Victoria Volina was too tired to go on. Excusing herself and showing us to the door, she muttered that it was exhausting business remembering the past.

When Stalin died Nikita Khrushchev decided to return the Soviet Union to its 'Leninist norms'. The country, claimed Khrushchev, was back on the road to the achievement of socialism in which all classes would merge into one. The state wouldn't be for one social class, it would be for all. It was a nice theory, but far from reality.

The economy was an out of control juggernaut. And though Khrushchev recognised the problems and introduced limited reforms, they only prodded the beast and made it angry. The ruling class which had managed to survive Stalin had became more self-protective, more determined, more conservative and unwilling to give up its privileges. Khrushchev's reforms threatened them, so the leader was unceremoniously ousted. In October 1964 he was brought back to Moscow from a holiday in the Crimea for a special meeting of the Central Committee at which there was only one report presented. In it, he was accused of mounting a meaningless reorganisation of the command economic system which, although not perfect, was functioning well and serving Lenin's ideals of equality. According to the party.

Leonid Ilych Brezhnev was a 'farcical trick of history', as Alexander Yakovlev put it, a leader for the times. The *nomenklatura* which had secured his ascension made sure he stayed in the job a long time— nearly twenty years—despite his laziness, stupidity and corruption. His reign allowed the *nomenklatura* to reverse most of the limited reforms introduced by Khrushchev and restore privileges he had withdrawn in his attempt to return the party to the people. In fact, Brezhnev's regime unashamedly used the catch-cry 'stability of the cadres' which everyone knew simply meant a more comfortable and profitable life for party members who would protect and provide for each other according to the rules of *blat*.

But little did the *nomenklatura* know that *blat* was about to extend itself beyond the ruling class. It was about to flourish.

A friend of mine openly refers to himself as *'blatnoi'*—the product of *blat*. He studied at MGIMO, the prestigious Moscow State Institute of International Relations which produced the bulk of the Soviet Union's diplomats and politicians from the 1940s until the 1990s.

Aliosha's parents were graduates of MGIMO and so it was quite natural, in the Soviet scheme of things, that their son would study there too. But they would have to go through the rite of entry.

First there was the ritual dance of *druzhba* [friendship]. This involves being nice to the person or people who can make decisions in your favour. This might involve friendly phone calls offering whatever it is that's available to you in a system of shortages. If you came across trousers made in Europe or magazines published in England, they could buy a little favour. Aliosha's mother 'washed a lot of hands', as the Russians put it, of those who were in a position to ensure that her son would receive at least a hearing at the oral entrance examinations. Even her stereo was sacrificed to her son's education. But there were books and magazines offered as well and private tutors hired, paid for in goods rather than money to ensure that Aliosha passed his orals.

The examination was the point at which you learnt whether the amount of *blat* you'd paid was enough to achieve success. Of course *blat* was not so blatant that only those who paid received entry. The institute was obliged to abide by the quota system which operated not only throughout the economy but also within the education system. It had to accept a certain number of candidates from the regions each year. But bright students from the regions were kicked off the list of entrants if they numbered too many or if they threatened those who had bought enough *blat*. And the method of ousting them was crude.

There's a joke at MGIMO about the oral examination which candidates have to undergo.

The first question of the exam is an easy one: 'When did the Great Patriotic War begin?'

'Nineteen forty-one,' answers the student.

'And how many Russians died in the war?' asks the examiner.

'Twenty million,' the student correctly answers.

But, 'Can you name all of them alphabetically?' is the clincher which ousts those not privileged enough to gain entrance.

Variations on the questions assured places for the *blatnoi*—the children of the growing *nomenklatura* with enough money and gifts to safeguard an ever-revolving cycle and the perpetuation of the ruling class.

Many have argued that the command economic system under which the Five Year Plan operated was kept in place so the burgeoning ruling class would remain well fed, well clothed and well travelled.

Irrigation projects which were badly designed, hopelessly unecological and criminally expensive were mounted, lauded and dumped. Grain silos were built in the middle of nowhere then left idle because the party's economic managers didn't think to build roads to carry grain to them. Despite its industrialisation, the system never really mastered the concepts of choice or abundance—and not only because they were considered bourgeois. The simple fact is that the command economy was mismanaged, corrupt and open to fraud. It was an abysmal failure. But it was maintained. Perhaps the shortages it produced were a necessary condition of the existence of the party. They nourished a flourishing class of the privileged which, because of its size and influence could effectively protect itself. And they kept the creative potential of the masses well and truly suppressed.

Whatever the reason, its failures gave enormous impetus to the counter economy. When the state couldn't provide, people stole and used what they had stolen to create their own system of patronage, their own form of privilege, their own *blat*. By the time Brezhnev shuffled off his mortal coil, *blat* had become generalised. It wasn't just a way of life for the privileged classes which numbered in the millions. It was the only way to live. Everyone from the most highly placed to the factory worker used connections and influence to survive.

In 1983, I took ill on a visit to Moscow. The Hotel National called in a doctor who thought I needed more expert attention. But he didn't know where to send me. There was a polyclinic for foreigners but it ministered to foreign correspondents and diplomats resident in the city. What to do with me, a mere tourist?

The dilemma led to several long phone calls, throughout most of which the doctor proclaimed *'da'* over and again, as though he were receiving instructions. But he wasn't. No-one knew what to do with me. In the end, it was decided I should leave the Soviet Union for my own good!

Instead, I used a connection. My friend Sasha, whose father was the party secretary for the republic of Kazakhstan, had an uncle who was a professor at the Medical Institute at Moscow State University. He agreed to see me if I pledged not to speak English as I walked into the gothic university skyscraper on Lenin Hills, overlooking Moscow. It turned out I had a cyst which disappeared with antibiotics prescribed by the professor to Sasha on my behalf. This was my very first experience of *blat*, though I was completely unaware of it. I needed something which was immediately unavailable to me so I called upon a connection to obtain it.

Anyone can bestow *blat* on another person. Sasha bestowed it upon me although strictly speaking the receiver should be able to return the favour or at least they should know someone who has something of value which can be passed up the line. It can become very complicated. In this case, the fact that I was foreign and likely to return to the Soviet Union was probably enough to have made the risk of helping me worthwhile. Perhaps on a return trip I could bring in letters or books.

The son of my acquaintance Lena was admitted to Moscow's prestigious School of Music in 1990 by *blat* bestowed by her neighbour who was owed some *blat* by a teacher at the school. In return, the neighbour received a constant supply of sugar, in deficit for years because of Mikhail 'Tachev's anti-alcohol drive which was forcing people to 'make their own'. The sugar Lena bought her son's placement with was stolen by her husband who worked at the warehouse where it was stored, though he didn't see it as theft.

Indeed, very few Russians considered the practice of *blat* to be corrupt or the theft it generally required to be, morally speaking, unlawful! They saw it more as a perversion of Marxist utopia in which everyone took what they thought they deserved because the economy couldn't supply them with what they needed and because the ideology refused to reward them for hard work.

Blat had become a way of life in a country where the shortcomings of the system threw up very real everyday problems—like not being able to buy or obtain enough food. My mother-in-law, Julia, tells the story of having formed a relationship with a store attendant at a state meat shop which meant she didn't have to rush to the shop in her lunch hour to queue for edible meat. She would simply wander in after work and offer her connection tickets to the Bolshoi Ballet in return for high quality meat at state prices. The tickets came from a neighbour who worked with the ballet company and who would benefit from the meat bought or often simply traded for the tickets.

'The front row of the ballet every week was filled with shop attendants,' said Julia, 'their pay-off for doing what the state couldn't.'

Even services could be bought with *blat*. When the plumbing system broke down you could, of course, phone the state plumbing service for help. But that would be a fruitless, hopeless exercise which would leave you exasperated. The call wouldn't be answered. Or they'd promise to send someone who would never arrive. Or they'd tell you the person you needed to speak with had *vyshel* (popped out). Or you'd be told that the service had closed down for repairs and reconstruction and would reopen in ten years' time. It was easier and more productive to phone your cousin Igor who knew a plumber who worked for the state who might do it to repay Igor for the muffler he'd obtained for the plumber's father-in-law with whom he worked two years earlier.

Once I threw out some old western glossies left in my apartment by a flock of visitors from Australia. But Lena who worked for me three days a week as a cleaner was horrified when she found them in the bin.

'Do you know I can get my child a new pair of boots with just two of these magazines?' she said.

How? *'Po znakomstvu'* ['Through acquaintances']. It was easy. Boots would appear in one of the local shops but what was made available for sale to the public would quickly disappear beneath the stampeding queue. Naturally, the larger share of what was actually received by the store would have been tucked away under the counter by an enterprising store manager and his co-workers for barter. Lena explained that there was every chance she or her husband would know someone who worked at the store or who was related to someone who worked there and she'd be able to offer the magazines as an inducement to get sympathetic consideration in the second round of under-the-counter sales which would inevitably occur.

There's no doubt that by the 1980s *blat* had become more important than money. In fact, a western study of former Soviet citizens who'd left the Soviet Union in the last years of Leonid Brezhnev's tenure concluded that *blat* was as much a precondition for success in life as outright bribery. Of the 1161 people interviewed, 42 per cent said *blat* was the essential ingredient for survival in the Soviet Union. A staggering 62 per cent said *blat* was the only reliable way of getting into university, 57 per cent said it was the only way to get a job and the majority didn't consider it to be corrupt behaviour. It was a means of survival.

Perhaps because *blat* was a system of favours which didn't necessarily involve money, it was the most obvious way Soviet people could go about getting even the most basic of needs, like food. In 1990, food shortages were acute across Moscow because the regions and the non-Russian republics were essentially boycotting the capital, refusing to allow their produce into the city for sale at the farmers' markets where prices were set by private sellers who had grown the produce on private plots. The prices were always higher than in state shops but food was usually available. This protest over the Kremlin's dogmatic refusal to countenance the prospect of a confederation of states rather than a socialist union of republics meant, at a grassroots level, that people were literally fighting in the streets over food. The sight was sickening. One afternoon in December 1990, I'd been to a press conference at the Foreign Ministry's press centre in the heart of Moscow. The deputy head of the Ministry of Foreign Affairs had been talking about the laws which the republics were breaking with their boycott. After the press conference, I walked down the road to the metro station and on the way noticed a crowd of people screeching at each other, huddling together at the same time against the wind and cold. At stake was a box of small, rotting tomatoes which one of the women told me the seller had grown in a hothouse at his *dacha*. It seemed as though the screaming would erupt into a physical fight. I walked away feeling terribly black.

That winter, the queues at city bread shops began at 4 a.m. Fresh fruit and vegetables were near impossible to find. The foreign media began talking of a famine while international aid agencies shipped in supplies. Russians knew better. It might have been close to a western definition of a famine, but it wasn't by Russian standards. *Blat* would ensure against disaster—as it always had.

The facts were, as the government well knew, that in Moscow and across the Soviet Union, bread factories were producing bread. Fisheries continued to can fish. The collective farms were still growing vegetables. The problem was that little was making it to the shop shelves and not much more was available in the farmers' markets. Food was being pilfered as Russians stockpiled for a rainy day. They would keep themselves, their families, their friends, friends of friends, and anyone else who had something to return as a favour fed (and quite often clothed) at the state's expense. And money was rarely exchanged.

Olga worked in the Department of Philology at the university. I met her when I was taking Russian lessons there. She and her sister had to keep their mother and father and, as well, another sister and her family who lived in Ukraine on two state wages. Together they brought in less than 500 roubles a month which at the time amounted to roughly US$40. They lived all together in a small two-room apartment on the northern outskirts of Moscow.

There was little I could do other than offer to supply, from the well-stocked hard currency shops, what they found impossible to buy—sugar and meat. The former because it was in deficit, the latter because it was so expensive. But Olga hated the fact that I knew of her family's predicament and she liked even less the idea that I might take it upon myself to help, so she warned me severely against it.

'We know how to make ends meet,' she told me. 'You really needn't worry. Come for dinner on Saturday night, I'll show you!'

The table groaned with food. Ox tongue, beetroot salad, borscht, spicy roasted chicken, beef stew. There was even vodka which had been difficult to find since 'Tachev's anti-alcohol drive began in 1986. And none of what the family proffered had been bought directly over the counter in any of the state shops, except for the vodka which had been put away by Olga's father who'd queue every week for one bottle bought with rationed coupons handed out by the central government as a means of controlling consumption.

But nor had any of Olga's offerings been directly stolen. The chicken came from the local produce store manager who lived next door. The meat was exchanged for tickets to a hockey game. The tomatoes and cucumbers had been grown the summer before at the family's *dacha* and pickled.

In the cupboard she had stashed away a veritable treasure chest of non-perishable food. *Kasha*, an oatmeal Russians eat for breakfast, had been rationed to one packet per buyer. Olga had sent out each member of the family. There was flour enough to ensure her street's bread supply for a month. The mill bordered their apartment block and her nephew, a mechanic, had repaired broken-down machinery there in return for sacks of flour.

As the satirist Mikhail Zhvanetsky put it: 'Our people are truly amazing. They're eating food that is not in the shops. They're wearing clothes not available in the shops. They're giving you things that can't be officially bought—anywhere. And they're getting paid

120 roubles a month but spending 250. People are stealing and the country is getting richer.'

Blat could even determine where you lived. For decades, until Boris Yeltsin officially disbanded the practice in 1995, Soviet citizens needed a *propiska* (a stamp of permission) to live in the big cities. It was mandatory registration which gave the state control over a person's movements. People couldn't pick and choose where they wanted to work or live. They had a blue stamp in their internal passports which confirmed their places of residence and employment. If they wanted to move to another city, especially to Moscow, they had to trek to the Interior Ministry to ask for permission which would invariably be refused unless they had a job to go to. Jobs in the big cities were doled out by the *nomenklatura* to their family members, friends and those who paid the price. Even to move apartment required an official change to one's *propiska*. There were literally thousands of laws under which the authorities were able to limit people's activity, even the laborious activity of moving house. But people found ways around just about all of them, including the *propiska* which was one of the more absurd.

I knew of a young couple from Rostov on Don in southern Russia who risked a jail term to live in Moscow. In 1979, they each married a Muscovite which made them eligible for a *propiska* to live in the capital. Then they divorced the people they married (who were in on the scam) and married each other which had always been their intention. And they boasted that it was the same clerk who divorced them from their Moscow partners who remarried them—a part-time marriage celebrant they'd met through the institute where one of them worked. They simply gave the clerk their 'gift certificate' which every young couple receives when they register to marry, entitling them to some household good not easily or openly available in the shops. They lived happily thereafter in Moscow.

There were other ingenious forms of *blat* devised to escape the tyranny of the regime. Soon after the *propiska* system was introduced by Stalin in 1932, the dictator extended it so that a person had no right to be away from home for more than three days without specific authorisation or travel documents. As the decades eroded the fear people felt during Stalin's reign, they would either blatantly ignore the decree or create ways to overcome it. They'd travel to wherever they wanted, despite the rules, and stay with relatives or friends or friends of people they worked with and had helped out in some way. This way they escaped having to stay in state hotels where their names would be registered and could be cross-checked for permission to travel. I travelled once to Tbilisi, the capital of Georgia, with a Russian friend who'd been given the name of a hotel clerk who had stayed with her colleague in Moscow for free. The clerk wasn't on duty when we arrived to check in so we waited. We waited for hours. But when the clerk arrived for duty, my friend was able to register as a non-existent person on a made-up passport registration number. *Blat.*

The authorities, if they bothered at all, would search for documents proving the existence of the fictitious person registered at the hotel for months before the system, or more likely laziness, forced them to give up.

Not long after I arrived in Moscow to live, I met a young artist from the Azeri capital of Baku who, try as she might, never managed to get official permission to live in Moscow. She'd lodged several applications in Baku but none met with success. Finally, she decided to take the gamble and move to Moscow without a *propiska*, rent an apartment and lie low. She provided the woman from whom she unofficially rented one room with unlimited accommodation in Baku whenever she wanted an unauthorised holiday as well as a permanent place in any food queue of her choosing. Lilia would queue for days for her landlord. She was queuing when I met her. She was *blatnoi*.

As Natasha would tell me, *blat* was, as I had first thought, a form of communal welfare in a state which couldn't provide what its people wanted and which trampled on their human rights. But sometimes it failed. And when it did, people had to find ways to reconcile themselves to the deprivations and official violations of their humanity.

CHAPTER 3

A QUESTION OF TRUST

This idealistic theory to create harmony in an ordered system had already turned into a dictatorship and we lived in terror of it. The laws of equality and fairness had become laws on the limitation of personal freedom and potential.

NATASHA YAKOVLEVA, 1996

In 1973, a diminutive, unassuming nuclear physicist told a Swedish journalist in Moscow that Soviet socialism was the maximum lack of freedom, the maximum ideological rigidity and maximum pretension about being the best system in the world. Only political reform could edge the Soviet people closer to a humane existence, he told the journalist. The Soviet Union needed multi-party elections, a free media and the decentralisation of the economy. Free hospital care and education were a chimera. Full employment was a cloak for political control. Socialism had delivered the Soviet Union little worth keeping. And he ought to have known.

The heresy was that of Andrei Dmitrovich Sakharov, a Hero of Socialist Labour, who helped create the first Soviet hydrogen bomb then spent his remaining years pushing openly for an end to the arms race, and with it socialism. He died too early, in 1989, less than two years before all that he'd fought for was actually realised.

'Sakharov said socialism brought us little worth keeping,' his wife Yelena Georgiovna Bonner told me in 1992, 'and he was right. We were really no different to the western countries which our leaders told us were the scourge of the earth. They'd highlight the murders, the robberies, the poverty of New York or San Francisco. But we had poverty, and we had crime. And we had—still have—what you don't really understand very well. Alienation. And a terrible fear.'

Sakharov's widow is a passionate Armenian Jew whose determination to protect her frail husband when he was alive had often been over-zealous, even frightening. Of course, she had cause to be protective of him. The system had honoured him when he delivered it a weapon of mass destruction, then virtually crucified him when he warned of its dangers, sending him into internal exile because he refused to play the party's war game. In the newspapers and on public stages, whenever it could, the regime denounced Sakharov as a slanderer of his Motherland. And worse.

Cooped up in exile in their one-bedroom apartment in the closed city of Gorky (now Nizhni Novgorod) in central Russia, Yelena Georgiovna and Andrei Dmitrovich had reason to think the Soviet Union was foul to its very core. If they were bored, they could stand on their balcony and watch the regime's political prisoners with shackles around their ankles carting heavy loads of soil and snow from one spot to another, only to be forced to take it back to where it had come from. They could read in *samisdat*—the underground literature movement in which dissidents wrote about the system and its inadequacies using carbon paper to make several copies—about dissenters who were persecuted in psychiatric hospitals and Jews who were jailed for applying for passports. They could see a strange phenomenon in action. The further away in time the Soviet people moved from the murderous years of Stalin, the more inward looking they became, even if they were not as frightened of the men who followed him. Nothing was getting better. The road to paradise was paved with bones and cemented with blood.

In 1986 when Mikhail Gorbachev allowed Sakharov and Bonner to return to Moscow from exile he freed more than mere mortals, for in Sakharov the people had found a fighter for human rights, a man who stood up to the party even when it was roaring at him. They had read his thoughts in *samisdat*. People patiently, faithfully retyped every word, and distributed it to an ever-growing circle of people who were locked away in the same jail as Andrei Dmitrovich—the Soviet Union. So they knew he was telling the truth.

I never met Sakharov. But I felt, as millions across Russia felt, that I knew him.

When Yelena Bonner finally assented to a meeting with me in 1992, we met in the apartment she had shared with her husband in central Moscow. It was cluttered and small, a shrine to Sakharov. Pictures of him were everywhere, his scientific manuscripts piled in bundles in every corner, his later political manifestos, many of them handwritten, lay on the kitchen table. Yelena Georgiovna lived as though he were still alive and engrossed in conversation, huddled with friends around the kitchen table, speaking in hushed tones about the party.

'The country has been a sham,' said Bonner, settling into an old chair in the living room, puffing away on the second cigarette she'd lit in the five minutes I'd been with her.

'We've been forced to believe that in the west capitalism is in crisis. From the time we were born we were told that communism was about to arrive and that when it did we would live well—not like you in the west. We were luckier than people in the west—we had Lenin. They [the party] were fanatics pushing us to the brink of our own minds. Do you know what happens to a person when a political system takes from you not just your right but your ability to think for yourself, to have information upon which you can make judgments about the world? It drives you into yourself, searching for sanity and safety.'

'But surely there must have been something good about Bolshevism?' I asked.

Bonner paced the room, from the chair to the window, from the window to the bookshelf. Repeating the words to herself, 'What was good about Bolshevism?', she reached for another Winston and settled back into her armchair.

'Nothing. Absolutely nothing. You know, it's time for the truth. And there were many people who wanted to tell it. But the intelligentsia in this country have always had to choose between staying and keeping their mouths shut, leaving, or becoming open dissidents like my husband.

'Too many picked the easy way out and kept their mouths shut and their families safe. And by their example, so we live, in the shadows, some of us committing unforgivable sins in the name of ideology, knowing that even if we'd been loyal to the system that might not have been enough to secure us a peaceful life.

Saddened, still grieving, her voice faded to a whisper. 'No, there was nothing about communism I thought or think now is good. And yes, we should feel pity for ourselves because the only safety we have known has been in our homes.'

In kitchens across the country, it was a common theme. The party allowed no opinion other than that which conformed with its false, distorted view of reality. Only actions and words which served its purposes were moral. As Alexander Yakovlev put it, the party psychologically crippled people while making them believe that their paralysis was good for them, for the state and for the shining future they were heading towards. So skilled had the party become at the art of moulding people's minds that when Stalin died there was mass hysteria and the people, his victims, went on to believe even more strongly in the brand of communism he had advocated. Only the terror stopped with his death. The system went on to bigger and better things. People might have mocked it in the privacy of their kitchens, but they held its preaching deep within their psyches. They knew the system was corrupt but they believed it to be legitimate because it was functional, albeit in a way which left them corrupting each other to survive. The party made them believe that there was an overriding benefit in the Soviet status quo, the corruption, the repression. It was psychological manipulation which stopped a mass uprising or even a move to create civil institutions to keep the party in check. And where the psychological mechanism fell short, fear chipped in.

Fear ensured that relationships, other than those which were corrupt, were confined to within the family or among close friends. As Bonner explained, the home as refuge from the system and the brutality it fostered had become a part of the Russian persona and remains so.

Natasha described the Soviet Union as a huge *communalka* in which literally millions of Soviet families lived. The *communalka* was a four or five-room apartment which two or three families would share. They would each have a separate room to sleep in but would share the kitchen and bathroom. Nothing was private. No word or complaint could be uttered, unless it was whispered. No discussion of the system could be had without an omnipresent, pervasive fear of being reported. People trusted their families and almost no-one else.

Was that why she and our extended 'family' of trusted friends had remained tucked away in the lounge room during my first *tusovka* (get together) in Moscow in 1990, distanced from the dining room where another, newer group of friends I had made since arriving in Moscow drank and talked?

'We don't know those people,' Natasha said at the time. 'They could be anyone—KGB, police, UPDK [the department for the diplomatic corps, notorious for using its staff to spy on foreigners]. How do we know what they want to hear and who they're paid to report it to?'

The next time I called a *tusovka*, Natasha stayed away. She preferred the safety and privacy of the kitchen—hers or mine—where we would talk for hours. She explained to me why it had to be like this.

'There are distortions,' she told me, 'caused by Stalinism. It turned this beautiful theory of communism into barbaric rule which has left us numbed by a fear not only of authority, but of people.

'Even after Stalin died and Khrushchev denounced his crimes, our subconscious was scarred. We kept going, believing we were marching to a radiant future with the party supervising every step. It was ruthlessly dogmatic and this was its most powerful weapon. I cannot think of a time when it loosened its grip enough for us to stop feeling afraid. There were always people whom we feared, whether they were KGB or just our neighbours. And over the generations this has turned us into a nation which actually fears itself. I am not only afraid to meet new people, I am afraid that my natural human instincts will cause me to stumble, let down my guard.

'You know, we have a saying in Russia. A good person is one who will do you over without enjoying it. Imagine living like that!' she said.

Yet even being able to sit in the kitchen and talk about fear was progress. In the early 1980s, when I had no apartment to retreat to and when visiting a Soviet citizen's home was not the safest of options, Natasha and I would walk the streets and talk quietly. If an old *babushka*, one of the self-appointed moral guardians of communist 'order', shuffled along or if a *militsiya* should walk our way, Natasha would stop talking and urge me to follow. She warned me that if we were ever stopped in the street by the *militsiya*, she would claim I was a visiting film archivist and she'd produce a phoney document stamped by her workplace to prove that I was an official invitee. It seemed ridiculous. But to have a foreign friend was dangerous. That would mean she had individualist ideas, that her mind was polluted by the bourgeois west, that she could leak information about the true nature of Soviet life, that she might get some help in trying to leave.

Fear of the police or the KGB had descended into farce by the time I moved to Moscow in 1990, but it was still present in a mild and almost subconscious form. Friends would still look to the ground and walk silently past the police guard at the front gate of my diplomatic apartment block, hoping that no questions would be asked about who they were visiting or what their business might be in the foreigners' compound where I lived. Others simply wouldn't visit me in my office because they believed our staff were UPDK-appointed. I remember one occasion when I tried to hail a ride on the streets and a little Lada pulled up, its driver an elderly Russian who put his foot on the accelerator and drove off in a hurry when he realised I wasn't Russian.

But what I found more disturbing were the looks I'd get from *babushkas* when (if my Lada was working) I'd call to pick up a friend. In the myriad laneways which divide the sea of prefabricated apartment blocks in Moscow, the *babushkas* walk and talk and wheel around their grandchildren, keeping watch at the same time on what's happening in the neighbourhood, prepared to report anything slightly mischievous or out of order. With their eyes peeled on my foreign number plates, they'd often slowly walk towards my car, shifting their gaze from their charges to me. Only once did I dare say good afternoon. The old woman gruffly responded, 'Who are you waiting for?'

It took the intervention of my friend's *babushka* to stop the paranoia. Maria Sergeyevna was almost ninety and she'd seen it all. Better still she didn't like what she'd seen and quite liked me so that when I visited the apartment where she lived with her granddaughter she would bring out old photograph albums which she'd kept hidden for decades and ply me with stories of a Russia I had only ever read about. Old sepia photographs of a young Maria Sergeyevna in Red Square with her father in a crowd watching Tsar Nicholas II ride by—it was an era the Soviet regime had not only politically demolished but attempted to erase from the country's collective memory. But Maria Sergeyevna hadn't forgotten.

'Life wasn't all sweetness and light before the Bolsheviks came, but it was better than this,' she would say.

'You must understand the old women here. Nothing is the same for them anymore. All they hear is that the principles they stood for are wrong. But the people who say this are young boys with leather jackets. These women were born thinking anyone who doesn't look like them are bad, subversive westerners,' she said.

Maria Sergeyevna called off the *babushkas* and for as long as I visited her apartment block there were no more questions asked.

But long before this I'd glimpsed what it must have been like to live in constant fear, never acknowledging who you knew. And I'd learnt the hard way. In 1984, on a visit to Moscow, a friend of a friend whom the authorities had placed in a psychiatric institution on a number of occasions, for refusing to stick to jobs he didn't want and for which he wasn't suited, had given me a letter to post to someone in Paris. It seemed a harmless favour to bestow and without further thought I put the letter in my travel wallet as I prepared to leave Russia. But when I got to the airport I was searched for no apparent reason and the letter was discovered. The customs officer made a phone call and within minutes I was being shunted into a backroom—the KGB room as the customs agent told me with a smile on his face. There, the letter which had been written in English was read aloud by men whom I assumed were KGB officers.

Having read that the KGB randomly picked out foreigners at the airport and photocopied their address books to check which Russians they knew or might have made contact with, I foraged in my shoulder bag for mine. As the officers joked among themselves, mocking my predicament, I quietly ripped out the back page where I kept the names and phone numbers of my Russian acquaintances. I still have the crushed page and indeed, at the time, my address book was taken and photocopied. Finding no Russian names in what remained of it, the officers insisted I tell them who had given me the letter to post. I said it was someone who had approached me on the metro and pleaded the truth, that I didn't realise it was a crime to take a letter out of the USSR. Finally, having missed my flight, I was released and got to spend another night in Moscow, confined to a hotel not far from the airport and a long way out of the city centre. Nothing ever happened to the person whose letter had been seized but that, no doubt, was due to the fact that he knew better than to divulge any personal detail which might have allowed the authorities to trace him.

Although the watchfulness of the authorities was always present, since Brezhnev's time it had been random. While most people assumed the 'watchers' were less interested in watching them than working as little as possible, they knew they could easily make their presence felt if ordered to do so. So fear was less a constant and more a protective companion, as Natasha described it. And no doubt this accounted for the schizophrenic character which so many people would comment about in the Soviet era. Almost everyone I knew was both Soviet and Russian. The same person could be warm, open and emotional, yet turn around and be cold and brutal if need be. And the brutality wouldn't always be directed towards those in authority. Often, I would watch my friends dispense with the care and emotion they displayed in private and allow the heavy wooden doors in the metro to slam into elderly women or children. The excuse would invariably be that they didn't know the person whose nose had just been flattened by their rudeness or, worse still, that they didn't care. Even more often in the bread shops I would see people scream at the *babushkas*, some in their eighties, who sat at the counters slowly serving the queue, yet with their own grandmothers they were meek and gentle, never raising their voices nor showing any anger or disrespect. Life was simply divided into public and private spheres.

More than once, and most often during the early years of my association with the Soviet Union, I felt that my relations with people were poisoned by a fear that they couldn't be trusted. On the one hand, they were my friends, people I liked. On the other, they were part of a system which turned people against each other.

I would often ask Natasha to check out some new person I had encountered who wanted to pursue a friendship. Should I doubt their openness and warmth? Was I just a foreigner to be used for my hard currency or to be reported on? How could you trust the private face knowing the public face could be so cold and self-serving?

'As a general rule,' Natasha would say, 'our public face is a sort of psychological barrier to protect what's really inside us. And you can safely ignore it. If you're invited to someone's apartment, you can be sure they want to show you what's inside and that means they're genuine. If they share their thoughts and better still their emotions with you, you are completely safe. If they don't, the chances are they're watching you.'

It was a good rule of thumb which I used almost without fail.

Soviet people battled not just political authoritarianism and fear but also the aesthetics of the country which, whether by design or other-wise, made people feel minuscule, insignificant, easy to erase. The boulevards of Moscow and St Petersburg are monstrous, many of them ten or twelve lane highways. The buildings which flank them are leviathan. Across Moscow, the so-called Stalin Wedding Cakes reek of authoritarianism, their stone spires jutting out as though to make the point that they are much more than mere *vysotnye zdaniya* (skyscrapers) no matter what an individually minded Russian might think. Their size is incomprehensible. Some of them are little towns. They make ants of humans. The Hotel Ukraine on the Moscow River, across from the old Russian parliament, has a 36-storey central tower with turreted wings on either side. Its spire which used to be crowned with a golden star, is 72 metres high. Sasha, who was just twenty-one when I met him, a child of *glasnost* as he liked to call himself, suggested when the tanks rolled into Moscow in August 1991 to return the USSR to its familiar authoritarianism that we go to the Hotel Ukraine and scream until its giant red granite boulders crumbled to the ground with fear of the hidden wrath of the mere mortals it had towered over and belittled.

And there were the statues and shrines which served not only to reinforce the ideology but to remind people of their place in Soviet life. The most dramatic of them still stand—Yuri Gagarin on Leninsky Prospekt in central Moscow and Lenin's Tomb which remains in Red Square at the eastern foot of the Kremlin wall, despite all the talk by Russia's post-Soviet leaders that the great man ought to be removed to a grave in St Petersburg. His physical presence in the centre of Moscow had been good for the Soviet leadership. They used the tomb to reinforce what they were preaching—that socialism was good, that communism when it arrived would be Lenin's nirvana on earth, that they, as Lenin's successors, wanted only the best for the workers. So important was the tomb, that one hundred and fifty scientists were employed to keep Lenin's body in mint condition in the mausoleum, by dabbing it with embalming fluid twice a week and removing it every eighteen months or so to the Moscow Brain Institute where Lenin would get a bath and a new suit. His brain was dissected into 30 000 sections between 1924 when he died and 1991 when the authorities decided that his grey matter probably held no profound explanation of why communism had been such a raging success. In any event, the process of keeping his myth alive cost the country one million roubles a year which, until the collapse of Soviet communism, would have been the equivalent of US$1 000 000, or enough to build apartment blocks, in chronic short supply, for one hundred families each year. But Lenin was more important than the people.

The mausoleum itself is a pile of red granite and black labradorite cubes with bronze doors, outside of which a guard of honour performs a slow goosestep and changes on the hour. On my first visit to Moscow in the winter of 1983, the queue to see Lenin was an hour long. Visiting delegations from Eastern Europe, whether they wanted to or not, would queue to show that they were respectful socialists. On special national days of honour, the Kremlin leadership and high-ranking members of the Soviet government would gather on the mausoleum's reviewing stand, reached through the Kremlin itself, to watch parades honouring Lenin, communism and the workers. But among ordinary Russians, feelings towards Lenin's Tomb were mixed. I knew some who treated it with genuine respect, a shrine to which they would regularly pay a visit, especially when the reality of Soviet life—the queues, the deficits, the oppression—left them yearning for reaffirmation of what they'd been taught life ought to be like. Others regarded the tomb with contempt and disdain, as a symbol of all that was wrong and farcical about the Soviet state.

Igor, my protest companion, thought it hilarious that Konstantin Chernenko, the third General Secretary of the Communist Party in three years, caught pneumonia while standing on top of the mausoleum watching the 1984 Revolution Day parade through Red Square. Chernenko subsequently died.

'You've heard the joke, haven't you?' Igor asked me.

'Two strangers are walking through Red Square, and one says to the other "Are you going to Chernenko's funeral?"

"Yes," says the other.

"Do you have a pass?"

"I have a season ticket."' Igor thought it hilarious.

But my favourite statue in Moscow was that of Russia's superhero Yuri Gagarin, the first man in space, who's buried around the corner from Lenin at the Kremlin wall. The monument to his greatness is some 60 metres high and made of titanium. My neck would crick, standing at Gagarin's feet, trying to take in the full view. The country's leadership no doubt believed Russians would find in the statue the resolve to continue on the path to communism. They didn't.

But while Yuri still stands vain and noble, others have fallen. 'Iron Felix' Dzerzhinsky, the Polish-born revolutionary who ran the CheKa as the secret police was called when it was formed in 1917, now stands dejected in a park next to *Tsentralny Dom Khudozhnika* (Central House of Artists) across the road from Gorky Park in

Moscow. But for decades before his fall, Iron Felix stood mightily in Lubyanka Square opposite the KGB headquarters—a sad testimony to some of the worst excesses of Soviet Bolshevism. His was the most awesome and disturbing reminder of how indifferent the state was towards its citizens. Russians used to say that Iron Felix had the best office views in Moscow. Out of his window you could see all the way to Siberia. The CheKa boss inspired pure fear. I knew people who refused to lay eyes on his statue when they were forced to walk past it. Some of them preferred to walk an extra kilometre, around the back of the massive buildings which housed the KGB, rather than come face to face with Iron Felix. His was the first Soviet monument which toppled when the 1991 coup attempt against Mikhail Gorbachev failed.

If, however, there was a monument to remind Soviet people that, in the regime's eyes, they were ants who needed to march in columns before the impact of their labour could be felt, it was VDNH—the Exhibition of the Achievements of the People's Economy in Moscow. It used to be a trade fair for Russian producers who would display specially manufactured items to show off the Soviet Union's self-proclaimed industrial superiority. So brazen was the regime that in the 1930s it even boasted a pavilion to commend the construction projects worked on by the millions of people Joseph Stalin turned into slave labourers in the Gulag.

But the point of the park's overbearing, larger-than-life Stalinist architecture was to reflect the people's dedication to collectivism and the communist planned economy and, in the process, denigrate them. At its entrance, a 25-metre-high statue of a muscular worker and a scarfed farm girl carrying sheaves of wheat fixes its gaze upon unsuspecting visitors. An avenue of fountains winds its way from the entrance towards the centrepiece of the park—the 'Fountain of Friendship of Peoples' with its fifteen gilded maidens in different national costumes representing all the former Soviet republics. I saw the fountain work only once before the state could no longer find enough light bulbs to replace those which had blown around its rim.

When it worked, it was a spectacular sight. Thousands of water jets showered the basin while hundreds of spotlights bounced off the flowing pool. In crushing contrast with the dilapidated state of the rest of the city, at VDNH the lawns, until the mid 1980s, were always beautifully clipped, the pavilions meticulously maintained.

Russians, however, saw beyond the sophisticated tractors on display, the aluminium space craft, the industrial washing machines. That was all pompous hyperbole, what the regime claimed it could produce to haul the masses into the modern era and towards the communist paradise. But, for most, it was a pretentious lie.

'We used to go to VDNH,' Natasha told me, 'it was somewhere nice to go on the weekends. But there was never any doubt in our minds that it was all *pokazukha* [for show only]. The longest queue wouldn't have pleased the party. We didn't want to see our Soviet advances in education, biology, physics or chemistry. We went straight to the pavilion for consumer goods,' she said.

Of course, Natasha hoped to see what consumer goods Soviet industry had invented to make her life easier. But rarely did the *pokazukha* on display make it into people's homes.

'But that was the point really,' she said. 'VDNH was all about making us feel that we were somehow not worthy of the things the Soviet state said it was capable of making.'

Beyond the monolithic buildings, far from the statues to myths and ideologies long defunct, tucked away in ugly prefabricated ten-storey apartment blocks with their badly made balconies precariously plastered to chipped and peeling outer walls, you could enter another Russia. The real one.

My friends' apartments were crammed with bits and pieces of non-matching furniture collected, swapped, passed down, bought and squeezed in wherever there seemed to be space. Usually there wouldn't be enough room to swing a cat. A corridor lined with books or boxes, from floor to ceiling, would wind its way from the front door through to each room. The sitting room would almost always double as a bedroom for the parents of the household and sometimes for the entire family. At night-time the couch would fold out into a three-quarter-size bed. In the morning, it would convert back into seating. Natasha could turn the wooden sitting-bench in her kitchen into a spare bed. All she had to do was flip open the lid on a shelf in the sideboard and out would pop a thin mattress, spare blankets and a pillow.

Those with some station in life, of course, had better apartments—a room each for the parents and child, perhaps even a study which could double as a spare room, a lounge cum dining room, a separate bathroom and toilet and a large kitchen. But generally, for the working class, apartments were small and cramped. At my friend Sasha's home, the lounge room was also his parents' bedroom while the combined bathroom and toilet was also used as storage space. Propped up next to the toilet bowl were the family's skis, while bottles of vodka his parents had been steadily collecting over the years were stacked around the bath and basin. In the kitchen, spare parts for the car sat in one corner, while in the other the kitchen table, the symbol of the safety of the home, begged for company which was rarely denied.

The very first time I was invited to a Russian friend's home for tea, on a visit to Moscow in 1985, I walked through the front door and immediately committed not one but two cardinal errors. I forgot to remove my shoes and slip into a pair of *tapichki* (slippers) always at the ready near the front door. And I walked straight into the lounge room where I assumed we would be sitting. Gently, my friend guided me back towards the front door and suggested I might be more comfortable in *tapichki* before leading me towards the kitchen where we spent the rest of the evening.

Being taken to the kitchen was a display of trust and warmth for only there did people seem not to be frightened or suspicious. Even though their complaints about their bosses or the party would still be limited, in the kitchen pervasive fear relaxed in the face of personal judgment about who could be trusted. But if your judgment was imperfect it could be dangerous.

'It's something you know,' Natasha said. 'Either people have a soul or they don't. If they don't, it's written on their faces.'

Through Natasha, I met a filmmaker from the central Asian republic of Tadjikistan. Mara had just moved to Moscow and was throwing a *tusovka* to celebrate the shift. I was invited as a friend of Natasha. But not realising the offence I was to cause, I took along a Russian friend whom I trusted, and who came because she wanted to break the old rules.

'You don't know or understand why,' Natasha took me aside to say, 'and you mustn't be offended by what I'm about to say to you. But you've spoiled the party. We don't know your friend and she doesn't know us. Why does she want to be here?'

We quietly left, the lesson learnt. Mara's kitchen was her only safety.

Friendship too was unlike anything I had experienced in the west. My friends and I would hear from each other every day, even if we had no news to pass on. They would call, or drop in. Or I would visit them. There was a personal obligation to always be there for friends, to put them first in every situation—before work, before your own needs. In the first few years of my posting to Russia, I often found myself explaining to one friend or another why it was that I couldn't abandon the office to talk over a particular problem. Or why it was necessary for me to go to a press conference when I could have spent the afternoon having fun or just being with them. Russian friendship demanded a loyalty and drew an intensity of commitment which was way beyond anything I had ever experienced.

To betray the trust of friendship was a crime worse than the overt, tangible crimes of corruption or theft. They were against the system.

To let down a friend was to turn on what was inside your soul. It was much worse than falling out with a friend in the western sense and stopping all contact. It threatened the core of a Russian's being.

So too did watching friends leave Russia, even if only for a brief holiday. I soon learnt that it was important for me to give lots of notice if I intended to return to Australia or go anywhere for a holiday. If I simply sprang my plans on the handful of people I was close to, they felt they were being locked out of an important decision, or, worse still, being abandoned. Natasha knew that times had changed and that when friends or relatives went abroad not only were they no longer exiled for life, but there was every chance they'd want to or would have to return to Russia. But old hurt had bitten deep. Each time one of her friends travelled abroad she became morose and dispirited. Whenever I left Russia for a short break, Natasha would question whether I'd actually return. She'd summon our circle of friends for a final, heartwrenching farewell which always made me feel guilty for going away and careful to repeat over and over that I'd be back in just a few weeks. But it rarely alleviated the emotion of the moment. There we would sit, Natasha and I, on my luggage for a few minutes for good luck. Over the years, I became so frightened of the emotional charge of leaving that on my last visit to Russia in 1996, I went out of my way to pretend that I would see Natasha again before leaving the country, even though I knew I wouldn't. 'Don't be silly,' she told me when she discovered what I was doing, 'I'm convinced the borders are open. We'll see each other again soon.' I'm not sure she believed what she was saying.

My close friends, and there were very few, were so involved with my life and I with theirs, they were so shockingly open, so eager to force me to show them something of myself beyond mere words that I often felt thoroughly exposed. I wanted to talk about what I knew. They wanted to talk about what I didn't know, the intangibles, the dark side somewhere inside me, beyond my conscious mind. Invariably they sensed my discomfort and tried to make me feel easier.

'You're more than just your past,' Natasha said to me as we sat one evening talking about the problem I had communicating with people who I thought wanted to expose me, warts and all.

'The warts are probably what we would find most interesting about you, whether you're capable of changing yourself. I'm not interested in what you are learning about Russia. I'm only interested in how Russia is changing you. Whether you are one of those people who can become a little bit like us,' she said.

My friends didn't want just conversation. They wanted someone with whom they could plumb the depths of the human condition. I still wonder whether perhaps they were looking for emotional affirmation, for someone to understand why they were the way they were, what it felt like to be the subject of a social experiment, to have been deluded, to have spent a lifetime chasing utopia only to wake up each day, every day, to Soviet reality. Or perhaps their probing and enveloping relationships were a defence against the intrusions of the state; something deeply personal to cherish against the absolutely impersonal character of everything the Soviet Union stood for. I often felt utterly incapable of reporting them as they were and utterly fraudulent for trying. And even when they gave me the words to use, I felt almost as though I were a KGB informer, only rather than telling Lubyanka about what I'd gleaned from the kitchen table, I was telling Australians. So often I found myself asking for express permission to write what they told me. Usually they gave it. But although they could laugh at the party and the stupidity of its mythology, and cry about its past excesses, they were still deeply frightened that it would rise up and bite them again. 'Use our lives, not our names,' they would say to me. It took the disintegration of the Soviet Union, not just *glasnost* to make them feel easier.

Perhaps ingrained fear was why they so loved physical closeness, the sort which would make most westerners feel decidedly uncomfortable. During my first few years in Russia, I remember feeling uneasy as, no matter the space available, my friends would sit cramped together, without any hint of self-consciousness or apology. Even if there were only three people, including me, at the table, the other two would insist on sitting terribly close by, almost on top of me. Closeness intensified the feeling of protection and refuge.

'When you trust someone, you don't feel that they're invading your personal space. You don't feel anything physical at all,' explained my young friend Zhenya.

One warm summer afternoon just before the 1991 coup attempt, I sat at the kitchen table of a tiny Soviet apartment in Filiovsky Park in the south-west suburbs of Moscow, not far from Stalin's *dacha*. The apartment was home to my friend Maxim and his parents. Vera, Max's mother, was fifty-three and tired of the deprivations of Soviet life. She wanted change even though change frightened her. I wanted to know her thoughts on all this talk about abandoning communism and establishing capitalism in what was then still the Soviet Union.

'Well,' she said, 'that's all very well. I know communism hasn't worked for us. I walked for a day yesterday and I found only toilet paper which was so thick you could write a letter on it. And I know they treat us like sheep. But we know how to get the things we really need and we know how to make ourselves feel like human beings. Capitalism will just take all that away.'

'But won't it give you more freedom to feel more like human beings?' I asked.

'Perhaps. But our homes won't be safe,' answered Vera.

The urge to protect what they knew was theirs, what symbolised safety and invulnerability against an awesome system which consumed every aspect of their public life, was overwhelmingly strong. And when the veil of repression lifted during the Gorbachev years, what people reacted most strongly to was the impact this seemed to have on their home life and the physical space of their homes. For so many years they'd been fed television pictures of the down-and-outers on the streets of San Francisco and the crime gangs of New York bursting their way into people's homes and holding them hostage as they stole whatever they could lay their hands on. Capitalism for many equalled poverty and crime and the link was proven when Mikhail Gorbachev loosened the economic strings and inflation, which had practically never been experienced, began to bite.

Between 1988, when the first shoots of private enterprise began to sprout, and 1991 there was an explosion of crime, most of it petty. But that was the problem. Petty theft and home burglaries were what affected Vera and millions of others like her. Ordinary people who worked in factories and shops wanted to know that no matter what hardships they faced on the streets as inflation bit harder and harder, they could go home to relative safety. All this talk of capitalism was fine but what if the thieves made off with the new boots they'd just bought, or the television set they'd finally acquired after twenty years of barely being able to dream about it. Their homes would be free of one menace and exposed to another! And there was no such thing as an insurance policy to protect them.

Comparisons of crime statistics are hard to make because according to the sanitised figures of the Soviet regime, there was almost no criminal activity before 1985. By 1989 when the obvious became hard to deny and a degree of honesty about the real nature of Soviet life was in vogue, the Kremlin put the number of crimes committed in Moscow alone at 1 094 000—of which 216 000 were serious. And that was one year's effort! More than three-quarters were crimes against ordinary people. The year after, the crime figure doubled and continues to rise steadily, although the nature of criminal activity is changing. According to the statistics of the Ministry for Internal Affairs, on average, in the period 1987–89, thirty apartments were robbed every hour across both Moscow and Leningrad.

At the local shops in the suburb of Krylatskoe where I lived, the *babushkas* talked endlessly throughout 1990 and 1991 about the 'criminal problem' and how it was undermining their way of life and robbing them of inner security which was all they'd been able to acquire after decades of virtual slavery to the system. The constant stream of articles in the newspapers about old people being killed for their city-centre apartments made them feel terribly uneasy. They didn't consider that the corruption and theft which had been the hallmark of Soviet life were what endangered their existence. For them the crime that capitalism brought to the Soviet Union was the only threat.

As Yelena Georgiovna Bonner told me at her kitchen table in 1992, 'All we ever had was corruption and theft, and an arbitrary bureaucracy which sometimes gave you what you needed and sometimes didn't. But we also had a sort of safety cone—our homes. Sure, they even bugged our apartments when they thought we were conspiring against them. But generally, our homes were a cure for the indifference they made us feel towards everything about our country.'

CHAPTER 4

AND THEN THERE WAS LENIN

The system needs a liquid that takes the shape of whatever vessel it is poured into.

YEVGENY YEVTUSHENKO, *FATAL HALF MEASURES*, 1991

In Soviet Russia, Lenin was omnipresent. Vladimir Ilych was inescapable. It seemed to me that the Soviet Union was one huge Lenin museum. He and the people were one, said the banners. He and the KGB, he and the Central Committee of the Soviet Communist Party, he and the queues were one, united in a historical half lie, half myth.

While across the Soviet Union, jokes at the Communist Party's expense were almost a cure for the more hideous and offensive effects of its all-consuming power and authority, Lenin escaped with just a few bruises. His powerful wife bore much of the brunt of the Russian habit of satirising life. There's the one about a film made to commemorate the eightieth anniversary of Lenin's visit to Warsaw. Leonid Brezhnev and the party high-fliers are sitting in the front row as the curtains are lifted. In the opening scene, shot in Moscow, Lenin's wife, Nadezhda Krupskaya, peers from beneath the sheets where she's snuggling with another man. 'But where's

Lenin?' bellows Brezhnev, lurching to his feet, irate, offended. 'He's in Warsaw,' said the film maker.

But all jokes aside, Lenin had a mesmerising, religious grip on people's lives. And not by chance.

Lenin was barely cold when the party leadership hit on the idea that if they turned him into a god they could achieve two goals at the same time. They could provide people with something to believe in—Lenin. And they could use the sacredness with which they would imbue him to impose whatever measures they liked on the people. They simply turned Lenin into a religion and called it Leninism.

The Bolsheviks didn't just preserve Lenin's body. As the Soviet general and historian, Dmitri Volkogonov, pointed out, they embalmed his ideas. Wrapping them up tightly into little pockets of wisdom, Lenin's worshippers could learn them by rote and repeat them mantra-like at every opportunity. His body, mummified and waxed to add a dose of surrealism to the picture, was a relic. Even the achievement of Lenin's vision the party distorted through constant revision, each new version aimed at securing one or another project, covering up failure or sometimes just the leader's whim. It was convenient to have a human god at hand, around whom the party could whip up a frenzied hysteria to ensure people remained subservient and obedient.

None of this was Lenin's fault. Indeed, Lenin had exposed human nature's inclination to exploit those without power. And his Marxist-based formula for wiping the slate clean sounded good too. Revolution would create a workers' paradise where each would reap the fruits of their labour in a triumph over capitalism and its exploitative tendencies. There would be a dictatorship of the proletariat where workers gave according to their capacity, and took according to their needs. Privately owned property would be usurped by the bureaucrats, as Marx had dictated, on behalf of its rightful owners, the people. To reject the basic tenets of communism, Lenin preached, was to reject the very idea of a just and perfect world and that, of course, would be to uphold exploitation and inequality. But his utopia turned out to be a cloak for a brutal totalitarian system, the seeds of which he himself sowed before he died in 1924.

For Lenin a just world in which the workers triumphed could only be achieved by crushing the exploiters—and the exploiters were not only the moneyed class and the owners of property. The workers too would be oppressed, if necessary killed, in the name of the Revolution. Unfettered dictatorship of one man, supported by an ever burgeoning bureaucracy owing allegiance to the Communist Party would create a new society.

Lenin created the Communist Party merely to carry out the ideals of the revolution. To do so its control had to be absolute. The party would have to transform itself into a state. Logically then, it would be a dictatorship not of the proletariat, as Lenin promised, but of the party and its apparatus. The party's *apparatchiks* would oversee the rules while the *nomenklatura* would work towards guiding the revolution and exporting it abroad.

But if Lenin noticed the party's drift towards totalitarianism, as some would later claim, he certainly didn't acknowledge it. Instead, he used more and more violence to achieve his aim. The secret Lenin files in the KGB's archives would reveal seventy years after he died that in 1920 Lenin said—and not for the first time—'We shall not hesitate to shoot thousands of people.' Indeed, just two months after he seized power, Lenin decreed that rejecting the Bolshevik program was a crime. He created the CheKa, the forerunner of the KGB, giving it authority to use the death penalty at will. He ordered his opponents to be shot without trial. His just and perfect world had to be violently imposed.

Even so, by the time of his death—6.50 p.m. on Monday 21 January 1924—the new world hadn't arrived.

But it was on its way. How could it not be? Everything—culture, education, industry, the law, the army, life itself—was being 'revolutionised'. New scientific theories were being written to suit the new order. A new moral code was imposed so that people could 'self-emancipate'. Women were given the same rights as men. Marriage was considered bourgeois, though if people insisted, they were free to indulge and even freer to divorce. It was a new society and to those who embraced it, it was a unique opportunity to completely rid the country of its past and replace it with 'a purely proletarian identity'. For Vladimir Mayakovsky, the giant of Soviet propaganda poetry who fathered the Futurist art movement in Russia, the revolution meant freedom from the church and the monarchy which had dominated Russians' lives. Out with the old, in with the new was his cry and that of Vasily Kandinsky, Alexander Rodchenko, Kazimir Malevich and Lyubov Popova—the Russian avant-garde who looked upon Lenin's revolution as a way of radically transforming life in Russia.

It didn't take long before each of them experienced Lenin and his revolution in a less blinkered way. The zealots would soon see that unless their efforts were channelled into one new idea—Leninism— then they would suffer. Some happily compromised themselves. Others, like Mayakovsky, couldn't. In 1930 he killed himself, unable to live with Soviet reality. He had watched in horror as the Red Guard roamed the streets of Moscow and St Petersburg shooting randomly. He watched as the poetry, the theatre and the art of his merry band of revolutionaries were subjugated, then consumed by socialist realism—party-filtered art and culture—all in the name of the revolution of the proletariat. He saw the lie and couldn't live with it. But when he died, the regime eulogised him, building a huge statue in the centre of Moscow to honour his propagandist art. They drummed his early propaganda poetry into the mind of every Soviet child, in the process turning many of them against him. But those who knew Mayakovsky also knew the truth.

As Winston Churchill wrote of the Russians, 'their worst misfortune was his [Lenin's] birth, their next worst his death'. The party's decision to use Lenin's death to secure complete psychological control was deliberate—as historian Dmitri Volkogonov discovered while foraging through the party's archives which had been opened to him in 1988.

Leaving Lenin in a crypt left 'the path to Lenin' open to everyone who wanted to renew their faith and know true happiness. All they had to do was visit him. The party built museums, statues, monuments to him. Petrograd (now St Petersburg) was renamed Leningrad. Whoever could mouth Lenin's words and apply them to the most situations received the best jobs, the best apartments, all the little luxuries.

So commonplace was the practice that by the 1960s and '70s, few climbing the party's career ladder even bothered to learn the mantra accurately. Even Boris Yeltsin admits to conjuring up a few socialist-like platitudes and claiming they were Lenin's words. In the end few knew the difference. But though Yeltsin and his ilk might have been duping their superiors, they were also duping themselves. With notable exceptions, people seemed to have separated in their minds the brutality of the regime and the image and myth of the man who led them through revolution. Lenin, they thought, was a kind and gentle visionary whose life was tragically cut short trying to deliver utopia to the people he loved. The shortcomings of the system, the corruption, the repression, they blamed on the bureaucrats and the party. Not Lenin. In the safety of their kitchens, as they berated the party and poked fun at its leaders, people would remember that Lenin had given them NEP—the New Economic Policy of 1921 which in essence restored private trading. When Mikhail Gorbachev came to power he tried to restore NEP. But by then the rot was far too deep. In 1921, there had still been a chance to rescue the situation.

Lenin's NEP kept heavy industry, banking and foreign trade in the hands of the state, but allowed workers to produce and sell. And with the profits of their labour they would be able to buy consumer goods produced by other private operators. But by 1927 NEP was dead. Private trading was again a 'bourgeois suppression of the workers'. When I arrived in Moscow, the catch-cry of the Leninists was that he had died too early to save them. They had managed to harbour the *svetloe budushie* (bright future) of Lenin's NEP through seventy years of totalitarianism.

Actually, it was only as the party began to lose its grip on power in the 1980s that the outward signs of mass belief in Leninism began to wither and the stories of Lenin's vision, his heroism and his kind and wise nature began to sound suspect.

As Volkogonov put it in 1994: 'Our view of Lenin has changed not only because we have found there is more than the stories that inspired us for decades. We began to doubt his infallibility above all because the "cause" which he launched—the party—and for which millions paid with their lives has suffered a major historical defeat. It is hard to write this. As a former Stalinist who has made the painful transition to a total rejection of Bolshevik totalitarianism, I confess that Leninism was the last bastion to fall in my mind.'

In 1991, I sat in the central hall of the Oktyabrskaya Hotel in Moscow and listened to several military generals condemning Dmitri Antonovich Volkogonov who had risen to the rank of Colonel-General in charge of the military's propaganda department, but had fallen from favour because of his 'new' history of the Second World War. He is a traitor they cried, a liar and a scoundrel. Who, other than a Judas, a lackey of western imperialists, could possibly accuse Stalin of being anything other than a brilliant military strategist or the Soviet state of being anything but militarily superior.

In the mid 1980s, Volkogonov, a gentle Siberian-born military general began a radical personal transformation and, in the process, helped destroy what for many Russians had been solid, immutable truths.

Volkogonov's father had been shot in Stalin's purges. He'd been arrested for possessing a pamphlet written by Nikolai Bukharin— once a colleague of Lenin who was tried under Stalin for allegedly 'undermining Soviet military power and helping Germany and Britain prepare an imperialist attack on the USSR'. Needless to say Volkogonov senior was sentenced to death. Volkogonov's mother—the wife of an enemy of the people—died in internal exile in western Siberia after what the Russians call the Great Patriotic War—World War II.

The young Dmitri Antonovich eventually entered the army and began studying Marxism/Leninism, rote learning the works of both Lenin and Stalin. Later, when his conversion was already underway, he reflected on his life with the journalist David Remnick.

'I was a young lieutenant when Stalin died,' he told Remnick, 'and I thought the heavens would fall without him. The fact that my father had been shot and my mother died miserably in exile, that didn't seem to matter; it was destiny, incomprehensible. My mind was contaminated. I was incapable of analysing these things, of putting the pieces together.'

But two years into Mikhail Gorbachev's reign, Alexander Yakovlev—Mr Glasnost as he was known among foreign correspondents— gave Volkogonov unprecedented access to the party and KGB archives which had been closed for decades. As he began to dig, depression and disillusionment set in.

His biography of Stalin, *Stalin: Triumph and Tragedy*, smashed a party truth which so many, including Volkogonov, had believed— that the NKVD (the precursor to the KGB) worked behind the party's back. To some extent, it had. But Volkogonov discovered that Stalin had more than passing knowledge of the activities of the secret police. Indeed, he had personally signed documents which sent literally tens of thousands of people to their death. He had ordered systematic executions. Still, in 1990, many people refused to believe Volkogonov, even those who had lost family to Stalin's terror. Perhaps a few thousand people were killed, they'd say. But not tens of thousands. Not millions. Even those who were prepared to accept that Stalin was pathologically murderous had chosen to look instead at what he had done for the country. And certainly, its industrialisation was to be applauded. But Volkogonov forced them to ask themselves 'but at what price?'. For Volkogonov the price was dignity, humanity. Stalin, for him, had moulded an indifferent, morally impoverished species which simply accepted his callous totalitarianism.

Volkogonov faced down his critics in the military. He ploughed on, digging through the vaults, writing furiously so that before he died the truth would be known. His history of Stalin and the Great Patriotic War infuriated the generals who sat in the Oktyabrskaya Hotel beneath a red silk portrait of Lenin—the father of the impending utopia. But they were not to know, not then, that Volkogonov had more to say.

The high priest Lenin also had a lot to answer for. In the party's archives, Volkogonov found documents the regime had always asserted had been lost. But they weren't lost. They were buried. And when he opened the boxes, Volkogonov found that Lenin had embraced terror and murder on a scale which only Stalin would later rival. Anyone who hadn't followed the revolution was killed without question or trial. When, in 1918, Latvia and Estonia established their independence Lenin wrote: 'Cross the frontier and hang 100 to 1000 of their civil servants and rich people.' And this was only the tip of the iceberg. He was disparaging of the Russians, his compatriots. As they starved to death at home, Lenin ordered trillions of roubles to be sent abroad to fan the flames of international revolution. The world deserved to live as the Russians allegedly lived.

On 6 December 1995, Dmitri Antonovich Volkogonov died, a self-avowed outcast among men with whom he had once shared so much.

Volkogonov was not alone in finding it difficult to debunk Lenin. I was bewildered in 1990 to find that despite the treacheries of the Soviet state constructed in Lenin's name, the repression and the deprivations imposed by his rapidly running out of steam Communist Party, so many people stood by Vladimir Ilych, choosing to hang onto their belief that he was the kindly Soviet tsar. They wanted to believe what they'd been taught from the moment of their birth— that Lenin was modest and good.

Despite the obvious lies of the Lenin myth and the lack of evidence to prove that, as Lenin had preached, socialism would mean that each would reap according to his or her needs, people blamed instead 'the system' as though Lenin himself had had nothing to do with its creation.

Perhaps this was because many people were too frightened to openly blame the party which controlled the system and which, although it was dying from a million cuts, still refused to lie down for good. Perhaps it was because the party was essentially Lenin's, so to criticise it would be to criticise Lenin. Perhaps it was simply because the party's policy of indoctrination and propaganda from the cradle to the grave had been thoroughly successful. I suspect the latter.

It didn't take too long to understand why that might have been the case. Tatyana Taptapova was fifty-six when I met her in 1990 in Moscow at a public meeting of the group Memorial which devoted itself to the revelation of Stalin's terror. Memorial had been given permission to hold a candlelight vigil outside KGB head-quarters at Lubyanka Square and Tatyana Vladimirovna had gone in memory of her parents. Both had been taken and killed in the 1940s leaving her to a desperately poor life in Russia's orphanages. Tatyana Vladimirovna was among the millions of Soviet people whose enqui-ries about their loved ones often met with a curt postal reply that 'they'd been relocated to the cemetery'. I approached her hoping she could explain why, in the face of this clear protest at the party's violent history, it had survived and why Lenin's myth was still intact.

Tatyana invited me to her apartment at Malaya Bronnaya not far from the Patriarchs Ponds in central Moscow where the writer Mikhail Bulgakov had lived.

'You go and speak with the scientists, or the historians, even the party people themselves, and they'll tell you the same thing,' she said. 'All of our history, our culture and worse still our potential was reduced to one goal—to achieve communism. And when the ideal-ism began to run out of steam, they used the belief that our leader, Lenin, from his tomb wanted only good for his people. He was the high priest of the Soviet Union. There was only one personality and that was his.

'Bozhe Moy ['My God'], they even named their kids after Lenin. There was the name Len, there was Ninel which was Lenin spelt backwards. To us, Lenin himself was a god, and the propaganda was so strong most people still believe he was something supernatural they could believe in when they were allowed to believe in nothing else. Maybe he wasn't as violent a man as those who followed him—I mean Stalin of course—but for a long time no-one wanted to believe that this violent system was his. And I for one didn't want to believe that those who came after him used his revolution and his name to hold together their regimes. Instead I thought we had a pathological liking for dictators who treated us like we were sheep cooped up in a farmyard. That's how little we thought of ourselves.'

The mother of a friend of mine, Natalia, explained how she also believed in Lenin's goodness, indeed Stalin's goodness, despite the brutality both had inflicted upon her family. Natalia's maternal grandfather had been taken to the Gulag for the crime of having worked in the last tsar's legal office. His origins weren't considered to be proletarian enough. When he returned from eight years' imprisonment, he joined the White Guard which had been fighting Lenin's Reds. The next anyone heard from him was through a distant cousin living in Argentina who wrote a cryptic note saying, 'Both of us are well.'

Natalia showed me a photo of her highly decorated maternal grandfather which her mother kept hidden. Only her grandfather's head remained in the photograph. Her mother had scratched away everything below it so that no-one would ever know he had been awarded medals by the last monarch. Natalia's mother feared she herself would be taken had anyone seen her father was a member of the tsar's army.

'Like my mother I always thought it was the party which was wrong, not Lenin,' Natalia told me. 'I even cried when Stalin died. Stalin seemed to me when I was a child to be such a strong leader. He was someone who wanted to carry out Lenin's ideals. That's what they told us over and over. And I can't say that I recognised Stalin's violence as violence. It was something completely different. It was the menacing threat of those who opposed communism which caused the violence.' Natalia picked up the kettle to pour a little more water over a drop of black tea. 'At least that's what I believed,' she said.

Lenin's violence, of course, was ignored by the thousands of Soviet history books and official biographies which were constantly revised according to the latest ideological twists. Instead, a lifetime of studying Lenin was inflicted on everyone and, as Volkogonov put it, was as compulsory for every Soviet citizen as the Koran is for an observing Muslim. 'Imagine if we'd been as good at everything else as we were at eulogising Lenin? We'd be a true superpower!' Natalia told me.

Indeed the bookstores teemed with Lenin's writings. In 1990, the records show that there were more than 653 million copies of Lenin's works published in 125 languages. In 1983, on my first trip to Moscow, I went to *Dom Knigi* (House of Books) which was a massive three-storey shop on Kalininsky Boulevard not far from Lenin's Library, Lenin's Museum and Lenin's Mausoleum. As I stepped inside, I was ushered by an elderly attendant away from the technical and academic books which made up much of the store's stock, towards the 'ideological literature'. There were mountains of books and pamphlets at bargain-basement prices. The more people bought, the more the state produced.

'From the moment he died,' my friend Igor told me, almost giggling with embarrassment, 'they began building factories to mould and manufacture statues of him at all ages. You could buy him in bronze, steel, granite or marble.'

His monument graced the central square of every village, town and city from Siberia to Estonia and the Arctic Circle to Tadjikistan. The biggest statue of Lenin I ever saw in the Soviet Union still towers on its pedestal in one of the busiest metro squares in Moscow—Oktyabrskaya—through which thousands of real people scuttle daily to their offices or to the factory nearby called *Krasny Proletariy* (Red Proletariat). While other revolutionary heroes toppled in the aftermath of the failed coup attempt against Gorbachev, Lenin mostly survived.

Lenin smiled down on schoolchildren as they entered their classrooms to be taught about the world according to Lenin. My husband tells a joke of the hundredth anniversary in 1970 of Lenin's birth when saturation propaganda clogged the air-waves, and bombarded the streets, school lectures and university halls. In Lenin's Primary School Number 36 the teacher challenges her pupils to tell her what is furry, has long ears and jumps from spot to spot.

'Can you tell me Masha?' she asks. Masha, barely eight, can't. 'What about you Zhenya?' Zhenya looks befuddled. 'Someone must know,' implores the teacher, 'what about you Sasha? What is furry, has long ears and jumps around?' Bold and proud, Sasha replies,

AND THEN THERE WAS LENIN

'Lenin!' Everything came down to Vladimir Ilych.

There were Lenin Libraries all over the Soviet Union which stored hundreds of official biographies. His bust watched over the sick in hospitals built in his name. Banners were hung across massive buildings proclaiming 'Lenin Lived, Lenin Lives and Lenin Will Live'. In 1983, when I tried, during my first visit to Moscow to find the Lenin Museum, an imposing, unmissable building on the edge of Red Square, I was led on a wild-goose chase by buildings from which monstrous portraits of Lenin were draped. None of them were the Lenin Museum. But the face of this benevolent demigod smiled down upon me everywhere.

Years later when I finally found the Central Lenin Museum (which also boasted branches all over the Soviet Union), I found a living shrine, an alternative to the mausoleum on the Kremlin side of Red Square where he lay pampered and plugged. Inside the three-storey museum hundreds of party researchers and propagandists worked constantly to update and keep in order the 10 000 pieces of Lenin memorabilia which had been collected since Lenin's death in 1924 and sent regularly on visiting exhibitions to Lenin memorial sites in Paris, Leipzig and Krakow. I often took visitors to the museum to look at Lenin's black Rolls Royce roadster, by far the best car in Russia until capitalism hit the place. Issues of the revolutionary newspaper *Iskra* (*The Spark*) which was another Lenin brainchild hang from the walls of the museum's exhibition halls with the articles the leader wrote himself highlighted—'The Urgent Tasks of our Movement', 'Where to Begin', and, a favourite of the propagandists whose job it was to further Lenin's teachings, 'What Is To Be Done', the first copy of which was printed in Stuttgart and sent secretly to Russia in a false-bottomed suitcase which is also in the museum. And holding pride of place, for reasons I cannot fathom, in the centre of the main hall is a replica of the printing press in Leipzig where *Iskra's* first issue was published.

In 1992, I went to the museum to compile a story for 'PM', one of the current affairs programs I reported for at the ABC. Galina

Arsenievna who was the propagandist assigned to me for the excursion, and the person to whom all my questions were to be directed was a petite woman of about fifty. Her blonde hair knotted tightly into a bun sat at the nape of her neck. She wore what I came to think of as the standard uniform of the female Soviet office worker—a heavy woollen skirt, sensible shirt, thick tights and ankle-high plastic boots with a thick zipper up the side. Galina Arsenievna knew everything the party allowed her to know about Lenin—what Lenin told the Second Congress of the Party in July 1920 when he delivered a report on the International Situation and the Fundamental Tasks of the Communist International; what Lenin thought about his comrades, about the Russian people, about the civil war. Confidently she told me in an interview I recorded for 'PM': 'The titanic workload involved in Lenin's leadership of the party undermined his health and in 1922 he had an attack which led to the sharp deterioration in his health. The doctors forbade him to do any work or read newspapers and magazines. But he insisted. Although he was severely ill, Lenin retained a clear mind and immense willpower and was highly optimistic about the Soviet Union's chances of achieving a perfect society.' It was pap.

The Central Committee archives when they were finally opened to Dmitri Volkogonov in 1987 told a completely different story. Volkogonov writes that a rare and inherited neurological disease had left Lenin unable to speak other than in monosyllabic words. Nadezhda Krupskaya, his wife, spent hours each day trying to make him repeat words which one imagines the leader of the Russian revolution would have known very well—words like 'workers', 'revolution', 'peasant'. Lenin managed to respond only with 'vot vot' ['there, there'] and spent his last two years in a dacha at Gorky just outside Moscow, according to Volkogonov, wrapped in a blanket, looking through people with a helpless, twisted smile. His arms and legs were paralysed.

Galina Arsenievna's spiel was identical to the recorded messages the museum gave to scores of school students taken there to learn yet more about Lenin. But she went on to explain, no doubt inadvertently, and only when I asked, how the lie about Lenin's ability to work even when 'stricken with ill health' was manipulated to induce workers to strive even harder to build a new, technologically advanced Leninist world. The ideology was running out of steam. But if Lenin could work till his death—no matter how untrue the claim—so too could his 'children' for the ultimate prize of his utopia.

'The way Lenin was is the way *we* must be in order to build communism. Without dedication, and the will to go on and fight, we will never get there,' said Galina Arsenievna.

Even in 1924, the year he died, the cry was 'Back to Lenin!'. It became the communist mantra. It still was in 1990 when I climbed underneath the huge iron gates of a Soviet metal and tube factory in the south-west suburbs of Moscow, having been told it had some of the best Soviet worker propaganda billboards in the capital. It was a 'dark Satanic mill' of epic proportions. Huge chimneys billowed black smoke. Intense heat radiated from the workshops. Monster billboards ten-metres high proclaiming 'Communism = Soviet Power + Electrification of the Entire Country' and 'The Party and the People are One' seemed to pour scorn on the men and women who worked in ten-hour shifts, around the clock, for a pittance. 'All Power to the Workers' said the posters.

But the workers Lenin claimed had won political power, smashed the old bureaucratic regime, annihilated private property and owned the country lived very poorly and seemed to me to have very little power. In the workplace, at workers' rallies and on marches through Red Square on national holidays they were reminded of the power they knew they didn't have. But no matter how great this lie, an even bigger one could always be used to mask the truth.

Joseph Stalin, who eventually succeeded Lenin, used Lenin's words to persecute anyone he thought was engaged in anti-Soviet activities. Among the few pieces of Soviet kitsch capable of making my Russian friends laugh are the portraits I've picked up along the way of Stalin and Lenin together. Everyone knew that Lenin thought Stalin was incapable of taking on his mantle.

Then Nikita Khrushchev, who followed Stalin, used Lenin to highlight the capricious cruelty of the Georgian dictator.

In his not so 'secret' speech of 1956 when Stalin was officially exposed for the first time, Khrushchev said: 'And who will say that Lenin did not resort to the cruellest measures against the enemies of the revolution when really necessary? No, no-one can say that. Vladimir Ilych called for the harsh punishment of enemies of the revolution and the working class and when the need arose he used such measures with utter ruthlessness. But Lenin used violence against *real* class enemies.

'Stalin,' he said, 'showed irreverence to Lenin's memory.' Of course, when the *nomenklatura* who had put Khrushchev in the top job wanted him out, they also invoked Lenin's name. Khrushchev, they said, had driven the country off the Leninist path with his reforms of the system. Lenin would not have approved of the 'thaw' in relations with the west, they said, nor of Khrushchev's frequent travels there.

The simple-minded Leonid Brezhnev, a trick of history as Alexander Yakovlev called him, assumed the throne when Khrushchev was overthrown and quickly sent the country to sleep for almost twenty years with his dull, self-indulgence. But until his death, he would say to anyone who bothered to listen, 'Lenin's cause lives and will be victorious!'

The next in line, Yuri Andropov, broke through Brezhnev's era of stagnation and tried to fix some of the problems making people's lives miserable. But his remedy was a return to law and order which allowed the *nomenklatura* to hark back to Lenin to justify their excesses and their corruption.

Konstantin Chernenko, senile when he assumed the party throne, used Lenin to encourage the people to work harder.

And last, though certainly not least of the Soviet leaders, Mikhail Gorbachev, in his more confused moments before the attempted coup against him in 1991, talked of returning to Lenin for guidance. In long, winding speeches to audiences of breathless, admiring foreign journalists and diplomats, Gorbachev would remind us that the Russian revolutionaries, led by Lenin himself, had exposed exploitation and inequality. But Gorbachev was unable to take the final leap and admit that the Leninists created violent totalitarianism. Gorbachev knew the truth but he could not accept that the Leninist social experiment of which he was a product had failed. For Gorbachev, no amount of time, blood or fear had tarnished Lenin's image.

As the Russians put it, Lenin's legacy was the party which produced leaders who followed him to the 'T'. Vladimir Ilych Lenin was the *titan* [titan], Stalin the *tiran* [tyrant]. Khrushchev was the *turist* [tourist], Brezhnev the *tranzhir* [spender]. Andropov and Chernenko were *trup* [corpses] and Gorbachev the *treplo* [chatterbox]. Everything came back to Lenin.

Beneath the surface of the old Soviet Union there lay a complex society in which stereotypes were impossible to pin down. Who were the true believers and were they the only people who didn't want to watch Lenin fall from grace? Did everyone who became a member of the party really believe the party was right or capable of delivering the just, egalitarian society promised by Lenin? Even though some knew that the propaganda they were being fed about Lenin was fodder from a corrupt party machine, did they still believe it all?

To Yelena Fedorovna whom I'd come to know because she ran the local bread shop near the Krylatskoe metro station, not far from where I lived, Lenin was 'an earthly god'. He was certainly no mere mortal. 'We are mortal, he lives on through the party,' she would tell me. No matter what evil the party perpetrated, it was not in Lenin's name nor through his eyes and mind that it did so, though

Yelena Fedorovna couldn't tell me how it came to pass that so many had died during Lenin's time, on Lenin's orders.

'The commissars!' she said as though I ought to be able to simply accept this as an ultimate explanation.

'But even Krupskaya [Lenin's wife] wrote that her husband was capable of cruelty,' I retorted.

'Ah, you believe all the rubbish the party prints!' she answered.

To my old friend Natasha, one of the very few true believers I knew, Lenin was the greatest revolutionary of the century whose ideas were noble, based on commonsense and humanist values. Leninism, she believed, amounted to the creation by peaceful means and hard work of a new and perfect civilisation. These were not ideals which could be questioned. The problems of Soviet communism, she believed, were created by those who succeeded Lenin, even Gorbachev who she claimed unashamedly wielded Leninist dogma to ensure the survival of a political and economic system which propped up the party and, in turn, kept him and his cronies employed and living well. Natasha, like dozens of other people I knew to be intelligent, thinking, honest workers believed wholeheartedly in the holy infallibility of Lenin.

Once, sitting in the privacy of her kitchen in 1989, Natasha showed me a film script written by a young producer which postulated that Lenin was merciless not just towards his political enemies but to anyone who was at odds with the 1917 revolution.

'Of course, it's fantasy,' she said, 'but it's an interesting interpretation of history.'

'But Lenin himself said that his new order could only be built with the help of violence,' I responded.

'That's not to say he didn't want the very best for workers,' she replied. And perhaps she was right, only Lenin's idealism was built on coercion and the cement which kept it together was propaganda.

Other intellectuals I came across held no particular ideological belief but they paid the party the lip service needed to get by.

I knew a young graduate in political science who worked in the prestigious International Department of the Central Committee of the Communist Party. Yuri would openly ridicule both Lenin and the party at gatherings he'd often be invited to by foreign journalists.

'The pressure to conform is enormous,' he told me. 'If I'd opted to dissent, I'd have been sent to Gorky [a reference to the exile of Andrei Sakharov] rather than New York for conferences.'

Yuri was content to use the party to climb the career ladder. He enjoyed the privileges of party membership. He had learnt the benefits of George Orwell's doublespeak, where the mind thinks one way but the mouth utters something else. When the Soviet Union finally collapsed, this *apparatchik* became a leading light of the new capitalist order. By the mid 1990s he was a dollar millionaire, using his party contacts and authority to cash in on the country's wealth.

The tragedy for the Soviet Union was that for people like Yuri the party was fallible. But he knew the CPSU was also capable of ruthlessness. He understood the party's monopoly of power and of thought and that this was, perversely, also its most vulnerable point. Open the way to unfettered, independent thought and the system and party could fall apart. The party had been his passport to the good life and he wasn't going to do anything to undermine it. Not yet, anyway.

Across the country, millions of people felt the same way. As a result they seemed prepared to accept that the state and the party were one even though they knew that if the party were to fall, the Soviet Union would survive.

The director of a small *kolhoz* (collective farm) I visited in 1991 on the outskirts of St Petersburg sat in his huge office with a massive portrait of Lenin on the wall behind his desk. I asked whether he was disappointed with the questioning of Leninism.

'The country won't collapse if Leninism collapses. But the *kolhoz* will,' he said. What he meant was that Leninism had been the backbone of the Soviet system, verifying, justifying, reinforcing it with a dazzling array of lies and distortions. If Leninism collapsed, the system it fed would collapse. If the system collapsed, who would provide funding for the *kolhoz* to continue operating at an enormous financial loss? His privileged position as the manager of a large agricultural enterprise and all the perks that went with it would disappear.

He was no different to the young man I knew who'd been given a choice when he finished school between working in a factory or joining the KGB. He joined the KGB, living in a well-appointed KGB apartment and driving a large black Chaika, second only in prestige to the Zil which the leadership were driven around in. Surely, he reasoned, it was better to prop up the party and with it an empty belief that the country was fighting off enemies in its effort to build communism so as to live well—at least in the short term.

But to many millions more, the party was simply a given. It was there. It ruled. It ran the factories and institutes they worked in, produced the food they ate, the clothes they wore. They had no desire to question its legitimacy or its morality because to do so was pointless. They saw themselves as cogs in the wheel. And as people would tell me over and again, even though the party was utterly deaf to their pleas for a better life, for more material goods, for better housing and health care, for a little less coercion, they believed what they were told. The state had been seized in their name. Private property had been abolished to give them the national wealth. Private enterprise was exploitative. And there were still capitalists and crooks out there who would again try to reclaim the country. So to make demands was to jeopardise the means by which they lived.

'Why?' I asked Natasha in 1990. 'Why don't people rise up against this system, against the party?'

'Sometimes I think you're so naive,' Natasha answered. 'When you get snowed under with electricity bills, gas bills, medical bills, mortgage payments, do you ever think to yourself communism is a better way to go? I know you don't! When we've been crushed by our system do you know what we thought? We thought about how far we had to go before we achieved Lenin's communism which would get rid of all the problems. We didn't think that communism was a bad thing, or that Lenin was to blame.

'When you ask why we don't rise up against the injustices of communism, you are asking why we don't question our own convictions! There is probably nothing harder for a human being to do in this world. Our past is still alive. We are it. Find me more than one million Russians who think that private ownership of property is anything but exploitative. Show me the Russian who believes that I have a right to live better than he does, even if I work harder.'

'But utopia is gone,' I insisted, 'surely Gorbachev has proven that!'

'Utopia is gone, I admit that. But Lenin's not to blame. The party is to blame. It might have been better except that the party limited the choices we could make about our lives, and about our future. What choices did we have to achieve what Lenin wanted? None at all! There was obedience, dissidence or the fine line between them which your George Orwell called "doublethink". And if you play the game of doublethink, you're not free.'

CHAPTER 5

GENERATION VS GENERATION

You are blind, like young kittens. What will happen here without me?

JOSEPH STALIN TO HIS FAITHFUL LIEUTENANTS JUST BEFORE HIS DEATH, 1953

The system was brutal with those who didn't play the game. Officially problems were hidden and when they were too obvious to hide, then the party performed verbal acrobatics and punished those who refused to help it turn bad into good, black into white. Anyone who couldn't or wouldn't think like the party was squashed like an ant. Everyone knew that unless you had official party rank or some kind of status bestowed by the party then it was better to keep quiet about one's apprehensions.

But even some with status who recognised the problems chose to surrender. Soviet history is littered with their crimes. The poet Yevgeny Yevtushenko whom the party trusted, and whom some in the west hailed as a brave dissident, admits in his book *Fatal Half Measures* (written when the blood of others' bravery had already been spilt), that sometime in the mid 1970s he was asked by Andrei Sakharov to sign a collective letter to the authorities calling for the death penalty to be repealed.

'I too was for the repeal,' he wrote, 'but back then I did not believe in the effectiveness of collective letters. The authors were individually called. Some recanted, claiming that they had been led astray, and repented. The bureaucracy did not simply punish, it also bought people and created schisms. The era of executions had passed—this was the period of quiet choking in the back alleys. People were blacklisted for humanistic initiatives, not only for speaking out against the government.

'Part of the liberal intelligentsia,' he wrote, 'followed a Soviet modification of Galileo's last cry, "It still revolves nevertheless" but added the forced, "only on orders from the party".'

In 1990 I rang Yevtushenko to speak to him about dissent. He talked about how dangerous it had been to think freely and to follow one's conscience. He said a few of those who had been brave—and he counted himself among them—now knew definitely that they had been right. The party was wrong. I asked him whether he felt, in hindsight, that he should have signed the collective letter for which so many of his comrades had been punished.

'No!' was the abrupt answer before he paused, drew a few expletives from his extensive English vocabulary and hung up.

Complete dissent was rare even if one felt utter disdain for the party. I can understand why. But a form of secret dissent was always possible—the type with which Yevtushenko and others of his generation flirted without any hint of self-consciousness. They knew the truth. They were born to propaganda. All that remained was to find a safe path between the two.

It could only ever have been in the middle and upper echelons of the party—as Mikhail Gorbachev proved—that the seeds of change could be sown. But there, in that self-perpetuating, mind-numbing abyss of ideological pap and falsehood, the party men who knew that their positions were built on violence and fear lived double lives. They had careers to further and families to feed. They were as much the product of Leninism as the party's true believers. Yet the force of their intellects and their access to the truth wouldn't let them ignore the lies. They too noticed what Andrei Sakharov had noticed years before, that the further in time the Soviet people moved from the years of terror, the bigger the gap became between the reality of their lives and reality as the party saw it. By the 1960s, there was no similarity at all between them. To be a secret dissenter was rather like waking each morning after a bad dream and pinching yourself into reality—only in reverse! It was a way to remain sane. The only puzzle which remained was why those who knew the truth were trusted by the hardliners. Perhaps in the abyss of Soviet communism, all one needed to know was the Leninist catechism and how to speak it with complete conviction. Real belief had long since disappeared.

In Russia, they were called the *shestidesyatniki* (men of the sixties). They would make up Gorbachev's inner and outer circle when he finally came to power. They helped mastermind the reforms of the late 1980s, mapping out the second revolution, allowing the non-Russian republics to express national pride and loosening the reins of the media so that dozens of newspapers independent of the state suddenly flourished. They not only told the truth, they challenged the old Leninist norms, questioned the economic system over which the communists reigned, and stood guard as Gorbachev slowly moved to build what he called a 'state of laws', a country in which arbitrary state power and repressive laws were dismantled.

The *shestidesyatniki* also understood by the 1980s that there was no point in holding onto Eastern Europe given the problems at home. They knew what the empire had cost, and they knew the price was too high, so one by one the satellite countries were allowed to go their own way. All the while, Gorbachev tried to calm his hardline Politburo colleagues in a bid to convince them that not only could Moscow no longer afford its empire, but that to attempt to maintain it would jeopardise the very foundations of *perestroika*, designed in part to give the party a chance to revive itself. The Soviet Union, he told them, needed western co-operation and an end to the Cold War to restructure the command economy. There would be no question of dumping socialism. Never! But, he told them, if the Berlin Wall tumbled, there was a chance of building socialism with a human face. Socialism could and would be renewed.

Reforms of great international significance gave way to more domestic changes like holding what looked like genuine elections for the old Supreme Soviet (the Soviet parliament) which had always simply rubberstamped the Politburo's decisions. It's true that the candidates fielded in the 1989 campaign were mostly communists, but, after all it had only been a few years since democratic movements had received permission to organise. Democracy would come in time. In the same year that the first democratic elections were held, the *shestidesyatniki* advised Gorbachev to create an outer parliament—the Congress of People's Deputies—which would meet twice a year to legitimise the changes agreed upon by the Supreme Soviet. The Congress would also be responsible for electing candidates to the Supreme Soviet in the future.

The Congress's creation heralded the end of the Politburo's capacity to call the shots. The Politburo could make as many decisions as it liked but it had fewer ways of enforcing them. Its members began feeling like flies trapped in a closed jar! And even their stranglehold on the economy was being shaken loose. In a moment of weakness, they'd agreed to allow a degree of private trading. Gorbachev knew the changes were necessary. Unless something changed, socialism would collapse completely. And none of them, not Gorbachev, not the *shestidesyatniki* wanted that.

The *shestidesyatniki* were true believers, people for whom communism meant more than a means of climbing the career ladder. For them, communism was a perfect and just theory which hadn't yet been applied to the Soviet situation. Khrushchev's reign had given them hope. But then during the decades of deadness under Brezhnev, Andropov and Chernenko, they lied to themselves, and made compromises to preserve their sanity as they helped the party stay in power knowing that it could never deliver the humane and democratic socialism they dreamt of. They were the prototypes of Orwell's doublethinkers, the makers of half measures.

They cried tears of genuine distress on 6 March 1953 when the dictator drew his final breath, but then they joined the party to purge it of the Stalinists. A decade later they would read *samisdat*, the uncensored dissident literature distributed underground in which the truth without propaganda must have tugged at their consciences. But then they applauded the Soviet Union's ambition to export communism to every corner of the world.

These were people who understood the meaning of Moscow's march on Czechoslovakia in 1968 to crush the reforms of Alexander Dubcek's ruling Communist Party which had loosened the chains. 'Socialism with a human face', as Dubcek called it, was just a little too human for the hardliners who ordered the invasion. The *shestidesyatniki* who were then just junior *apparatchiks* would nonetheless blithely attend conferences on 'World Peace Loving Forces in the Communist World'.

For people like this, doublethink was more than an overused cliche. It was as real as breathing. They would think one thing but publicly articulate another, knowing that the moment they stopped they would find they were beyond redemption—stuck in a hell between their conscience and the terrible truth.

The accession of Mikhail Sergeyevich Gorbachev in 1985 freed the *shestidesyatniki*. They could put into action their long-nurtured ideas for a new Soviet Union, almost all of which stopped well short of ending communism and disabling the party. But reconstructing communism was tortuous, the path to Lenin full of pot holes.

I knew several of Gorbachev's inner circle of *shestidesyatniki*, among them Nikolai Shishlin who was a peculiar mix of *apparatchik* and academic. He worked in the influential International Department of the Central Committee.

Shishlin was a man of dry humour and towering intellect whom foreign journalists loved for his wit and near perfect English. He in turn enjoyed receiving foreigners. Invariably they would bring him a bottle of whisky, and he loved a drop. He would talk for hours about his great passion in life—the reconstruction of the Communist Party, an idea which had been locked inside his mind for thirty years.

'The 1917 revolution was the first great moment for change this century. The second is now. Now we can become true communists,' he told me one day in 1990, sitting in the Foreign Ministry press cafe over a glass of state-subsidised cognac.

Often he'd forgo the prerequisite of a gift and meet me at five o'clock at the end of his day's work at Central Committee head-quarters in Moscow to explain his ideas. I'd arrive in my red Lada and park in the area reserved for party cars, not far from the build-ing's heavy revolving front doors so he could see me as he walked out. I would simply say I was waiting for Shishlin and the objections of the *militsiya* instantly vanished. Shishlin barely even recognised the inequity when I brought up the matter. He didn't see anything wrong with the way mere mortals were furiously waved away, refused parking spaces for blocks around Central Committee headquarters.

'You're altogether too sensitive, my dear,' he would say as we drove off in search of an open cafe where we could talk about the dilemma of the *shestidesyatniki*.

'Every day for thirty years it has been the same for us,' he would tell me. 'We did things we were and still are ashamed of. I've written works denouncing the west, praising Brezhnevism. I worked as a propagandist even when I knew the propaganda was a lie. I worked for the party knowing it was built on the bones of my own people. But to actively think this, to acknowledge it, that's like being con-scious as you watch yourself die.'

Secretly, at the kitchen table at home, Shishlin had worked on his manifesto outlining a new and less treacherous order, a humane socialism in which press censorship would be loosened and the republics were allowed to make their own economic decisions based on their own needs, not Moscow's diktat. But even he, like others in his set, drew the line at anything which undermined the power and authority of the party. That was unthinkable. The party would be renewed and it would take the Soviet people to real communism. When I asked what made him think the party could be trusted to change anything, he shrugged his shoulders.

'It's the power of Leninism, the force of its goodness. Would you argue that egalitarianism is wrong?' he asked. It was like arguing against motherhood.

'Why can't we simply reconstruct communism? The idea is a good one. It's just the people who are bad. So we can just make a few simple moves. We can atone for the sins of our past, purge the party of its reactionaries and start again,' Shishlin said in 1990.

But to simply forgive past sins and reform the party would be the greatest compromise of them all. Stalinism had done barbarous things to people's minds. Too many party people had too big a stake in the way things were. It took many more years of struggle for Shishlin to later admit to me that his burning ambition to reconstruct the party was purely a way to calm the conscience while the beast continued to fight for survival. In any event it was already too late for the party. It reigned but it didn't rule, as Alexander Yakovlev observed when he tried to convince Gorbachev to split the party in two, into a reform camp and a reactionary rump.

A new parliament had been created and it looked democratic even if it wasn't. A limited degree of business outside the state structures was permitted and was dealing the state's monopoly on economic life a powerful blow. And all along it was the party leader carrying out the reforms, dragging behind him a resentful, brooding mob of ageing men in badly cut suits who hadn't thought that 'change' would mean they'd lose status and privilege. But still, the doublethinkers stood resolute, some of them simply afraid of their own thoughts. Life without the party? Impossible!

As another member of the *shestidesyatniki*, Georgi Shakhnazarov, an adviser to Gorbachev, told me just before I left Moscow in 1994, 'If you come back in ten years' time, we'll still be here, writing our memoirs with greater or lesser degrees of honesty. And we'll still be saying that there was a way to rebuild communism without the coercion and the fear and the corruption.'

Vitaly Korotich was the editor of the weekly magazine *Ogonyok* when I met him in 1990 in his editorial office in central Moscow. Korotich, also a product of the 1960s, was a big man with a big voice and forceful opinions. He seemed to fully support Gorbachev's push for reform and indeed had been appointed by the leading reformer Alexander Yakovlev, who was spending more time tearing Marxism apart than anything else. But on the calendar on Korotich's desk were noted the birthdates of all the Politburo members. 'So we can write tributes to them,' he told me without a hint of embarrassment or irony.

Korotich spoke of the 'evil' party hardliners who were trying to undermine *perestroika* and *glasnost* but he himself compromised reform by publishing a condemnation of the young men of the reform movement who in 1989 began pushing for the abandonment of Article Six of the Soviet Constitution which enshrined the Communist Party's dominant role in Soviet society and made illegal the formation of other political parties. In other words, Article Six entrenched the one party state.

'But I supported Gorbachev's decision to televise the proceedings of the Soviet Congress in 1989 [in which the major issue of debate was the abolition of Article Six] which our people watched in unbelieving awe! This was *glasnost* in action.'

Only the country's fledgling democrats and the dissenters who wouldn't surrender to the party were brave enough to say in increasingly loud voices and on every platform they could climb that the abolition of Article Six was an essential step in the creation of a new civil society. The *shestidesyatniki* understood that Article Six had to be abolished. But they were frightened of the inevitable reaction from the hardline camp. The time for internal reform was passing.

Andrei Sakharov, a Hero of Socialist Labour, led the charge against Article Six. It would be his final battle with the party. He wanted the CPSU to subject itself to regular elections in which parties would have to compete for votes. He wanted an elected government to be answerable to the parliament. And he wanted the party to dissolve its operations within the KGB, the media, the bureaucracy and the military. It was a big ask and not one which Sakharov had just thought up. He'd long ago advocated the same reforms but had been exiled. Now he had the green light of *perestroika* and *glasnost*.

But as absurd as the party hardliners thought his ideas, Sakharov had let the genie out of the bottle. Article Six was on everyone's lips whether they agreed with its abolition or not. Suddenly, people waiting for buses and trains or in queues for food were talking about the possibility that the giant, all powerful CPSU might leave them to their own lives and their own thoughts. Some were excited. Others cursed Sakharov and the young democrats for their blasphemy.

My younger friends who openly mocked the party and cautiously mocked Lenin suddenly found themselves watching hour by hour relays on television of the Congress proceedings. They laughed as they told me what it felt like to listen to young democrats call the party hideous, criminal and irrelevant while others called members of the Politburo incompetent sycophants undeserving of the high office they occupied. But they were saddened, even appalled, when they watched how difficult it was for Mikhail Gorbachev, the father of this new found freedom, to break with his past and treat Sakharov as most thought he deserved.

Gorbachev had allowed Sakharov to join the committee drafting a new constitution for the Soviet Union, one which everyone assumed would write the party out of government. He even allotted Sakharov more time than other members of the committee to speak to the Congress about what he thought the constitution should contain.

'I was watching with my father,' said my friend Zhenya, 'and suddenly Gorbachev told the old man that he'd spoken for far too long. But Sakharov didn't listen to him. He kept talking, saying Article Six had to be abolished. Gorbachev asked him whether he respected the Congress but Sakharov said he respected the people and humanity. It was incredible. Truly inspiring. And when Gorbachev switched off his microphone to stop him talking, well, that was that. I had to start doubting Gorbachev.' Zhenya was genuinely upset, moved enough to begin going to rallies whenever work permitted.

At a Moscow protest 200 000 strong, people screamed their anger at Mikhail Gorbachev for delaying the abolition of Article Six. They wanted him to impose its repeal on the party. They needed proof of his reform credentials if they were to continue to trust him. They wanted him to order the party out of the KGB and the military. They wanted more, much more than the half-hearted, half-baked economic reforms which had so disturbed the old command system that the shop shelves were all but bare while the party felt it still controlled the show. People wanted to know how it was that Gorbachev had allowed Moscow's puppet governments in Eastern Europe to fall, while he let the party at home cling to power. They had literally taken Sakharov's political manifesto to the streets!

Sakharov died before the party agreed to his demands. And in a show of bad faith, the Supreme Soviet, made up of party cronies, refused to suspend its usual business on the day of Sakharov's funeral when thousands of mourners wore badges bearing a '6' with a red mark through it. If further proof were needed that the party was out of step with the people, thousands more flocked to the Moscow building in which he had lived with his wife Yelena Bonner after their return from exile in Gorky. The dissident who'd been labelled a pariah in the 1970s had become the new demigod for democrats, reformers, and the party's secret opponents whose dissidence had been limited to the *fig v karmane*, a thumb pushed between the second and third fingers—but hidden inside one's pocket. Now Sakharov had a new place in Russia as a martyr.

'It helped that the party looked like a fish with a hook in its mouth, caught and left lying on the grass to dry out, gasping for breath,' said Igor with a delight he didn't feel at all obliged to constrain as he related the heady events which had consumed people in the first few months of 1990.

Finally, under enormous pressure, Gorbachev persuaded the Central Committee to abandon Article Six. He really had no other choice. To maintain people's faith, he had to strike at the party. The facts were as clear as they could possibly be. The party was corrupt. Limited economic reform at home meant that rouble millionaires were sprouting all over the place, providing, through the workers' co-operatives they had formed, goods and services the command economy couldn't. Inflation was beginning its rampage under the force of essential economic change. Political fronts had formed even though strictly speaking they were unconstitutional while Article Six remained on the books. The Soviet Union was falling apart and no-one dared deny the fact. If the party had any hope of surviving the chaos it had to at least put on a show of democracy.

But Gorbachev too was a doublethinker. There would be compromise even in this, the party's surrender.

'For a moment, we thought the party had just given us democracy on a platter—multi-party elections, the prospect of a new government which would have to answer to us and to the parliament,' said

Igor. But when I arrived in Moscow in October 1990, the fight was far from over.

Article Six had been dumped but Gorbachev had managed to create a new position—President of the Soviet Union—which he promptly awarded himself.

'He's a smart man,' said Natasha. 'He has the party over a barrel now. All he has to do to ruin it completely is resign as General Secretary. If he does, the party has no link to real power other than through the bullet.'

Natasha reasoned, as did most of the *shestidesyatniki*, that Gorbachev was now protected by the presidency he had created.

Artyom Troitsky was one of the first people I met when I arrived in Moscow in 1990. I sought him out because of his reputation as a leading expert on Soviet art, culture and rock and roll. He was an author and the music director at Russia's national television broadcaster. I thought he might be able to explain to me why it was that with decreasing power, no authority and fewer followers, the party seemed still to be in control of the Soviet Union. Artyom was perfectly placed to explain what appeared to me to be a problem of the generation gap.

He was born in 1955 and in his own words discovered the true face of communism when he was still in his teens. That made him allergic, he told me, to politics and communist ideology.

In the 1970s, when the Soviet Union was more or less asleep under Leonid Brezhnev's rule, Artyom was putting together Russian bands which would roam from apartment block to apartment block playing, in the basements, what might loosely be called 'underground music'. But no doubt what made life as a self-proclaimed Soviet misfit a little easier for Artyom Troitsky was the fact that he was the son of a member of the *shestidesyatniki*—educated, well travelled and well connected.

Like most people of his generation who deplored the party and its tactics, Artyom was ecstatic when Article Six was abolished. But he was also deeply sceptical that Gorbachev hadn't gone to the people to ask them if they wanted him to be their president. Artyom, and millions more, would have voted for Gorbachev. But in not risking the verdict of the people, Gorbachev had sown the seeds of a mistrust which would spread like a cancer. To Artyom, by not calling an election, Gorbachev was simply trying to preserve the power of the party he led which was crumbling beneath him. Unlike Natasha who was barely three years older, Artyom didn't see the presidency as a way of protecting *perestroika*. Indeed, *perestroika* didn't need protecting as far as Artyom was concerned. 'I'd like to see the party try to reverse it,' he'd say.

'I think Russia is doomed by the generation gap,' Artyom told me in 1990. 'There are millions of people who just want to slap the party's backside and censure its bosses. But they don't want it to go. The only people who want it to die are the young and perhaps more and more people of my generation. But there's not enough of us.'

As it turned out, the generation gap was devastating for the country. And nowhere was this more obvious than on the streets. The mood of protest affected more and more people as the 1990s dawned. And during some demonstrations there were clashes between older people who wanted to retain the totalitarian structures minus the repression, and the young who wanted absolute freedom—minus the party. For the elderly, only the order the CPSU could provide would stop the chaos which had already begun to make life uneasy and even unsafe. For the young, the very notion of order induced as strong a reaction as communism had given Artyom in his teens.

I had always assumed that young people blithely followed the system, but a few weeks after I arrived in Moscow to take up my posting, something happened which changed my mind.

I'd been invited to what was billed as the first open rock and roll concert of Soviet bands in Moscow. It had taken the Moscow GORKOM, the city's Communist Party committee, weeks of delib-eration to finally approve the event, so it must have been a bewil-dering prospect for its members. But more so for the thousands of young Muscovites who first queued for days and nights to buy tickets, then for hours behind police barricades to be allowed inside the stadium on the night of the event. They waited and waited. Almost two hours past the time the concert was scheduled to start, impatience overtook them and they began to push their way forward, knocking over the barricades in their eagerness. The author-ities, in particular the *militsiya* which was unsympathetic to those they called 'hippies', interpreted this as a riot and the police batons began to swing.

In Moscow just a few weeks, I couldn't understand what had pro-voked this furious reaction. I thought, naively as it turned out, that even though some in authority might not approve of a rock concert, the fact that it had been sanctioned meant it would go ahead quietly. I was almost numb with shock when my friend Masha laughed off my naivety, explaining that the death of Article Six was just the beginning of the battle.

'The new parliamentary Congress might look like the USSR is on the road to democracy but the party is still everywhere,' she said. 'You don't think the *apparatchiks* in the Department of Internal Affairs and Vladimir Kruchkov [the head of the KGB] like the idea of this concert do you?'

Indeed it would have been no less to them than a dangerous dalliance with western values foolishly approved by the Moscow party.

When the kids were finally allowed inside the stadium they were systematically and very publicly picked out and bashed. 'This is *glasnost*,' said Masha as we watched an ugly and disturbing episode in Gorbachev's new Russia. Right before our eyes, teenagers out to see their favourite bands were being knocked to the ground and dragged outside. At the end of the night, the stadium looked like

a war zone. Ambulances whizzed in and out to attend to the battered who lay on the grounds surrounding the stadium, behind
bushes, in police cars. One of those in the group I was with disappeared for the night. He turned up the next morning badly
bruised. He'd been bashed and held in a cell overnight. Needless
to say, *glasnost* ended when the batons stopped swinging. There
wasn't a word about the incident in the media the next day. Even
the independent press was silent.

In a strange way, it all made sense. The system was fraying.
The old *nomenklatura* had been undermined for more than a decade
by their own children who'd been able to travel and live abroad
and who'd digested western pop culture with its rock and roll
music, drugs and less than austere fashions. And what they didn't
bring back with them arrived through other routes—foreigners or
sympathetic parents who smuggled back cassettes and magazines.
Slowly, over the decades, western culture had penetrated the Soviet
Union's closed borders and given Soviet youth all sorts of ideas,
not least among them the notion that they too could create music,
fashions, even ideologies which were interesting to others their age
and, of course, outside the limits the party found acceptable. The
appeal was powerful. In a country where consumer goods were as
scarce as hen's teeth and where Western values were condemned
as bourgeois, there was every chance of defeating Leninism. The
break between generations couldn't have been anything other than
sharp and painful.

Artyom's experience of the generation gap was obviously more
profound than mine. He saw the problem as more fundamentally
agonising than the break-up of a rock concert.

His father wanted the USSR to live on through a reformed party.
He knew the old one was rotten to its core. But as a member of the
shestidesyatniki, he'd listened to Khrushchev's denunciation of Stalin's
crimes and, rather than being repulsed by communism, like others
of his generation he had actually joined the party, eagerly seeking
that bright shining beacon of communism which he was certain was

burning somewhere ahead, and which would defeat the forces of darkness.

Artyom's father had decided to invest his life in the system. So sure was he that Lenin's ideals were worth fighting for that even after he was sacked from his prestigious, party-sponsored institute for 'political shortsightedness', he remained committed to the party. All he had done to attract the party's wrath was bring a group of Che Guevarists from Moscow University to work with him at the Institute of World Economy and International Relations. The students were subsequently charged by the KGB with 'forming an underground anti-communist organisation' which, of course could not have been further from the truth nor more indicative of the extreme paranoia which afflicted the regime.

'I'm not sure I can explain it to you so that you can understand what I mean,' said Natasha as she desperately groped for the words to make sense of the generation gap.

'It's impossible for you to know the strength of indoctrination that this generation underwent. For us, Lenin's ideal of socialism was the car engine and the car body was the Communist Party. There's no point having an engine without the body, is there? You can't move! What do you do when you realise the car body is rusted but you know the engine is still good?'

Alexander Yakovlev explained the dilemma in party terms. 'Since *perestroika* started out inside the party, it could announce itself as an initiative aimed at strengthening socialism and the party, as an effort to bring about a more accurate understanding of Marxism–Leninism, and as a struggle to cement the socialist and communist nature of society. We tried to destroy the Church in the name of a genuine religion and genuine Jesus, only vaguely aware of the fact that our religion was false and our Jesus an imposter.'

When the *shestidesyatniki* came to power in the late 1980s as part of Gorbachev's administration, they were frightened not only of their own thoughts, but of their children. For them there could be no real progress without socialism and socialism would not work without the party. For their children, there could be no meaningful progress until both socialism and the party were buried. The men of the Prague Spring gave Gorbachev their support in the late 1980s on the understanding that he would never be tempted to abandon socialism. Their children supported Gorbachev believing he would bury the party in the dustbin of socialist history! For men like Artyom's father, the nascent nationalism of the Soviet republics which Gorbachev's freedom had unleashed, especially in the Baltic states, was dangerous because it would lead the outlying republics to believe they could live without the empire which was glued together by the party. For Artyom, the empire had long ago crumbled.

'I remember arguing with my father about this thing he still thought of as an empire,' Artyom told me in 1990.

'It dawned on me that although the men around Gorbachev talked as if the Cold War were over they didn't really believe it, because to believe this would be to admit that there is nothing left to protect—no empire. That's why even the more liberal of the military hierarchy won't agree to reducing the military budget or changing what the military–industrial complex produces. It would be a major psychological defeat. They'd be lost, completely.'

Gorbachev convinced his colleagues he could reform and renew the old system. He purged the bureaucracy of untalented Brezhnev toadies, freed the media, allowed democratic elections for the parliament. And all the while the more hardline of his comrades believed the party would survive because they knew that their leader, whom *Time* magazine had hailed as the Man of the Century, never really accepted that the system was bankrupt. He couldn't. Gorbachev was a product of communism. To him, as to his colleagues, the system could be fixed.

But as 1990 drew to a close and 1991 dawned, it became painfully clear that things were spinning out of Gorbachev's control and perhaps communism would fall. Perhaps this was inevitable.

The party's psychological hold on the people was slipping. Millions were relinquishing their membership. They no longer needed it to live well and do better than their neighbours. The shrewd ones were using their party connections to make money and, given the party had reluctantly approved a degree of small-time trading, there was nothing to stop them. But in keeping with Soviet tradition, some of them took rather more than the state allowed them and stole resources under their control. By the end of 1990, there were dollar millionaires in Moscow and just about all of them were party men who were on-selling to unscrupulous western businessmen what the state had given them to protect.

Others simply turned their party skills to the art of political provocation. Among them was Boris Yeltsin, silver-haired, bullish and Russian to his very core. Once a member of the party, indeed the head of the Communist Party organisation in the Urals city of Sverdlovsk, there were two sides to this man, both of which he kept in healthy competition with the other. He was, on the one hand, a reformer as Gorbachev had correctly identified. That's why Gorbachev had invited Yeltsin to Moscow in 1985 to head the Moscow GORKOM, the city's Communist Party committee, which gave him considerable power because it also entailed a seat on the Politburo and the Central Committee.

But by October 1987, a little of the man's other side had become obvious. Reading his fellow Russians like a book, he sensed their anger and frustration and most of all their mistrust of the party. And he cashed in. Yeltsin wasn't a party loyalist. He was a careerist. And in 1987 he could see the writing on the wall. The party was increasingly unpopular. So he launched the most scathing of attacks on one of its more hardline members, Yigor Ligachev, a member of the Politburo.

The Yeltsin–Ligachev feud erupted when Gorbachev discussed with the Politburo what he would be saying in his speech to celebrate the seventieth anniversary of the October 1917 revolution. Yigor Ligachev was absolutely determined that Gorbachev would not call Stalin a criminal. And that he would not detail how many millions Stalin had killed. It was not that Ligachev was a Stalinist, simply that reappraising the past was a deviation from socialism.

A few months later, Ligachev told an audience in a small Russian town that Stalin's reign had been troublesome but had also been a time of great achievement. He condemned people like Dmitri Volkogonov who, he said, told Soviet history through closed eyes, as though it were a 'chain of mistakes'. Yeltsin exploded. Ligachev, he said, was not only a reactionary committed to protecting the party (of which Yeltsin himself was a leading member), but also that he and half the Politburo, including Gorbachev, were obstructing *perestroika*. He was, of course, correct. But there were limits to the truth in Gorbachev's time.

For his crime, Yeltsin was expelled from the Politburo and sacked from his position as Moscow party chief. The divide was created; the battleground set. Gorbachev and Yeltsin had become ideological enemies.

From his seat on the Central Committee, Yeltsin sat, watched and waited for his moment. And in 1989 it came. He won overwhelming grassroots support in the first multi-candidate election for delegates to the Soviet parliament, the USSR Congress of People's Deputies. Yeltsin found, in the Soviet parliament, a new perch from which to carp at Gorbachev and vie for authority if not power. This infuriated not just the General Secretary but also the party he was dragging along behind him.

Gorbachev was being exposed as a maker of half measures. Private business was acceptable so long as the party got its cut. Independent newspapers were a good thing so long as they weren't too critical of the party. But Yeltsin would change all of this and force the General Secretary into the open.

In March 1990, elections were held for the Russian parliament, the national legislature of the Russian Republic and, as expected, Yeltsin triumphed. Before long he would be its chairman and under his tutelage it would adopt a 'Declaration on Russian Sovereignty', in effect signalling its belief that Russia wanted control over its own affairs. Yeltsin wasn't saying the Soviet Union was no longer viable, he was just offering an alternative to it—one in which there would be no need for a Soviet tsar like Gorbachev because each of the republics would have its own centre of power and own leader. Yeltsin was trying to write Gorbachev out of the picture and Gorbachev was mightily unimpressed.

Yeltsin quit the party altogether, denouncing its criminality for, amongst other things, crucifying dissidents like Andrei Sakharov. History had begun to repeat itself. As Stalin and all who followed him had ridden on the coat-tails of Lenin, Yeltsin would cling to Sakharov's, the man whose bravery had weakened the party and challenged the very core of Leninism—the premise that those who believed in him wanted good for the people.

In the 1991 referendum which Mikhail Gorbachev called to try to end the talk that the Soviet Union was no longer a viable entity and ought to give way, in Russia at least, to a sovereign republic, there were only two simple questions put to the people—Do you want the Soviet Union to continue to exist? and Do you want a Russian President? The second question was devised by Boris Yelstin who stood to win the position, if created, at the upcoming June parliamentary election.

Artyom Troitsky's father said 'yes' to the Union and 'no' to the Russian presidency. Artyom said 'no' to the Union and 'yes' to the presidency.

Natasha voted to keep the Soviet Union *and* to create a presidency to make sure the reactionaries learnt a lesson. 'Let us have two presidents,' she reasoned, 'one for the Union and one for Russia. That way they'll never cheat us again.'

But the truth was Natasha couldn't accept that freedom from all that was evil about the party might not just cost the party its life, but the Soviet Union its existence. That seemed to her too high a price to pay.

'You watch,' she said, 'the young people will say they want a Russian presidency with no USSR. And everyone over forty will say they want both even if in their kitchens they tell you the USSR is on its knees and the party put it there.'

She was right. In Russia, the referendum result was as evenly split as any result could possibly be. It was carried that the Soviet Union should continue as a sovereign entity but that a Russian presidency ought to be created nonetheless.

As the next era was about to begin, Artyom was asked to write a story for a new glossy monthly, *Moscow Magazine*, on what could be done to save the Soviet Union.

'What a useless question,' he wrote. 'Don't worry about saving the Soviet Union, or maybe even better, please don't save the Soviet Union! If you don't get it, I can spell it out for you: don't try to save the Soviet Union or you're in big trouble.'

Indeed, he could see absolutely nothing worth saving. His father disagreed.

CHANGE

PART TWO

CHAPTER 6

AN UNEASY DEATH

The clock of communism has tolled its final hour. But the concrete structure has not completely collapsed. Instead of being liberated, we may be crushed beneath the rubble.

ALEXANDER SOLZHENITSYN, 'HOW CAN WE REVITALISE RUSSIA?' 1990

Something very strange happened in May 1990. The traditional May Day parade to celebrate the labour of the workers in the workers' paradise was declared voluntary. There would be no floats of factory workers coerced or bribed into attending by their workplaces, no pompous odes to leaders dead or dying. The Soviet Union could no longer boast employment for everyone or monthly packages of produce for the proletariat or shop shelves sporadically full of food. Indeed, the leader himself had exposed the workers' paradise as a sham. So Gorbachev's decision to declare May Day of 1990 a low-key affair was nothing short of smart given the speed with which the Soviet myths long rammed down the workers' throats were exploding. Had it been anything other than low-key, then the antici-pated contingent of protesters (by now a daily phenomenon in Moscow) might not have agreed to join the parade rather than protest elsewhere in the capital, where they would have attracted more attention and shown up the official parade for what it was—a communist relic.

Mikhail Gorbachev looked calm, even proud as he walked onto the reviewing stand on top of Lenin's mausoleum where the Kremlin bosses usually watched the parade. And from his perspective there was a lot to be proud of. There he stood with a handful of young, democratically inclined leaders about to watch the first parade in Soviet history in which both advocates and opponents of communism would march across the cobbled stones of Red Square. And God only knows, Gorbachev needed something to spruce up his image. He was beginning to look a tinge Stalinist against the democratic glow which bathed Boris Yeltsin.

There hadn't been a day in the past year when protesters' voices hadn't been heard in Moscow. Everything Gorbachev did—and didn't do—enraged people. Even what he thought would be a goodwill trip to the Baltic republic of Lithuania sent people into frenzied apoplexy. He had gone there to help the Lithuanians 'celebrate' the fortieth anniversary of their country's annexation by the Soviet Union, in a poorly disguised attempt to calm the Baltics' surge of nationalism. This stunning failure of diplomacy was surpassed only by his attitude to protesters in Vilnius, the Lithuanian capital, 'mourning' the annexation. To their call for the Soviet Union to give them their freedom, Gorbachev replied: 'If that's the way you feel, then we have nothing to talk about at all.' *Glasnost* had its limits for Gorbachev. People were also incensed that Gorbachev, who had opened up the Pandora's box of party hatred, had been so slow to convince the party to surrender its constitutional monopoly and abandon Article Six. To most people, Gorbachev wanted democracy, just not too much of it.

For a while, it looked like the May Day march was all going to plan. But then the protesters filed onto Red Square and they were anything but orderly.

'Do you think this is the first time Gorbachev has been to a protest?' my regular protest companion Igor asked his son as thousands of flag-waving, shouting protesters filled the square.

'I'm not sure. But I bet he doesn't stay for too much of it,' his son replied.

But Gorbachev did. He stood and smiled while the crowd watched in disbelief.

Had the protesters marched straight past the podium, it might have been a non-event. Instead, they stopped and began shouting their protests at the leaders, staring them down. Surely these people in whom fear had been bred, people who had whispered their anger at the kitchen table among close friends, surely they must have been frightened? But with their protest placards that read 'Gorbachev, you are finished!', men and women of all ages had decided that the time had come. The party's time! If Gorbachev thought this was just another protest, the hardliners who stood reluctantly alongside the democrats Gorbachev had invited onto the reviewing stand certainly didn't.

'It was as though the crowd—and there must have been at least ten thousand—had Gorbachev on trial, right there on Lenin's tomb in whose name we had believed this rubbish about a workers' paradise. And you know, Gorbachev looked like he was listening to the charges as though he were trapped, handcuffed in a courtroom dock,' said Igor.

'I made my way towards Lobnoe Mesto, and I thought about how appropriate it was that I found Boris Yeltsin there. You know Lobnoe Mesto was where Ivan the Terrible tortured people. He even staged a festival of torture there—hundreds of people were fried in a human-size frying pan. Anyway, the party was being fried now and Yeltsin was being mobbed by fans and he loved every minute of it.'

So it had come to this, thought Natasha. May Day, a celebration of the workers, marred by anti-party protest. 'The people never were terribly smart,' she told me many months later as we talked about this day. 'They thought Gorbachev was a Stalinist just because he led the party and they think Yeltsin is the new living Messiah, on this earth to carry out Sakharov's unfinished work, because he walked behind his coffin at the funeral procession.'

Back at Red Square Igor managed to ask Yeltsin, 'How long do you think this confrontation will go on, Boris Nikolaevich?'

'Not long,' he told Igor. But he was wrong. The crowd booed and jeered as Gorbachev sidled away. But the party was far from over.

The first 'co-operatives', a Gorbachev initiative, appeared in 1988. They were essentially a bubble of private enterprise in a turbulent storm of ailing state monopolies and at first they managed a healthy trade. The restaurants, hairdressers, butchers, grocery shops and other enterprises which sprang up all over the Soviet Union—providing people with consumer goods and services the state couldn't— were an economic achievement. But most important of all (as far as the democrats and economic reformers were concerned), Gorbachev had allowed the whiff of capitalism to seep into the air and a lot of people liked it, especially the well-connected and street savvy who could cash in.

But there were problems—not least among them the fact that the co-ops were reliant on the state for almost everything.

It was illegal to own property so they were forced to rent premises from the government which meant they had to deal with bureaucrats who extorted and bribed their way through negotiations. Unless the co-ops paid up, they'd have to move on, no matter how long their leases ran. They were reliant on state credit too, which meant they had to hope not only for efficiency, but for uniformity from a system which didn't understand commercial investment. The USSR State Bank operated like most of the state's monopolies. It would create a rule, then break it the next day to suit its own needs or the demands of the system. And the co-operatives were utterly dependent on the state to supply them with goods to sell or resources from which to make the goods themselves. This meant they were forced to pay corrupt bureaucrats, factory managers and distributors to divert goods from the state sector to their own.

The co-op owners, eager to make profits, were not unhappy about paying the necessary bribes and didn't find it morally difficult. They were, after all, Soviet. To them, the new environment was a means of making money. If Gorbachev could manage somehow to provide them with legal certainty (there was no commercial or contract law to speak of) then perhaps they would change their modus operandi and lower their prices. But until then their prices would stay high to cover the cost of 'doing business'.

In the eyes of the authorities and most ordinary people the co-op owners were *spekulanty* (speculators), a derogatory term referring to people who make clear profit. Furthermore they were adding nothing to the goods they got, legally or otherwise, from the state to on-sell. So even though it was easier to buy from the co-ops, 'why pay more for the same stuff' was the guiding principle for average consumers. When people were forced to queue outside state shops for substandard goods in chronic short supply, they blamed the co-ops for 'stealing' their food and clothes from the state system. They didn't blame the system or the command economy for the shortages. Most people had a stake in the status quo and they didn't like it being disturbed by private enterprise.

Though there was never anything like an egalitarian society in the Soviet Union, there had been at least the pretence of one. With the advent of the co-ops social divisions created by money, not party patronage, came into existence—and rankled. People who worked within the state system, for factories, plants or institutes, earned poor wages and generally thought twice about buying at the co-ops. People who went out on their own generally made a lot more money and lived accordingly. They bought at the co-ops, wore fashionable clothes, ate in co-op restaurants and suffered the reproaches of their fellow countrymen. I heard of a young girl who managed to find a job in one of the co-ops which sold clothes imported from Europe.

Every morning she would leave her Soviet apartment on the outskirts of town dressed as if heading for work at the Red Guard cigarette plant. Along the way she'd change into something more chic, more suitable for her real job in the co-op. She was no different to the round-faced Georgian who owned one of the first co-op restaurants in Moscow at the Patriarchs Ponds. He was so frightened of what he called 'soviet jealousy' he had two burly thugs stationed at the entrance to his restaurant. The notion of someone doing better than anyone else was still utterly unacceptable.

Then there were the *raketiry*, members of protection rackets specialising in extortion, arson and murder, phenomena the Soviet Union had previously only experienced at the hands of the state apparatus, like the KGB or the special police. Once you opened your doors for free trade you suffered what went with it and invariably that included the threatening demands of groups of men in brightly coloured rayon tracksuits offering protection from 'criminal elements'—like the KGB. The old certainties had been turned upside-down.

But the old certainties were especially destabilised for the old *nomenklatura*. They had agreed to a measure which was undermining their authority to rule the economy. Some saw the benefits of open capitalism and began cashing in, making their fortune in the early days of the co-operatives. Others stuck by their Leninist prejudices. Gorbachev dithered, not knowing what to do. Even if he never admitted it to his party colleagues, he could see that the legalisation of small-time trading was dealing the command economy a blow it could barely sustain. He'd sown the seeds of capitalism and more and more people, especially the young, liked it. His economic advisers wanted him to make a decision—either outlaw the co-ops and repair the old system, or smash the old system and let the market economy flourish. Gorbachev's mind was telling him to pursue the free market. But his heart was beating to the party's drum.

In mid 1990, Gorbachev flirted with the idea of a total transition to the free market economy. A team of young economists was set to work on a formula which would allow the Soviet Union to shed its Marxist economic values and shut down the command system in favour of all-out capitalism. They came up with the 500-Day Plan which proposed obliterating seventy years of centralised economic planning in a little over a year. Preposterous though it was, Gorbachev at first liked the idea.

The party was enraged by the threat to its power base. It conjured up conspiracy theories about how the plan would kill off the Soviet Union, force massive unemployment and the closure of red factories and, more importantly, the military industrial complex. The threat of revolt caused Gorbachev to abandon the idea. The party, of course, thought it had won.

But though he caved in on the 500-Day Plan, by the time I arrived in Moscow in 1990, Gorbachev still hadn't made a clear decision about whether to stick to the command economy or embrace capitalism. He still hadn't outlawed private trading. And the co-ops— their owners tired of being captives of a corrupt bureaucracy—had brazenly moved out of the shops and into aluminium sheds perched on the streets.

In the Moscow suburb of Kuntsevo, just around the corner from where I lived, a line of burnt-out wreckages was testimony to the ferocity of the battle being fought over the economy. Across the road from the metro, one co-operative which remained was a knick-knacks store doing a roaring trade in paper, paper clips, pens, pencils and school texts, all of which were in chronic short supply in the state shops but which the owner told me he'd acquired from a government supplier which had them tucked away in a warehouse outside Minsk, the capital of faraway Belorussia.

'You tell me what you need,' Mikhail Borisovich told me when he learnt I was a journalist, 'and I'll make sure that within a week it will be here for you.'

It was service I could usually only dream of in Moscow in 1990— a ready supply of paper, note pads, typewriter ribbons, even computers if you gave enough notice. But a month after our conversation,

I drove past Mikhail Borisovich's shop where the embers still smoked. The man who ran the state-owned cigarette kiosk on the corner of the street told me to look for Mikhail Borisovich in the state-owned cafe across the road. And there he sat, drunk and dispirited.

'I paid all the bribes to the factory managers, to the drivers' bosses, even to the drivers themselves. I never once missed a payment to the Kuntsevo racketeers.

'The KGB came around a lot asking me where I got the stuff from and I told them. So it can't have been the KGB who did this,' he said, puzzled, ruined, defeated.

But the KGB *was* waging a campaign against the co-operatives and many small-time entrepreneurs were driven out of business. If the KGB wasn't putting the small entrepreneurs out of business on the party's direct orders, it was doing so on the implicit understanding that the party didn't want people to make money unless its cronies were getting a cut. Still, many of Russia's current millionaires persevered and made their way to the top via the co-operatives, keeping afloat the idea that if you wanted to make money through business you could. But they also took with them an increasingly sophisticated *raket* (racket) that not only protected them from rival racketeers but from competition. People became frightened to open up a shop or restaurant because it had become a dangerous game.

The state cafe where I found Mikhail Borisovich the day after his shop was torched was run by a barrel-chested woman called Galina Vladimirovna with whom I spent many hours talking. She kept the locals in line, refusing alcohol to the drunks who'd stagger through the door in the middle of the day having *vyshel* (popped out) from their offices for just a moment. None of the younger set would willingly cross her either. But as well as an iron fist, Galina had a wicked mind for business. She'd done a deal with a caviar cannery in Gorky and each month would traipse off to the railway yards where she would collect her illicit supply from which she made a very healthy and regular personal profit. Once she co-opted me in her jaunt to the pick-up point, although I didn't know it at the time.

Galina had told me she needed to collect the cafe's state-allotted supply of coffee because the truck which normally delivered it had broken down. And I believed her!

Despite the reminders across the road of the perils of private business, she thought long and hard about applying for a co-operative licence and refurbishing the drab, dark, dank basement of the office complex in which the cafe operated and could be extended.

One afternoon in December 1990, I was working in my office when the phone rang. It was Galina. 'Come quick,' she said, 'there's trouble.'

'If you need a ride to the railyards, forget it Galina,' I said.

'No, no,' she implored, 'really, I'm in trouble.'

A group of youngish thugs from a suburb on the other side of Moscow had heard about Galina's desire to operate her cafe privately and they'd crossed town to threaten her. When I arrived, they'd only just gone. But they'd left a calling card. A few windows were smashed and Galina's well-worn coffee pots had been thrown against walls so they were dented and unusable.

'They wanted protection money! And I haven't even got a licence to operate yet!' said Galina.

'How did they hear you've been asking about one?' I asked.

'I suppose Ispolkom told them,' she said.

Ispolkom was the equivalent of an Australian local council and it was there that Galina had gone to ask what she needed to do to operate as a co-operative. Later, when I asked Vladimir Tikhonov who was then president of the controversial United Co-operative Alliance whether it was possible that the party through its control of local council bodies had jumped into bed with the private mafia to stop the co-ops, he said simply that privatisation was a dirty word. The councils too felt threatened by private trading. For the grey men who ran them, the co-ops were direct competition. They fell back on the old Leninist argument that private ownership corrupted humanity.

By 1990 privatisation was so dirty a word that Mikhail Gorba-chev's parliament declared that the co-operatives could sell only 15 per cent of their goods at 'free prices', and the remaining 85 per cent would have to be sold at 'state prices' which were literally etched into the bottom of everything. Prices for resources needed by the little entrepreneurs were set much higher than for state enter-prises and free traders were forced to pay extraordinarily high taxes on imports. The party made sure private business was unprofitable. But no matter how hard the government made it, the private business people persisted.

This was the Soviet citizens' first experience of capitalism. It was hardly encouraging. Every step would be difficult. It was just as *Pravda* and 'Vremya' (the nightly state-run television news) had said it would be. Night after night, 'Vremya' would relay pictures of co-operatives in flames, which only made people worry more about the new economic order the young democrats were talking about. And it didn't make those who were entertaining the idea of leaving their state jobs to work in private enterprise feel any easier. The television campaign was a clear disincentive to those who might have been thinking of starting a business. And because so many people who did take the risk were driven out of business, their workers were thrown into unemployment.

At the same time, the state and independent media were telling people the truth about the Soviet economy. People knew the economy was in crisis. Gorbachev had taken a number of halfway measures to reform the state sector which still accounted for some 90 per cent of the economy. But his measures were disastrous. State enterprises which were productive and could finance themselves were allowed to operate outside the central planning system, which meant they didn't have to meet quotas laid down by the planners. But the problem in telling these enterprises that they could produce according to the demands of consumers was that the consumers' needs were still dictated from on high. Not only were the producers refused permission to sell directly to the retailers, most of the shops remained state owned.

Gorbachev tried to fix the problem by making wages dependent on output. But because what factories produced depended on the resources they could acquire (usually very few because the command system was almost completely defunct), they soon began producing fewer, but more expensive, goods. The result was nothing short of an unmitigated disaster. Wages skyrocketed and the government had to print more and more money to pay the bill. The crisis only hit workers when they noticed that month after month fewer affordable goods were available in the shops. By 1990, thanks to Gorbachev's half-measures, basic consumer goods had literally disappeared from the shop shelves and hyper-inflation loomed.

Almost every day I'd go 'shop watching', either walking to the local shops or driving to the nearest farmers' markets to see how dramatically prices were increasing and what people were saying about it. Almost every day I'd listen to people's tales about how hard they were finding it to make ends meet, and to their creeping bitterness with *perestroika* and Gorbachev whose idea it had been to allow the 'thieves' who ran the co-ops to rob people so openly. Few people seemed to blame the party which was forcing the government to impose measures which were paralysing an otherwise natural movement to the market. Nor did they blame the party for not being able to cast off its Leninist prejudices and preach that a market economy wouldn't necessarily lead to the 'exploitation of the workers'.

Whether it was a collective lack of imagination or sheer frustration, shoppers seemed unable to blame anyone other than the *spekulanty* and the man who'd legitimised their trade. Time after time, I'd hear stories about shoppers going to the farmers' markets to buy their fruit and vegetables only to find that by the time they got to the end of one row of stalls, asking each stallholder the price for a kilogram of tomatoes, the price at the first would have literally doubled. People simply couldn't manage.

In September 1990, just a month after his Soviet citizenship was returned to him, *Komsomolskaya Pravda* published an essay written by Alexander Solzhenitsyn called 'How Can We Revitalise Russia?'.

In it, the bearded, self-proclaimed prophet called on Russia to search within itself for its lost Russianness and the strength to rise from the ashes of communism. He wanted a return to a mystical, spiritual Russia. Bolshevism, he wrote, was a disaster and he urged Moscow again to give the republics which made up the Soviet Union their freedom, deserved after years of torment and the 'equality of poverty' which communism had delivered them. Explicitly, Solzhenitsyn rejected the legitimacy of the Soviet Union. He'd done it before. But the party was vulnerable now.

The tone of his essay, like its author, was self-righteous, but having been tailed, jailed, banished and lied about perhaps Solzhenitsyn had cause to feel this way. He had challenged the giant decades before in his books *Cancer Ward*, *The First Circle* and *August 1914*, all of them suppressed in the Soviet Union but published in the west and inspired by the eight years he'd spent in prison for so-called 'anti-Soviet activities'. When his sentence of exile was annulled he wrote *A Day in the Life of Ivan Denisovich* which, when it was printed in the Soviet Union in 1962 by Khrushchev's direct order, inspired hundreds of people to write to him about their time in the Gulag. From these personal accounts of misery and torture, he wrote *The Gulag Archipelego*, irrevocably angering the party. Thrown out of the Soviet Writers' Union, he spent much of his remaining time in Moscow trying to evade the KGB, which in 1971 attempted to take his life. His apartment was under constant surveillance; his friends were blackmailed. In February 1974, Solzhenitsyn was finally deported to the land of the exploiters after years of goading the regime. His enemies had found the perfect punishment for a Russian patriot.

But even exiled in the United States, the terror didn't stop. Solzhenitsyn watched and listened as the Soviet press crucified him as a traitor who had lied about his own country to the west. *Pravda* denounced him as a reptile with a hatred for everything Soviet. And this he certainly had. Solzhenitsyn's self-avowed mission was to rescue Russia from communism.

But as life as they knew it began to disintegrate in the Soviet Union, few people were interested in what the Russian patriot had to say. They wanted solutions and to hear something positive about their recent history—needs Solzhenitsyn had never been able to meet in his books.

In the autumn of 1990, at the Krylatskoe metro station in Moscow, a middle-aged man threw open the back of his truck to reveal volumes of Solzhenitsyn in Russian and English. 'Going cheap,' he bellowed at a completely indifferent crowd which had gathered the moment the truck arrived to inspect what it was carrying, hoping for something they could make use of. While I stood watching, no-one bought a book.

I found it strange then to listen to the concern some in the party hierarchy were expressing about Solzhenitsyn's latest tirade in *Komsomolskaya Pravda*. Why were they worried? No-one read Solzhenitsyn, or even liked him.

Igor Malashenko was an *apparatchik* in the Communist Party's Central Committee but he was different to most of the grey old men who served time in the various departments which determined policy. Malashenko was young, urbane and smart and had landed himself a secondment with Mikhail Gorbachev whom he was helping to mount a public relations campaign against the enemy, Boris Yeltsin.

Out in the villages, Malashenko told me, people would have read Solzhenitsyn's essay, because 'he's reminding them of a part of their history they have reduced to anecdotes and stories which seem too brutal to be true. He's offering them a route to redemption which our people want and need and are searching for.' For Malashenko the party's reluctant acceptance that the country could no longer be a one party state, a closed totalitarian regime, was an admission—and one he welcomed—that it had little left to offer people by way of hope or vision.

'But God won't save us,' he told me. 'We need more than whatever it is He has to offer. Telling the Russians to look within themselves to find their Russianness is fraudulent. We need political solutions otherwise we'll be praying on battlefields as our country explodes into flames of violence.

'Why do we fear Solzhenitsyn? Because maybe our people won't see him as a raving, delirious madman from a Russia they can't remember. They might begin to see him as a saviour *just* because he's able to speak freely. Maybe they'll invest some hope in this imaginary Russia he speaks about.'

Young people I spoke to at the time disagreed almost completely. Some of them read Solzhenitsyn's essay but they couldn't understand a word of it. His Russia was unrecognisable. It was a mystical entity moving backwards into centuries past. Not at all what young people wanted to hear. They wanted discos and Coca-Cola, good clothes and wholesale capitalism—everything Solzhenitsyn despised. 'He doesn't speak our Russian,' they'd say. But they liked what he'd written about the bells having tolled for communism's final hour.

But for the middle-aged and the elderly, Solzhenitsyn's words reminded them, if they needed reminding, that their duty was to remember their history, the sins of a brutal, evil system. And in doing so, the bearded prophet was undermining what Gorbachev was trying to do—remake and preserve the Soviet state despite its history.

Solzhenitsyn's call to memory brought to mind a story a lot of Soviet people had told and retold at their kitchen tables about Joseph Stalin's purges of the 1930s and 1940s. The dictator was looking over a list of people to be executed. One of his aides expressed concern that the killings, now numbering millions, might cause problems down the line.

'Problems,' said Stalin, 'what problems? Who will remember all this rubbish in twenty or thirty years? Who remembers the names of the boyars Ivan the Terrible killed?'

The problem for the system Stalin bequeathed Gorbachev was that people did remember. And Solzhenitsyn, no matter that he came from a different era, was prodding their collective conscience.

The seventh of November 1990 was to be the last time Red Square would host the official Revolution Day parade, though at the time no-one knew this. Gorbachev and a few of the party leadership stood on the reviewing stand as usual and watched, hoping no doubt that they wouldn't suffer the same humiliation they'd felt on May Day, just six months earlier.

There were floats and dancing girls and acrobats. Red flags lined the streets of Moscow and little girls with huge bows in their hair skipped along the metro tunnels, excited to be off to an event which wasn't a protest. But the day took on another dimension by the time it came to a close.

The mastermind of the anti-Gorbachev counter-revolution revealed himself, and he was none other than the chief of the KGB which was still, despite all the fuzzy rhetoric that came with *perestroika*, an army able to both plant informers in high places and keep watch on growing political movements at ground level. And Vladimir Kruchkov looked like he was watching.

Below the reviewing stand, next to the front gates of Lenin's tomb, an area had been partitioned off for high-ranking party faithful and their wives. Even Raisa Gorbachev was there. She chatted with Eduard Shevardnadze, the reform-minded Foreign Minister whose job it was to sell *glasnost* and *perestroika* abroad, and with Alexander Yakovlev, 'Mr Glasnost', the Central Committee secretary in charge of propaganda. But Raisa Maximovna kept her back towards the rest. Just inches away from her were her husband's enemies—Valentin Pavlov, the Soviet Prime Minister; Gennady Yanaev, the Vice President; Anatoly Lukyanov, the Chairman of the Supreme Soviet and an old university friend of Gorbachev whom Raisa had long distrusted, and Vladimir Kruchkov, the head of the KGB. The two groups didn't mix—not at all. But Kruchkov's eyes didn't wander from the small reform camp.

In a segregated area next to the party faithful were the foreign media. I stood chatting to David Remnick of the *Washington Post* who, like me, was intrigued by this obvious stand-off. David was sure that Kruchkov was the most evil of the hardliners and the man to be watched.

'It'd be good to speak with him,' said David.

'I've had requests in for months,' I said, 'but whenever I ring, I get the same answer—yes, he'll talk *skoro* [soon].'

'We could try to get to him now,' said David. I thought he was joking.

It would be an act of boldness not entirely dissimilar to open dissent to sneak through the metal barricades which divided us from the upper echelons of the party in order to approach the chief of the KGB. So we planned carefully.

We would watch the conspicuous KGB minders and, at an appropriate moment, David would quietly lift a metal barricade to separate it from the others which blocked our path. Within minutes, he had separated one barricade from another. I waited for him to sneak through. But before we could make another move, the mighty hand of authoritarianism landed on our shoulders and the barricades were closed on us again.

Kruchkov noticed the hubbub and grinned a grey sort of smile.

The party was on its way down but it had been replaced by an even bigger party—the party of non-party people, as Yevgeny Yevtushenko called it. By December of 1990, it was still hard to tell whether this new 'party' would force the Union of Soviet Socialist Republics to fall along with the Communist Party which had kept it glued together. Perhaps the KGB and the internal security forces would crush the non-party people first. I struggled to make sense of it all. But everyone I spoke to simply blamed Gorbachev for the uncertainty. It was all his fault. If he went, everything would get better.

He had opened the floodgates and allowed open dissent knowing this would anger the party, people would tell me. Yet despite his actions, he danced to the party's tune and slapped the protesters down, calling them 'mobs'. And there could be no disputing the fact that in his arrogant belief that the party could survive, Gorbachev had failed to heed the threatening messages coming not just from the major towns and cities of Russia but from the non-Russian republics as well.

Before I arrived in Moscow, there'd been riots in the central Asian republic of Kazakhstan (1986) when Gorbachev replaced its local party chief with a Russian. There'd been uproar in Tbilisi (1989), the Georgian capital, when Soviet troops opened fire on a peaceful demonstration. And Armenia and Azerbaijan were in open warfare over Nagorny Karabakh, a once tranquil passage of land wedged between the two republics. But neither the party nor Gorbachev were overly concerned about any of this. Or, if they were, they weren't showing it.

But by 1990, when Gorbachev could no longer ignore the danger signs, it was too late to do anything about rising nationalism outside Russia and the Kremlin panicked. The Baltic republics of Estonia, Latvia and Lithuania were roaring their discontent.

Yevgeny Kisilev, the presenter of the popular television program 'Itogi' ['Results'] and a friend of the ABC bureau, thought the party would tolerate the noises coming from the non-Baltic republics because few of them would want to stand independent and alone.

But, he explained, the Baltic republics were different. Their dissent would bring into question the communist dogma and lies which had brutally forced them into the Soviet Union.

Indeed in the Soviet Union's melting pot of nationalities, the Baltic republics had always been a problem. They refused to be tamed by the heavy hand of authoritarianism. They hated the Russians, the communists, the command economy. By the time *perestroika* and *glasnost* struck the country, they had harboured more than forty years of barely disguised resentment at their violent annexation under the secret protocols of the Molotov–Ribbentrop pact which the party refused to acknowledge until 1989.

The Balts considered that Stalin and his murderous lot had not just taken them by force, but had raped their culture and their language. They weren't wrong. In their millions, the Balts had been arrested and sent to labour camps during Stalin's forced collectivisation of farms. To add insult to injury those taken were replaced by Russians. By the time Gorbachev came to power, more Russians had immigrated to the Baltic republics than to anywhere else within the Soviet Union other than Kazakhstan, which was almost completely Russified. In Latvia—which the party had identified in the late 1980s as the most radical of the Baltic states—the population was so Russified that only 52 per cent were of Latvian origin.

So angry were the Latvians that they demanded in 1988 that they become a truly sovereign state, a demand which, as it fell short of a complete declaration of independence, didn't overly worry the party.

Yet in their thousands the Latvians protested and through their sheer volume and persistence forced the Latvian Communist Party to accept the formation of a Popular Front in Support of Perestroika, which in essence was no less than a front to force Moscow out of Latvia. The Popular Front's agenda was overwhelmingly anti-Soviet and one wonders why it wasn't crushed the moment it appeared. It wanted to make Latvian the official language of the republic rather than Russian and to stop any further Russian immigration to Latvia.

It demanded that Latvians be given a majority on all local committees and boards and that Latvians due for conscription to the Soviet
army be sent instead to the defence of these 'democratic and liberal
objectives'. It was radical stuff.

Still Gorbachev sat back and watched. Even if his mind told him
to let the Balts go their own way (they had been, after all, the last
to be brought into the Soviet fold), his heart beat to the party's
drum. But for the Russians who lived in Latvia, Gorbachev's refusal
to act was more than they could stand.

By 1990, shadowy organisations calling themselves National Salvation Fronts came together in Latvia, Lithuania and Estonia. They
were political organisations in which Russians from the republics'
armies, police forces and KGB organs planned to either coerce
Moscow into putting out the nationalist blaze or to put it out themselves. They were shadows of the party. They wanted Gorbachev to
impose presidential rule to bypass the elected governments of the
three republics. They wanted nationalism to be crushed. Unless their
demands were met, they threatened they would take power—violently if need be. Again Gorbachev did nothing.

Eventually it was Lithuania, not Latvia, which led the way towards
the break-up of the Union. The reason was Vytautis Landsbergis.

Landsbergis led the *Sajudis* movement which was Lithuania's
Popular Front. Its moment of victory came in March 1990 and was
delivered by Gorbachev's own hands. He permitted elections to be
held for republican parliaments and regional and local councils across
the Soviet Union. The elections were far from democratic in some
regions where only one candidate was allowed to run and he or she
was a communist. But in the Baltic states, the Communist Party had
already split into pro-Moscow and pro-independence camps. People
had a real choice. In Lithuania, the new pro-independence parliament elected Landsbergis as the country's first president.

A musicologist at the Vilnius Conservatory, Landsbergis was not
only anti-communist, he seemed to speak only to himself. Discussion with him was circular. He would chant the same mantra over

and over. The Baltic states were violently, illegally annexed. They were occupied territories and Russia was a foreign country. Of course he was correct. But the Kremlin wasn't yet in the mood for the truth.

Gorbachev had hoped that by admitting the existence of the 1939 Molotov–Ribbentrop pact, he would calm the Lithuanian bid for freedom. Instead, Landsbergis declared Lithuania's independence. The party was furious. All Gorbachev could do was condemn Landsbergis for 'threatening the integrity of the USSR'. But the party couldn't be calmed. It forced Gorbachev's 'democratically elected' parliament—loaded to the gunwales with party men—to pass a law which outlined the steps any republic would have to take in order to secede.

Landsbergis predicably wouldn't play the game. 'There is nothing to negotiate,' he told the world.

Within weeks, Estonia and Latvia followed Lithuania's lead and in all three republics there were two sets of laws—Soviet and republican law—and two sources of authority—the elected republican government and the Soviet government. The scene was set, the western media thought, for Moscow to take action, on the premise that if it didn't then in all likelihood there would be confrontation and blood would be spilt. The world watched.

So too did Vladimir Mikheiyev, an English-speaking journalist with *Izvestiya*, a newspaper which had managed a remarkable transformation from party mouthpiece to reasonably fair-minded journal. Mikheiyev had spent many years in Australia for the paper so we had much in common and often we'd meet to talk about what was happening and how it all might end up. I asked him what the talk was in *Izvestiya*'s editorial offices about the Lithuanian crisis. Might the party force Gorbachev to roll out the tanks and quash the Baltic independence movement?

'We're asking the same question and no-one will give any answers. Probably no-one knows what can break the impasse. Just think,

Gorbachev is anxious not to harm his considerable international reputation as a man of peace and the party knows that the Soviet Union
needs financial help from the west. To roll in the tanks would be
yet another fatal half-measure because the Balts will never give up
their fight.'

It was a crisis which threatened the very existence of what
remained of the Soviet empire.

Gorbachev tried imposing an economic blockade. But it was a
dangerous move. A centralised economy meant that factories across
the entire Soviet Union depended on parts made elsewhere in the
country, including the Baltic republics. If Moscow blockaded Lithuania, the pain would be felt in Russia, in Tadjikistan, in Moldova.
But the Balts weren't worried. The Lithuanian and Estonian governments took over the factories and plants where they commanded a
majority of the workforce, literally ousting the Russians and with
them the Communist Party's propaganda cells. In the end the blockade lasted only a few weeks, long enough to make the Baltic republics feel they could win this battle of wills against the Kremlin if
they simply kept up the pressure.

Moscow's will had certainly never before been challenged with
quite this level of infectious resolve. And it was spreading to other
republics, among them Azerbaijan, Georgia and, to a lesser extent,
Armenia. Gorbachev needed to win the fight with Lithuania to prove
that the party was invincible, that Moscow wouldn't look on helplessly as its empire fell apart.

By December 1990, the counter-revolution in the Baltic states had
taken up arms. There was a series of explosions, many of them in
Latvia. The casualties were much lower than expected, which made
us think the explosions were professionally planned by the army or
the KGB. But there was no proof for the outrageous thought that

perhaps Mikhail Gorbachev, unwilling himself to stain his hands with blood, was allowing his hardline ministers for Defence and Internal Affairs to mount a campaign against Baltic independence.

I remember one night receiving a call from a Danish journalist who lived in the same building. She wondered whether I had seen in the English translations of TASS (the official Soviet news agency) a story about OMON (the well-trained and mostly vicious special assignment police) seizing a publishing house in Riga, the Latvian capital.

My Danish colleague said she was alarmed to read in the Russian version of the TASS story that the director of the publishing house had claimed the seizure was ordered by Alfred Rubiks, a Politburo member who happened also to head the pro-Moscow wing of the Latvian Communist Party.

I checked my English translations and the publishing director's claim had been omitted, no doubt discovered by the censors in the Russian to English translation. We pored over the two versions and the wire stories which had come before and after it with growing apprehension that there was some sort of Kremlin cover-up going on. If a member of the Politburo had been involved, then surely his ideological brothers in the Central Committee were aware. And if that was the case, how could Gorbachev not know?

When I rang off, I sat confused and dumbfounded until a few moments later John Bruce, the executive producer of 'AM' phoned. He wondered what we should make of the explosions in the Baltic republics. Was there anything to them?

I told him that as strange as it sounded, a lot of people thought Gorbachev had either lost control of his ministers or he was turning a blind eye to what they were doing. There could be no other possible explanations.

Indeed, on the face of it, it seemed Gorbachev was an accomplice. He had been dancing intimately with the right, reshuffling his ministry and appointing a number of party hardliners who held the confidence not only of the party, but of the Baltic Salvation Fronts.

Gorbachev sat in the Kremlin like a mushroom accepting advice and intelligence from these men on the state of the country.

A day later, Dmitri Yazov, the Defence Minister, and the new hardline Interior Minister, Boris Pugo (whom Gorbachev had only just appointed to replace a liberal), signed an order which allowed joint military and paramilitary patrols of the streets of the Baltic capitals. The move was apropos of nothing, other than whipping up fear. It wasn't clear whether Gorbachev knew of their decision before it was announced. But within days, the order had been used to seize all Communist Party buildings in the three republics.

A week later, the Soviet Prime Minister Nikolai Ryzhkov issued a decree ordering the governments of the Baltic republics to round up their young for conscription in the Red Army. Military rollcall had been down since *perestroika* began. Now, young Balts, many of them with no Russian blood, were being told that rather than defend their parents who wanted independence from Moscow, they would be forced to take up arms against them.

The morning of 13 December 1990 was frightfully cold and I wished I were at home in Sydney in the sun. I could think of nothing better. Since October when I'd arrived in Moscow, the temperature had steadily dropped till it hit minus ten in a notably cold December. And the work was gruelling. If you blinked, something would happen. The Soviet Union was unravelling at an almighty speed. Gorbachev's reforms were going badly wrong.

I'd gone that morning to the office to find the wire services running stories about Victor Alksnis, a leading light of the anti-nationalist Latvian Salvation Front.

The 'Black Colonel', as he was called, was also a leading member of the *Soyuz* faction of the Soviet parliament which was absolutely opposed to *perestroika* and *glasnost*. Not smitten with shyness, Alksnis would meet journalists in his 'office' on the tenth floor of the Moskva

Hotel in the Manezh Square to peddle his anti-Gorbachev, anti-*perestroika*, anti-democrat lines. He talked openly about how the Salvation Front would seize power in the Baltic states.

But now, Alksnis had upped the ante. If Gorbachev wasn't prepared to stop the rot, then a Salvation Front would be formed in Russia to do the job. The republican parliaments which had been democratically elected would be disbanded. The Soviet president himself would be ousted. A state of emergency would be declared. It was a performance designed to both threaten Gorbachev and put the west on notice that its adoration of Gorbachev was doing the Soviet Union no good.

I rang Alksnis and asked whether he'd meet me for an interview. He was always easy to find, the most accessible of the hardliners. He agreed to an interview but not for two days. I asked whether he might, on the spot, tell me who would carry out this 'state of emergency'. 'No-one who you don't already know about,' he answered before hanging up.

That night, after the late-night television news, a sombre announcer appeared to introduce Vladimir Kruchkov, the KGB chief. 'Recent changes in our country have led to a sense of disorder which many comrades do not like, and I appeal to you to follow the path mapped out by our predecessors. Without order, there will be no Union,' Kruchkov told tens of millions of people from Siberia to the Baltics. The chief of the KGB declared himself against *perestroika* and against *glasnost*. It was extraordinary. He was calling on people to rise against Gorbachev and return to Lenin.

As I sat in the office preparing to file Kruchkov's announcement to Sydney, a friend who worked for the KGB rang to see whether I'd been watching.

'Vsio panyatno [All is understood],' he said. 'They've watched long enough. They've been keeping Gorbachev in there at the Kremlin, feeding him bullshit and lies. But still, Gorbachev won't do anything to stop what's going on.'

Only a day earlier, my friend had been assigned to keep watch over a democratic protest at Mayakovsky Square in the centre of Moscow at which demonstrators carried placards labelling the party criminal. There was nothing new about this.

'The only thing that's changed is that the message has begun to sink in. The Baltic republics are driving it home,' he said. It was the simplest of explanations but probably the most accurate.

Everyone was worried. Everyone had an opinion about what they were seeing and hearing. But few interpretations of what might happen in the crumbling Soviet empire had been as dark or as explicit as that of the Black Colonel. I wondered whether he might repeat his warning about a state of emergency in the parliament. So day after day I sat in the parliament's all but empty press gallery and waited. On 20 December I went without an interpreter and so had to concentrate hard to make sure I wasn't missing anything, or at least that I was catching everything important. Alksnis sat in his usual place, surrounded by other *Soyuz* members who'd become regular guests on the television current affairs programs. But Alksnis didn't budge. He sat chatting to his colleagues, no doubt waiting for a break in the parliamentary session to swan outside where he'd drop a few more lines designed to shock.

Quite suddenly, Eduard Shevardnadze, the silver-haired Foreign Minister, much loved in the west for his 'gently gently' approach to this new 1990s version of détente, walked to the podium. He was one of the few reformers who remained in Gorbachev's government.

In his thick Georgian accent, he threw a political bombshell. He was resigning.

I looked to my colleagues and back to the podium. 'What did he say?' I asked.

'He's resigning,' said Jeanette Mathtey from the Canadian broadcaster CBC.

Shevardnadze was visibly distressed. He accused the military of pretending to like the idea that the Cold War had ended but he said they hated the United States as vehemently as they always had. And the Interior Ministry, he said, had pulled off a series of blasts in the Baltic states to discredit the new order and make it look like a farce.

'A dictatorship is coming,' said Shevardnadze, 'and the democrats have scattered to the bushes.' The big talkers with epaulets on their shoulders—a not so vague reference to Alksnis—would soon win the day and Gorbachev all the while would do nothing to stop them because he was being fed 'provocations' by a deceitful KGB chief, backed by a bevy of deceitful hardline ministers.

I have to confess my most immediate thought was how to get the story to air, rather than what Shevardnadze's resignation would mean for *perestroika*. There were no international phones in the parliamentary building. I'd have to drive all the way back to Krylatskoe to the ABC office. But first I'd have to run fair across the Kremlin to get to my car which was parked at the Kremlin's eastern gates. By the time I got there, I thought I was having a heart attack. And never before had I driven so fast, using what foreigners in Moscow called the KGB lane reserved for the authorities whenever I could, ignoring the *militsiya*'s attempts to pull me over to the side of the road. When I arrived at the office, I threw off my coat and bags as I walked through the front door. Tanya, the translator and office secretary, was white with shock.

'Shevardnadze has resigned!' she said.

Everyone except the hardliners felt black. People talked endlessly about the showdown just around the corner, winter making it no easier to be optimistic.

Food shortages were causing anxiety that few who weren't there could possibly understand. That winter, people queued at four in the morning for bread. Moscow City Council imposed rations so that only those who could prove they lived in the capital could access the little which was available. Of course the old ways of *blat* ensured against famine, but the state shops were mostly bare—a few dozen cans of pilchards imaginatively displayed in a shop window testimony to the shortages. At the farmers' markets, the situation was only marginally better. When Article Six went by the bye, the cities and regions outside Moscow along with the non-Russian republics began to assert themselves by deciding to take care of their own needs first. Feeding Russians was no longer a priority. So the markets were unusually bare in the winter of 1990.

Foreign embassies were helping out their own by importing food directly, rather than leaving people to buy at the hard currency shops which were finding it hard to get their trucks across the icy roads leading into Moscow. The Australian embassy flew in frozen Australian T-bone steaks and legs of lamb which it distributed to the handful of Australians in the Russian capital. It was like winning Lotto. My freezer could barely cope with the basket-loads of frozen Aussie meat, more than enough to feed myself and my friends sumptuously for months. Leg of lamb cut into lean pieces for *plov* (a Tadjik meal of meat and rice and whole garlic cloves) would take everyone's mind off what was happening on the streets, at least for a few hours.

But nothing could stop the fear, a deep abiding apprehension that all would end very badly. It was the overriding emotion that winter. I knew no-one who didn't think obsessively about what would resolve this terrible stand-off between the dithering Gorbachev and the party hardliners. Young and old knew that Shevardnadze was right when he said the democrats had scattered to the bushes. But what else could they do? They were disorganised and fractured into small groups whose platforms differed, in most cases, very slightly. But the right to disagree with party diktat had gone to their heads rendering them helpless against the growing wrath of the party. They were shooting themselves in the foot and they knew it, their lack of unity making them vulnerable targets for the party. Zhenya, one of my younger friends, said he'd heard people substituting the word 'perestroika' with 'perestrelka' which meant to shoot-out!

Sergei Stankevich, the youngish democrat who'd made his name as a one-time Gorbachev adviser, had defected to Yeltsin's side. He recognised that by the time the penny had dropped for the movers and shakers in the democratic camp, it was too late. Stankevich talked openly on television about being sent to Siberia.

'Don't joke about things like that,' said the interviewer, Sasha Lubimov, almost as though he was trying to reassure himself.

'I'm not!' said Stankevich.

Perestroika was in crisis. Little could have made the situation worse other than an uprising in Russia itself. And people knew this. But so too did the Communist Party.

The crisis in the Baltic republics was a point from which there could be no return. The Balts wanted freedom but to grant it would have undermined the very foundations of the USSR and, with it, the party. 'If there's blood spilt in Lithuania we will not escape bloodshed here,' said the democrat Stankevich. 'It's a simple equation. Freedom has its price. The Balts want freedom from the USSR. We want freedom from the party.'

Something in Victor Alksnis gave me to believe that he and his hardline cronies agreed and were moving closer towards a willingness to pay the price for the party's unfettered control. He walked around Moscow smiling like a Cheshire cat.

I'd organised to meet him for an interview for 'AM' at the Moskva Hotel in the Orthodox Christmas holiday period of early January. 'Come tomorrow. Tomorrow night I'm going to Vilnius,' he said.

How unusual, I thought, that this Latvian was going to the Lithuanian capital for the public holiday break.

This time, Alksnis didn't invite me into his office. The interview was conducted in the lobby. 'It's busy in there,' he said with the mischievous grin of someone about to pull off a major stunt.

'The Lithuanian crisis is of Gorbachev's own making. He is not for the Soviet people. He doesn't know what he is for. Let him dance. It won't be for too long,' he told me.

I asked whether he was in contact with the KGB chief. 'There are things that as a woman you don't understand,' said Alksnis.

Alksnis specialised in shocking people but I hadn't banked on his sexism. I put the question again.

'We talk all the time,' said Alksnis with an absolutely blank look of resignation on his face, as though what he'd just said ought to be a perfectly acceptable fact of Soviet life.

But the head of a minor faction in the Soviet parliament would have little to talk about with the head of the secret police unless, of course, the two had something in common.

Bloody Sunday, as the Lithuanians called it, began in the wee hours of 13 January 1991. The Christmas season was barely over as Soviet tanks rolled into Vilnius. In Iraq, American bombs were searching out Saddam Hussein.

On Monday morning, when news of the Lithuanian assault broke, Natasha phoned. 'Do you think your people in Australia will want to hear about this next chapter or do they just want to watch the first televised war on CNN?'

I was surprised by the question but actually wondered myself. So I called Sydney. But no-one disagreed that on the face of it, it seemed as though *perestroika* and *glasnost* were about to sustain serious injury, and if they survived then life in what remained of the Soviet Union would change dramatically. Natasha and I took the next available flight to Vilnius.

The city looked like a war zone. On route from the airport to the city centre, we saw Soviet tanks rumble through the suburbs while people shuffled around in minus thirty degree cold, bewildered and frightened.

Two nights earlier, the National Salvation Front had declared a state of emergency and attempted to seize the Vilnius television tower, backed by forces under Moscow's control. They clearly hoped that if they seized all means of communication they could impose their will. But the Lithuanians came out in their hundreds. Ground forces fired at them, killing fourteen people and injuring scores more, but ultimately withdrew.

Around the parliamentary building, Lithuanians had built a wall of defence with sandbags and concrete blocks. They believed the Soviet troops would soon return to crush all resistance. They put up a shaky razor-wire fence on which people spiked Politburo pictures of Gorbachev which they had splattered with red paint. As far as the Lithuanians were concerned, Gorbachev the peacemaker was no less a murderer than Stalin. He had blood dripping from his hands.

Some Lithuanians, no older than fifteen, carried Kalashnikov rifles across their shoulders as they patrolled the perimeters of the compound. They were prepared, they told me, to use their weapons, pilfered from the Soviet military bases scattered throughout their country, against the KGB or the ground forces which had tried to take the television tower. One told me that Moscow would have to douse them with radioactive waste to kill their hunger for freedom. 'And what will you westerners think then of Gorbachev?' he asked.

Entry to the parliament was by the express permission of Vytautis Landsbergis. He would see no-one. He was holed up in emergency meetings with his cabinet, planning the defence of the Baltics with the leaders of the Popular Fronts in Latvia and Estonia which everyone suspected might become the next targets. But other members of the parliament shuffled from room to room, some panicky, others resigned to the war it seemed they were now fighting with the Kremlin. Kazimiras Uoka, a member of the leadership of *Sajudis*, looked pale and shaken when I asked for an interview.

'You now have to ask what freedom means for Gorbachev and his Communist Party. Does it mean smashing down everything which gets in their way? Or does it mean sane negotiation to end what millions of people are telling them is an intolerable situation?

'Maybe now the intelligent people of the party will lose what little faith they had in him and this "humane socialism" Gorbachev has duped you all into believing he wants. Maybe now you will ask what does he really want?

'He wants the Union of Soviet Socialist Republics. He wants the party which nurtured him. All that is needed to kill it forever is the acknowledgment that the Soviet Union is an illegal entity built on blood and Gorbachev won't do that. When you stop seeing this man as an icon and see him the way we see him—as someone caught by his own past—then you can look in the mirror and not spit at yourselves.'

I felt a terrible shame. I can still hear Uoka's words in my ears, just as I can still hear the conversation I had with the young Russian conscripts riding the Soviet tanks which patrolled the city.

Many of them had been born in Lithuania of Russian parents and their allegiances were confused. They'd been unable to escape the orders given by the Defence Minister to answer the annual military rollcall because they'd been bred to believe that the Soviet Union was the Motherland. But they were of a new era. They didn't want to fight the party's causes. In the days following the assault, many of them defected from the Red Army and went to the parliament to defend Landsbergis.

Others were from the different non-Russian republics which, they thought, might suffer the same fate as Lithuania. A young Georgian soldier perched on one of the dozens of tanks which were parked around the television tower asked me if I'd heard of any reaction to the Lithuanian invasion by his republic's parliament. I hadn't. 'But why do you ask?'

He shrugged his shoulders and looked towards the ground. 'I have a fear that one day soon I'll be ordered to defend the Soviet Communist Party against Zviad Ghamsakhurdia [Georgia's first democratically elected president].'

'What will you do if you are asked?'

'I don't know,' he answered.

The Lithuanian assault might have sent a clear message to the republic's parliament that its anti-Moscow behaviour wouldn't be tolerated much longer. But it was an abject failure in what most assumed was its ultimate objective—to frighten the Lithuanian people away from *Sajudis*. Lithuanian hatred of Russia deepened. They had withstood annexation, the humiliation and heartache of Stalin's forced collectivisation and the Russification of their country. They had watched as their plea for freedom was ignored. Now they had been slaughtered—again—and they would take no more. Natasha and I could almost feel their hatred of all things and all people Russian.

The Intourist Hotel where we were staying was almost deserted. A few correspondents from Moscow were staying there but the staff had decamped almost entirely. There was no food in the hotel restaurant, the fast food automatic bar in the foyer was empty. At the front desk, the attendant—a Lithuanian—thought we'd find it hard to find food. 'But try the bread shop down the road. Only don't speak to them in Russian!' she warned.

Of all the shops which normally sold food and groceries only the bread shops were open. At the first we went to, the women refused to sell us bread because we'd asked in Russian, the only language we had in common.

'But we don't speak Lithuanian,' I implored. The women shrugged their shoulders and turned away. We tried another shop and then another. Each time the reaction was the same. During the four days we spent in Vilnius we ate only the chocolate bars we'd brought with us from Moscow and a packet of dry biscuits, and drank endless cups of tea.

CHAPTER 7

BLINKERED AND BLIND

The Soviet Union could not exist without the image of the empire. The image of the empire could not exist without the image of force.

BORIS YELTSIN, *THE VIEW FROM THE KREMLIN*, 1994

The question everyone wanted answered after the bloodshed in Lithuania was whether Gorbachev, who had been awarded the Nobel Peace Prize in October 1990, approved the assault. Was it his hand which signed the paper ordering Soviet tanks to crush the Lithuanian independence movement? The assault had changed everything. It had not only worsened the tension in Lithuania, it had sent *perestroika* and *glasnost* reeling, and re-established the determination and ruthlessness of the hardliners in the party.

The morning Natasha and I returned from Lithuania, I called my friend Masha to report in safe and sound. Masha was concerned by everything she'd been hearing on independent radio stations about what was happening in Lithuania. She had never really believed that reform was possible. 'You know,' she said, 'when Stalin died, all his cronies stood and looked at him for hours because they thought maybe he's not dead, despite the fact that he wasn't breathing. I don't know what makes Gorbachev think he can kill the system, or kill the party with a few half-baked ideas. All he's done is make life harder than it ever was.'

'We'll see what Gorbachev has to say,' I told her. 'If he had nothing to do with what happened in Lithuania, then maybe there's still a chance.'

'Whatever he says, don't believe him,' she replied.

As I watched him walk towards the speaker's stand at a media conference he called that afternoon at the Foreign Ministry Press Centre in Moscow, Mikhail Gorbachev seemed washed-out, a little grey. He looked like he'd been dragged there under sufferance. He's a man with a gun at his head, I thought.

He spoke for three minutes. I remember because I looked at my watch wondering whether Gorbachev the chatterer would finish speaking before six o'clock when peak-hour traffic would bring Moscow to a standstill, forcing me into semi-criminal acts like driving on the footpath to make it back to the office through the lines of traffic belching out black exhaust fumes.

Gorbachev didn't jabber endlessly as we expected. He made a short sharp statement in which he blamed the Lithuanian government for what had happened at the television tower in Vilnius. Nor would he condemn the National Salvation Front for masterminding the assault. The army escaped unscathed too. It was the media, he said, which was to blame for whipping up false nationalist sentiment and encouraging the vacuum of respect for the sovereignty of the USSR. Then he left, refusing to take questions. Gorbachev had become a prisoner of the hardliners, mouthing their rhetoric even if he didn't believe it.

He was someone you'd think was on his way to a factory job if you saw him in the metro. But in fact Nikolai Travkin was a Hero of Socialist Labour and a member of the party faithful—until the first time he travelled overseas and was struck by the lies he'd been told about the non-communist world. He liked and supported Gorbachev until 1990 when he, like millions of others, left the Communist Party. Travkin took the freedoms Gorbachev had granted literally. He formed his own political party—the Democratic Party of Russia—and by the day became angrier with the Communist Party. At the huge anti-party, then anti-Gorbachev rallies in Moscow he would tell protesters how they'd been belittled and made fools of, urging them to join his group. But many people thought Travkin was just one of a whole army of former party people who'd become anti-communist and pro-nothing. As Natasha would say of Travkin and others like him, 'It's easy to denounce communism. We all do in our own way. But what do they really stand for? How do they think they're going to fix the country? The democrats say we need millions of people to become businessmen. But who's going to plough the fields and collect the harvest? Or maybe they'd like us just to sell the USSR to the highest bidder?'

In January 1991, following the assault on Vilnius, Travkin and his democrat friends found a rallying point. Finally, the democrats who in Shevardnadze's words, had scattered to the bushes, came out united, full of hatred for the party and misgiving towards Gorbachev whom they believed had ordered the troops into Vilnius. Travkin's message was especially scornful.

'And now, what are *perestroika* and *glasnost?*' he screamed from the back of a truck parked on the footpath outside the Moskva Hotel on Manezh Square, opposite the Kremlin, to a crowd of perhaps fifty thousand. Is this humane socialism? Is this what we can expect from Gorbachev—that he will lead this slow creeping coup against us, the very people his new thinking is meant to protect?'

The crowd roared. I'd been to dozens of protests in Moscow, in Lithuania, in Azerbaijan, in Armenia but never had I seen people so angry. They'd come out in freezing temperatures, carrying pictures of Gorbachev with red paint splattered across his face. They believed he had blood on his hands. They demanded an election for his post of Soviet president so they could give him a swift boot up the backside, strong enough to send him all the way to America where he was so adored. The bitterness was unmistakable.

Sasha Lubimov also took the microphone. Lubimov hosted a television current affairs program called 'Vzglyad' ('Opinion') which was pacey, honest and anti-Soviet. Sasha was one of the *glasnost* darlings, using his language skills to talk up the need to protect the reform process at any cost. He told the crowd 'Vzglyad' had prepared a program on what Shevardnadze was talking about when he warned of a creeping dictatorship. The program was pulled before it got to air and 'Vzglyad' was axed. Behind the decision stood the conservative Leonid Kravchenko, whom the parliament had appointed to head the Soviet television and radio network, *Gosteleradio*. According to Lubimov, Kravchenko would personally edit stories before they were aired on 'Vremya', the nightly news, and needless to say anything that implied party guilt was left on the cutting room floor.

But not all media still dependent on the state for money toed the party line. *New Times*, under its editor Alexander Pumpyansky, went as near to the truth as it could about what had happened in Lithuania. Pumpyansky went even further in an interview he gave me for the ABC. 'It is important that our readers are left in no doubt that the Kremlin backed the Lithuanian Salvation Front, and fourteen people lost their lives as a result,' he said.

Mikhail Sergeyevich Gorbachev was an icon in the west. At home, he was despised. But as Natasha would say, 'You have to be Soviet to understand why.'

For decades people had been degraded by the Soviet experiment.

They had known civil war and famine. They had lost family and friends to Stalin's perversions. And because they believed the Leninist propaganda, they had allowed themselves to be beaten by a system which denied them the most basic of needs like good health care and decent food. Gorbachev ended their nightmare by smashing the old structures and allowing a few of the myths to crumble with them. But corrupt as they were, the old structures at least provided certainty.

'He was like a bulldozer. And for what? Did he want to fix the old command structure, did he want to introduce capitalism, or did he want something in between the two? To tell you the truth, not even I am sure,' said Georgi Shakhnazarov, Gorbachev's close aide.

'By 1989 it was clear the command system was dead. But Gorbachev couldn't bring himself to dump it for a capitalist market economy. So he tried to steer a middle road which he thought would give the Communist Party time to renew itself. But the party was incapable of reform and, even worse, it was angry,' Shakhnazarov told me in 1994.

Indeed, it was growing angrier by the day with the economic and social freedoms which Gorbachev bestowed and which were, in any event, negatives for the great majority of people.

'His freedom is not freedom. There is no freedom to live in peace, no freedom to eat properly, no freedom to know that tomorrow I will have a job. I am not even free to say whether I want to be a guinea pig in this ugly experiment with freedom,' said Natasha.

'I can't travel to Georgia to see my sister because there's a civil war going on there. I can't afford to buy meat for my parents at the free markets and there's none in the state shops. And I haven't been paid for a month.' It seemed trite to argue that Gorbachev meant well.

Nor did the young completely support him. He had removed the certainty from their lives as well. 'If you're not cunning enough to sell, then you're unemployed,' my young friend Zhenya told me as he sat morosely in his family sitting room pondering the point of life. 'If you think about it,' he once said, 'I'm a member of the lost generation. I have nothing at all. Gorbachev has even changed the history books from which I received my education. So I know nothing and I can do nothing.'

Faced with the hardship his half-measures were creating, Gorbachev could only point the finger back at the people. Communism, he told them, had turned them into *Homo Sovieticus*, dependent on the state for everything.

'Don't ask me about *perestroika*,' he warned one Russian journalist in a fit of anger. 'I should ask you about it. I gave you full freedom to act as you would consider necessary. So act! The trouble is in the workforce. They don't know how to work, they don't want to, they're too old, they're too tired and they're incapable!'

It was pointless arguing that the measure of Gorbachev's success was the chaos which was now swallowing people's lives. So many times in conversation on the topic, which needless to say dominated people's thinking, they'd scoff at me when I'd say that Gorbachev had simply been left behind by his own reforms. Life was changing very fast, I'd say, you ought to be happy Gorbachev has allowed himself to be overrun by events.

'What does that mean?' Natasha would come back at me. 'You really think that if Gorbachev had moved faster he would have beaten the forces of Soviet power who knew from the start how deeply they were being threatened by this reform-crazed guru? You don't really believe he had a chance do you?'

Perhaps it was simply, as Natasha insisted, that you had to be born Soviet to understand. Only they could really comprehend what was inside the Pandora's box which Gorbachev had opened—the Communist Party ruling elite, the dogma, the bureaucracy which carried out the party's word, the KGB and the military which punished those who didn't obey the party, the barons of the Soviet Union's centralised industry who oversaw the party's economic system and those of the military–industrial complex who produced the party's weapons. It was an unfair war from the beginning. Gorbachev had taken on the Soviet Union. He'd managed only to make the country's organs weaker; the body was still twitching. As Masha said, the system was a little like Stalin after he stopped breathing—not yet dead, but terminally ill.

The Communist Party had been unceremoniously dumped from its central place in Soviet life. It was no longer the only party constitutionally allowed to govern and by no means the only party people thought capable of governing. But it had regrouped in several republics, taking political advantage of the hardships the reforms had caused. The barons of Soviet industry were threatened by economic reforms, but they still presided over enterprises which were overseen by the central government in Moscow. The outer reaches of the Soviet empire had given way to velvet revolutions but the generals who returned to Russia angry at the loss of empire and the arms concessions which had left the military–industrial complex floundering were able to drum up considerable support for the conservative cause among their troops who were forced to live in makeshift housing in the countryside. And the presidency Gorbachev had created to protect his reforms was not healthy enough to continually ward off the attacks. He had not been elected to the post and he was holding onto the party for support.

Throughout it all, people felt like they were pawns in an almighty tussle for power. They'd been given the freedom to protest but when they snatched the chance to hate the party, Gorbachev slapped them down. To most of my friends, Gorbachev was the sum of his past. He was born to the Soviet Union, educated by it. He believed its dogma and followed its leader. When he mouthed the democratic mantra, people didn't believe him. They knew that Gorbachev truly believed the Soviet Union should remain united under Russia's control. And Russia had always dominated the union of 'equal' republics. Even the clocks in railway stations and airports in the far-flung empire were set to Moscow time. Russians ran defence factories, the republican KGB services, the military, the economy. Russians dominated republican governments. For Gorbachev, it was the natural order of things.

Driving in search of a cafe in February 1991, with freezing winds gusting around the car, my passenger Nikolai Shishlin of the International Department of the Central Committee, tried to explain that Gorbachev was one of the few real communists left in Russia, but one who was trying desperately to reconstruct himself to fit the times.

'Communism is built on monopolies of thought and political power. Gorbachev thinks that to be a reconstructed communist means you claim a monopoly on reform,' he said. It seemed to explain why Gorbachev felt only his reforms aimed at preserving the party could lead the way to a new shining future.

What other explanation could there be? He had given his blessing to new political movements, which after all, was what *glasnost* was meant to be all about. But when these groups, naive and vulnerable, decided to break the rules and operate outside the realm of socialism, Gorbachev turned his back on them. And even if his instincts were to accommodate the demands for bigger and faster reforms, to usher in capitalism, he couldn't. He was roped into a corner by his background as a member of the party which claimed his allegiance.

People wanted him to resign from his post as General Secretary of the Communist Party which would have caused the party, if not its cells within the other organs of power in the USSR, to collapse. Gorbachev was, after all, the party's only remaining official link to real power, unless of course the party resorted to the gun.

For most people I knew there could be only two reasons why Gorbachev didn't resign from the party leadership: either he didn't want 'good' for his people or, if he did, he was frightened of losing power and so couldn't break with the party. Either way, he was damned. By 1991, after the bloodshed in Lithuania, after the abandonment of the 500-Day Plan and Gorbachev's promotion of a cabinet of hardline deceivers, people could only believe that Gorbachev's struggle to hold onto power clashed head on with their struggle for a better life with or without the party.

Yet continually Gorbachev would argue that the people's struggle for human dignity was Lenin's struggle. They baulked.

'I don't know why he thinks like that,' young Zhenya said one day. 'He must know better. He's not a stupid man!' Stupid, certainly not. Just blind.

People thought Gorbachev vain too. He loved the adoration he received whenever he travelled abroad. Jonathan Steele in his book *Eternal Russia* writes of a conversation he had with the hardline Politburo member Yigor Ligachev about Gorbachev. Gorbachev had returned to Russia in 1989 from a trip to Italy and Ligachev went to the airport to meet him.

'The whole of Milan, the whole of Rome came out to meet me,' Gorbachev boasted. Ligachev replied: 'You should go to Sverdlovsk and Nizhni Novgorod and talk to people there.' Ligachev wasn't exaggerating the point, for had Gorbachev travelled to Sverdlovsk or Nizhni Novgorod or anywhere else within what remained of the Soviet empire he would have found people who literally spat his name in disgust.

He recognised none of this. Talking to his own people was below him, although when he was abroad he happily answered questions about how people at home were coping with change. But he didn't know. He was isolated. He could even become angry with foreign correspondents when we pushed him on the point at his media conferences during which his opening statement could take an hour and would be anything but self-effacing. 'Gorbachev knows the people,' he would tell us, 'Gorbachev is the first Soviet leader to listen to the people.' He was nothing of the sort.

On International Women's Day—8 March—my old protest friend, Igor, called to bestow upon me the traditional congratulations on being a woman. 'Monica, I have something to tell you,' he added, 'but promise not to laugh at me.'

'Sure,' I agreed.

'I wrote Gorbachev a letter. He says he listens to the people. Well,

I wrote to him about his ministers. I told him not to trust Pugo, or Yazov and I told him that everyone on the streets is talking about Kruchkov. Do you think he'll listen?'

Gorbachev didn't listen, at least not to any of the enlightened in his midst. The liberals in his entourage—Alexander Yakovlev, Eduard Shevardnadze, Vadim Bakatin—had all told him that he was surrounded by men who were deceiving him. They told him that a right-wing counter-revolution was underway and it had only one aim—to destroy *perestroika* and *glasnost* and put the country back to sleep. But Gorbachev insisted he knew what was going on in his country.

I could listen to what people said about Gorbachev for hours and understand every word, every betrayed emotion. But the moment I walked away, I would revert to type. I was a westerner. I had placed all my faith in this 'reform-crazed guru' and I couldn't accept that the man who allowed Eastern Europe to determine its own fate could possibly be scheming against his own people. But yet more proof was to come.

Boris Kagarlitsky was a socialist, but of the democratic persuasion. He'd been jailed in 1982 for his honest account of Soviet intellectual life from 1917 to Brezhnev's era which had been published in *samisdat*, the flourishing underground press. By 1990 when I first met him, Kagarlitsky had long emerged from the Soviet netherworld and had taken to intriguing against Moscow's democratic mayor, Gavriil Popov, whom he wanted dumped in favour of more socialist-minded candidates. He lost that battle. But he was predicting another.

Kagarlitsky believed the final showdown would not be between Gorbachev and the party. Gorbachev clearly supported the KGB, the military and the party. The showdown, Kagarlitsky predicted, would be between Gorbachev and Yeltsin and it would come in June when elections would be held for the Russian presidency, the position Russians had overwhelmingly voted to create in the March referendum which had supported the continued existence of the Soviet Union.

'Russia cannot have two kings,' Kagarlitsky said, 'and Yeltsin will be elected president of Russia. That means we'll have two presidents, just like the republics have two sources of power. Something has to give. Which one do you think will surrender?'

Both men readied their weapons. The party gave Gorbachev his ammunition—intelligence from his cabinet of deceivers (led by the KGB chief, Vladimir Kruchkov) that protesters would try to take power violently by the most absurd of means. They would scale the Kremlim walls, Gorbachev was told, and physically remove him from power and assume control of the whole USSR.

Gorbachev wasn't the only person to believe the lie. Sasha, my KGB acquaintance, asked me whether I'd heard anything of the rumour about the assault on the Kremlin. 'Are you crazy?' I asked. 'Where did you hear that rubbish?'

He pulled out of his pocket a scrap of paper from which he read Kruchkov's call for the KGB to decide which side it was on. Was it for the treacherous democrats or was it for the face of order and certainty?

'You don't believe this do you?' I asked him.

'Well, I'm not sure what to believe. But the point is that this sort of stuff is being sent to every person who works in the KGB, Internal Affairs and the police. Something's happening!' he replied.

The next day *Pravda* published the rumour and Gorbachev slapped a ban on all protests and demonstrations for three weeks—a half-hearted attempt to appease both sides.

I was writing the story for the morning news bulletins when Kagarlitsky came to my office for a pre-arranged interview.

'There's going to be a protest, a big protest on 28 March,' he blurted out as he walked through the door.

'But what about the ban? They're just going to ignore it?'

'Gorbachev is ignoring us. Why not?' he said. It would be a major test of Yeltsin's authority. Kagarlitsky thought fifty or sixty thousand people would turn out in support of Yeltsin and in defiance of the General Secretary of the Communist Party and President of the Soviet Union. 'But there'll be no bloodshed,' he predicted.

The night before the expected showdown, Interior Ministry troops in military trucks and public buses blocked the streets around the Kremlin.

My young friend Zhenya rang to ask whether he could come to the demonstration with me as I had a press card which would give me access to all parts of the city. He wanted to take photographs of the action. And action was certainly on the Kremlin's agenda. As 28 March dawned, Moscow Radio news was full of portentous warnings. The authorities, it reported, would use all means at their disposal to ensure order was maintained and the safety of the Kremlin was not breached. It was high farce.

On the streets where the protesters gathered, danger was far from imminent. 'It feels like a street party,' said Zhenya as he raced around snapping shots of the troops sitting helplessly on their buses and trucks, no doubt wondering what they were supposed to do if anyone tried to break past their barriers. The protesters chatted and ate pizza from the takeaway Pizza Hut outlet on Gorky Street which had just opened. I caught up with fellow foreign correspondents who, like me, had been buried in the story for months. One middle-aged woman climbed on a bus blockading Gorky Street to test whether the police would remove her. They refused.

By June when Russians would for the very first time elect a president from a genuine list of candidates who'd collected their one million signatures to validate their run for the position, there could be no doubting that Boris Nikolaevich Yeltsin would win and win handsomely. Russia was about to have two kings.

I knew only a handful of people who didn't vote for Yeltsin, and they voted for a leading reformer, Vadim Bakatin, whom Gorbachev had sacked as Interior Minister and replaced with a hardliner. But as far as the people I knew were concerned Yeltsin could do no wrong. He wanted only 'good' for his people. He could say nothing undemocratic. He was the people's light, hope and vision for the future, leading them out of their fearful wilderness into a new world of fast cars and profitable factories, full shops and a truly egalitarian life where 'to each according to their labour' would actually mean something.

The day of the poll, I was driving into the city to watch Yeltsin cast his vote. Again Zhenya was with me to capture the event on film. As we drove through the back streets of Filiovsky Park, we were stopped by the *militsiya*. They had nothing much to say, standing there almost mute until I asked whether we might be on our way if there was nothing they required from us. 'Who's the Russian in the car?' one of the officers blurted out.

'Who wants to know?' I replied as Zhenya jumped out of the car and confronted the startled officer. 'My name is Zhenya Krylenko and I'm going to cast my vote today in the first presidential election in Russia. I'm voting for Yeltsin. And you?'

I burst out laughing. The officers scowled and shuffled away and off we drove to watch Yeltsin vote for himself.

Masha voted for Yeltsin too, but what distinguished the occasion for her was that it was the first time she had voted in her life. She'd ignored what she called 'the mock democratic elections' for the Soviet parliament in 1989. There were lots of candidates, she said, but they were all communists. And she wasn't around to vote in the polls for the Russian parliament in 1990. But this one, she wouldn't miss.

Boris Yelstin, with a huge dose of ego, wrote in *The View from the Kremlin* that people voted for him because they felt they were voting for the end of Soviet history. 'Even the very word Soviet was no longer possible to pronounce; it had exhausted its resources. The image of the USSR was inseparably linked with the image of military power. As Gorbachev changed our image in the world community within the framework of our global strategy by silencing our tanks, so he continued to babble on and on about socialism, the friendship of the Soviet peoples, the achievements of the Soviet way of life which must be developed and enriched—never realising that he was up the creek.'

The euphoria of Yeltsin's victory made those who supported him think Gorbachev would be forced to see the light. Perhaps now he'd give up the party and join Yeltsin. But that was just wishful thinking. Gorbachev was blinkered and blind. Only he couldn't see Russia had a president, ruling from the same city in which he was trying desperately to keep together his empire, and that people no longer needed or trusted him.

Boris Yeltsin's office was in disarray, overwhelmed by the presidential victory and the prospect of a clear run for power over Russian affairs. None of his aides knew who would issue passes to the inauguration which was to be held in the Kremlin's Palace of Congresses, right under Gorbachev's nose. In desperation I rang my minder in the Soviet Foreign Ministry, the man to whom I had to report my every move and who bestowed passes to official events. 'I don't know and I care even less where the inauguration will be held,' he said, 'but I'd like to know why you want to go.' I'm not sure why I was shocked but I was. After six years of *glasnost*, the concept of a free media, not to mention a free foreign media, was still not entrenched. Maybe I too had been swept up in the euphoria of Yeltsin's victory!

On the day, I just turned up and was given entry to the press gallery for a most extraordinary event. The massive red backdrop upon which Lenin's face was etched in silver thread had disappeared. In its place, the red, blue and white Russian flag floated freely. Gorbachev looked out of place, redundant.

The reality was that Gorbachev was no more than the General Secretary of a party which was split and had lost its totalitarian control over the country. He was president of a union of republics demanding sovereignty. The outer empire had long gone. Now the Soviet Union looked like going the same way. If there was to be any hope at all that the Soviet Union would survive the chaos, the Union would have to be renegotiated, and Gorbachev would have to begin some old-fashioned bargaining in order to keep the republican presidents interested.

Gorbachev's preference was for a confederation of states, each of which would have some independence, but not so much that Moscow lost control of the Soviet Union. There would still be a centre—Moscow—and a president called Gorbachev. The talks, however, were farcical. Yeltsin insists Gorbachev was asserting his superiority over the republican presidents. He treated them like naughty little boys. They, in turn, deluded themselves that Gorbachev's gesture of negotiation meant that he was thinking about relinquishing control.

The tension was extraordinary. It seemed that even the protesters had decided to call a moratorium on their anger while they watched and analysed what was going on.

For Gorbachev, it was all a question of power. It was one thing for the republics to demand sovereignty, another for them to want to snatch Moscow's powers and determine their own foreign policies, or create and operate their own financial systems, despite the size of the mandate of independent-minded governments all over the country. And which of the western powers, he asked, would like to see the Soviet Union fracture into fifteen new nations each with their own armies? Would the west surrender global security to the democratic 'whims' of the people?

Of course he had a point. The west was frightened of the prospect of a splintered Soviet Union. And so long as it remained frightened, Gorbachev would continue to receive its support. He would be allowed to do whatever was needed to keep the USSR whole. It was a point which didn't escape the hardliners and no doubt this was a major part of the reason they didn't dump Gorbachev. He was still their best bet.

The party leadership was confident of success in the Union treaty talks. It had suffered some devastating blows but it still had Gorbachev's ear. It had managed to convince him that the strength of the USSR depended on the military, the KGB and the internal police and even if Gorbachev, in his heart, had wanted things to be different, he'd given the party enough evidence to prove that he wouldn't act on his feelings. It was, after all, Gorbachev who had so willingly thrown away the principles outlined in the 500-Day Plan which aimed to carry the Soviet Union out of the Marxist wilderness. It was Gorbachev who defended the military and the KGB after the Lithuanian bloodshed. And now the party thought it would simply string the General Secretary on a little longer. It would persuade Gorbachev to be strong in the negotiations, ceding the minimum required in order to renew the Union and so restore peace and order.

Ivan Polozkov, a moderate conservative given the position he held as the First Secretary of the Central Committee of the Communist Party would argue quietly with Gorbachev that what was enveloping the Soviet Union was not democracy. It was anarchy and only the party could bring it to heel. The hardliners, of course, made the same point more forcefully. Democracy, they told Gorbachev, had developed far too quickly in the Soviet Union and must be reined in. This was a far cry from the way the people saw things.

I spoke with Polozkov during a break in proceedings at the Soviet parliament just after Yeltsin won the Russian presidency and he told me that Gorbachev seemed to understand and agree with the party's general line that 'the people of the Soviet Union have a common history, firm blood and family relations and an interdependent economy. So we have no choice but to work together'. In other words, the republics were free to proclaim their independence, but their declarations would be meaningless.

Gorbachev, Polozkov told me, didn't disagree at all with the party's proposition that a new Union treaty needed to preserve the central powers of the USSR, not let them devolve to the republics.

But at Novo-Ogaryovo, one of Gorbachev's many Moscow residences, where the republican presidents were negotiating the future, Gorbachev was giving away more in the treaty talks than the party would ever condone. The Baltic leaders were boasting that the treaty included clauses which would allow them their freedom. The remaining republics were to gain some control over their finances. It was sounding to many less like a new treaty and more like the beginning of the end.

Still, the party moderates weren't worried. Indeed they cautioned their more reactionary colleagues to stay calm. They thought Gorbachev was simply bargaining, taking a little here, giving a little there. For the party hardliners the story was very different.

Victor Alksnis, the 'Black Colonel', explained why the Union had to be preserved. 'There is no alternative to the CPSU,' he told a group of journalists who mobbed him at the parliament during the final rounds of negotiation. 'Of all the political parties which have emerged, none possesses real power. Only the Communist Party has power because it has property. The democratic parties offer disintegration as a solution. But disintegration means economic chaos because economic divorce is impossible. And this Union treaty! What rot! Why? A confederation of states might have been possible if our republics were made up of only a few nationalities. But they are not. Each of the republics is multi-racial and a Union treaty is just a nice way to say disintegration which would mean racial conflict.'

No doubt the Baltic declarations of independence compounded

the hardliners' deepest fears. The thought that the hundreds of races which co-existed in the Soviet Union might splinter and go their own ways raised the spectre of the final defeat of the party.

Boris Yeltsin was a paranoid man. The affliction coincided with his falling-out with the party, many assuming that as a one-time party boss he was all too aware of what it could do to silence its critics. But his antics since arriving in Moscow were decidedly over the top. After he was sacked from the Politburo he was convinced that KGB operatives had tried to push him into the Moscow River to drown him. And after he was elected to the Russian parliament he claimed that the secret police had staged a motor vehicle accident which was intended to cause him serious injury, 'perhaps even death'. It seemed that election to the Russian presidency had done little to soothe his nerves.

In *The View from the Kremlin*, Yeltsin describes the last Union treaty meeting, held at the end of July at Novo-Ogaryovo, just before Gorbachev was to leave Moscow for Foros in the Crimea for his annual August holiday. Nursultan Nazarbayev, the president of Kazakhstan, was also there. The draft treaty was all but on the printing presses so that when Gorbachev returned from his holidays on 20 August it could be signed.

Yelstin decided to test the water, to see whether the concessions Gorbachev had made in the Union treaty were a genuine acknowledgment of the independence of the republics or whether he was merely paying it lip-service in order to give the party a chance to bite back.

As Yeltsin tells it, 'As soon as we began addressing topics which were extremely confidential I suddenly stopped talking. "What's wrong Boris?" Gorbachev asked in surprise. It's hard for me to now recall what feeling I experienced at that moment. But it was an inexplicable sensation, the kind you feel when someone is constantly spying on you behind your back. I then suggested that we go out on the balcony because I thought we were being bugged. Gorbachev protested somewhat unconvincingly but followed me outside.'

On the balcony, Yeltsin told the Soviet president that if he wanted the treaty signed he'd have to promise to get rid of some of his 'odious entourage'.

'Who would believe in a new Union treaty if KGB chairman Vladimir Kruchkov who had the attempted coup in Lithuania on his conscience was to remain chairman? Not a single republic would want to join such a Union. Or take Defence Minister Dmitri Yazov. Could such a hawk from the old obsolete days be in the new commonwealth?' wondered Yeltsin.

While they were on a roll, Nazarbayev added two more names to the list of people Gorbachev needed to behead—Boris Pugo, the Interior Minister, and Leonid Kravchenko, the chairman of *Gosteleradio*.

Yeltsin looked at Nazarbayev who looked at Gorbachev. 'And while we're at it,' said Yeltsin, 'what kind of president would [Gennady] Yanaev [the Soviet vice president] make?'

In Yeltsin's account, Gorbachev agreed that Pugo and Kruchkov would definitely have to go. But as usual he would keep a foot in both camps. He urged Yeltsin and Nazarbayev to calm down and wait until the treaty was signed before making any firm demands.

CHAPTER 8

SUMMER HEAT

This wall is rotten. When you hit it, it will just fall down.

VLADIMIR ILYCH LENIN ON THE TSARIST EMPIRE, 1907

The summer of 1991 was hot. By the beginning of August, Moscow was almost empty as people packed their Ladas and Nivas and headed out of town.

Every year at this time the Soviet Union's class structure went on display. Ordinary people would pack what they needed and head off to their little wooden cabins which were mostly unheated and lacked water and toilet facilities. Non-party professionals would decamp to their rather less modest country homes built by the institutes they worked for or the unions governing their employment which would allocate holiday accommodation as reward for good work or loyalty. The VIPs holidayed in considerably grander surroundings.

In Peredelkino on the south-west outskirts of Moscow, rambling two-storey *dachas*, many of them with attached tennis courts and *banyas* (saunas) were reserved largely for the literary elite, although over time a few KGB generals had sneaked in. The writer Yevgeny Yevtushenko lived much of the year in his well-appointed, heated *dacha*. Boris Pasternak, the Nobel Prize winner who wrote *Doctor Zhivago* also lived in Peredelkino until his death. Academics and middle-ranking government officials went to Nikolina Gora, west of Moscow, for a dose of escapism.

But the party leaders rested like kings. Stalin preferred the mansions and villas of the Crimea. Khrushchev must have been too exhausted from his international travelling to want to go too far. He returned the party elite to the two-storey country homes of Zhukovka, not far from Moscow, which were built originally by Stalin for respected scientists, among them Andrei Sakharov who was rewarded with a *dacha* when he invented the first Soviet hydrogen bomb. Khrushchev broadened the residential base of Zhukovka, allowing in cultural figures like Dmitri Shostakovich, the composer, and even the cellist Mstislav Rostropovich who was never much of a fan of the communist order and was forced to leave the USSR for having harboured Alexander Solzhenitsyn in a cottage in the backyard of his *dacha*.

Brezhnev kept up the tradition and neither Andropov nor Chernenko were around long enough to change it had they been so inclined.

But even though the sort of *dacha* one had and where it was located was a clear reflection of one's place in Soviet life, the *dacha* ritual crossed social boundaries because just about everyone escaped to one every summer, including this summer of 1991.

For most people I knew, 1991 had given them more reason to escape than usual and I had no difficulty understanding why they wanted to leave Moscow behind. It was a crazed and frightened city. But Gorbachev? Why was he thinking about a holiday at the villa he'd ordered built for his family at Foros in the Crimea when his empire was falling and his chief lieutenants were traitors?

It's not that the Soviet president and General Secretary of the CPSU hadn't been told by enough people that he was in strife. Tens of thousands of protesters had tried to send him a message. His closest aides and oldest friends were telling him that the KGB chief Vladimir Kruchkov, the Defence Minister Dmitri Yazov, the Prime Minister

Valentin Pavlov, the Vice President Gennady Yanaev and an assortment of others were planning a coup. Gorbachev listened but ignored the warnings.

Victor Alksnis too had tried to warn Gorbachev. His threats of an emergency committee to save the Soviet Union were becoming shriller by the day. By August he was almost completely unabashed about his plans. He'd ring foreign correspondents with increasingly graphic details of how the committee would take the country. In the newspapers, his cohorts talked of patriotic forces 'seizing the country'. The only detail they didn't reveal was when this would happen.

But those close to Gorbachev felt it would be soon. Alexander Yakovlev, the Central Committee Secretary for Information had been close to Gorbachev since the birth of *perestroika* and *glasnost*. He listened to the hardliners as they complained to him about Gorbachev. He watched as their resentment boiled into fury.

'I told Gorbachev,' Yakovlev told Russian television in September 1991, 'I told him that some in the government were seriously listening to people like Victor Alksnis, that they wanted to put up roadblocks on the democratic path to paradise. But Gorbachev didn't listen. Or he listened and didn't believe me.'

In the summer of 1991 I was exhausted, too exhausted to go anywhere for a holiday, and in any event my friend in the KGB had given me good reason to hang around Moscow.

Sasha had been trying to leave the organisation for more than a year but with no success. Like others in the service, he wanted to try his hand at *biznez*—the free market world which showed no sign of dying despite the best efforts of the hardliners. Sasha wanted to start a personal security business which in 1991 was a growth industry given the level of extortion and mafia-style murder the KGB had been unable to stamp out as private trading flourished. But the KGB simply said 'no' to his request. Sasha was needed. Until the KGB could afford to lose men, he would have to stay. He knew better than to argue. After all, the KGB was not used to dissent. And it duly noted Sasha's desire to leave.

At the beginning of August Sasha became terribly worried. He suspected he was being slowly isolated. He and other officers who wanted to leave the KGB were being excluded from meetings of similarly ranked men which by the beginning of August were being held almost daily. More curiously he was taken off 'protest duty' where he'd be required to produce written reports on those he recognised. I remember feeling utterly betrayed when I spotted him sitting in a car on the Kremlin side of the grey Moskva Hotel while on Manezh Square, which bordered the hotel, demonstrators voiced their anger with Gorbachev in the winter of 1990. He assured me then that the reports his masters required him to produce during the turbulent demonstrations of 1989 and 1990 had been full of 'manufactured' names.

I'm not quite sure I ever really believed the story until August 1991. After all, if the KGB had discovered he wasn't sympathetic to the hardline cause, it would hardly have levelled an accusation against him or sacked him—that, after all, would be obviously anti-*glasnost*. More likely, he'd be isolated.

In any event, by August the 'us' and 'them' regime was impossible for Sasha to ignore. And every day he grew more anxious.

As the city emptied itself of Muscovites and foreign correspondents, he asked me whether I could organise a meeting for him with Oleg Kalugin, who had been the KGB's chief of foreign counter-intelligence in Moscow but had been retired early for expressing unorthodox opinions and being resistant to reform. In 1980 Kalugin attacked the KGB's demonisation of the American CIA. For this he was sacked as deputy head of the Leningrad KGB. Back in Moscow, he delivered a thinly veiled attack on the party, accusing it of looking for an imaginary 'hostile encirclement' by western anti-Soviet forces (presumably the CIA) which wanted to see socialism dumped.

It was dangerous stuff and Kalugin, the youngest general in counterintelligence in Soviet history, looked like he was on a career path to oblivion.

But in 1990 even oblivion seemed out of his reach. He attacked the grey shadow of authoritarianism personified—Vladimir Kruchkov, the KGB chief. As Kruchkov battled to convince Gorbachev, the parliament and the west that the KGB was mending its ways of its own volition and didn't need to be brought under parliamentary scrutiny, Kalugin piped up with the truth. The KGB's shadow, he said, was in absolutely every sphere of life. 'All the talk of the KGB's new image was no more than camouflage.' Kalugin was forced out of the service and into retirement at the age of fifty-five. His life as a KGB general was over and he would spend the next few years writing his memoirs in his KGB apartment in the suburb of Kuntsevo, which he managed to keep through bureaucratic incompetence.

Kalugin was a fiery character, smart and urbane. He'd spent many years in the Soviet Embassy in Washington where he refined his near perfect command of English. Since *perestroika*, Kalugin had decided to speak his mind. He knew what was wrong with the Soviet Union. When I arrived in Moscow he was among the first people with whom I made contact. And our first meeting is hard to forget. He organised to meet me in the hard currency bar of the Hotel Savoy which I thought strange not only because it was just around the corner from Lubyanka, the KGB headquarters, but because I assumed a retired KGB general in 1990 wouldn't have a lot of hard currency at his disposal. He drank whisky and chatted openly for more than an hour about what was wrong with the KGB, how professional the CIA was, how its staff weren't prone to extreme judgments as were his own former colleagues. He also relived his attempt to nip the Prague Spring in the bud.

Kalugin was the KGB resident in Washington as Moscow was preparing to pounce on Alexander Dubcek's 'socialism with a human

face'. The KGB had sent more than thirty operatives into Czechoslovakia to gather evidence that Dubcek was mounting a counter-
revolution at the west's behest. But each returned empty-handed.
The intelligence they gathered showed that contrary to what the
KGB leadership was telling the Kremlin, there was no western
inspired plot to undermine the Communist Party. The KGB ignored
the advice. They also ignored Kalugin who had accessed what he
claimed were 'absolutely reliable documents' proving the CIA was
not prompting political change in Czechoslovakia. Indeed, Kalugin
told KGB headquarters that Washington was shocked when Soviet
tanks eventually rolled into Prague in 1968.

'You know,' Kalugin told me as he hit his fourth whisky in the
Hotel Savoy, 'when I returned to Moscow in 1969, I found that
Lubyanka had destroyed my messages. They hadn't shown them to
anyone.' And so began his life as a dissenter, albeit a secret one for
the next twenty years.

I phoned Kalugin on 5 August 1991 to ask for an interview about
the 'current situation'. He was, as usual, happy to talk and that afternoon I went to his apartment.

Kalugin repeated what he'd said publicly at a democratic rally only
a few months earlier, for which he'd been stripped of his military
rank and decorations, making his forced retirement even more humiliating. Kruchkov, he said, was planning a coup. He'd been lying to
Gorbachev since December 1990 and unless the young dissenters in
the KGB rose in defence of *perestroika* and *glasnost*, democracy would
soon be finished.

'But are there enough young dissenters in the KGB?' I asked.

'Kruchkov has more dissenters than he has supporters but many
of them don't know how to disobey and even if they did, they're
too frightened. But unless they act, no matter what their number,
they're going to be crushed.'

I told Kalugin about Sasha. Kalugin said he'd been in contact with
dozens of young officers who were in the same boat as my friend

and just as concerned. 'Tell him to follow his conscience, not their orders.'

I included Kalugin's remarks in a story for 'AM' but played them also to Sasha. It seemed only to make him more anxious and when on 18 August he called at my apartment, he was not only agitated but unusually circumspect about what he said. I thought it a little amusing that after a year of openly poking fun at the KGB's inability to mount a decent internal surveillance operation, he was now worried about who was listening. He signalled that we should go for a walk down to the Krylatskoe Olympic Stadium where we sat in the viewing stalls built for 20 000 spectators. We were definitely alone!

'Have you been in contact with any of the hardliners from *Soyuz* recently?' he asked.

I hadn't. But I didn't think I needed to be. They were signalling their punches quite clearly in the newspapers.

Sasha pulled from his pocket a crumpled piece of paper and asked me to take notes as he read.

'Our nation needs a real leader. We are at the mercy of fate at this dire time of our history. Moral damage is being committed to our great Motherland and it is your duty to stop it. Be prepared to act.'

It was issued, Sasha said, by the fifth directorate of the KGB which dealt with matters concerning ideology. 'I called a friend of mine in the third chief directorate [this dealt with military counter-intelligence] and he wasn't home. His wife told me he'd been sent to the Baltics but she wasn't sure where.'

Sasha seemed sure that the mobilisation had begun. And it had.

CHAPTER 9

COLD REVENGE

Fear, which picks out objects in the dark,
Guides a ray of moonlight to an axe.
From behind the wall comes an enormous knock—
What is there? A spectre, a thief, or rats?

ANNA AKHMATOVA, FROM 'THE SEVENTH BOOK', 1921

On 17 August, Boris Yeltsin was in Almaty, the capital of Kazakhstan, where he was signing a bilateral treaty with the Kazakh leader Nursultan Nazarbayev. Nazarbayev was happy. The two republics had just made a substantial step towards taking hold of their own affairs. Gorbachev's central government had played no part in this event. The Kazakh wanted to eat, drink and be merry. Yeltsin, however, felt a heaviness he couldn't ascribe to anything physical. He had a 'sense of vague, unfocused anxiety'.

In Moscow a powerful group of men close to the president were anxious too. The day before the KGB chief Vladimir Kruchkov, the Defence Minister Dmitri Yazov, the Prime Minister Valentin Pavlov, and the Vice President Gennady Yanaev had gathered in a Kremlin office to talk over the 'crisis'. To them, the situation seemed hopeless. The country was falling apart. Gorbachev had refused to return 'order' to the country as far as they were concerned. Protesters had all but done away with the authority of the party while Gorbachev had allowed its power to be constitutionally whittled down. He'd abandoned Article Six. Yeltsin was gnawing at what was left of the party's once almighty hold on power. He'd even outlawed its propaganda cells in all Russian workplaces. And in three days' time, Gorbachev would help Yeltsin bury the USSR by signing the Union treaty when he returned to Moscow. Together they would consign the workers' paradise to the dustbin of history.

All of the coup plotters except Vladimir Kruchkov felt frustrated. Only the grey man of Lubyanka had given serious, strategic thought to what to do. A few of the plotters were assigned the gruesome task of confronting Gorbachev. He'd be given an ultimatum: either support a state of emergency or step down.

In the afternoon of the next day, 18 August, there was a knock at the door of Gorbachev's Foros villa. The leader had visitors.

Gorbachev began to sweat. How unusual, he thought, to receive uninvited, unexpected visitors. He picked up a phone to call Moscow to see what all this was about. But the line was dead. All lines into the villa had been cut. 'Noo vsyo,' ['Well, that's it'] Gorbachev told his wife, Raisa Maximovna, as he went from phone to phone with mounting despair.

The delegation which had come to Foros from Moscow was rude, according to Gorbachev. They told him that a State Committee for the State of Emergency had been formed. It was called the GKChP. The plotters showed Gorbachev a list of its members. Gorbachev was shocked, 'deeply hurt' he would say later. Finally, the penny had dropped. He had been betrayed. The ringleaders were men he had nurtured and trusted.

The delegation told Gorbachev, incorrectly, that Boris Yeltsin had been arrested and they urged him to put his name to the GKChP. He refused. 'Then resign,' one of them demanded. Gorbachev told them they were criminals. If they were really worried about the crisis which had gripped the Soviet Union, they should convene the parliament and discuss the problems in an open forum. He was, of course, dithering, his mind darting through all the possibilities and consequences of his refusal to go along with the coup. But to this suggestion Gorbachev received a reply he didn't want to hear. The delegation muttered concern about his health which they claimed had suffered during the *perestroika* period. Gorbachev knew what they were up to.

'General Valentin Varennikov, the commander of the ground forces, spewed out the usual line,' said Gorbachev after the coup attempt was defeated and he was brought back to Moscow. 'The country was being torn apart by extremists and people were tired. I told him I'd heard all this before. And I said to them they must be mad if they think the country would simply follow another dictatorship. People are not that tired.'

When the delegation returned to the Kremlin, Yanaev, Gorbachev's vice president, wanted to know—incredibly—whether Gorbachev had agreed to the GKChP. Told that Gorbachev was angry and had dissociated himself from the hardliners completely, Yanaev began to worry.

A year later, as he sat in his apartment waiting to be tried for treason, he told me that he had wanted to speak with Gorbachev himself. The bottom line was that he didn't want to assume the presidency and with it responsibility for the coup and worse still for running the country. I wondered whether the question of morality had played any part in his anxiety. But the man who sat before me was no moral beacon. He was a drunk who mouthed the Leninist mantra for a bit of payola—a huge apartment, a car, free airfares and power. It was more likely that his sudden concern for Gorbachev's welfare was born of pure fear that no-one would take him seriously. And nobody did.

'To be honest, I wasn't up to it. The country was in a mess, I knew I couldn't fix the problems. So how can they blame me for the coup?' he asked me.

Indeed, Yanaev was the consummate Soviet—subservient not just to the party but to any form of authority, unable to make decisions, unwilling to accept responsibility. On the night before the GKChP seized power, Yanaev sweated over a document sitting on the table before him. It had been drawn up by the KGB chief and declared to the country and to the world the formation of the committee and the state of emergency. It would use as its justification the lie that Gorbachev was too ill to rule. Yanaev procrastinated but eventually succumbed to habit.

'You see, I was ordered to sign the document and I am telling you, I never believed that responsibility for the GKChP would be mine alone. Lukyanov [Chairman of the Supreme Soviet] told me the parliament would support me,' he said.

All the plotters signed the document as it was passed around the table. All except Alexander Bessmertnykh, the Foreign Minister appointed to replace Eduard Shevardnadze. He was too frightened. He wanted to see the medical reports to prove Gorbachev was too ill to rule and, of course, there were none.

So Bessmertnykh left the room. He didn't protest. He didn't send the message to his ambassadors across the globe that Gorbachev was being ousted, that the plotters would say he was sick but that this was a lie. He didn't call for help. Bessmertnykh did the only thing his Soviet conscience would allow him to do and kept silent.

I'd had a late night on 18 August, talking to Sasha, my KGB friend, then sharing his concerns on the phone with Natasha who didn't believe the hardliners would be so stupid as to mount a coup. 'I'm telling you,' she said, 'they know that this is not 1956 or 1968, and it's not 1981 either [when Solidarity was crushed in Poland]. They can't just roll out the tanks and hope for the best. There are Mercedes Benzs in Tadjikistan for God's sake!'

At 1 a.m. I rang off and went to bed. At 4 a.m., Gennady Yanaev, drunk and, according to Russian newspaper reports after the event, unable to find the toilet in his office suite, assumed control over the Soviet Union and its military arsenal.

At 4.30 a.m. all military units were put on high alert, ordered to occupy Moscow, and be prepared for battle. An elite unit was ordered to arrest Boris Yeltsin, though the order was later rescinded.

At 6 a.m., a television announcer broke the news. Barely able to disguise his anxiety, he read out a statement issued by the GKChP. The country had lost its way, it said. The law of the USSR was being violated by people who were trying to grab dictatorial powers. They were preparing to stage an 'unconstitutional coup'. The people were demanding that something be done to stop it. Vladimir Kruchkov was speaking.

As the news flashed up on wire services across the world, my phone blasted me out of my sleep. 'Monica, it's Kerrie Weil. Where's Gorbachev?'

The executive producer of 'PM' had heard the news about the GKChP before I had.

'I'm fairly sure he's in the Crimea. Why?'

'According to AFP [Associated France Press] he's sick and some sort of committee has been formed to run the country.'

I grabbed my bag and bolted for the door, in my panic forgetting even to change out of my pyjamas. It had always been handy having our office and apartments in the same block and within two minutes I was wading through the masses of stories which Reuters and TASS had spat out in the fifteen minutes since the GKChP had declared itself. My hands were shaking uncontrollably as I looked for the one story on TASS which would confirm what we suspected had happened. It was the simplest of statements.

'A state of emergency has been declared on the territory of the Union of Soviet Socialist Republics. The president Mikhail Sergeyevich Gorbachev is ill and in his absence a State Committee for the State of Emergency has been formed. The committee consists of: Gennady Yanaev, Valentin Pavlov, Vladimir Kruchkov, Dmitri Yazov, Boris Pugo, Valeri Boldin, Yuri Plekhanov, Oleg Shenin, Oleg

Baklanov, Alexander Tizyakov and Vasily Starodubstev.'

I'd never even heard of Tizyakov and Starodubstev! I fumbled through my Soviet version of *Who's Who* and found them. Tizyakov was the President of the Association of State Enterprises, no doubt violently opposed to the recommendations coming from the reform camp that subsidies to state enterprises be cut. Starodubstev led the Union of Collective Farm Chairmen, a group also intractably opposed to the notion of private enterprise and what that meant—private farming.

I stared at the copy for several minutes. So that was that! Everyone was expected to believe what the GKChP said and watch as six years of *perestroika* and *glasnost* were dismantled. Over and over I read the line that Gorbachev was too ill to continue his duties. It sounded like a fabrication. The phones began ringing hot. Kerrie Weil, the sub-editors in radio news, other journalists from around the ABC, public radio in France, everyone wanting to confirm what the international wires were saying—that Mikhail Gorbachev was sick, that a state of emergency had been declared across the Soviet Union.

I switched on the television but could find only midnight to dawn movies. I tried calling the Foreign Ministry but the guard on duty knew nothing and he said the building was empty. I woke Nikolai Shishlin, my old friend from the Central Committee's International Department. 'I wouldn't be surprised if there's a coup,' he said. But was Gorbachev ill?

'Not when I last saw him,' said Shishlin.

The minutes were ticking away. I'd have to file for news and go to air for the early edition of 'PM'. I couldn't confirm that Gorbachev was sick but I could say that a state committee had declared itself to run the country.

I wondered what my parents would think when they heard me report that a coup d'etat was underway. Just two days before, I'd canvassed the possibility in conversation with my father who'd said that if the hardliners tried to get rid of Gorbachev, they'd have to be vicious and determined because the world would come to Gorbachev's defence.

As I tapped out my first story for the noon news bulletin, I dialled my parents' number. Begging them not to worry seemed pointless. 'As long as we hear you, we know you're OK,' said my father. My mother just felt anxious.

At Archangelskoe village, just outside Moscow, Boris Yeltsin was asleep when the coup was declared. His daughter Tanya flew into his room with the news: 'Papa get up. There's a coup,' she told him. 'That's illegal!' Yeltsin said in an astonishing display of naivety. Tanya told him about Kruchkov, Yanaev and the others. 'Are you kidding me?' asked Yeltsin. Within minutes, his phone too would begin to ring hot. His faithful lieutenants urged him to leave his *dacha* as soon as possible because, 'no doubt, there'll soon be an order for your arrest. Come to the parliament'. Yeltsin thought for a moment. Would Russian soldiers arrest him or would they disobey orders?

By eight o'clock, Moscow was a city occupied by its own forces, besieged by columns of tanks and armoured personnel carriers taking up positions around the Russian parliament, rumbling down two of Moscow's main boulevards, Tverskaya and Kutuzovsky towards Manezh Square on the edge of the Kremlin. By nine o'clock the Manezh would be the main focus of tension. Tanks, APCs and soldiers armed with assault rifles filled the square while elsewhere in the capital motorised rifle and tank divisions perched outside important buildings—the Foreign Ministry, the Finance Ministry, the grey Stalinesque *Gosplan* building and the Central Telegraph Station.

I called 'PM' and suggested that we pre-record coverage of the

GKChP's declarations for the early edition of the program in case the international phone lines were cut. The program's presenter Paul Murphy bolted for the studio and we began recording. He asked about Gorbachev: Was he still in the Crimea? Did he know what was happening in Moscow? Did he approve? I had no idea whether Gorbachev was still at his villa in the Crimea, nor whether he had any idea of what was happening in Moscow but instinctively I was sure that he hadn't handed the State Committee the power to carry out his duties, nor would he have sanctioned the deployment of tanks to the streets, if for no other reason than that he didn't have the stomach for violence. Indeed there was no word on Gorbachev's whereabouts until much later in the day when Kruchkov told Yeltsin that he was in the Crimea under house arrest, cut off from the world by three platoons of forces—the navy, air force ground services and border guards. Later, Gorbachev would tell us that he tried negotiating with his captors to send a message to Moscow, but to no avail. He walked around the villa, desperately apprehensive, furious, frustrated, but above all incommunicado.

While he stewed, the cabinet in which he had for so long stubbornly placed his faith was tripping over itself in confusion. Yanaev was getting drunker by the hour and by the time some of Gorbachev's old allies got to him in the Kremlin, three hours after the State Committee was declared, he was completely disorientated—and apologetic. He'd been roped into the whole affair he told them. The Prime Minister Valentin Pavlov wasn't in much better shape. He'd long suffered from anxiety but now he was overwhelmed by the enormity of what he'd undertaken. He too was drunk but had the sense to go home sick, where he tucked himself into bed, unable to do anything—not even watch the chaos.

That left Defence Minister Yazov and KGB chief Kruchkov as the brains behind the operation.

The ABC's phones weren't disconnected, which was good news. Surely no serious coup plotters could have overlooked the important detail of ensuring only their version of events left the country? In fact not only were the phone lines not disconnected, they seemed to improve in quality—a phenomenon not of my imagination but observed also by the few other foreign correspondents who'd remained in the city over the holiday period. So good were the lines that just about every producer at the ABC was ringing for an account of what was going on. In the end, it was impossible to give them any news because their demands had stopped me from getting to the city centre to see things for myself. Finally, I asked Kerrie to call them off. I thought of racing back up to my apartment to get out of my pyjamas but in the end I didn't have time. Just as I was about to walk out of the office, Sasha, my KGB friend, turned up.

He'd decided to take Oleg Kalugin's advice and wasn't prepared to take part in Kruchkov's coup, nor did he want to be at home when the phone call came for him to report for duty at KGB head-quarters. 'I'll drive you around Moscow,' he said which, under the circumstances, was a brave offer on his part and one I couldn't refuse, particularly as his KGB pass would get me to places I'd have been otherwise barred from. But first we wanted to make sure our coterie of friends was safe. Masha and her husband Rob were away. Natasha was at her home in Belye Stolby not far from Moscow. As we discussed who to call first, Zhenya arrived with a young man I hadn't met. His name was Nikolai and he was in his second year of military service. Nikolai was in Moscow on leave and didn't want to have to go to battle for the GKChP. 'Can I stay in your apartment?' he asked.

I didn't know what to do. As I ran through the possible conse-quences, Natasha called to see whether I was alright and whether I needed any help. 'What will I do Natasha, I have this young boy with me who doesn't want to answer Yazov's call for soldiers to return from leave. What am I going to do?'

'If this is a serious coup,' she said, 'and they begin rounding up correspondents and find a defector in your apartment, so what?

There won't be enough room in the jails for you, my friend. They'll deport you.' Nikolai stayed.

On our way to the city centre we stopped to pick up Max, who'd also rung offering help. The three of us made our way to town.

Perhaps not everyone had heard the news, perhaps they didn't think the tanks on the streets meant serious business, perhaps they simply were too tired of all the politics to give a damn, but that morning as we drove to the Kremlin, past the Russian parliament, the people we saw seemed relaxed. With their mandatory plastic carry-bags in hand in case they came across a good buy on their travels, they strolled along, looking nonchalantly at the APCs and the soldiers atop them armed with rifles. A few protesters had gathered outside the parliament but hardly enough to constitute resistance, which was probably a good thing because Kruchkov and Yazov, on the morning of Day 1 of this very strange coup, were still serious about their actions and might have used force to quell any protests.

But in the hour it took to drive through the traffic and the tanks from the parliament to Manezh Square near the Kremlin (which are separated by no more than a ten-minute walk), Yeltsin had set up resistance headquarters at the parliamentary building and written an appeal to the people which was being broadcast on Moscow's independent radio station. Echo Moscow had been calling on people all morning to come to the parliamentary building and it seemed they'd been slowly answering its request, because by the time we reached the Kremlin, Boris Yeltsin had mounted a tank back at the parliamentary building and in a booming voice told a sizeable crowd that 'the legally elected president of the country has been removed from power. We are dealing with a right-wing, reactionary, anti-constitutional coup d'etat. We appeal to all citizens of Russia to turn back the putschists and demand a return of the country to normal constitutional development.' My Russian friends were leaping with joy.

'They didn't think to take Yeltsin!' crowed Max. (In fact the putschists had organised to have Yeltsin arrested, but the usual Soviet combination of inertia and incompetence meant the order was never carried out.)

Whether the thousands of people who answered Yeltsin's call came to defend the Russian president they'd just elected or whether they came in Gorbachev's defence, I'm not sure. Certainly that first day of the coup at Manezh Square, it was Gorbachev the people were screaming for. If Gorbachev was too sick to rule and had abdicated power to the GKChP then why were there tanks on the streets? This was no constitutional abdication. This was a coup and everyone knew it. 'Where's the proof that Gorbachev is sick?' people asked the troops. Why was there no medical certificate or message from Gorbachev to confirm that he had handed power to the hardliners?

As the tanks stood motionless in their columns, the crowd swelled and women and men of all ages clambered towards the young soldiers who manned them. 'Go home to your mothers,' one woman begged. Another grabbed at the arm of a young guard and asked him to look her in the eye: 'Do you know what you're doing?' she asked him. He shook his head. 'Then go back to your barracks like a noble Soviet soldier and leave us in peace!' An old man was waving a photograph of Gorbachev at one young soldier: 'Where is he, you fool? If you follow blindly, you'll end up blinded, just like Gorbachev. But remember, you've been free for six years now. Turn your tank away—and go get Gorbachev!'

The stand-off seemed to go on for hours, but in fact it was only thirty minutes or so before the tanks and APCs began to move ever so slowly. Suddenly the crowd became hysterical. '*Noo ladno, spokoyno*,' ['OK, be calm'] the commander of the tank I was nearest bellowed to the crowd. All I could think was that times had changed.

'Can I jump up?' I asked the tank commander. He offered me his hand, pulling me on board where he and his subordinates were listening to Radio Echo. Somehow I felt safe, knowing that they were listening to the voice of resistance. Yeltsin was calling on troops to 'throw down your bayonets'. Clouds of terror and dictatorship are gathering over Russia, he told them, 'do not take part'. And these troops were listening.

The commander slung his rifle over his back and propped himself next to me, watching intently as I recorded Yeltsin over the little portable radio sitting on the edge of the tank's circular hatch. He was a very ordinary young Russian. We started chatting quietly as around us the chanting grew louder and louder. He told me he came from Leningrad, that he had no idea if his parents knew what was happening in Moscow and that he had no idea whether his commanders agreed that *perestroika* had led nowhere as the putschists claimed. I asked if I could record our conversation. After all, here I was, sitting on a tank near the Kremlin, talking to its commander as though he were one of my friends. Surely he wouldn't mind if I turned on my tape recorder. And he didn't. He wasn't at all coy or fearful of being interviewed in a situation which was meant to be frightening, threatening. He wanted to talk.

'Do you know who's behind the coup?' I asked him.

'Only from what Yeltsin's been saying,' he replied.

'When did you first hear anything about occupying Moscow?'

'This morning at 3 a.m. when they woke us and gave us our orders to come here?'

'And did they tell you why?'

'They said Gorbachev was sick and a committee was taking over?'

'Did that sound right to you?'

'I didn't think about it really. But Yeltsin says it's not true. Do you know anything?'

'Have you asked where Gorbachev is?'

'No.'

'What did your commanders tell you was the purpose of this exercise?'

'They told us nothing at all, other than the fact that we had to preserve calm in Moscow.'

'If they ask you to shoot to preserve the peace, will you?'

He stopped and thought, then looked at me. 'You know, I'm

Russian, just like all of them,' he said, nodding his head towards the swarm of people who now surrounded the tanks. 'I think I'd rather go to jail for treason than shoot at my own people.'

Before I could ask another question, his walkie-talkie began blaring a message I couldn't decipher. He politely asked me whether I wouldn't mind jumping off his tank. 'Another minute if you wouldn't mind,' I said as, still in my pyjamas, I began recording what I was seeing from this vantage point.

The declarations of the GKChP had it that tanks and APCs had also occupied Leningrad. The author David Marr was holidaying there, enjoying the book shops of Nevsky Prospekt when the GKChP seized power. While I was in the city centre, he'd phoned Moscow several times looking for me, to offer help.

'Are there tanks on the streets there?' I asked him when we finally spoke.

'Not that I can see,' he said. But that's not what was being reported on the news cables and by Yeltsin's team who had put out a document claiming that the Defence Minister had issued orders to his deputy ministers across the USSR, to the commanders of military groups from the Baltics to Siberia and to the chiefs of directorates to follow the edicts of the GKChP and to quash all resistance. That meant that tanks would be needed everywhere, not just in the capital.

David's mission in Leningrad was to find those tanks. But he circled the city several times and there were none, another small detail the plotters had overlooked in their drunken, confused haze. Leningrad, with its liberal mayor, Anatoly Sobchak, would also have been expected to mount resistance.

I managed to sneak a call to Natasha between filing stories to Sydney. Her opinion was that the coup would soon be over. 'As soon as Nazarbayev [in Kazakhstan] and all the other leaders throw their weight behind Yeltsin, that'll be the end of it.'

But resistance, I argued, was not a word in the Soviet vocabulary. Subservience yes. Submission yes. But not resistance. 'We've come a long way,' said Natasha.

The reaction of the republican leaders to the GKChP indicated they had a long way yet to go. They had watched Anatoly Lukyanov, the Chairman of the Supreme Soviet, declare that the Union treaty they had been about to sign was unconstitutional and that the parliament would ratify the GKChP and the state of emergency, and they remained neutral, refusing to condemn the coup, refusing to offer Yeltsin support in calling for workers across the country to strike and bring this hideous committee to its knees. Of course the Baltic leaders vowed to resist come what may. But that wouldn't be enough. Perhaps the non-Baltic republican leaders, as they later claimed, were engaging a clever diplomatic tactic, but it looked pretty much like lack of courage. They could have demanded evidence of Gorbachev's whereabouts and his state of health at the very least.

There was, however, plenty of courage to be found elsewhere. In the Kuzbass coal-mining region of Siberia, workers went out on strike. In the huge military–industrial complexes of Gorky, workers called meetings on the shop floor and walked off the job. Throughout the day, region after region across Russia reported that they'd refuse to obey the GKChP's decrees and its orders to keep working.

In Moscow, as the tanks continued to roll into the city centre the news slowly sank in and more and more people walked out of their offices and institutes, out of their plants and factories and went to the Russian parliament. By late afternoon, as the putschists were preparing to hold their first media conference, protesters were stopping tanks as they tried to cross the bridge across the Moscow River which led to the parliament. They had commandeered state buses and parked them across the city's side streets to stop troop movements. They had brought razor-wire fencing and old tyres from their suburbs which they used to erect barricades around 'resistance headquarters'.

Kruchkov, the brains of the GKChP, had banked on people showing respect for the re-emergence of Soviet order. He was wrong. To have any hope of succeeding, Kruchkov and his only sober colleague in the GKChP leadership, Defence Minister Yazov, would need to use force. Instead, they committed another cardinal sin in the putschists' litany. The orders the tank commanders were receiving as they encountered obstacle after obstacle on their manoeuvres around Moscow were to 'stay calm'. Perhaps Kruchkov and Yazov too had learnt a thing or two from the post-Stalinist gospel according to Gorbachev.

That afternoon, the coup began to look like a nonsense. As more and more army units arrived in Moscow, Yeltsin swore in a 'war cabinet' and assumed the office of the Supreme Commander-in-Chief of the armed forces in Russia. After all, no-one knew where Gorbachev was and the troops on the streets couldn't be asked to obey Yeltsin unless he was their commander. No sooner had Yeltsin assumed his new powers, than eight of the APCs parked outside the parliamentary building went to his side. It was a turning point.

At 'plotters' headquarters' there was anything but order. In fact there was complete disorder. The Defence Minister Dmitri Yazov and KGB chief Kruchkov were arguing. The others were drunk.

It was the rift between the two arms of force in the Soviet Union which was the most serious, though not entirely unexpected, setback to the putschists' cause. Logically, Defence Minister Yazov needed, in Yeltsin's words, 'a real fully fledged full-throated putsch that would once again force the world to believe in the might of the Soviet tank'. The KGB chief Kruchkov needed 'as clean and as sophisticated a transfer of power as possible to ensure respect and compliance'. But neither was possible for the same reasons—the people had resisted and the troops were divided. *Perestroika* had changed people and the biggest failure of both men left carrying the GKChP burden was that they failed to realise this. Instead, they argued with each other about what to do next.

At six o'clock on the night the tanks rolled into Moscow, the plotters held a media conference. They were about to break another rule in the putschists' handbook. None of their predecessors had tried to publicly justify their actions. With my 'Russian guard' of Max and Sasha, I weaved and bobbed my way back to the city centre, to the Foreign Ministry press centre on Zubovsky Boulevard where, in January, Gorbachev had sheepishly refused to answer questions about his role in the Lithuanian assault. There too, at the press centre, tired, angry soldiers who'd been dragged from their sleeping quarters in the early hours of the morning sat on top of tanks and APCs, wondering, no doubt, what they were meant to do if a foreign correspondent tried to defy their orders!

Again, I asked permission to board one of the tanks and again permission was granted. Only this time, the commander began pumping me for information. Had I heard anything of Gorbachev's whereabouts? Was the parliament supporting the GKChP or not? Could I confirm that eight APCs had defected to Yeltsin's side outside the Russian parliament?

Yes, troops were defecting I told him and turned the tables: 'Would you defect to Yeltsin's side if you were asked?'

'I wish he would ask!' he replied. It was sad and Kafkaesque.

Inside the building he was protecting, the putschists were trying to hold themselves together for a performance which would either make or break them. They had to convince the media and the diplomats who'd crammed into the press centre that what they were effecting was a constitutional transfer of power. With straight faces they had to lie and say Gorbachev was ill. And they had to convince everyone that this was not the end of reform and that they were capable of leading the country. Of course none of this was possible because none of it was true.

I squeezed into the foyer where a huge screen had been erected to beam the putschists out to those unlucky enough not to be sniffing the same air as the committee members still on their feet. Valentin Pavlov was still sick in bed, apparently treating himself with increasing doses of alcohol. Yazov, the Defence Minister, was watching the charade on television in his office and Kruchkov didn't even bother to turn up. It was all left to the weak Gennady Yanaev, inarticulate at the best of times. Now he looked pitiable. He sweated profusely and his hands quivered. He could barely speak for the anxiety which was clearly overpowering him.

'Who has control of the nuclear button?' asked a reporter from *Moskovski Novosti*.

'The Minister for Defence,' answered Yanaev.

'Is this a state coup?' asked another reporter.

'No, this is a constitutional transfer of power from the hands of the Soviet president who is unable to carry out his duties,' answered Yanaev, fumbling for the words.

At the Defence Ministry where Yazov was watching what was meant to be a display of certitude and strength, he must have felt a broken man. He'd apparently laughed at his hardline colleagues when they'd talked of getting rid of Gorbachev. Now he was one of them. According to Yeltsin, Yazov's wife who had gone to ask her husband what was going on begged him to give it all up. 'Dima,' she said, 'who are all these people you have gotten mixed up with? Call Gorbachev,' she urged him.

'That's impossible,' he told her as he wept over his desk.

That night, 'Vremya', the state-controlled television news was the only fare going. The other channels had been reduced to dramatised Russian fairytales and opera. But on 'Vremya', a scintilla of truth broke out. An uncensored report on the day's events made it to air. There was Yeltsin astride a tank outside the Russian parliament, and Yanaev's shaking hands as he faced the world. Thousands more left their homes for the parliament or 'White House' as people called it.

At the Russian parliament some ten thousand people huddled around camp fires and waited, sure that Kruchkov and Yazov would eventually send their tanks to storm the bastion of resistance. Every now and then, a member of the Yeltsin coterie would emerge from the building to encourage the crowd to stay on.

I spent much of the night there until I had to return to the office to prepare for a live cross to 'AM'. Wandering among the crowd were the gliterati of Soviet and Russian politics and culture—Mstislav Rostropovich, the cellist, Father Gleb Yakunin, the dissident Russian Orthodox priest whom Russians adored, and Yevgeny Yevtushenko with whom I hadn't spoken since he told me to fuck off when I asked him about the politics of dissent a year earlier. I put the same question again: did he regret not having supported the country's dissidents when he was asked to in the 1970s, when there weren't tens of thousands of people huddled in the darkness, preparing to throw themselves beneath tanks to protect their right to decide their own future. Yevtushenko ignored me and walked towards the front of the building. Ten minutes later he appeared on a balcony to read a poem he'd written for the moment.

As the night wore on, more minds were being convinced of the benefit of resistance. The republican presidents, one by one, sent word of their support to Yeltsin. No doubt they'd seen Yanaev's trembling hands and watched as the number of protesters in Moscow swelled. Better to be on the winning side, after all! And that night, 19 August 1991, the resisters looked like they were winning. The barricades were constantly being strengthened and by midnight included the Mercedes Benzs of the rouble rich who were offering their copiers and fax machines to help Yeltsin get his word out to the people.

That night, my friends stayed at parliament while I returned to the office to file reports and catch a few hours sleep.

At five the next morning, I woke Max and Sasha. They'd fallen asleep where I'd left them, not far from the statue of Pavlik Morozov, the thirteen-year-old who'd been turned into a bronzed hero for having reported his father for hiding grain from the state during Stalin's forced collectivisation. Pavlik's murder by farmers who opposed Stalin had given the regime another hero.

'It's been boring here,' Max said, 'nothing's happened at all, except the rumour is that the parliament will be stormed before the end of the day.'

It hadn't been boring at the putschists' headquarters. Kruchkov had been sent a memo by KGB analysts detailing the 'grave errors' which had been made in attempting the coup.

The ground troops commander, Valentin Varennikov, offered a solution—liquidate the protest at the Russian parliament. But this would turn out to be easier said than done. Support for the move in the upper echelons of the military was clearly waning.

Alexander Lebed was a member of the Central Committee of the Russian Communist Party and the second in command of the Tula Airborne Division. Before the coup he and his commander, Pavel Grachev, had told Yeltsin that in the event of trouble, they and their troops could be relied on for support. Now both men were making good on that promise. In Yeltsin's war room, Lebed told the Russian leadership that there was utter chaos within the military. Chains of command had been broken. The KGB's elite Alpha commando unit, trained to carry out the most difficult acts of terrorism, had pledged not to take part in any blockade or storming of the Russian parliament. The Dzerzhinsky Division had gone back to sleep after the initial convoy left barracks to take Moscow. On the morning of Day 2 when Lebed called the base to ask how many tanks were leaving for Moscow, a sleepy junior sergeant told him, 'Nobody's going anywhere!' Nor was the Tula Division moving.

The division commanders no doubt were swayed by the support for Yeltsin. *Komsomol*, the Young Communist League, was appealing to young people, especially soldiers, not to take part in the putsch.

According to Yeltsin, academics, institutes, artists, unions, even the fledgling Russian stock exchange—all urged people to disobey the GKChP's decrees.

The putschists now knew that unless they acted decisively, they'd fail and spend the rest of their days behind bars. Kruchkov and Yazov desperately tried to persuade the generals to follow their orders.

The planned storming would take place at 2 o'clock the next day. The army, the KGB and the Interior Ministry troops would surround the parliamentary building and block all access to it. Paratroopers would drive a wedge through the protesters, leaving a path for the Alpha Division to penetrate the building using grenade launchers. They would then find Yeltsin and arrest him. Interior Ministry troops would move around Moscow, taking resisters to KGB headquarters where they'd be charged.

It didn't take long for the commanders of the divisions meant to carry out the task to give Yeltsin each and every detail.

I was at the parliamentary building when word of the plan to storm it leaked to the resisters. At first I thought it was just another rumour, whispered from person to person. But this was more than rumour. A middle-aged woman handed out fliers prepared inside the parliament. They stated that Yeltsin had intelligence that plans were underway to storm the building and arrest him, and that afterwards the resisters would be rounded up and taken to prison.

An eerie sort of calm descended. So far, throughout the ordeal, not once had I felt physically threatened. But as I looked around at people reading Yeltsin's flier, I wondered whether we'd all be mowed down by the Alpha group as it lobbed its grenades up the front steps towards the parliament. Or might we be crushed by the tanks that encircled the area, or by the stampede of resisters as they tried to flee? I must have turned white because Max looked at me and, putting his arm around my shoulder, led me over to the embankment of the Moscow River where I sat and cried. He thought I should leave and return to the office. But I couldn't.

As we pored over Yeltsin's information, there was silence. People were listening for the unmistakable rumbling of tank treads. And at one point, it sounded as though they were close. But as they rumbled down Kutuzovsky Boulevard, it was soon obvious that the tanks weren't turning into the street which would bring them to the parliamentary building. They were going to the Kremlin.

We waited and waited—it surely must have been close to an hour—but nothing changed. I decided to dash back to the office briefly to file for 'PM' and the news bulletins. But as I started to walk down Kutuzovsky Boulevard to a point where I'd be able to flag down a car, I decided to ask CNN whose offices were just across the road from the parliament if I could use their phones. As I began dialling Sydney, one of their Russian interpreters came rushing at me with some copy from TASS, in Russian. A factory in Pskov on the Russian border with Latvia and Estonia, not far from Leningrad, had been ordered to send to Moscow urgently a quarter of a million pairs of handcuffs. And Kruchkov had ordered two floors of the Lefortovo Prison in central Moscow to be cleared. Until now, I'd thought the coup a sham.

Back at the parliament, women and children were asked to leave. Those who were left had no means of finding out what was happening because the military had closed down Radio Echo. The only information we had was coming from prominent Russians who had access to the military and KGB intelligence, being leaked to Boris Yeltsin. But even that was very little. A parade of luminaries tried to help tired resisters understand the need to keep up the pressure. Yelena Bonner, the widow of Andrei Sakharov, wasn't worried by the GKChP. 'They will fail,' she told the crowd. 'But you must begin to take responsibility, shed your Soviet past. Ask yourselves where is Gorbachev. Tell the troops we want Gorbachev back,' she bellowed through a microphone to a crowd of 20 000 or more. 'It's not that we suddenly support him but the people have the right to vote him down in free and fair elections.'

The only question which remained was how the generals would convince the division commanders to obey their orders and attack the parliament.

By evening, the tension was overwhelming. Max would say every few minutes: 'Soon, very soon.' Sasha was more optimistic. He'd been phoning people he knew in the KGB and it was clear to him that there was division not only in the military but within the KGB. So we waited.

At the Kremlin, desperation was setting in. The ground forces commander had drawn up the plans and disseminated them to his generals. But he reported that no matter how willing, the generals themselves couldn't clamber into the tanks and drive them to the parliament. The division commanders had told the top brass that they were deeply worried. The GKChP was making moves which would not be supported by the troops. Some were already retreating to their bases.

If only the resisters had known the truth. At the parliament, there was mayhem. Many more thousands of people had come to resist and protest. And now they had broken their silence.

I found Eduard Shevardnadze in the crowd, making his way towards the parliament. He was distraught. I walked by his side for a few minutes, not saying anything. I didn't know what to ask him. In the end I thought he might offer some news of Gorbachev. But he clearly felt no pity for his old friend whatsoever.

He gave me a stern look of disapproval as though I'd just mentioned the name of the devil, the man whose fault this whole mess was in the first place.

'I have no idea where Mikhail Sergeyevich is, nor in what state of health he is, other than "not sick".'

The ABC's new Moscow correspondent outside the Kremlin in 1990.

Natasha Yakovleva, who became my closest friend and mentor. Natasha was an honest communist who understood all that was wrong with her country.

Masha Stubblebine—a guiding light. Soon after I arrived in Moscow, she told me: 'The Soviet Communist Party is a mafia. Once you understand this, everything else will make sense'.

The house that Stalin built. Known as the House on the Embankment or the Fraternal Grave, this is where the old Bolsheviks once lived. It gave way in Stalin's time to party men, many of whom disappeared from the building in the dead of night.

Negotiating with the police. This encounter cost my friend $20. He was stopped for no apparent reason, a routine event for drivers in Moscow.

An old man begging, Ukraine 1991. 'I am one of those lucky enough not to die in the KGB's basements. In 1927-28 I was sent to the gulag and in my life I saw horrible crimes committed by the party. NUREMBURG 2'

Troops try to stem the crowds in the streets of Moscow during Gorbachev's protest ban, 1991.

The police try negotiation. An officer pleads with an elderly protester at a demonstration during Gorbachev's protest ban, Moscow 1991.

Gorbachev's troops try to seal off access to the Kremlin during the protest ban, 1991.

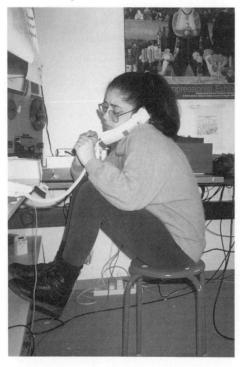

Filing a story from the ABC's Moscow studio, which was in the same building as my apartment.

Sergei Stankevich, the democrat who rose to prominence as a Gorbachev adviser in the late 1980s, leading a protest against Gorbachev in 1990.

The Russian Parliament, better known as the White House, the focus of resistance to the Soviet Communist Party and later Boris Yeltsin's economic reforms.

Red Square, where tens of thousands of people protested between 1989 and 1991 against Mikhail Gorbachev's regime.

A protest in Kiev, the Ukrainian capital, against the Commonwealth of Independent States formed by the three Slav republics in December 1991. The protesters called the union 'death'.

'Gorbachev shares in the Nobel peace prize with Saddam Hussein.'
Protesters condemn Gorbachev's role in the 1991 Lithuanian onslaught.

Grigori ('Grisha') Klumov in front of the Kremlin. I met Grisha through some Australian friends in 1992 and we married in Moscow in 1993.

Ten years ago this contrast between old and new may have shocked some people. Military school graduates on a ritual visit to Red Square, 1996.

Natasha at her dacha outside Moscow in 1996. Most Russians have summer dachas but their style and size varies according to one's status in life.

A far cry from the dacha—city living in pre-fab apartment blocks. My apartment and the ABC's office were housed in a similar building at Rublevskoye 26.

Boris Yeltsin and friends in Ivanova, 1992. The President visited one of the worst hit regions during his dispute with the parliament over the pace and extent of economic reforms.

A sign of the times. Babushkas selling their clothing and shoes at a second-hand market in Moscow in 1992.

Carrying her icon with pride. An old woman turns out in the town of Ivanova in 1992 to greet Boris Yeltsin.

A pro-communist protest at the foot of Lenin's statue in Oktyabraskaya Square, Moscow, 1995. The banner reads: 'Russians: Save your Children'.

Paid for doing nothing. A state worker remains on duty as a gate attendant even though the gates are now permanently open.

Better than begging. A man sells old news-papers, *Sovetskaya Rossiya* and *Pravda*, in Moscow, 1995.

Voting day, 1996 presidential election. Voters' names are crossed off the roll after voting. In the old days, even if you didn't turn up, your name was counted along with those who had voted.

Election graffiti, 1996. Other slogans included 'Yeltsin's head on the railway track' and 'Death to Jews!'

A Yeltsin voter. In the uniform of the kiosk owner or minder, this young man represents a typical Yeltsin supporter.

A Zynganov voter. This elderly woman told me she would vote for the communists because Yeltsin had delivered only chaos.

1996 election poster: 'Think and choose'. The old, portrayed in depressing black and white images, versus the new, scenes of happiness and prosperity in glorious colour.

A family of beggars, Yeltsin's new poor, Moscow 1996.

Moscow 1996. The Bolshoi Theatre gets a facelift and the streets are bombarded with western style advertising.

A private fruit seller sets up shop in Filovsky Park, where Stalin once lived. After four years of reform, visitors to Moscow could see material benefits — fresh fruit and fully stocked shops — even though most ordinary Russians couldn't afford to buy basic goods.

Soaking up some summer sun and western culture, central Moscow 1996.

A babushka relaxes at 'home'. With the advent of capitalism, many elderly people became homeless.

Building new churches from the old on the outskirts of Moscow. Many were paid for by rich businessmen in return for tax perks.

A gypsy and her child begging at a metro entrance, Moscow 1996.

An old corner of Moscow gets a facelift after decades of neglect. Thanks to initiatives by Moscow Council such as giving children paints to decorate hoardings and granting entrepeneurs licences to operate sidewalk cafes, parts of the city looked almost Parisian in 1996.

Neither Shevardnadze nor the crowd which was mobbing him had any idea that the coup d'etat was about to take a turn for the worse, even though many of the tanks around the city were actually retreating.

Ilya Krichevsky was 28 years old when the hardliners mounted their coup attempt. Not quite a decade earlier, he'd been a tank commander in the Taman Division, which now encircled the White House.

On 20 August, as Ilya's father sat reading *Obshaya Gazeta* (Common Newspaper) which journalists from newspapers banned by the GKChP had decided to print and distribute themselves, the phone rang. It was Ilya's friend Nikolai who wanted to go to the city for a look at the protest. Radio Echo was again broadcasting news of the pockets of resistance around the city which were growing by the hour as fears heightened that the parliament would soon be stormed. Ilya's father told his son to stay home, urging him to obey the curfew the GKChP had imposed. But the two young men went to the city nonetheless, Ilya reluctantly.

As they emerged from the metro tunnel near the parliament, they were swept up by a huge crowd of people. This was no small protest! So they found themselves a safe spot and watched for about an hour.

A few metres away from where they sat there was a sudden roar of protest. At one of the many underpasses near the bridge over the Moscow River, just near the parliament, people were screaming and shouting. The two young men went to investigate.

Tanks were trying to drive through the underpass tunnel only to be stopped by a barricade of trolleybuses which the resisters had commandeered and brought to the area.

Ilya weaved his way through the protesters and came face to face with a line of tanks rumbling towards him, their tread throwing up black smoke, their noise in the echoing tunnel thunderous. He jumped to safety onto the pavement.

I was walking over the underpass when I heard the commotion. I zigzagged through a thick crowd of people who had jammed the footpath and roadway leading down into the tunnel. I could see the trolleybuses and behind them soldiers bobbing up through the hatches on their tanks, but I couldn't see exactly what was happening. Next to me a woman with a carry-bag full of hard-boiled eggs to feed the resisters grabbed my arm and started weeping. 'They're going to mow us down,' she was saying through her tears. 'Our sons are going to kill us!'

The stand-off in the tunnel lasted no more than five minutes. Enough time for some of the commanders to give up and leave their tanks standing empty and idle. One of those who had surrendered brushed past me, a bottle of Coke in his hand. The crowd was urging the soldiers who stayed in their vehicles to get down and join the protest. I could hear them screaming at the soldiers.

But deep in the tunnel, one tank had refused to give up. It was still rumbling. It surged ahead and was pounding the trolleybuses in its way. Three men jumped aboard as the tank violently rammed back and forth. Its manhole cover flew open, and 23-year-old Dima Komar jumped inside. A few seconds later his body was slumped over the hatch. The soldiers inside had shot him in fear. The other two men tried to drag Dima's body off but the tank again violently jerked forward and one of them was thrown off. Vladimir Usov, 38 years old, was crushed beneath its tread.

Panic turned to fury. 'Murderers, murderers,' I could hear people bellowing. But still I could see nothing. I could only hear gunshots. The lady with the eggs clung to me as hard as I clung to her.

Five soldiers jumped out of the tank and ran for cover, firing pistol shots randomly into the air.

Only the tank commander remained. Caught between his trapped tank and the wrath of the Russians he'd been ordered to crush, he too began firing his pistol as he prepared to run through the crowd.

One of his bullets went astray and Ilya Krichevsky became the third victim of the GKChP's attempt to turn back the clock.

I ran from the tunnel opening back towards the parliament hoping to find my friends in the masses. But I couldn't. I was terrified and on the verge of hyperventilation. There was a thick crowd of people lining the road above the underpass—shocked, angry, disappointed, frightened, defeated. Some wept. Others swore. A vehicle was trying to drive a wedge through them and from where I stood it sounded ominous. I heard the panic in people's voices. An old man muttered: 'Ne mozhet byt!' ['It couldn't possibly be!'] But it wasn't a tank. It was a car carrying Eduard Shevardnadze, who'd been sent out by Boris Yeltsin to investigate when word reached the president that blood was being spilled.

I pushed through the crowd towards Shevardnadze, almost losing my tape recorder which was being dragged back by the people who were crushing against me. Shevardnadze sat in the back seat of the car, the window open, his tired eyes with black bags beneath them full of pity and sadness.

'Eduard Amvrosievich—they say people were just killed near the tunnel!'

'I don't know,' he answered, 'but if they've killed people, they'll be our martyrs.' He paused. 'They will have single-handedly buried the Communist Party forever.'

When I escaped the crowds, I looked down at my tape recorder and the end of the microphone cord was crushed. It had been pulled from its socket during the mayhem near the tunnel and I hadn't recorded a thing.

CHAPTER 10

THE FALLEN

When they come to bury an age,
And no psalm rings out above the grave,
Only thistles and nettles
Are doomed to adorn it
Only the gravediggers toil apace.

ANNA AKHMATOVA, FROM *THE SEVENTH BOOK*, 1921

By dawn the coup attempt was over. At least everyone thought it was. But no-one could be sure. There was a chance, albeit an outside one, that the coup leaders might have been terror stricken by the bloodshed and were thinking of striking hard. But I knew no-one who really believed that Pavlov, Yanaev and Yazov were capable of hard-core Stalinist cruelty. The KGB chief perhaps, but not the others.

David Marr had arrived in Moscow from Leningrad and we nutted through the possibilities. David wondered whether the hardliners had hated Gorbachev so much throughout his six years in office that they'd listened to nothing he'd said, seen nothing positive in the relaxation of party oppression.

As it turned out, the putschists had realised their efforts had gone very badly awry. Defence Minister Yazov must have taken fright when he looked in the mirror that morning, for at a meeting with his chief divisional commanders, some of whom had been advising

Yeltsin, he asked what they thought of the situation. They told him the coup had been a terrible failure.

At eleven that morning of 21 August, I was walking down Teatralny Lane from KGB headquarters towards the Kremlin when a horrific roar of engines stopped me in my tracks. The tanks which had been patrolling the area around the Kremlin were starting up and taking off. That's it, I thought, the coup's over. I ran to the nearest phone booth, near the Savoy Hotel, not far from the KGB, and called Igor Malashenko of the Central Committee of the Communist Party who'd been assigned to work with Gorbachev in the few months before the coup. He'd managed to hold onto his office in the Kremlin, a few doors away from the room the KGB boss had taken over. 'Do you know what's going on?' I asked him.

'They're going to Foros to beg for forgiveness,' he said, roaring with laughter. My God, I thought to myself, I have a fabulous scoop and no international phone to call Sydney!

Within minutes I was in my car making my way back to the office. Not far from Lenin Museum I was stopped in tank traffic and two young women and a man jumped into the car—overjoyed, jumping out of their skins with excitement. 'Give us a lift to the Pizza Hut?' they asked. 'We have to buy flowers to throw at the convoy as they leave.' What could I say? 'With pleasure!'

Back at the office with the latest wire story in one hand, the television remote control in the other, I dived for the phone to ring David Marr who was upstairs in the apartment. I could barely contain my excitement. Together we watched as Boris Yeltsin told a session of the Supreme Soviet of Russia, which he had specially convened, that Vladimir Kruchkov had phoned and asked him to go with him to Foros to see Gorbachev. Yeltsin's parliament didn't want him to go. Instead it sent the Russian Vice President Alexander Rutskoi and a handful of other Yeltsin loyalists. With them travelled a team of heart specialists in case Gorbachev really was sick and a handful of journalists. On another plane sat the putschists, defeated, hung-over, exhausted.

At his villa in Foros, Gorbachev would speak only with the Russians. And Lukyanov, his old friend. Lukyanov tried to tell Gorbachev he hadn't supported the putsch, that he'd wanted the Supreme Soviet of the Soviet Union to meet to condemn the coup attempt, but that the hardliners would have nothing of it.

At last the scales had dropped from Gorbachev's eyes. *'Shto vye mne lapshoo na ushi veshaete!'* ['Don't hang noodles on my ears!'], Gorbachev said to him in possibly the best line of this drama.

Mikhail and Raisa Gorbachev returned to Moscow the next day, the event broadcast on national television. Gorbachev stepped out of the plane, his face sun-tanned from all the pacing around the villa talking in the open air for fear that the building was bugged. He looked exhausted—perhaps even a little embarrassed.

As the putschists left their aircraft, they were arrested. The first of them to be led away was Vladimir Kruchkov, the grey man of the Lubyanka.

The Russians went back to 'resistance headquarters' inviting Gorbachev to go with them. He refused. He was going to his office in the Kremlin. He didn't feel any need to thank people for staying out for three days and three nights to protect the tiny morsel of democracy they'd been given. Gorbachev wanted to ring and cable the international leaders who had sent messages of support for his continuing rule. Australian Prime Minister Bob Hawke was on his list.

He chose to give his first audience not to ordinary Russians but to journalists at a press conference. I sat in the front row.

Gorbachev's monologue went for two and and a half hours. It was a detailed, nitty-gritty account of what had happened, how he felt. He told us how concerned he was when told he had visitors on 18 August, how he'd refused to lend his name to the GKChP, how he told them to take their differences over the reform process to the

Congress of People's Deputies (the *nomenklatura*-dominated Soviet parliament which sat twice a year). He watched our faces as he repeated the ultimatum he had given the putschist delegation at Foros: 'I'd rather kill myself than agree to your demands.' His big brown eyes filled with emotion as he described how he felt about the enormity of the betrayal he'd suffered.

'But how can you feel so betrayed, Mikhail Sergeyevich, by the actions of your entourage when you had been warned so many times?' he was asked when he finally threw the conference open to questions from the floor.

He thought long and hard. It was a curly one, but Gorbachev managed to turn his shortcoming to a virtue. 'Somehow, I think it is easier to mistrust than to trust.' He paused. 'Yes, I was gullible.'

Then a reporter from *Nezavisimaya Gazeta* asked him what he now thought of the Communist Party. It had not condemned the coup, nor shown any concern for his welfare, though he was its General Secretary. Would he now, finally, distance himself from the party? Perhaps even resign?

The party, he said, ought to be purged of its reactionaries and reformed. Socialism, he told us, is still the only way forward. We gasped audibly. Surely confinement had sent the man mad!

Outside the Foreign Ministry press centre where Gorbachev had held court, my waiting friends were desperately anxious to know what the great man had said. All I could do was blurt out his line that he wanted to reform the party. There was stunned silence. 'Did he laugh after he said it?' asked Max. I shook my head.

'Only seven people in the whole damn country haven't changed. Six of them are in jail and we spent all that time and energy saving the last remaining lunatic in the USSR!' he said.

Someone suggested we head straight towards Central Committee headquarters because there were thousands of people there, celebrating the putschists' failure right under the party's nose. At Oktyabrskaya Square, a huge crowd of people were daubing a statue of Lenin with red paint. There was anti-communist anger everywhere.

At the Central Committee building, lights flickered through drawn curtains. Someone inside pulled back a curtain to look out onto the street where a huge crowd had gathered. He quickly took fright and scurried away. On the street, people threw eggs at the building and screamed obscenities at the minions inside who were hauling fax machines, typewriters, computers and photocopiers out the back doors to waiting vans. 'Mostly they were shredding documents,' said Igor Malashenko who was on the phone to his colleagues from his office in the Kremlin. 'They were taking care of business.'

I was dog-tired by 11 p.m., but there was 'AM' to go. At midnight I reported that Gorbachev had spoken but perhaps was still dazed because he seemed to think he could breathe life into a corpse. I reported that no-one agreed this was possible, least of all the people who'd stood at the Russian parliament for three days and nights as tanks circled around them, determined that the coup d'etat should fail. They had taken matters into their own hands. They were at Central Committee headquarters watching as the *apparatchiks* cleared out the building. Others were at Lubyanka Square, KGB headquarters, where they wanted to rip Iron Felix Dzerzhinsky from his plinth but couldn't. They had to wait until the next day when a crane sponsored by the Moscow City Council did the job for them, consigning the terror and fear he'd wrought to history. And I reported that the party was under siege. It, like me, would soon collapse.

The next day, Gorbachev was asked to go to the Russian parliament to answer the questions of deputies to the Supreme Soviet of Russia. He gladly obliged and the event was televised for all to see. The Russians have a saying, 'Revenge is sweetest when it's cold.' Yeltsin was about to taste revenge for his ousting from the Politburo in 1987.

Gorbachev was about to be humiliated. He had been kept in isolation for three days while his cabinet of deceivers did what everyone had been telling him they would eventually do. The situation had been saved by his arch enemy, while the party he'd refused to relinquish to the will of the people had allowed him to languish under house arrest without so much as asking a question. While he allowed Yeltsin to rightfully take all the glory for having ended the coup d'etat, Gorbachev pledged himself to the party's reform. Now, he had willingly stepped into enemy territory, hoping that his international reputation or perhaps just his charisma would somehow plug the seepage. Now he stood before a truly democratic parliament, unlike his own which was loaded with *nomenklatura* cronies who'd submitted themselves to the mercy of the electors secure in the knowledge they were the only horses in the race.

Yeltsin asked Gorbachev to read out loud the minutes of the last meeting of the Soviet government. Gorbachev did. The government in its entirety had supported the GKChP—and all but one of its members belonged to the party. Before the eyes of the Russians, and of the world, Yeltsin signed a decree which suspended the activities of the Communist Party in Russia. Gorbachev was stunned. A day later he resigned from the party. That was it. The party was over.

'Well, Masha, that's it. A new era has begun,' I said.

'Not yet,' she answered. 'The most important corpse of all hasn't yet been buried.'

I'd forgotten all about Lenin.

In the days following the collapse of the coup, Gorbachev's military adviser, Marshal Sergei Ahkromeiyev, killed himself. I'd watched Ahkromeiyev in the Oktyabrskaya Hotel berate General Dmitri Volkogonov in 1990 for his truthful account of Stalin's leadership during the Second World War. Soviet history was littered with lies and

Volkogonov had been charged with the very important task of unravelling them. Facing history, for Gorbachev and the *shestidesy-atniki*, was a crucial part of the recuperative process the country had to go through if it had any chance of emerging whole. But Marshal Ahkromeiyev was resisting the bad medicine even then. Now at the end of August 1991 he was ill with grief for a country he no longer knew or understood. In his suicide note to his family he wrote: 'I cannot live when my Fatherland is dying and all that I have made my life's work is being destroyed. My age and all I have done give me the right to leave this life. I struggled to the end.' As the news of Ahkromeiyev's suicide came through on the wire service, I cried. I liked him. He was at least a true believer, an old man with conviction.

Nikolai Kruchina must also have felt defeated. Kruchina had administered the finances of the Central Committee. Just before the coup I'd gone to see him about the persistent rumours in the Russian newspapers that the party had been stealing the country's gold reserves and tucking their proceeds away in foreign bank accounts throughout the *perestroika* years. He denied it all, of course. His office was littered with boxes, packed to overflowing with papers and folders. 'Are you moving office?' I asked him. He didn't answer. 'Perhaps only the papers are leaving the building?' I asked.

'Perhaps you are right,' he replied. Kruchina, it was claimed, jumped from a window in his apartment in Moscow when the coup collapsed. But like the bookkeepers of Cosa Nostra, perhaps there was more to the story.

And Boris Pugo, the hardline Interior Minister who had ordered the crackdown against the Baltic republics also found the prospect of a jail term overwhelming. Gorbachev had called him a man of integrity. When investigators went to his apartment to arrest him, Pugo was dead. He'd also shot his wife. He wasn't to know that although his colleagues were arrested and charged, none were ever to face trial for their actions.

'Are you relieved that it's all over?' I asked Natasha when I finally managed to snatch a moment for conversation.

'And what do you think I ought to be relieved about?' she asked. 'What's there to be happy about? Or maybe I've missed the point. Do we stop dancing in the streets when every communist in the USSR has killed themselves? You know what's going to happen? People are going to feel lost, more lost than they have been these last six years, and we'll lose the weakest of them. The ones who will survive will end up hating the anti-communists more than they hated the communists.'

I felt black.

CHAPTER 11

TALKING FREEDOM

The Belovezhsky agreement was not a 'silent coup',
but a lawful alteration of the existing order of things.

BORIS YELTSIN, *THE VIEW FROM THE KREMLIN*, 1994

In the autumn of 1991, people were truly exhausted. There was no fight left in them. Winter was coming and with it the fear that every Russian winter brings: of cold, of food shortages and, in the last few years, of uprisings as discontent spilled onto the streets. This year, the people would have something else to contend with—uncertainty over whether the USSR would survive.

One by one the republican leaders had declared the independence of their countries. First the Baltic republics, then Georgia, Moldova, Armenia and Azerbaijan. But still Gorbachev couldn't see the wood for the trees. He wanted the republics to sign his blessed Union treaty. He wanted a new decentralised Union with a common defence force and foreign policy. The republics wanted their own seats in the United Nations. They wanted their own armies.

But still the talks went on. We in the foreign media corps wondered what they were negotiating towards. Clearly a Union was out of the question. Logically it couldn't have existed without a centre of power controlling a few vital functions on behalf of the participating countries. And the republics were certainly unwilling to accept this. The most they seemed prepared to accept was a Confederation of Independent States with a figurehead in Moscow holding even less power than the Queen of England has over Australian affairs. So what was Gorbachev talking about to the republican leaders throughout September, October and November of 1991?

By 25 November the staying power of the republican leaders was exhausted. Their love of *razgovory* (talk) had run its last mile. Gorbachev tried the old Soviet tactic of imposing a decision, telling the media that the Union treaty was ready to be initialled, the first stage in the long process which would ultimately result in its being signed by all the leaders.

When Gorbachev returned to the next round of talks, the leaders were furious and demanded much more of what little was left of the central powers Gorbachev wanted. Gorbachev could take no more. He was furious, embarrassed and impotent. It was rather like telling your adolescent children that they had to abide by a curfew they were rejecting! He stormed out of the talks only to be invited back by Yeltsin and the President of Belorussia, Stanislav Shushkevich. But none of the leaders initialled the draft treaty, and none of them ever would.

When the Soviet president went before the media to give his final account of the negotiations, he carried with him the draft, unsigned.

At the end of November as Ukraine prepared for a referendum which would ask one simple question—'Do you want a free and independent Ukraine?'—I went to Kiev. It was freezing and the train wheels threw up a flurry of early snow with every turn. In the Ukrainian capital, protesters were walking through the streets silently, wrapped up against the icy winds, carrying placards calling on Gorbachev to stand down with dignity and allow the people of the Soviet Union their ultimate freedom, the freedom to choose their own sovereignty. Ukraine's Defence and Foreign Ministries were already preparing for freedom. They were issuing passes to foreign correspondents on Ukrainian letterhead and giving us permission to travel to military bases, previously a tightly controlled function of the central government in Moscow.

I was heading towards a base not far from Kiev where the nuclear missile warheads on Ukrainian soil were kept. On the way, the taxi driver thought I might be interested in seeing something else. 'Wouldn't you like to see where we're training our own army?' he asked.

On 1 December, Ukraine chimed the final bell in the slow death of the Soviet Union. It voted overwhelmingly for its independence and a few days later pulled out of the treaty talks. It was a brutal blow to Gorbachev who'd watched as the republics one by one left the fold, never believing that Ukraine would follow in their footsteps. For Gorbachev the Soviet Union would continue to exist despite the defections so long as Ukraine, the country's breadbasket, remained loyal. For Gorbachev, a Soviet Union without Ukraine was not worth having at all. What would be the fate of the millions of people across the country who were not living in their national homelands but in neighbouring countries which, though disparate, were united by the Soviet Union, he asked. Gorbachev didn't seem to understand what was happening.

Early in December the three Slav leaders, Boris Yeltsin, Stanislav Shushkevich of Belorussia and Leonid Kravchuk of Ukraine went to a hunting lodge in the Belovezhsky Forest near Brest and decided to make the point more clearly. They agreed to form a commonwealth because the Soviet Union was dead.

All three Slav leaders were determined. There could be no turning back. The Communist Party had built a country on blood and terror.

It had tyrannised people for seventy years. It had corrupted all institutions and organs of power. It had conducted a social experiment which the subjects themselves had declared a hopeless failure. It had failed categorically to deliver the people to paradise.

For my young friend Zhenya, news of the 'secret coup', as it would come to be called, was music to his ears.

'The Soviet Union was corrupt anyway. It was an illegal entity. Now we can perhaps think about how to live normally, like people do in normal countries,' he said.

His father, a military man, felt utterly betrayed. What made a country legal, he asked me. A secret agreement voted upon by nobody, or the blood, sweat and tears of 360 million people united by a common ideology and a single economy?

'But isn't this historical justice?' I asked.

'Historical justice for whom?' he replied angrily. 'For you in the west so that you can now dance on our grave and claim to have won the Cold War? Is that what you call justice? My grandparents supported the revolution. My parents worked all their lives in steel and tractor factories to build a country where no-one would be exploited. They believed we would get there finally. And so did I. I've fought in two wars. And what do I have to show for it now? Where do I come from? A country which no longer exists—and not because I voted for that. Your democracy is a sham and Gorbachev is a traitor.'

Zhenya's father was going through the first stages of grief—profound shock tinged with anger.

'First he lost Eastern Europe. Now he's lost the Soviet Union. And I've lost my identity. My God, next you'll tell me it's a good thing if there are discos in the centre of Moscow, and that drugs aren't such a bad thing. Or maybe you think we should just open up Lenin's tomb to evangelical groups!'

I left the argument at that, defeated.

Out at Belye Stolby, south-west of Moscow, the two local shops were bare. A few old cans of sprats and spiced pilchards looked like a fair enough reason to try a new political and economic system.

I'd gone there to rest for a few days, out in the woods which separated the town of Gorky where Lenin died, from Moscow. Natasha had lived and worked there for twenty years, ever since finishing her studies at the Moscow Film School. The state film archives, *Gosfilmofond*, had allocated Natasha and her family two apartments in the town. For more than a year, she had been forced to ask the unthinkable—for me to buy her sugar from the hard currency stores, which she detested for their links with capitalism. But there was no choice. There was so little available on the streets for average Russians. For more than a year she'd watched the political mayhem, telling me all the while that the Communist Party had made lots of mistakes, but all it had to do was go back to Lenin and he would point the way to the future.

When the coup d'etat began, Natasha sat tuned to her little radio in the kitchen, listening intently as it creaked out the edicts of the State Committee which had toppled Gorbachev. She wanted to come to Moscow to join the resisters because she felt instinctively that what the hardliners were doing was wrong and un-Leninist. But the radio announcers at Radio Echo said the situation looked as though it might become dangerous. She had elderly parents and a more or less dependent family. Best if she stayed at home until the danger was over. So she rallied her workmates, most of them extremely conservative, to send protest telegrams to the Central Committee, and as secretary of the local Belye Stolby Communist Party cell, she phoned headquarters and protested.

Natasha hadn't counted on her country collapsing and it seemed to her a high price for the Soviet people to pay for the mistakes and indiscretions of the party. Despite everything that had happened, she remained committed to the struggle for the communist ideal. Like Gorbachev, she believed the party could be reformed once the plotters were punished, and could continue the struggle towards the *svetloe budushie* [shining future].

'Listen to me,' she said after the coup attempt. 'In a few months life will settle down again. Gorbachev is a man we need. Let them hate him. He's given them the freedom to hate him and that's good. But he'll lead us back to a humane socialism. Soon, you'll see, the Soviet Union will be a normal country.'

The notion of a normal country was something everyone, including Boris Yeltsin, held up as the benchmark of ultimate success. But what they meant by the term still baffles me. A country of neat tree-lined streets marked off into suburbs, with local shops brimming with consumer goods and food? Two kids per family with two cars in the garage and a lawn-mower tucked away on the side? What was a normal country for the Russians who had been born to a frighteningly depraved netherworld in which only corruption was rewarded?

'A normal country is one in which no-one exploits another,' declared Natasha. 'It's where people work collectively towards the creation of a state which has a single ideal—to live better. A normal country is one where people don't feel frightened to speak, where they travel easily and want to return to their own country. It's where everyone—even those who can't defend themselves—is taken care of by a state which cares.

'That's not the Soviet Union. But it's not this stupid Commonwealth of Independent States that they're talking about either. Do you think the factory in Ukraine which for seventy years has produced oil pipelines is going to give them to Russia for free now that we're all independent? Do you really believe Russia will still give Armenia cheap oil now that it's not ours? The economy will collapse. We have all been tied together for far too long. People will starve and as they're dying on the streets you can go up to them with your microphone and ask them where they come from. They'll be able to say nowhere and your leaders will be happy.'

George Blake had a lot to lose as well. He was Russia's only living western spy, out of the same melting pot as Kim Philby and Donald Maclean.

For more than twenty-five years he'd been living in a KGB apartment in a grotty part of Moscow, on the Kremlin side of the river. But it was home to Blake, who in 1961 had been busted as a Soviet mole working within the British Secret Intelligence Service. In nearly fifteen years of service to the Soviets, he'd given the KGB a copy of nearly every important document which had passed through his hands. The court which sentenced him to life imprisonment for treason was told he'd caused the deaths of forty-two western and Soviet agents.

But Blake wasn't long for Wormwood Scrubs in England. After an escape which even the Soviets admired for its audacity, he made it to the Motherland—Russia—where he was confronted with the reality of the ideology he had so fervently believed in. Instead of the new society Lenin promised, Blake found queues, food shortages and a chronic housing problem which left divorced couples living together in one room with their in-laws for twenty years. Instead of paradise he found a society riddled with inequality, envy and corruption.

When I met Blake in December 1991, he was very much a Russian. He'd married a Russian woman, had a Russian child, lived in a Russian apartment, and had worked in a Russian institute for more than twenty years. He walked around his bigger than average apartment wearing *tapichki*, the Russian house slippers, and poured boiling water over a dash of old tea as the Russians are in the habit of doing. There were no western products in his refrigerator, no western furniture anywhere in the apartment. Everything he had was prescribed, bought and delivered by the KGB.

He disliked the democrats with an intensity I could understand.

After all, they would now begin the process of dismantling all the old certainties, among them that George Blake would have refuge in the Soviet Union to his dying day. Never would he be deported, he had thought. Never would his ideological mentors surrender him as he had surrendered the lives of the agents and moles he'd betrayed. But if the Soviet people were now denouncing Lenin and Marx, surely they wouldn't spare Blake.

'I have forty years' imprisonment left to serve in Great Britain and of course I am frightened that Yeltsin and his lynch mob will send me back there. What Russia needs now is western money and my escape has been such a sore point in relations between the Soviet Union and Great Britain, even though the KGB didn't help me get out of Wormwood, that I wouldn't be at all surprised if the Brits demand my return before they offer aid,' he told me.

'But as you sit here feeling frightened, do you also feel remorse, Mr Blake?' I asked, watching his steely blue eyes. 'Do you ever feel guilt, have you ever questioned Marxism?'

'I felt the condemnation of my country very strongly. But I started out on the road which led me here and it was impossible to turn back,' he said, reaching for his autobiography and pointing me towards quotes which might answer my questions. As I asked whether he'd ever had cause to think that his actions had been wrong, immoral, he again resorted to his book, as though a spontaneous answer might incur someone's wrath.

'I'm able to separate in my mind the personal from the official just like the best of the Soviet *apparatchiks*. I didn't act in my own personal interest. I never accepted money from the KGB for my work for them. And my activities weren't directed against those I worked with. They were directed against the capitalist system.

'The only question I was able to ask myself in the years I have lived here is what went wrong. It was a perfect theory. Communism was there to be built and we all would have lived better. But when I came here and saw the gross lack of human respect in people who were servile towards anyone in authority, I knew nothing could be done to retrieve the situation. But I was stuck.'

Watching the Soviet Union unravel caused his heart to ache, that much was clear. His adopted homeland had succumbed to the call of capitalism—'godless, bourgeois and contemptible' as he called it.

'If they come to get you, will you go willingly, surrender?' I asked. He looked uncomfortable, but answered without the assistance of his book.

'If there is any hint they will come for me, I will go willingly, though perhaps not to Great Britain.'

As I left Blake, he offered to lend me his copy of his autobiography *No Other Choice*. I thanked him and promised to return it. But a few weeks later when I phoned his number, a Russian man answered the phone claiming he'd lived for twenty years in the apartment where I'd met Blake and he'd never heard of the foreigner I was looking for.

When he returned to Moscow, Boris Yeltsin didn't bother to call Mikhail Gorbachev to tell him that he and the leaders of Belorussia and Ukraine had just dissolved the Soviet Union. He left that task to the Belorus president. Instead, he phoned George Bush in Washington to deliver the news.

With a flick of the pen, President Yeltsin had hammered the final nail into the Soviet Union's coffin. Russia had long before stopped paying federal taxes and other republics had followed its lead, so the Soviet coffers were empty. Yeltsin had won the hearts and minds of the officer corps by promising them a massive wage rise. Now he transferred the Kremlin to Russian management.

Gorbachev protested. If he hadn't forced the central parliament to dissolve itself in the few weeks after the coup collapsed, perhaps he could have called it to session to declare the act illegal. But there was no parliament. Actually, there was no Soviet Union. Gorbachev wanted the Russian parliament to protest. But it didn't. In the end all he was left with was the fading hope that the west would object or that the Soviet people would rise and demand their country remain unified. But they didn't. He was a president without a country.

On Christmas Day 1991, there was nothing I was looking forward to more than the turkey and ham lunch we'd prepared. The Sydney-based writer Sasha Soldatow was staying with me in Moscow and we'd invited over some friends, among them Masha and Rob, to indulge for the day.

We'd just settled into a post-gorging slumber when one of the greatest anti-climaxes of the twentieth century took place. Mikhail Gorbachev, president of the Soviet Union, appeared on television to announce that the Soviet Union would soon cease to exist, and that he was resigning. That was that! The Soviet president had thrown in the towel. Max, Sasha and I went to Red Square that night to watch the red hammer and sickle flag be lowered over the Kremlin for the last time. But by the time we arrived, it had already been replaced by the Russian flag.

Six days later, on New Year's Eve, thousands of people went to Red Square to see in the New Year, most of them simply oblivious to the real portent of the occasion. Perhaps they were too tired to notice that Russia was now independent, free of the party. It had an elected president and ahead was the prospect of a normal life. Champagne bottles popped, glasses were thrown onto the square's cobblestones, drunken youths clowned around wishing each other a happy new year while fireworks donated by the recently unified Germany blistered into the cold winter air. And so they drank in the first year of a sovereign, independent Russia.

Television news coverage of Gorbachev's retirement seemed obsessed with the fact that he had barely had time to pack up his

Kremlin office and take his name off the door before boxes of Boris Yeltsin's papers were shuffled in. And there was a sort of unseemly glee in the news that none of the republican leaders had bothered to come to Moscow to say goodbye.

RUSSIA
PART THREE

CHAPTER 12

HOPE FADES

Russia's trouble was never a shortage or an abundance of reformers. The trouble was an ability to adhere to a consistent policy. Whether Czar or General Secretary, everyone wanted to distinguish himself in history.

BORIS YELTSIN, *THE VIEW FROM THE KREMLIN*, 1994

Not that Mikhail Gorbachev had ever wanted it to, but *perestroika* had turned into revolution. And it's not that Boris Yeltsin had ever intended the revolution to kill off the Soviet Union. But it had and Russia was left alone, without an empire, heading towards a new *svetloe budushie* [shining future] called capitalism. Communism was still alive, but it would have to battle to recover. Without fear to keep people in line, the corpse of Leninism might never revive. And fear had definitely vanished.

But revolution is an exhausting business and as 1992 dawned, the Russians were tired. By the time Boris Nikolaevich Yeltsin assumed power, he—and hope—were just about all the Russians had left. The economy was in tatters, millions of people had been displaced by the collapse of the Soviet Union, and winter was brutal. There were worse than usual food shortages. Seven years of political mayhem had not only derailed production. They had further broken the lines of supply and distribution. The shops were bare and the queues long. The same old complaints were muttered person to person down the line about the system having failed everyone. Only now, the country's moral guardians, the *babushkas*, weren't blaming the party or the *nomenklatura*. The communists might have reigned but hadn't ruled for some years they reasoned, and although they had finally accepted that it was the communists' political and economic system which had caused shortages, corruption, theft and laziness, it seemed much easier to point the finger at the so-called democrats who had refused to allow the Bolshevik experiment to go on any longer. Talk quickly turned to whether the democrats had enough experience and strength to create what they had promised—a 'normal' country, a market economy and a real democracy. In short, a new future to replace the lie Leninism had become.

'If you can't eat it what good is it to you,' the *babushkas* would say of their new freedoms in the inevitable conversations about what was going to happen next. 'Unless these democrats can think of something good, something which will feed and clothe us and not leave us begging on the streets for a few spare roubles to buy bread, or with our hands outstretched to the Americans for a few kopeks to buy sausage, then the Bolsheviks will be back.'

For a few months, as the country slumbered in exhaustion, it was almost as though only the *babushkas* had energy to think about and deliver a prognosis on the sickness which was ailing Russia. The democrats, savouring their victory, seemed to have hidden themselves in the Kremlin to work out a formula for Russian capitalism. For a few weeks after the Soviet Union collapsed, it felt as though Russia might easily slide back to a collective lack of responsibility, a collective jealousy, a collective deception that Lenin's utopia was just around the corner and was worth waiting for. As survey after survey showed, slipping back to the old ways would have been much easier than experimenting with capitalism. Far fewer people supported the market economy than opposed it.

The generation problem which had haunted Gorbachev would haunt Yeltsin too. Life for the Russians had always been a matter of absolutes. In the era only just past, communism was good, capitalism was bad. Now the young reasoned that socialism and its command economy hadn't worked, so capitalism must be good. If everything the communists had said about the United States of America was untrue, then everything about it must be wonderful! The elderly found this sort of thinking annoying, and many I knew would tell me of an old Russian children's story. If one looks into a crooked mirror, they'd say, at the proper angles and from an appropriate distance, imperfections are turned into beauty. And vice versa.

The idea of democracy was of course enticing to everyone, even to the old. While they grumbled in the queues and worried about what was around the corner, few older people relished the thought of returning to the days of fear and oppression, even though they hungered for the old certainties when supplies of food and vodka were delivered on the same day every month. But if they had a good word to say about the democrats, it was that they had defeated the culture of fear, and no-one wanted to feel fear again.

Julia Arsenievna, my mother-in-law, saw it as starkly as most. The price for having conquered fear would be high, she said, but any price was worth it. 'Once when Grisha was just a little boy, he was walking with his father on the streets and Grisha asked him whether he liked Brezhnev. Of course, his father said yes, lying but trying to hold his heart in its place! What a question to ask someone on the street! Do you love Brezhnev? But Papa, Grisha went on, that's not what you say when you see him on TV! He was so frightened, he grabbed him and they almost ran home.'

Natasha's father, his chest weighed down with war medals, was obsessed with questions about the immediate future—if the communists weren't running the plants and factories and the farms then how would they produce enough to feed the country, chief among them. But to accept, and even welcome change, all he had to do was remember when the party cadres had visited his home in Kazan on the Volga River years before. They'd heard that he had taken up some private work fixing musical instruments, a natural extension of the work he did for the state pedalling around the streets on a three-wheeled cycle playing his accordion for the 'pleasure of the masses'.

'We had four daughters to support on a miserable state wage and they wouldn't let him do some extra work because they said he was exploiting the masses,' grumbled his wife. 'And what were they doing? Relaxing in their saunas in their big *nomenklatura* apartments, buying food in special shops.' For Natasha's parents, the idea that the younger generation had won the freedom to express themselves and work towards something of their own which they would have to take responsibility for was a ray of sunshine breaking through a bleak Russian winter sky. It was more than enough to overwhelm their doubts about capitalism.

As the bells of St Basil's Cathedral on Red Square chimed out on 7 January 1992, marking only the second time in more than seventy years that the Russians had been allowed to officially celebrate the Orthodox Christmas, Oleg Borisovich stood in his uniform at the foot of the belltower and listened. He was a colonel in the ground forces division of the Soviet Army, though he wasn't at all sure whether the Soviet Army still existed now that the empire had collapsed. I'd watched him for a few minutes as he stared silently at St Basil's. He seemed lost in reflection and I wondered whether it would be insensitive to walk up to him and ask what hopes he held for the future.

'Imagine what it is like to lose everything,' he asked me when I finally struck up conversation. 'How would you feel if Sydney mounted a Bolshevik-style revolution and you separated from the rest of the country and suddenly you had to live under communist rule?'

As we walked away from the Kremlin he poured out his concerns. 'Of course not even that is a comparison with what we're facing. We lost our influence over other socialist states outside Eastern Europe and that was fine because we didn't really care about them. But then we lost Eastern Europe itself which, well, that wasn't too bad either because we couldn't afford to keep it any longer. But now we've lost the whole country. The Soviet Union. There are dozens of new "centres" now. Every republic thinks it can run its own show. Yerevan thinks it has real power, so does Kiev and even Dushanbe. And here in Russia, we have a contrived democracy being run by people who are old party people. I am happy that totalitarianism has gone. Who isn't? But the way I see it is that the old party people—people like Boris Yeltsin—they'll have to let us do what we want just so they can prove they're not communists. And without order how are we going to keep things in control?

'We have thirty thousand nuclear weapons and that's not counting the chemical and conventional weapons. I know how badly corroded the system of command is within the military, so if you think about it, the world is in danger unless these pseudo-democrats act fast. And because they're not really democrats, they can't do it alone. We need international help to disarm and rebuild. But can you imagine how the military generals are going to react when they see American consultants in the Defence Ministry giving advice on how to destroy our nuclear arsenal? If they are patronising and see what they are doing as dividing the spoils of victory, then there'll be trouble because no-one will listen to them and we'll end up hating them again while Yeltsin and his boys do their best to pretend we don't. It'll be chaotic and remember how much the communists hated chaos.'

Despite the disorder of the old Soviet Union, chaos was about as frightening to the average Russian as the prospect of unprotected nuclear warheads was for the west. The Russian love of *poryadok* (order) had allowed the cult of personality to develop unchecked. People had willingly followed the leader despite his incompetence or predilection for terror, because he promised and delivered order. When they were given the freedom to protest, the elderly who'd lost their parents to Stalin's terror would instead carry his picture glued to placards held high, hailing him as the leader who delivered victory in war and order from the economic chaos of industrialisation. That much was true. But they had allowed themselves to be ruled by the arbitrariness and mean-spiritedness of a bureaucracy which imposed rules created in the thousands to keep the population marching in line, because their need for order was so strong.

'The danger now,' Oleg Borisovich muttered as he pulled open the huge wooden doors to his apartment block, 'is that the Russians will sit back as they always have and allow themselves to be led. They see themselves as the *narod* (the people). The communists sold us a lie on the basis that they were maintaining order for us and we followed them. Now the democrats can sell us a new lie—that they are taking us somewhere—and we will follow again.'

'Tell me how a bank account operates and what relationship it has to a credit card,' my friend Igor asked anxiously. 'You put all your money into an account. What happens then? If the bank can use the money to lend to other people, what happens when you want yours back? And I'm not sure I understand how it is that you can go into a shop and buy what you want with a little card then the bank pays the bill!'

It was so easy a concept for me that I wasn't even sure what Igor was asking. He had answered all his own questions. The process was simple, I said, and explained as best I could.

'But if it's so simple, why haven't we been doing it?' asked Igor in a legitimate question I couldn't answer. Nor was it easy explaining that western economies, to some extent, were reliant on giving concessions and publicly funded subsidies to big corporations while the workers often paid a higher level of tax.

Igor began to look depressed. So it wasn't the case that everyone who lived in the west had an equal capacity to make a million dollars.

Just the day before, Igor had read an interview in *Komsomolskaya Pravda* with a representative of the International Monetary Fund who said that an iron-clad law of free market economics was that enterprises which were inefficient should be allowed to go bankrupt. Pulling the article out of his work bag, he looked seriously worried.

'That would mean every enterprise in Russia would have to go bankrupt,' he said, 'and how many people would that leave out of work? Which political group in Russia is going to make sure that doesn't happen? The communists are outlawed and Yeltsin says he believes in western capitalism.'

The thought was frightening. Entire towns would be thrown into chaos and poverty. Millions of people would be out of work. Igor wondered whether the international community would make it a precondition of aid to Russia that state enterprises which were unprofitable be forced into bankruptcy.

He also wondered how Boris Yeltsin intended to fix all the problems, create a new economic system while at the same time people like him struggled with the new concepts of business, profits, trade and commerce.

'We have to do more than simply move goods from one point to another, don't we? We have to actually generate the means of production as well, as Marx would have put it.'

Igor's assessment wasn't lost on those a generation below him. In mid 1991 *Izvestiya* newspaper published the results of a survey which showed that a majority of the teenage girls of whom they asked the question: 'What do you want to be when you leave school?' answered that they wanted to be prostitutes. When asked why, they said it was the only way they could think of to earn money.

It seemed incredible to me that such a large proportion of soon-to-be school-leavers wanted to get on the game. Masha laughed at my outrage. 'Just think about it for a minute. They know that if they go to university or spend years at an institute, the best they'll come out with is a piece of paper and a job that pays 200 roubles a month [roughly US$30].

'If they sell themselves to hard-currency-paying foreigners, they earn real money and they'll meet a lot of people, maybe even someone who'll take them away from all this.'

At Krylatskoe High School, near where I lived, the news was shocking. Of the twenty or so schoolgirls I put the question to, fourteen said they had thought about prostitution as a profession, or wouldn't be hostile to the idea. Such was freedom!

As Mikhail Gorbachev moved out of the Kremlin, Boris Yeltsin moved in, and wondered which of the many problems facing the country he ought to tackle first. The man everyone entrusted with the responsibility of digging them out of the economic hole they were in was carrying not just the expectations of his people, but their anxieties. It was a tough job. But he had a lot in his favour. He was all that the Russians admired. To the young he was a man prepared to give up the privileges of the *nomenklatura* in order to stand by basic human principles. He was prepared to dump the party. And he was a hero for having mounted resistance to the GKChP. For those older, even though he'd abandoned the party, he was above all else a *muzhik*, a real Russian man who spoke the same language as the people. He was unlike his predecessor, Mikhail Gorbachev, whom most had considered rather too intellectual for their liking. Yeltsin promised in simple clear words that everyone would soon live well, in a 'normal' country in which people were paid properly for their work and would be able to buy good food, clothes, washing machines, televisions and new cars without queuing or waiting for years. The party and its corrupt practices were dead, he told them. And because he was one of them, one of the *narod* (the people), they believed him.

But Yeltsin needed to find the right person to plot the new order, someone who thought beyond the Communist Party's Five Year Plans and understood the mechanisms of a market economy which the president had promised his people. There weren't that many candidates for the job. Economists trained in the Soviet Union had studied socialist economic principles; their exposure to market economics was limited to books written by the party's *apparatchiks*. Yigor Gaidar was one such economist, although he had also been involved with liberals whose thinking had evolved beyond that of the socialist planners. He came to the Russian president highly recommended by the man who had engineered the 'silent coup' against Mikhail Gorbachev and delivered Russia its independence—Gennady Burbulis. Once a professor of Marxist philosophy in the Siberian city of Sverdlovsk, Burbulis had become the champion of all things anti-Marxist. The 'grey cardinal', as he was called in the corridors of power, had masterminded Yeltsin's campaign for the presidency just six months earlier.

Gaidar, the man he spirited into the top economic job, was a short, stout man who spoke in spluttering bursts of words grouped together in a way which made it hard for the listener to understand or keep up with anything he said. Born in the year Soviet tanks rolled into Hungary, he had studied economics at Moscow State University but had been associated with people who had devised the doomed 500-Day Move to Capitalism which Gorbachev had dumped two years earlier. Yeltsin appointed Gaidar as his deputy prime minister in charge of the economy.

'A lot of shock and little therapy,' became the description people attached to his economic reforms. Gaidar, people would say, wanted only to destroy the old political system once and for all by making sure that the command economy had absolutely no hope of seeing the light of day again.

On the face of it, burying the command system looked like a relatively easy task. The economy was very near to broken. Production had been plummeting since the late 1980s. Gorbachev had borrowed money from the west which only added to the old Soviet Union's foreign debt, now Russia's responsibility. The communists had sold much of the country's gold and the old Soviet trade bank had collapsed, leaving massive debts to foreigners importing goods—among them Masha's American husband Rob who could scarcely afford to lose his earnings. But the most sinister effect on the economy resulted from the definitions of 'sovereignty' applied by the former republics. Producers across the old USSR, once tied together by the command economy, decided that independence meant asking whatever prices they wanted for goods whose prices had always been pegged at low state-subsidised levels.

The result was chaos. By January in Russia's first year of true independence, I was queuing at 3 or 4 a.m. at the local petrol station so that I wouldn't have to wait for three or more hours in the daylight. Because the train lines were so decrepit, supplies needed to produce the basics slowly dried up in the capital and elsewhere, so that even bread was becoming difficult to buy. And, unlike in the Soviet era, the shortages of food were impossible to negotiate because now there simply was no produce for shop attendants to tuck away and sell later on.

Gaidar's task was to salvage the economy by crushing its old institutions and precepts. Price liberalisation, to be followed by privatisation of the state's property, was the medicine he prescribed with the blessing of the International Monetary Fund. Gaidar reasoned that in a market economy, the government had no right to determine prices. They would find their own equilibrium. Selling off the state's factories and enterprises once prices were freed would have a double impact, thought Gaidar. It would free the government of the financial burden of keeping them afloat, while giving Russians the chance to become property owners with, it was assumed, the incentive to work hard and make the system operate efficiently.

The second of January 1992 was the most miserable of days. It was particularly cold with temperatures hovering around minus fifteen and threatening to drop even further. By 3 p.m. it was dark. Driving to the city to see the first effects of Gaidar's price liberalisation, my car wheels skidded on the packed ice and I was sent hurtling towards a parked car. Turning the steering wheel one way then another, I managed to avoid catastrophe. But only just.

In the city centre, calamity had already struck. State price controls had been removed from most goods. The cost of everything—a loaf of bread, a piece of sausage, a kilo of sugar—had just risen 500 per cent. Gaidar had promised price rises of closer to 20 per cent. Of course, wages remained at their old levels. So too did pensions.

Grisha, my husband, hopped into a taxi. He wanted to go only a few kilometres. The meter clocked up 5 roubles but the driver asked for 100.

Babushkas wailed as sullen-faced shop attendants gave them the bad news. They simply didn't have enough money to buy what they needed to feed their families. Some wouldn't have enough to feed themselves that night, let alone tomorrow. A basket of bread, potatoes and sausage which was the normal staple would cost them double their monthly pension. Suddenly, with the stroke of a pen, Gaidar had made Russian shops more expensive than the luxurious hard currency shops which imported western food. Of course, most Russians didn't have the hard currency required in those shops, but for those that did, there would be a double insult. Some of the hard currency shops, anticipating a rush on their products which they might not be able to meet, made it illegal to buy with cash. Only credit cards were accepted and this locked out most Russians.

And nor could *blat* do its normal work because the problem was no longer a shortage of goods. It was inflation, indeed hyper-inflation, on goods which, by the end of February 1992, two months after price liberalisation sat on shop shelves in unprecedented abundance because no-one could afford to buy them.

It's difficult for the average westerner to comprehend the shock of price liberalisation. The Soviet economy had been spared the sometimes rampant inflation suffered in the west. People could ride the metro for the equivalent of 3 US cents. Their rents were fixed at around US$3 a month. Potatoes cost some 4 cents a kilogram. Meat cost an average of 6 cents a kilo. There had been a huge outcry when the price of a bottle of vodka went from around 7 cents to 12 cents in 1970. Even moderate price increases would have terrified the Russians, and made their lives extremely difficult.

Perhaps if people had more energy, they might have protested vociferously against the price rises in 1992. But you got the feeling that after three years of protesting against the Communist Party, most people believed the worst was over. Natasha certainly did. Price liberalisation, she hoped, was a bad dream which would pass. But she wasn't sure.

She came to Moscow the day after prices were freed and wept. It seemed to her a monstrous travesty of justice that the mighty Soviet Union would come to this. Her monthly wage was not quite enough to feed herself for a week.

'It's OK for those Parisians from the International Monetary Fund to recommend how we should go about reform, but how would they know what it's like to be a Russian in 1992?'

They'd lost their country and now they were losing the little dignity which had been returned to them by the defeat of the communists.

'I heard Gaidar say on the radio that people shouldn't panic because prices will fall when the sellers realise no-one is buying anything. Do you think that's true?' Natasha asked.

The laws of a market economy would seem to indicate Gaidar was correct. But in Russia the laws of the market were far from mature. I saw truckloads of cabbages sitting on back streets around Moscow, left to rot because they were too expensive for anyone to buy. Rather than lower their prices, the owners would watch their produce decompose. At a flea market in the city centre, a friend searched for a radio. Two kiosk owners, neighbours, boasted that they'd been able to get their hands on a small consignment of radios which had been sitting in a factory in Ukraine for years. One of the sellers wanted 600 roubles and the other 1500 for the same radio. My friend pointed out to the seller with the more expensive radio that if he lowered his price to better his neighbour's, he might buy his radio.

'Buy his,' he said, 'eventually he'll run out and they'll have to buy mine.'

A hideous distortion of market principles tinged with the old laws of Soviet jealousy was dictating the course of the emerging Russian market and there was nothing the government could do about it.

'You don't need to be Einstein to figure out what's going to happen in a few months,' said Natasha. 'They're going to have to increase our wages so that we can live. And where will the money come from or are they going to do what they've always done and print money when they need it?'

The government not only printed more money, notching up inflation, it began a process of belt-tightening which hurt average workers even more. The only thing which might have stopped the gallop of inflation was the forced closure of factories and enterprises. But that would have created mass unemployment which most political and economic analysts knew would lead to civil unrest.

Instead, the factories were kept open even though they were unable to keep up with skyrocketing prices for raw materials they needed to manufacture their output. They simply produced less, but charged buyers more for it. So every day inflation increased by a further 5 per cent, which to most westerners is incomprehensible. It was to me. One day, a set of Russian-made pots and pans cost 200 roubles. The next week they might cost 5000.

The roubles people had stashed away under their beds throughout the Soviet era disappeared in a few months. Natasha's sister, Luda, had saved for years to buy a washing machine, but suddenly was further from her goal than ever. The blow to morale was devastating.

The government managed to avoid closing down the bigger factories which consumed entire towns, even cities, but because most factories were producing less, they needed fewer workers and people were laid off. Many were women who had worked in what amounted to the old Soviet welfare system—the children's creches and subsidised food shops attached to most factories, which simply disappeared.

Out where Natasha lived in the village of Belye Stolby, the kindergarten attached to *Gosfilmofond* closed down just as more and more women had to start looking for work to subsidise their family income. And the local polyclinic shut its doors because there was no money to pay its employees, which meant that sick villagers had to travel fifty kilometres by electric train (the Russian version of a cattle train) to Moscow in search of medical help. The few gifts of the collective system were being snatched from beneath them and the Russians were angry.

On the nineteenth floor of the old Comecon building next door to the Russian parliament sat Jean-Paul Foglizzo, the IMF's representative in Moscow. The presence of his office in this building was enough to send *Pravda* into paroxysms of fury, for it was here that the Communist Party had sifted through and integrated the economies of its Eastern European satellites. Now it was where the organisations which the more conservative in Moscow called the 'agents of western imperialism' plotted the destruction of the command economy.

Foglizzo was a worried man when I met him in March 1992. He understood how hard it was for Russians to live with hyper-inflation which western analysts estimated would hit 2000 per cent by the end of the year.

I asked him whether it had been wise to liberalise prices before privatising the state-dominated economy. Of course, he said, it might have been better to create a private sector first so that people had at least an ability to earn more money. But, he went on, the mistake had been made. It was too late to do anything about it.

'Lucky,' said my friend Igor when I played him the interview I'd recorded with Foglizzo, 'that he doesn't have to support five kids in Russia today on what I earn. I'm already more than halfway through the money I've been saving for ten years!'

Even Boris Yeltsin admitted that the effects of the economic shock therapy administered by Gaidar had depressed him and caused him numerous second thoughts.

By May, the snow had melted into sludge. It was that time of the year everyone hated in Moscow. No matter what you wore it was guaranteed to be filthy within a few minutes of leaving your apartment block. But this year, people I knew complained less about the weather than about the cost of living and the *spekulanty*—those who made a profit by selling goods for more than they had been bought. They weren't wallowing in poverty. Many of them were doing very well. Indeed, anyone with sufficient energy and connections began to cash in on the freedom to be entrepreneurial.

On the streets of the major cities like Moscow and St Petersburg, kiosks were flourishing and they were no longer just co-operatives dependent on the state for their wares. They were businesses which were privately owned, selling all sorts of products—tea, coffee, batteries, calculators (for which there was a fresh and novel demand), ladies' underwear, make-up and perfume. Some of it was made in Russia but most was imported by enterprising *biznezmeny* in brightly coloured silk track-suits. They would either travel to Turkey or China themselves to buy clothes and other consumer goods by the bale, or they'd buy from networks of middlemen who did the travelling and buying for them. Anywhere else, they'd be called self-employed entrepreneurs. In Russia they were *zhuliki* (scoundrels) because they bought at one price and sold at a profit.

My friend Nikolai made a small fortune by hiring a jet from Aeroflot and going to Beijing where he'd scour the markets and buy ten or twelve bales of silk shirts and men's boxer shorts which he distributed among the kiosk owners who would sell them on commission. Everyone ended up happy. The sellers in China were delighted that a new market had opened up, Aeroflot was eager to rent out its aircraft given its safety standards had fallen so far below what was internationally acceptable that no-one wanted to fly with them, and the consumers in Moscow and elsewhere were delighted. Of course only those who no longer worked for the state could afford silk shirts and boxer shorts, but as the state went broke and more people went out on their own, business grew. In any event, the goods were sold for very little because they'd been bought so cheaply in China. Nikolai was ecstatic—just a year before, he had finished his studies in diplomacy and economics at the prestigious Moscow State Institute for International Relations where he was being groomed to take up a foreign posting. Now he was becoming rich instead.

Max, Vera's son, hopped onto the China route as well. He'd travel to Beijing on chartered Aeroflot flights with a group of twenty or thirty others and hit the markets. The Russians even developed their own language with which to communicate with the Chinese. 'Chippa, chippa,' meant 'Can I have it a little cheaper please?' and 'doga, doga' from the Russian word *dorogo* (expensive) meant 'it's too expensive'. Max and his cohorts imported literally hundreds of cheap padded jackets. Of course they weren't the only ones doing this kind of business. Within months, all over Russia, I began noticing a change in the general colours on the streets. Rather than the drab brown, black or grey coats which people had worn to death, they were donning new and brightly coloured Chinese jackets!

As the new businessmen began making more money, they became more adventurous. By the end of 1992, there were canned vegetables imported from Scandinavia in the kiosks, along with coffee and pasta from Italy. It seemed suddenly that you could buy anything in Moscow. The problem of price remained overwhelming, but as people saw that it was possible to freely import goods, more of them—mostly the young and able—left their state jobs and entered the new world. As their businesses grew, they hired people to travel abroad for them, to distribute the goods at home, to oversee the marketing process. People were earning better money than the state could afford to pay them, if indeed they were paid at all. For many, the decision to enter the capitalist world wasn't hard to make.

Even Natasha dipped her toe into capitalist waters. She kept her job at the State Film Archives, but started selling her knowledge of Russian film to western filmmakers who were eager to shoot films in the newly opened Russia. 'It helps to keep the dogs fed,' she said defensively.

At least Natasha was using her knowledge. Others weren't so lucky.

The giant brown marble Mezhdunarodnaya Hotel on the banks of the Moscow River used to be where visiting delegations from Eastern Europe were put up in the 1970s when they came to Moscow for trade talks. By the 1980s, western businessmen would also stay at the 'Mezh' as it was called, which had opened Moscow's first shopping mall. There were lots of western clothes shops, a Christian Dior outlet, a hard currency supermarket importing food from Italy, restaurants and bars and various airline companies including an Aeroflot counter where, although there was no discernible change in the attitude of the staff, one could at least queue in relative comfort, inside rather than on the street in the cold or stifling heat.

The Mezh was a western haven in a city with few luxuries. Moscow had two Pizza Huts, even a McDonald's, but few 'shopping malls' other than the rows of Russian kiosks on the streets. The Mezh was different. It was an oasis of consumerism which warmed the soul and satiated the intense desire to spend which almost every foreigner I knew in Moscow had in a more than healthy supply.

But it wasn't six months into economic reform that the administrators of the Mezh decided to charge westerners for the right to park anywhere near the enormous structure. The fee started at US$1 a half hour, then went to US$5 an hour.

It was a price I was happy to pay for a reprieve from the gloom which had descended on most of my friends, including Natasha, who I convinced to come with me to the Mezh one frightfully cold day. Despite her protests against entering a world not affordable to the average Russian, she came. We were stopped at the new boom gates by a man in his fifties who asked me for the parking fee.

'Aren't you ashamed to be charging foreigners to park here?' Natasha barked at the man, leaning across me so that he could better hear her. 'You are doing exactly what the party told us the west did—exploiting people for money. Don't you feel shame?'

'Of course I feel ashamed,' the man answered much to my surprise, 'I'm barely able to sleep at night. But this is my job. And I've got to feed my family, so do me a favour lady, and don't make it harder than it has to be.'

Misha, the parking attendant, was 59 years old and an economist. All of his life he'd worked as a researcher for the Institute of Socialist Economies of the World. But price liberalisation had claimed his career. He was unable to survive on the 500 roubles (US$60) a month he earned at the Institute. In any event, he hadn't received his salary for several months. His neighbour worked for the businessman who received the contract from the Mezh to cordon off the area around the hotel and turn it into paid parking and so Misha got a paying job. It was the new Russian version of the old Soviet *blat*. Misha felt deep shame at his situation, as though he'd rather be churning out propagandist analyses of western economies than standing in a shed collecting dollars from westerners. But such was life in the new Russia.

'I have a chance,' he told us, 'to start a little business of my own, selling car accessories but I have to earn real money first. So until then, when you come to the Mezh, it's my doomed face you're going to see here at the gates.'

The hardships faced by some were depressing for everyone, even those who were making money and doing well. It was as though the country had been thrown into the arms of humiliation for the sake of a new *svetloe budushie* [shining future] which they knew would chew them up and spit them out if they were not capable of fighting back.

In Dorgomilovskaya Street near the centre of Moscow, a man with one leg, dressed in shabby clothes, sidled up to my car window begging for a few roubles. He wasn't alone. All over Moscow beggars became a routine sight.

Boris Yeltsin's new order had a long way to go before Russia began to look like the United States and before the Russians began to live like Americans, but it seemed only the beggars and the *babushkas* understood this.

Masha and Rob were in the city shopping one evening in April 1992. They were looking for furniture, feeling increasingly frustrated that they couldn't afford what they found, not even on Rob's reasonably good salary. They phoned me from Gorky Street to tell me some three hundred *babushkas* had decided to protest at price liberalisation.

The din of their protest was very different to what we'd heard in the years before the collapse of communism. There were no placards this time, no speeches from the back of trucks, and no calls for the party to get out of the business of government. Now it was the clang of pots and pans being beaten with wooden spoons by an army of old women in felt boots and huge grey woollen scarves, condemning the democrats for their cruel hoax.

CHAPTER 13

BUT NOT FOR ALL

The state is the private property of the bureaucrats.

KARL MARX, *CRITIQUE OF HEGEL'S PHILOSOPHY OF RIGHT*

For decades under the Soviet regime, money held no particular meaning. It was merely paper given to workers in return for their occasional effort. They could stash it under their mattresses, count it on a dull Saturday night and pretend they were millionaires, or use it to buy the few consumer goods available to give to the doctor or dentist in order to secure an appointment. But money wasn't the major currency. *Blat* was what kept people alive and the wheels of the Soviet economic and political system turning.

Price liberalisation meant that money acquired meaning for the first time, and suddenly people needed a lot of it just to survive. It was natural for them to think that life was better when they queued for goods which were in short supply but were affordable, not to say cheap, when they finally arrived. They knew when goods would be distributed to the shops, who had food tucked away under the counter and who to bribe to get anything done. Capitalism was a whole new ball game and, apart from the *spekulanty* and the racketeers, not many people seemed to understand the new rules.

The newspapers were full of stories about *babushkas* so desperate for money to buy food that they sold their apartments, which the Yeltsin government had decreed they owned, for the proverbial song to spivs in shiny suits. Others were cheated in different ways. Alcoholics, always numerous in Russia, would be visited in the middle of the night by racketeers offering to ply them with the vodka they could no longer afford. They'd be taken to hideaways far from their homes and kept drunk while the racketeers bribed officials to falsify property documents. The victims would get their hit, but when they were dumped in the city centre they'd have no apartments and their official documents would show they'd transferred them to someone else. Others weren't lucky enough to make it back alive. *Moscow Times* reported that by August 1992, some 8000 people in the capital had mysteriously disappeared, presumed to have been the victims of extortion and murder. Capitalism was getting a bad name and the government had to act fast.

Voucherisation seemed at first a stroke of genius. In September 1992 Yeltsin and his savvy young Minister for Privatisation, Anatoly Chubais, introduced a scheme which would give every Russian citizen a 10 000 rouble voucher (at the time equivalent to about US$60). The idea was to give people something—anything—so they'd begin to see the merits of capitalism. With their vouchers they'd be able to buy a stake in the factories where they worked, or in any other enterprise they thought could become profitable.

Giving people a share in the state's assets gave them a base from which they could enter the world of capitalism. The more entrepreneurial could buy the vouchers of those who didn't want them and, in the process, a system of market pricing for assets which had never previously been valued could be established. The government's burden of keeping factories, plants, enterprises and institutes afloat would be magically lifted once they were sold. But perhaps more critically for Boris Yeltsin, voucherisation was good public relations. Centrally controlled state-owned property was to be given to individuals. After years of toiling for an idea that had not only gone bust but had sapped them of any initiative, the workers in the workers' paradise were to be given something back. They were told that if they owned shares in their workplace, they would have the incentive to work harder. And if they worked harder, what they produced would be of better quality and they'd be able to sell more of it. Eventually they'd turn a profit and their share values would increase. Finally capitalism—not communism—was to reward the Russians and its image was looking better by the minute. There were risks of course, chief among them that the voucher process would be corrupted by the people who had always corrupted the system— the *nomenklatura*.

Among the first factories to go up for sale was Bread Factory Number 37 in central Moscow. So enthusiastic were its workers about placing some truth in Lenin's promise that the workers would triumph that there was a near riot on the day of the share handout. They not only snapped up the 51 per cent of shares that by law were reserved for them, they wanted more. They wanted 80 per cent.

'Who'll buy what we don't?' demanded Ivan Alekseyevich of his manager, baring his yellow teeth in a half grin as though to answer his own question.

With his finger shaking wildly a few centimetres from the factory manager's nose he went on, 'If you think for one minute that we don't understand what you managers are up to, then you're mad! You'll buy up 49 per cent of the stock, then when we need money you'll offer to buy our shares. What'll be the difference between the old *nomenklatura* owning everything which was meant to be ours, and you? You were *nomenklatura* and you still are!' spat Ivan Alekseyevich.

Workers in their white coats and overalls clapped madly as though they were trying the *nomenklatura* after decades of subservience. Ivan Alekseyevich had hit on what would become a seemingly insurmountable problem for the new Yeltsin order—how to stop the rise and rise of the *nomenklatura*—well-connected and powerful, and now wanting the biggest slice of the cake being divided up. Soviet norms were outdated but the tactics of those the Soviet Union had bred for privilege hadn't changed at all. As the Soviet state economy was unravelling, they were moving at a rate of knots to carve out a place for themselves. And their capers paid off. As Boris Kagarlitsky, the socialist who'd spent years in jail for his contributions to *samisdat*, put it, 'The manager had been sacked but the master remained in place.'

Before the workers had even collected their vouchers from the state, factory managers in their thousands had begun siphoning off what their workers produced by forming private daughter companies which would either distribute or export the factory's produce. Other managers didn't even bother to form subsidiary companies. They simply got their mates in the old *Gosplan* structure to write out export licences for them. Precious raw materials—aluminium, oil, rare metals, copper, steel, coal and tin—were illegally sold outside the country, with the profits going directly into bank accounts overseas. The first of the new really rich were born.

The system had always been open to theft and corruption. Now, theft and corruption was an open system. One case in point involved a student at the Chemical Institute in Moscow who capitalised on the fact that Russia wasn't selling abroad the inert gases it produced despite their superior quality. The reason Russia couldn't sell the gas was because it couldn't manufacture the heavy metal containers needed to hold the gases during transportation. So the student borrowed money and went to Germany where he bought four used containers. Bringing them back to Russia, he convinced the institute's director that they could get rich fast exporting the gas which was still cheap to buy in Russia as not all prices in the energy sector had yet been liberalised. The pair paid for an export licence and were soon on the way to becoming millionaires. Germany bought the gases at below world-market prices, which were hugely inflated, however, by Russian standards. Using the same containers over and over, they made a million dollars a month until the Ministry of Chemistry realised the price for inert gases was artificially low and that the new entrepreneurs were making a fortune semi-legally. It had taken them months to cotton on to the scam, but when they did they not only raised the prices but began doleing out export licences, often corruptly, to the managers of other factories and institutes which manufactured the gases.

This was *nomenklatura* privatisation and it was sinister and common, leaving a lot of workers feeling that privatisation was just another bureaucratically controlled means of cheating them. There seemed to be no limit to the number of scams, just like in the old days. The only difference now was the scams were being conducted in the name of democracy.

Three generations of workers on the Red Tractor Collective Farm in southern Russia would no doubt have sympathised with the fears of Ivan Alekseyevich of Bread Factory Number 37. The farm was slowly going broke. Its equipment was old and run-down. Its young were more interested in getting to the big cities to make some real money now that trading had been legalised. Selling chewing gum in Moscow was more exciting for some of them than staying on the farm. But the farm was in dire need. The only people who wanted to stay were the elderly who couldn't work. In desperation, the collective's managers asked the state for help. But in 1992 the state had little money to hand out, especially to enterprises which had no hope of producing or paying back the debt. So the government asked the local authority to appoint a receiver to sell what the farm had managed to maintain, and to distribute the profits among the residents. The receiver appointed was a local bank, the board of which was made up of the region's bosses—the people who appointed the bank the receiver. The board appointed a former *Komsomol* leader to break up the collective. Instead, he reorganised the farm into a collective of a different sort. Enticing some of the younger people born on the farm back to the land by promising them a healthy cut in a new collective experiment, he divided the land into small farming units and food-processing enterprises which paid the bank good money for the rent of the equipment which was owned by the state. In return, the farmers received 10 per cent of the profits. The rest went to the receiver and members of the bank's board.

Ivan Alekseyevich's fears about the percentage of shares the *nomenklatura* would snatch through the voucher system were also realised. Many of the public auctions appeared to be rigged. One I went to in Moscow for shares in the Bolshevik Tube Factory was attended mainly by office workers in suits and ties rather than workers, and the auctioneers seemed in a hurry to conduct the business of the day and close their doors.

Slowly I moved among the bidders, asking who they were and whether they worked at the tube factory. Aware that I was a foreigner reporting on the privatisation process, they were reluctant to answer, but a general picture did emerge. The 51 per cent of shares reserved for workers had all been claimed. The plant's managers had snatched up the remaining 49 per cent, as they were legally entitled to do. But now an auction had been called for the shares which workers at the plant wanted to sell. And the buyers were the factory managers or their proxies.

For several weeks after the voucherisation process began, the especially poor could be seen selling their pieces of paper in the streets, sometimes for as little as 15 000 roubles, a mere 5000 rouble markup. But even 5000 roubles (around US$35 at the time) was a windfall for some given the job losses and surging inflation. They knew the real value of the asset the state had given them, and they knew they were being ripped off. But times were hard. Kuznetsky Most, just around the corner from the Bolshoi Theatre, became a favourite place for voucher sellers. They'd hang cardboard placards around their necks offering their vouchers for whatever price they thought they'd be able to get on the day. It was a sad sight and one which attracted the attention of those who wanted to make fast money, in particular the managers of 'investment funds' which suddenly seemed to sprout everywhere.

The role of the investment funds was to invest vouchers for workers unsure of how to exploit them. But most were fly-by-night outfits hastily set up by shonky types who'd left their jobs as office workers in the state system. One of the investment funds was called the Einabean Fund which backwards spells 'naebanie'— Russian for 'to fuck you over'. Yet people flocked to it when it opened its doors, entrusting its officers with their vouchers which soon disappeared along with the fund's directors. In a system without any checks and balances to keep it honest, vouchers given to the working class quickly made their way into the pockets of the *nomenklatura*.

What I was witnessing at the Bolshevik Tube Factory share auction was the purchase by employees of the Einabean Fund of vouchers on behalf of the plant's managers. The managers ended up owning more than 85 per cent of the plant, and they got it at a bargain price—around US$5000 instead of its independently esti-mated worth of half a million dollars.

As usual in matters concerning capitalism, Natasha was sceptical. She dragged me to the Central Privatisation Office where the vouchers were being distributed and together we waited in the queue for her 10 000 roubles of paper.

She marched up to the counter and signed for her share in the state's assets, insisting when she had the paper in hand that the clerk officially witness her giving it to me.

'You can't do that,' insisted the clerk with a look of horror on her face, 'she's a foreigner!'

'If the *nomenklatura* can take workers' vouchers, then a foreigner has every right to them because it's no longer a fair process. So you watch me. I am giving my voucher to my friend here from Australia and she can do what she wants with it.'

Slightly concerned at the attention we were attracting, I gently tried to coax Natasha into leaving the office. But she was angry.

'You want to play your part in turning us into a capitalist country?

Let me help you because there is no way we can trust these democrats to do it for us.' She almost spat out the words.

She wasn't far from wrong. By January 1993, more than 60 per cent of Russia's large factories had been turned into privatised companies and their controlling interest was in the hands of the men who'd always run them, the *nomenklatura*.

The element of genius in the plan, as told to me by the young economist Grigori Yavlinsky—who would years later run for president—was that Boris Yeltsin had left the task of dismantling the old Soviet economy to two young men who despised communism. Yigor Gaidar and Anatoly Chubais had smashed what remained of the old system and with it the old ideology, because even though property was being transferred into the hands of the old communist ruling class, it would be theirs to manage and make profitable.

Gone were the days when a new BMW or Mercedes on the streets of Moscow would attract a phone call of shock and surprise. They were everywhere by the end of 1992 and their drivers weren't the young who'd gone out on their own to open up kiosks on the streets, but the middle-aged who were getting rich off the state's resources. *Apparatchiks* were swapping their tacky brown and grey suits for Armani and Boss. The *nomenklatura* were opening bank accounts abroad in their own names, rather than in the names of fictitious companies run by the Communist Party.

The government seemed unconcerned about their incredible wealth. But it reasoned that if the old party men were making money, it was, at least, an investment in capitalism. They'd presumably be unlikely, as capitalists, to join the escalating emotional protest coming from the Russian parliament about the 'young boys in pink pants', as Gaidar and Chubais were known due to their youth and openness to western economic values, who had thrown the country into poverty.

There were two broad camps in the parliament. One backed Boris Yeltsin and his reform team. The other backed Yeltsin's vice president Alexander Rutskoi and the Chairman of the parliament, a Chechen by the name of Ruslan Khasbulatov.

Rutskoi and Khasbulatov whined about the rise of a new wealthy class though they didn't mind that the new rich were the old *nomenklatura*. They seemed to protest only against the speed of the reforms and the lack of legislation to prevent those who were getting rich from stripping the state of its assets so rapaciously and dumping their profits overseas.

The parliament had given Yeltsin and his 'boys' a free hand in sweeping Russia clear of communism. The president had been ruling by decree since the collapse of the Soviet state. But if the president wouldn't listen to the cries of the people, or to the complaints of the legislators, then the parliament would consider removing that power. Or so Khasbulatov and Rutskoi threatened.

The contest for sovereignty began. Yeltsin claimed the country needed a strong president with unfettered powers—a sort of benevolent dictator, as some were asking for. The parliament claimed that Russia was becoming ungovernable and that there was something very wrong with the economy. Capitalism was fine, argued Rutskoi and Khasbulatov, but its creation had to be humane and democratic. People ought not be left to beg on the streets or humiliated into selling to tourists for a few miserable roubles the Orders of Lenin earned by their grandparents.

If the truth be known, the grandchildren of Lenin's heroes were delighted to be palming off Soviet memorabilia to gloating tourists. And they were happy to sell it all for very little.

'Come and look at my statues of young Lenin!' For a few hundred roubles you could pick up Lenin—at any age—in bronze, or Stalin in marble, or Brezhnev on a red silk wall-hanging. Military uniforms and caps, epaulets and the regime's deliberately misleading maps of Moscow and St Petersburg were scattered over makeshift tables on the footpaths, crying out to be bought—just so their owners could declare the Soviet era dead. Even watches made by Faberge for the pre-revolutionary well-heeled which had been long tucked away beneath wooden slats under the lounge suddenly made a public appearance, only to be snatched up for less than US$50.

With a sort of skip in their voices, young men and women selling Soviet kitsch would beckon passers-by, calling out 'Gospoda' or 'Gospodin'—the customary greeting of pre-revolutionary times which had been replaced by 'Comrade' in the Bolshevik era. The first time anyone referred to me as *Gospoda*, I was walking down the Arbat, a narrow cobbled street with an old tramline down the middle. A century ago, the nobility occupied its neo-Gothic apartments painted in light pastel shades of pink, green and blue. They'd stroll down the street, comparing the number of serfs they owned and counting their wealth. The revolution turned the Arbat into the heart of bohemian Moscow where writers and actors would drink coffee in street cafes buzzing with new ideas and new art. But as the first flush of revolutionary fervour passed, the Arbat's grand homes were divided into communal flats and left to the carelessness of collective irresponsibility.

By 1992, the Arbat was again bursting with bohemian flavour. Portrait artists and actors peddled their talents for dollars while stallholders took delight in shocking anyone who thought Russia might want to remember its Soviet past. As one of them bellowed, 'Gospoda, come see what I have here! An Order of Lenin, very cheap', my friend Max looked around to see if anyone had heard the heresy. That an Order of Lenin could be bought was nothing new. Party sycophants had been able to buy them since the Brezhnev years. It was the use of 'Gospoda' which shocked Max. It was the first time he'd heard anyone openly referred to as madam, rather than the unisex 'comrade'.

But there were some people who wanted to remember and relish

the recent past. A group of communist deputies in the Russian parliament decided to ask the Constitutional Court to rule on whether
Boris Yeltsin had acted legally when he banned the Communist Party
of the Soviet Union in the days after the collapse of the hardline
coup attempt against Mikhail Gorbachev. Lewis Carroll must have
been lurking somewhere in the background spinning the unfathomable out of the unbelievable. It was Gorbachev who insisted that
the Soviet Union become a law-based society. But it was Yeltsin
who created a Constitutional Court to get it there.

The court heard two petitions at the same time. The communists
were claiming that Boris Yeltsin had acted outside his constitutional
power in banning the party, while Yeltsin was claiming that the party
had never been a political party. He insisted it was a special entity
created for the purpose of seizing power and establishing dictatorial
control over the country. But preoccupied with Russia's 'wild'
capitalism, as people called it, few seemed concerned about the case
at all.

'So what's new?' was Masha's reaction when we discussed the latest
development. 'Some people think the party should be, others don't!
The only thing that's interesting is that the communists themselves
want the court to decide. That's news!'

On the day the court convened, those who cared—pro-communist demonstrators, most of them aged over sixty—unfurled their red
hammer and sickle flags and called for both Gorbachev and Yeltsin
to be tried for treason.

'Beware,' they bellowed to Yeltsin's team as they made their way
into the courtroom, 'you are next!' For them, the democrats had
destroyed the Soviet empire, ended the glorious and honourable life
of the Soviet Union, plunged its people into poverty and now were
selling off the people's property. The time would come, shouted one
man standing next to me, when Boris Yeltsin the dictator would ban

the democratic parties. *'Bozhe moy*! ['My God!'] He's already ruling by decree!'

Valeri Zorkin, the Chairman of the Russian Constitutional Court, was a skinny, drab-looking man, and until the 1991 putsch, a member of the party. Anyone who had reached any degree of standing in society or the professions had been.

I sat through days of the court's proceedings, heard in the building which used to be home to the Central Committee, watching the pained look on Zorkin's face as Yeltsin's team argued persuasively that the CPSU was not a political party. It was, they argued, an organisation designed to deliver Lenin dictatorial control. Lenin's claim that only a dictator could express the will of the working class was rubbish, argued Yeltsin's team. The will of the working class had never been expressed. It was suppressed. Workers had no rights, not even the right not to be a member of the party, for if they failed to join their lives were made miserable. Lenin's dictatorship created Stalin. And Stalin killed people, ordinary workers. Throughout it all, the bureaucracy had meticulously documented everything. Dmitri Volkogonov had found the archives. But most disturbing of all, the party never believed what it had done was immoral. And it never believed it would lose power. Nuremberg was not on its mind. But it must have been on Gorbachev's because he refused to give evidence.

By 1992, Gorbachev had officially become a bad guy, especially since he'd spoken his mind about the first of Yeltsin's reforms, telling whoever would listen that 'Yeltsin came to power with more goodwill and support from his people than any other leader in the world in recent history. Everyone trusted him. And in just a few months, he's lost that trust!'

Yeltsin's lips must have curled in rage for from that moment his aim was not just to humiliate Gorbachev but to punish him.

'He's in the United States now,' sneered the state-subsidised Moscow World Service newsreader one morning in April, 'touring the country on a corporate jet', as though such capitalist activities were repugnant to Yeltsin's camp.

Gorbachev had become a turncoat, the newsreader reported. For six years he'd refused to allow the Communist Party to die, leaving his people living in fear, bemoaning the injustices against what he called the most just society in the world. Now, bellowed Moscow World Service, he was dining with Ronald Reagan, the former enemy who just five years before had blundered before open microphones and labelled the Soviet Union an 'evil empire'.

On the evening television news there were shots of Gorbachev being cheered by crowds of American fans, thanking him for killing the Soviet Union and ending the Cold War; the pictures were intended of course to anger the older generation at home, some of whom saw the end of the Cold War as the defeat of all they'd worked for. The tactic worked. And as a throwaway line at the end of the news, a broadcaster suggested people get up early and buy a copy of *Izvestiya*, the newspaper which the party had used as one of its mouthpieces for decades and which was now trying to find its way in the new world. It was a spiteful advertisement which must have sent Moscow's phones into meltdown that night with the curious wanting to know what else Gorbachev could have done to betray his people.

Kris Janowski, the correspondent for Voice of America, called to ask whether I knew anyone at *Izvestiya* who might give us an advance copy of the morning paper so we could beat our deadlines. I did, and by the end of the evening we had a copy of the story which would help to turn people's minds against Gorbachev once and for all.

As we pored over the document, Masha called to see if I knew what *Izvestiya* was going to print.

'You wouldn't be able to guess, Masha,' I told her.

'He's surrendered himself to the authorities and wants to be charged with treason? He's apologised to Yeltsin for kicking him out of the Politburo? Just tell me!'

I could barely conceal my horror but Gorbachev, according to *Izvestiya*, had bought a two-storey house in Florida.

It was big news, the worst sort of treachery. The last leader of the Soviet Communist Party shacking up in Florida, dining out with the rich and not so famous, while at home the devastation left behind by *perestroika* made people's lives utterly miserable. News of the Florida acquisition was grist to the mill of a frenzied campaign to discredit the man who'd bartered a little freedom for Russia for the chance to renew Soviet communism. But it was untrue, a complete fabrication designed to do the impossible—make Russia more anti-Gorbachev than it already was.

He had no friends other than those who had worked within his immediate circle in the early years of *perestroika* and who now made up his workforce at the Think Tank he had established in a marble castle on Leningradski Prospekt in central Moscow. There, he and his cohorts wrote political and economic papers which they passed on to Boris Yeltsin. But the new president not only dismissed what Gorbachev and his friends had to say, he took enormous glee in telling the media that he'd just received another piece of fanciful rubbish from the last *GenSec* (General Secretary) who, he would say, seemed to be slipping further away from reality by the day.

In self-defence Gorbachev told anyone who would listen that he was now a mere pensioner. His only privileges were those which accrued to anyone who'd held high office. He was living in an apartment in Moscow granted him by the state and he had a car and driver as well as his institute. Certainly he was paid highly to speak on the international circuit, but which former state leader wasn't? In any event, he said, everything he earned he ploughed back into his institute to pay its workers so they could produce treatises which might help the new government, if only it would listen.

But if the story of the Florida house was an invention, others weren't.

Since his fall from power, Mikhail Sergeyevich Gorbachev had become a prolific author, writing several books, the first of which began with a series of accusations against Boris Yeltsin and the two other Slav leaders who'd plotted the downfall of the Soviet Union. His subsequent books were written to suit particular audiences. One was intended for Russian eyes only and was vaguely apologetic. It admitted that some of his economic reforms could have been a little more decisive. Another—his autobiography— was written for western consumption and for this effort he was paid handsomely, rumours have it in the vicinity of US$1 million. Page after page of newspaper editorial was devoted to pouring scorn on him for making money out of a botched attempt to reignite the flame of communism.

Gorbachev, by 1992, was not only hated, he was bored. He was accustomed to power and now he had none. His ego was suffering terribly. He loved the adoration he received abroad for his accomplishments, but even his most ardent fans were now treating him as a relic rather than someone with more to contribute. He must hate being nobody, I commented to Nikolai Shishlin in his office at the Gorbachev Think Tank.

'That's a massive understatement. If you were to walk into the office directly above us now, you'd see him pacing the room, wondering how he's going to get his next hit. He is addicted to power and Yeltsin has put him on methadone.'

If someone had said to me a year earlier that Gorbachev would become so bored with life that he would take up where his new friend Ronald Reagan had left off before becoming a politician, I would have laughed. But take to the big screen is exactly what Gorbachev did. Wim Wenders used the last General Secretary of the Soviet Communist Party in his film, *Wings of Desire*, with Gorbachev playing himself in the opening sequence. Sitting at his desk, he reeled off his thoughts on the state of the world. *Wings of Desire* played to a capacity audience in the giant main hall of the Hotel Rossiya in Red Square, not far from where Gorbachev's Zil limousine, only a year earlier would have whisked him in and out of the Kremlin. Watching Gorbachev make his film debut, it was as though Wenders had pushed us through a time tunnel into one of the long-winded media conferences of the 'great man', as foreign correspondents would refer to him, listening to him ranging across subjects, searching for answers to the imponderables, coming up with lucid, if verbose, answers to his own questions.

Natasha sat with me thinking the same thing. 'He's just found a new way to get his message across,' she whispered. 'He has to defend himself. They'll blame him for everything now. It's the way things are here. First the Tsar was to blame for everything that's wrong. Then it was Lenin who was evil. Now it's Gorbachev! Soon, they'll say Gorbachev bastardised the Communist Party and I'm sure that if you ask people who's to blame for price liberalisation, they'll say Mikhail Sergeyevich, as though he wanted capitalism.'

Little wonder that Gorbachev refused to be dragged before the Constitutional Court. 'I won't take part in this shitty little trial,' he told foreign journalists. For his obstinance he was fined 100 roubles (around 30 cents) and his passport was impounded so that he couldn't travel. He felt he was being treated as a common criminal and in many ways he was correct. The Yeltsin regime thought that by stopping him from leaving Russia for Italy where he was to deliver a series of lectures, they were sending out a message which told Russians, and indeed the world, that Gorbachev would rather abscond to the indulgent, capitalist west where he would make hundreds of thousands of dollars than meet his obligations at home. For his part, Gorbachev was sending out a message that he wouldn't support the party to which he owed everything, not even if he was deprived of the right to a couple of his favourite pastimes—travelling and being adored.

The hardliners were furious. One after another, they took to the stand before Chairman Zorkin and blamed Gorbachev for every-thing. Yigor Ligachev, one of the longest-serving members of the Politburo whose falling out with Boris Yeltsin had led to the Russian president's dismissal from the party's leading body, said Gorbachev's intention had always been to destroy the party.

'And what evidence do you have for this proposition?' asked the big-bellied Andrei Makarov, who led the Yeltsin legal team even though he looked each day as though he'd had a hard night on the vodka.

'It was clear to us,' answered Ligachev.

'And because you had convinced yourself of this, you were threat-ened, so threatened that you conspired against him?'

'What conspiracy are you talking about? I was not against change. I only wanted it to happen slowly,' replied Ligachev.

The hardliners' deep-rooted immorality had left them unable to see the truth. To slow down the reforms, the party men had done more than protest. They had mounted a coup which left three people dead. They had sent tanks onto the streets to control their own people. Ligachev cut a sad figure.

Even sadder was the fact that in defending his ban on the Com-munist Party in whose name the coup attempt had been mounted, Boris Yeltsin, the chief democrat, was relying on a law created by Stalin in 1932. Under Stalin, any political party could be abolished by decree, without resort to legal redress. Moscow was hosting a mad hatter's tea party.

By the end of 1992, children as young as seven were dropping out of school to weave in and out of lines of traffic at major intersections selling bottles of warm Coca-Cola or plastic-covered copies of old *Playboy* magazines. University students were leaving their studies to start up kiosks or businesses in fields where they had connections. Ukrainian *babushkas* were hopping on the midnight train out of Kiev bound for Moscow to sell a miserable sausage or some homemade cakes. Outside the main television complex, Ostankino, graffiti condemned the wave of new western television programs—among them the raunchy Australian series 'Chances' which aired at 8.30 p.m., just after the children's cartoon program, 'Spokoinoi Nochi, Malyshi!' ['Goodnight Children!']. And while they were at it, the *babushkas*, who'd taken to the art of graffiti, painted slogans accusing the Yeltsin government of kowtowing to the west, doing whatever it demanded no matter the implications for the Russians. But perhaps the most worrying change was the daily escalation of crime.

My KGB friend, Sasha, had finally received permission to leave the organisation. Now he was on the streets looking for something to do.

He was not without qualifications. He'd spent ten years spying and wiring telephones for tapping operations. He had an extensive network of contacts and was extremely adept at getting hold of secret information, especially about enemies. These would be useful skills in the new world of Russian business. Nor was he alone. Hundreds of former security agents were on the loose, searching for a way to make use of their talents. They hit on the obvious—they would protect the new rich, collect money owed to them, make sure that troublemakers disappeared and that competitors were stopped in their tracks. Sasha laughed at the look on my face.

'There's a new joke going round. Two hitmen arrive at the apartment of the man they've been sent to kill. They knock on the door but there's no answer. So they wait. After a few hours, one of the hitmen turns to the other and says, "Hey, this is very strange! It's 2 a.m. and he's not home yet. Maybe something bad has happened to him?"'

The pity was that both of us chuckled at the joke. I'd seen Sasha sit on the edges of anti-party protests during the day, closely watching the demonstrators who he was meant to report on. At night, he'd mingle with the same party haters. I'd met other security agents who'd kept watch on dissidents, reporting the people who visited them and the phone calls they made, all the while bringing them vodka or caviar they'd managed to lay their hands on through *blat*. It didn't seem strange that the very people who were moving into racketeering and the 'security' business should feel concern for their victims. In the old days, they were all victims.

'You're leaving one criminal organisation to join another. You can't do that. You've got to find something to do that actually helps Russia,' I said.

'I'm helping Russians make money and in the process I'll make money too. That's what Moscow is now. There's a new system of classes and they're all criminal, except for the poor and I don't want to be poor.'

On the day Boris Yeltsin decided to hammer Mikhail Gorbachev a little further into despair by withdrawing the few privileges remaining to him, I was without a car. So I thumbed a ride, as was the custom, to avoid the walk to the metro. 'Gorky Street, if you don't mind,' I asked the driver, hoping to be able to meet up with a friend before the kerbside press conference Gorbachev had called to air his outrage commenced.

'Don't know that one,' he replied.

'What do you mean? Where are you from?'

'Moscow. But there's no Gorky Street anymore. It's Tverskaya now,' he laughed.

The Moscow City Council was flexing its muscles, throwing out the old names and bringing in the new to make sure the door was closed and bolted tightly on the Bolshevik era. From the council's foyer I tried phoning the man whose job it was to rename Moscow's streets and suburbs but he was too busy to take my call.

Waving down another car to take me to Gorbachev's Think Tank, I apprehensively asked the driver whether he knew Leningradski Boulevard. He looked at me as though I was quite mad.

'What building do you want?' he asked.

'Number 55.'

'Ah! The lunatic asylum,' he laughed.

Outside Gorbachev's marble castle, a horde of journalists was waiting. 'We'll soon see Gorby pedalling to work on a bicycle,' quipped one of my colleagues. But it was no joke. Yeltsin had just stripped Gorbachev of his car and driver and, to rub salt into the wound, much of the marble castle was to be taken back and turned into hard currency watering holes! Before us stood a man who if he'd been any less strong might have broken under the pressure of pure hatred and disdain being heaped upon him.

'They'd be happy if I left the country,' said Mikhail Sergeyevich, 'but I won't go!'

The old Central Committee building where the Constitutional Court was deciding the future of communism had to find extra chairs for the hundreds of people, most of them journalists, who filed in on judgment day. Such were his lowered circumstances, I sat next to Vladimir Ivashko, the former Deputy Secretary General of the Soviet Communist Party.

He made me very nervous. The only other times I'd seen Ivashko he'd been on the podium of the Central Supreme Soviet where he often sat in for Gorbachev, wielding his temporary authority like a whip. Now his hands were shaking and beads of sweat dripped from his forehead as we waited for Chairman Zorkin to read out his verdict.

I thought for several minutes about striking up conversation before deciding to take the plunge. After all, what could he do to me now? He was no longer powerful and mighty.

'Are you nervous Comrade Ivashko?' I asked.

He turned towards me and with a forced grin answered that he wasn't. Not at all. There is every indication that the court will be fair. And if it's not, then democracy will pay the price.'

I wasn't sure but I guessed he meant that Chairman Zorkin had granted the Communist Party rooms in the court building during the hearing, two million roubles and access to government cars so that it could adequately mount its case before him, and that if the ruling was unfavourable the party could always claim that democracy in Russia didn't extend to political tolerance. But maybe he meant that if the ruling was negative the communists could try to again seize the country.

'Of course,' I ventured, 'some people don't believe the Communist Party should be given the benefit of fair judgment. Some people say it is a criminal organisation.'

Ivashko let out a quiet laugh. 'Criminal, you think! Yes it committed crimes. But at least it was repenting. And what about that gold-digger Gorbachev—so far I have heard no apology from him for lying.'

Leaning towards me to make sure I heard him clearly, Ivashko went on.

'Young lady, let me tell you that when Gorbachev began the changes in 1985, the Politburo supported him. It thought change was necessary. But Gorbachev didn't want change. He wanted to destroy the communists. The only criminal is Gorbachev. He lied to us.'

As Chairman Zorkin entered the courtroom to deliver his verdict, I wanted to sneak some final questions to Comrade Ivashko—If Gorbachev had lied to the Politburo in 1985, if *perestroika* was a calculated attempt to kill communism, why did Mikhail Sergeyevich fight so hard to save the party? And why would he have remained faithful to Lenin even after the coup attempt? But it was too late. Chairman Zorkin began to read his judgment.

Zorkin found that President Yeltsin had acted legally in banning the activities of the Communist Party's ruling bodies. But he had no right to ban the party itself. That was undemocratic. Indeed, the party was now free to regroup and its property, at least that which hadn't been used by its ruling bodies, should be returned to it.

None of it made sense. In the name of democracy, the communists were back in business!

CHAPTER 14

GOD INSTRUCTS US TO SHARE

The connections between the mafia and government are very well settled because for work to be profitable we need good government connections.

CHIEF OF THE BRATVA CLAN, MOSCOW, 1992

On Pushkin Square, McDonald's was doing a roaring trade, keeping its prices artificially low, doing its bit to shelter people from the cruelty of inflation. The communists were appalled that Russians liked Big Macs, and even more distressed that the Canadian chief of McDonald's in Moscow had moved into a luxury apartment on the top floor of Stalin's House on the Embankment, once reserved for the Soviet elite. But such were these peculiar times. For most people there were bigger things to worry about.

As the queue for burgers weaved around the corner onto the newly named Tverskaya Street, old *babushkas* stomped the pavements, their hands stretched out for a few spare roubles. As they blessed themselves and promised redemption for the more generous, the words on the lips of those who dug deep to help them were 'Khozyaina nyet' ['No-one is in charge'].

There was a new order, as Yeltsin boasted almost daily, but there seemed to be no-one making laws or rules to ensure it was imposed fairly. Inflation was stampeding people into poverty while the *appa-ratchiks* and the *nomenklatura* turned the old socialist empires they ran into private companies. They'd had a lot of experience at lining their own pockets with the proceeds of their corrupt scams. But the need to keep up appearances and at least some degree of grudging deference for Leninism in Soviet times had meant there had been an upper limit to their gall, above which their corrupt practices might be exposed as 'economic crimes'. Now they were stealing as much as they wanted openly without the slightest hint of fear or shame.

Strolling home from the shops one day, I chatted with a middle-aged woman eager to share her thoughts on privatisation.

'It's theft,' she said as we stopped at a corner waiting for a safe moment to cross the road. 'They're not privatising at all, they're grabbing whatever they're closest to as always. You weren't around to see it but the party has always had the first bite of the cherry in this country. It's never been any different. We worked, they reaped the profit. The state was our property but they owned it. They're like the upper crust of the mafia freeloading off everyone else, thieving what they can. But you wait until the next layer finds out what they're doing. It'll be war here.'

As we stepped onto the road, a black BMW whizzed around the corner, catching my companion's eye before mine. She stepped forward to grab me, tripping on a crack in the asphalt. The driver didn't bother to stop.

'I feel sad for my mother,' she said, dusting herself off as she struggled to her feet. 'She believes the communists bequeathed us some morality to see us through this new experiment. But I don't think she's right.'

She wasn't. The old party mafia had corrupted and stolen while the KGB and police protected them, punishing anyone who competed with the elite for a cut of the action. They jailed tens of thousands of people wanting to live a little more like the *nomenklatura*, but the party bosses, at the same time, relied on these 'economic criminals' to supply whatever the decrepit state system couldn't. But the Soviet criminals couldn't complain. For services rendered, they got to do a little non-party business themselves, using state resources to build virtual industries operating in the shadows of the real, command economy.

Of course, the bearers of Lenin's legacy—the party men—invariably got a cut of the profits made by the entrepreneurs. And more often than not they pooled resources to pull in even bigger money. They were caught in a symbiotic web of criminality.

The same party men and criminal traders were now the new rich, men with no personal experience of basic decency or virtue. For them only one factor had changed. Power was no longer doled out by the party. Now property was power.

Boris Yeltsin's government could think of no more imaginative way to move to wholesale capitalism. In a country which needed to create capitalists out of the so-called red directors (the men who had run industry on behalf of the Communist Party), what better way than to turn a blind eye to their activities. Perhaps one day they'd pour their profits back into Russia. Instead, old enterprises which the new rich couldn't make a buck out of were left to wither, their workers thrown into unemployment, making the gap between rich and poor more obvious by the day.

'What's wrong with former members of the Communist Party taking over the factories and trading resources?' asked the Privatisation Minister, Anatoly Chubais. 'After all, they have the skills to manage and trade.' And he was right. The only problem was that literally thousands of other Russians wanted to manage and trade as well. And now there was no Communist Party or KGB to get in their way. It was just a matter of time before the new order erupted into a battle for resources.

If the government didn't see the problem, the parliament did, but Boris Yeltsin's feud with his vice president, Alexander Rutskoi, and the Chairman of the Russian Parliament, Ruslan Khasbulatov, had paralysed the legislature. While the *nomenklatura* were stashing away millions of dollars from resource selling in foreign banks, the parliament battled with the president over who should be making laws to stop them. The result was mayhem. When the parliament passed laws, the president annulled them. When the president issued decrees, the parliament wrote laws to override him. Both sides watched helplessly as right under their noses the Telecommunications Ministry, among others, turned itself into a private company, signing joint ventures with western companies which would bump up the prices average Russians paid for phone calls by 3000 per cent. Not a rouble of the profit went back to the state. And what the Telecommunications Ministry had done was merely the tip of the iceberg. It was no secret that some people were making lots of money off the state. But to defend their ideology, Boris Yeltsin and his 'boys in pink pants' chose to shut their eyes, just like the party bosses did under Brezhnev.

'I think Yeltsin believes nothing has changed here,' complained my shopping companion, struggling with her heavy bags of cheap potatoes as we made our way down the road. 'Before, we kept our mouths shut and watched them live the good life. But we had no choice then.

'If I'd complained to anyone, they would have reminded me that I had a husband and child and a mother who was getting old. But now? Well, I'll remind them of some of the things they got away with then and tell them that if they think they can start building themselves palaces with our money, then they're going to have a fight on their hands and not just from the black marketeers. They can go to hell.' The woman had become so incensed, she turned back for a last dig even after she'd said goodbye.

'Do you know the party bosses in the Central Asian republics had huge villas with dozens of rooms and even gold taps in the bathrooms—and we lived like trapped mice.'

But just as they had lived ostentatiously in the old days, so too would those prospering in Yeltsin's new order. Like Brezhnev's breast heaving under the weight of the dozens of medals of honour he had bestowed upon himself for services to socialism, the new rich flaunted their wealth at every turn, driving around Moscow and St Petersburg in their brassy new foreign cars, their fingers barely able to hold the steering wheel for the gold dripping from them. They were utterly shameless.

They shopped at Galeries Lafayette and Benetton which had opened up in GUM, the central department store on Red Square, flicking out crisp new hundred dollar bills for skimpy jumpers they might have bought elsewhere for an eighth of the price. The wives of the rich, with their emerald and diamond rings, were chauffeur-driven in Rolls Royces to the new shopping arcades seemingly built exclusively for them, since foreigners were paupers by comparison and average Muscovites certainly didn't have the money to shop in them. It was almost sport to watch the rich spend an average monthly wage on a haircut, then walk into the next shop where they'd blow forty or even fifty thousand dollars on a few Versace or Chanel outfits.

I remember thinking how much emotion I'd wasted feeling like a bloated capitalist pig in the socialist capital because I had enough money to travel to London for my shopping needs. I had walked into a flashy clothes shop in the Petrovsky Passage, an elegant mall on one of Moscow's most aristocratic streets, and eyeing a dress that I quite liked, I asked the shop attendant if I could take a closer look at it. Clearly I didn't look like I'd have the sort of money needed to buy it. Literally looking me up and down, she crooned, 'Oy! It's three thousand dollars you know. You'd probably be better off looking in the street kiosks.'

If the rich dressed to kill, they'd have to eat better than most as well. In the hard currency food shops you could scarcely move for full-length mink coats and silk suits. Loading their trolleys with hundreds of dollars worth of exorbitantly priced goods, the rich would pay in cash or with corporate American Express cards. Their plastic carry-bags groaned with New York cut sirloin, whisky and cognac, but I wondered whether they cooked at home all that much. It didn't seem possible given the number of nouveaux riches, or New Russians as they were called in Moscow, who crowded into the more expensive restaurants in the major cities every night of the week, hiring private rooms or more often entire establishments while they paid US$40 for a teaspoon of black caviar they could have bought in the kiosks for US$5.

Image counted for a lot. It wouldn't do to be driven around in a Rolls to the most expensive shops and restaurants in town if, at night, you returned to a drab, small apartment on the fifteenth floor of a monstrous prefabricated Soviet-style block. One had to openly demonstrate one's wealth. That was almost as important as having the money to begin with. So those who could lay their hands on a chic apartment on the central boulevards of Moscow or St Petersburg did so. Others moved into the pre-revolutionary mansions not destroyed by the communists. Some were so grand they even had their own churches tucked away behind their red brick fences. But no matter how high the fences, the occupants couldn't escape a dose of reality every now and then. 'Moscow can be so depressing,' I overheard one woman comment to another as they stepped into their chauffeur-driven Mercedes, 'I'm tired of the beggars everywhere. Why doesn't the government do something about it? It's so ugly!'

Indeed it was. And unable to cope with the reality of capitalism Russian-style, the new rich opted for a little reprieve by chartering aircraft, if they hadn't yet bought their own, to fly them to Paris or London for the weekend. Flying on normal commercial jets was far too common. In Europe, they'd shop for real estate, buying up the very biggest in the very best areas. The poshest real estate agents in

London were bowled over by the enquiries they received within a year of communism collapsing. One of them reported that he sold five London mansions to Russian entrepreneurs, each of them for over £3 million. Many wanted homes near posh boarding schools where they'd pay £20 000 a term to educate their children. The New Russians were free to be filthy rich.

'At some point along the road to our conversion from communism to capitalism, there had to be a point where the robber barons came out of hiding,' said Boris Kagarlitsky, the socialist who a year before had predicted the showdown between Yeltsin and Gorbachev. 'It just so happens that the robber barons are the *nomenklatura* who have no real experience at producing. They can "manage resources", steal and live well. Actually, I think what we have here is not *nomenklatura* privatisation as people like to call it. It's state capitalism. A lot of western scholars have already identified it. It's where the state decides who can own what, how much money they can make and when. Otherwise, why isn't the government doing anything to stop them?'

It was a simple explanation and one which wasn't far from the truth. But on the streets, it was causing disquiet which was growing by the day. Outside McDonald's a *babushka* approached me for money which I gave willingly, asking her to spare me the anointment of redemption.

'Ah! You're a foreigner, you don't need to be saved. It's our own who need our prayers,' she said. It was an unusually calm and considered comment for the times.

Konstantin Borovoi was a maths professor in the old days but he'd also made a small fortune wheeling and dealing right under the regime's nose, selling the party his knowledge of computer software. When the floodgates opened, he started the Russian Commodities and Raw Materials Exchange and ended up indirectly controlling about 12 per cent of Russia's economy. Nonetheless Borovoi was a pessimist.

'It'll all end badly,' he told me, sitting in a salmon-coloured leather chair in his Moscow office.

'The majority of Russians think entrepreneurs are swindlers. For seventy years, they were driven underground so they don't have any business ethics. It's easy to think of them as criminals or the mafia because they operate now like they did in the old days. It's all they know. Even the ones who want to be honest won't have much of a chance because they need to make enough money *"na levo"* [under the table] to pay their taxes which are extraordinarily high, and inflation forces them to look for ways to make a killing and avoid long-term investment. It all leads to one thing—criminality, even if all they're doing is evading taxes. Everyone in business in Russia thinks like a criminal.

'I know a plant which produced construction equipment which, as you'd know, was in short supply in the Soviet Union for fifty years. But the director mysteriously found the supplies to start producing and he's been churning out construction supplies for the whole of 1992. He uses the same state plant, the same workers, the same equipment and the same supplies which should have produced the same product for the state. Only it didn't. He bribes government officials so that the books show the plant is operating at a loss. But nearly all the profits are going into the director's pocket.

'He figures, "Why should I work my backside off for the government?" And he's right. But why should the government just give him the plant? If it does, people will scream robbery. So he's doing what he learnt to do in the Soviet Union—steal! And he's helped all the way up and down the line by people, mostly bureaucrats, who also get a cut and can carry on their own business as a result. There are people who provide him with materials, trucks, trains, distribution points. That's state capitalism at play.'

Borovoi sat fiddling with a pen, shaking his head in despair.

'My question is this. Isn't this what Russia needs to get the country working again? And what would average people prefer? The old system which produced nothing and made everyone equally poor, or a new system which gives some of us a chance?

'We've taken the first step. That was easy. Now we have to take the second step which is much harder. That involves changing people's attitudes which they've developed over decades, and passed down to their kids—that business is bad and businessmen are criminals. A lot of ours are. But unless we have something of our own to protect, we'll never learn how to be honest.'

But the sense of unfairness most people felt was too pervasive to allow them to see that perhaps Russia was going through a stage from which it might emerge a more stable and wealthy nation.

'You tell your friend Borovoi,' said Natasha when I relayed his explanation of the new capitalist phenomena, 'that he might well be right, but by the time the theft has stopped, we'll be dead.

'Tell him that the people he thinks don't like business aren't full of envy. They're hungry, they're poor and they're unemployed. And they're getting very angry because they can't see the difference between the new rich and the old rich. The only difference was that before we had jobs, and we had food we could afford to buy. Ask Mr Borovoi whether he's sharing his millions with the people he used to sit around the kitchen table with, whispering about the time when they'd all live like Americans.'

As the new rich feasted at a banquet table provided by the state, tens of thousands of people in the old pyramid of Soviet crime began to scramble for a slice of the action. The Soviet *vory v' zakone*, the big-time criminals; the *tolkachi*, the 'grey area' traders; and even the *shushara*, the low-level black marketeers were regrouping, searching out new business.

In the old days, the black-market traders negotiated illicit deals between state agencies and enterprises for materials which 'on paper' had never been produced. Now, enterprises were free to trade between themselves, and without the need to meet quotas there was less need to fiddle the books. They were, of course, still needed to smuggle raw materials across borders and to finance illegal companies selling state-produced goods. But soon they wouldn't be. They were facing a brave new world. Unless they got in on the ground floor of Russian capitalism, they'd be left behind.

In the lower echelons of crime, racketeering was an obvious way to bolster the coffers.

The privately run kiosks sanctioned by Gorbachev had faced the first wave of racketeering. But that was small fare by 1992 when four out of every five businesses were paying racketeers just so they could keep their doors open. The police were at a loss.

There was little point trying to bust the racketeers. Not only was the problem too widespread, it was a dangerous game to play. Murder and hostage taking were not uncommon. In any event, there was money to be made and the Russian police had never been especially moral. They were on the take and obviously so. Rather than evade the law, the racketeers simply decided to pay it off. Police stations were targeted by clans wanting to take over a particular patch. In return for the right to operate, they'd give the police new Mercedes Benzs for their personal use and organise the importation of BMWs for use as squad cars, which the government gratefully accepted. If kiosk owners were inclined to complain about the ever increasing extortion demands made of them, they knew better than to go to the police. They'd be bashed or murdered by the standover merchants to whom the police were leaking information. By the end of 1992 police would refer applications to open street kiosks to the local clan leaders. The best the retailers could do was bump up their prices to cover their overheads. Again, average people paid the price.

Thuggery was on the rise. In Moscow alone, 3500 criminal gangs slaughtered more than a thousand people before 1992 came to a close and there seemed to be no sign of the violence petering out. The murder rate hit 64 a day in the last six months of the year.

Firearms offences were up 250 per cent. More than 300 000 'crimes of racketeering' were committed, in which standover criminals demanded protection money or profits from businessmen operating semi-legally out of the shadows of the old command economy. Contracts for supplies, services, distribution and exports which weren't fulfilled or which were changed, even minutely, often ended in gangland style assassination. Because there were no business laws for the courts to oversee, most businesspeople turned to criminal gangs to settle their commercial conflicts. There didn't seem to be a corner of the country nor any sector of the economy where criminality wasn't taking hold.

In Nizhnevartovsk, Russia's oil producing boom town in western Siberia, the central rigs had been privatised in a semi-legal way. The old bosses were simply given the opportunity to take more of the company than the workers. Appointed in Brezhnev's time, they had not only survived Gorbachev's purge of old party hacks, they were now shedding their ideological hang-ups, looking for foreign capital to help restart the engines which they hoped would soon spill out millions of dollars of rich black oil. Export licences were supplied by the Ministry of Natural Resources which was to get a 30 per cent cut of all profits. Everyone was optimistic. The directors would soon be billionaires, the ministry's *apparatchiks* who'd defied a parliamentary order not to issue export licences would soon be building *dachas* in the south of France and the locals would be employed. But then the old illegals came knocking.

Misha and Sergei were the region's ringleaders who for years had commandeered state trucks to move what little the plant produced across the Polish border, bribing police and customs officials along the route to reap the plant's directors a healthy and completely illegal profit. Now it was time to take a cut of whatever legitimate business the directors were about to engage in.

Needless to say, the directors were unenthusiastic about the 'invitation' they received from Misha and Sergei.

'You know, they basically wanted to keep everything for themselves,' Sergei told me in the Spanish Bar of the Hotel Moskva near Red Square. Two burly thugs sat at the table next to us with Sasha, my KGB friend, who had introduced Sergei to me.

'I've done my bit to cause Russia's bleeding, I admit that. But there was no choice before. We had business to do and they wouldn't let us do it. They couldn't even supply the factory with electricity, they were so incompetent. But things are different now and if this is meant to be a fair redistribution of this country's wealth I want my cut. That's fair isn't it?

'We asked only for 50 per cent of the profit which was a good deal for them. There are about twenty of us in our clan and we had all worked for them tirelessly, without fear of the authorities, for years. I even went to jail for them. There are only eight of them on the board. Half of the profit is actually quite generous when you count the number of people who need a cut,' he said, mocking Lenin's egalitarianism.

'And when they turned you down? What did you say?' I asked.

'I said nothing.' Sergei, snapped his fingers for the bill. The conversation was over.

Sergei and his cohorts allegedly murdered the chairman of the board, forcing his car off the road into an idle oil tanker. They leant on the rest of the board until they resigned. The clan members then installed themselves as the new directors. Of course they lost all interest from the foreign companies which had been eager to enter into a joint venture with the enterprise, but that, I suspect, wouldn't have bothered Sergei. As Sasha explained, the clan went on to make a fortune. With a well-established network of friends in important positions, they had all the export licences transferred to their own company.

'They're working out their patches,' said the Moscow Chief of Police, resigned and quite unashamed. 'When they've carved up the country, they'll stop!'

By 1993 when the old Soviet banking world had fractured into hundreds of new, independent banks, the number of assassinations was dizzying. My friends were excited when new banners were put up around Moscow advertising new products, new independent banks. But they were in mute shock when bankers, refusing extortion demands, were gunned down on the streets. The chairman of the new Rosselkhozbank, a director of the St Petersburg branch of the new Inkombank, the chairman of the new Pragmabank and the chief executive officer of the Kuzbassprombank were the first to go. Their deaths were just a part of life in the new Russia—simple, brutal solutions in a chaotic environment where the opportunity for instant wealth was always just a gunshot away.

'The war will end soon,' said Victor Yerin, the Interior Minister, 'it must, soon there'll be no-one left to kill.'

As I watched the news every night on television, the minister's words seemed not far from the truth because it was not only the top end of town which was being hit by the racketeers and standover merchants. By the winter of 1992, the gangs were hitting anyone and everyone for money regardless of their ability to pay.

Babushkas whined that they couldn't leave their apartments to look for food they could afford, they were too frightened. And for a time, Natasha also was too scared to come to Moscow. She was walking through one of Moscow's metro tunnels late one night when she heard a gunshot ring out. An innocent man had been shot dead, caught in the middle of a clan feud over who would control trade in the tunnel. The experience completely unnerved her.

'Now you have to admit,' said Natasha, 'that life is a little out of hand! Who's running this country? Where's the president, or is he drunk?

'Ah, I despair—just like Gogol. You remember what he said? "Russia where are you rushing to?" Well, if this is your capitalism and we are rushing towards it, then I'm getting off the train. I want to go home.'

Natasha's despair was heartbreaking but nothing was the same anymore. Friends had always helped each other out with connections to ensure access to products in short supply. Such were the human dimensions of survival in the Soviet Union. But it was different now. Some of Natasha's oldest Russian friends wanted her to ask her foreign friends for contacts to ease the way into the world of business. They were just doing what they'd always done. But the intensity of their need was different. It was more pressing and exhausting. Even I feared seeing some of my acquaintances because I knew they'd ask for money or contacts. Who did I know who wanted to buy this or that Soviet-made product? Did I have any friends in the west who wanted to 'invest' in one scam or another? My patience hit rock bottom when a friend asked me if I could carry a suitcase of stolen *spichki* (matches) to Australia on my next visit and find a distributor willing to handle them. My office fax machine suddenly started spurting out business proposals from factories in Siberia and the Arctic Circle. Some of my more business-oriented friends had clearly forgotten to ask me whether I'd mind the ABC's equipment being used for their private purposes.

'You work for the state don't you?' said one of them. 'What's the problem?' It was a lame but logical reply for *Homo Sovieticus*.

Nostalgia bit hard, even at me. I used to feel safe catching the metro at night, walking through Red Square alone at dusk, thumbing a lift home after a party. I couldn't have conceived of a time when people would be gunned down in the streets of Moscow. But by mid 1992 you could watch television footage of cars being blown to smithereens, or apartment doors being blown open with TNT while outside your lounge room window gunshots would ring out—and not only during the night.

Between courses one summer day at my favourite Georgian restaurant in Moscow, an almighty battle erupted between two clan leaders over which of them would take the last window table. The shouting soon produced clenched fists, which attracted the attention of the clan leaders' protectors who came running from their bosses' Mercedes parked across the footpath outside the restaurant. Before I had time to get out of the place, gunshots had shattered the window so that neither of the clan leaders could catch the view. Fortunately no-one was hurt.

In Moscow's soulless suburbs, it was a reign of terror. Racketeers moved into every corner of people's lives. In Krylatskoe, the suburb where I lived, the garbage was left uncollected for two weeks in the summer before numerous phone calls to the council uncovered the fact that racketeers had impounded the council's trucks until it paid protection money of millions of roubles. At the international airport, taxi drivers had created a brotherhood to extract a non-negotiable inflated fare to the city, half of which was siphoned off by the racketeers. Even the *babushkas'* finicky zeal for bureaucratic compliance didn't escape the mafia. Racketeers moved into the old Soviet public lawyers' system which had offices in just about every apartment block, set their prices as a collective and *babushkas* found themselves paying half their pensions to write their wills, copy their internal passports for their building administrators and to privatise their apartments.

The racketeers soon had competition from the growing army of young unemployed calling themselves bandits. They engaged in subsidiary criminal activities—procuring prostitutes, protecting brothels, mugging tourists, selling drugs—aberrant behaviour which had become normal in Russia's new capitalism. The younger, inexperienced bandits moved into the compounds where foreigners lived, reasoning that foreigners had money ready for the taking.

At first, my windscreen wipers were the target. Each morning I'd have to trudge off in search of a new set, the old ones swiped the night before. Seeing a way to double their money, the bandits were soon offering to sell me back what they'd stolen from me.

'It's up to you,' they'd say when I argued the point. 'You can go to the kiosk and buy new ones if you want, but we'll give you these ones for much less.'

'And if I don't buy them back? You'll just steal the next set I buy?' I asked.

'Yeah! But this must be inconvenient for you. Why don't you save yourself the hassle? For fifty dollars a month, we'll leave your wipers alone and we'll tell the *militsiya* not to pick you up around the corner for not having them on your car.'

Kafka couldn't have done the plot justice. Indeed some foreigners in the compound who refused to pay up, unlike me, were stopped by the *militsiya* who once or twice even threatened them with syringes unless they paid the bribe demanded.

Dishonesty was so firmly implanted, cynicism so ingrained in the Russian character that not even the young saw merit in working honestly for their own future.

'If we don't make money now, we'll have nothing when the communists come back,' one of them told me when I asked him why he didn't put his entrepreneurial skills to better use. They didn't believe that democracy would ever take root.

The bolder bandits didn't waste their time on petty crime. They moved into gun-running, selling the weapons stolen by the old racketeers to third parties, generally fruit and vegetable sellers at the farmers' markets who casually stacked them beneath sacks of potatoes. They were just another commodity to be sold.

'I have a very cheap Kalashnikov,' one Azerbaijani fruit seller told my friend Max, whom I'd sent to the markets to investigate. 'Two thousand dollars and I'll throw in the ammunition!'

Makarov pistols could be had for US$1200 each and F-1 hand grenades pilfered from Soviet army bases for US$50 a piece. Even a SR-25 sniper's rifle with a silencer, manufactured in the United States, could be snapped up for a mere US$5000. In the warped world of the new Russia, the buyers were businesspeople wanting to protect themselves, and one-time state security officers out on their own, marking out their patches.

The police made some effort to bust the arms traders and for a while took enormous pride every time one of their market raids was filmed by a foreign TV network trying to capture the new 'wild west' on film. But the police didn't see the irony in their demand for money in return for the right to film. And when a ban was slapped on foreign film crews paying officials for film access or interviews, the raids mysteriously slowed down.

The cry for order was bellowed from every corner of the country. Even Boris Yeltsin said he could no longer distinguish the business-men who were among the biggest arms buyers from the criminals who sold them. He created an Organised Crime Department, not dissimilar to that which tried to keep New York's gangs in check in the 1950s. But even though the number of crimes the department solved was quite high, it wasn't nearly as high as the crime rate.

The older criminal gangs—the so-called new entrepreneurs—had begun to look a little unsophisticated compared to the younger breed by the beginning of 1993. Once strong and proud district gangs were falling to the authorities. Ominously, the gangs decided to group together for more muscle.

In Voronezh, several members of one criminal gang were arrested and charged with committing thirteen murders when they raided the guard detail of a motorised infantry battalion. During their killing spree, they managed to steal 34 machine guns with silencers, 301 pistols, 4000 rounds of ammunition and a grenade launcher. They could easily have taken hostage what remained of the KGB. The Voronezh gang leaders were so angry at the apprehension of their underlings, they hooked up with a huge inter-regional gang which moved into the highly specialised area of underworld contract assassinations. The idea was to fight back. The group boasted that five of its members were OMON—the Interior Ministry's special taskforce.

In fact, no sooner would the special organised crime units infiltrate a gang than new members would be recruited to assume the responsibilities of those put behind bars. The new Russian criminal world was beginning to resemble the old *nomenklatura* very closely.

The Russian Businessmen's Club opened its doors in the winter of 1992. In the car-park, Saabs and Rolls Royces disgorged men in Armani suits for whom money still held no meaning. They handed over their heavy pure wool overcoats bought in Paris and Milan, along with their pistols, to stunned *babushkas* whose job it had always been to run the cloak-rooms at the entrances to public places. As they settled into huge leather armchairs to sip on Jack Daniels and nibble delicate, imported water biscuits topped with foie gras, they eyed each other cautiously, like mafia dons meeting to carve up New York. But, true Russians, they could still make jokes about the situation.

'Hey, Volodya, heard the one about the New Russian with the beautiful new tie? Ivan says to him: "Nice tie! How much did it cost?" Sasha answers: "It's Versace, I paid a thousand dollars for it!" "A thousand dollars?" says Ivan. "I know where you could have got it for two thousand!"'

As they snickered and gossiped, Konstantin Borovoi, the head of the Russian Commodities and Raw Materials Exchange, escorted me around the opulent clubrooms, explaining that there were myriad ways to get rich in Russia and not all of them involved criminality. Some people were honest, said the chief patron of Moscow's latest 'money club', others just well connected to people in high places.

Borovoi often spoke out against the criminalisation of the new Russian economy. 'The mafia will kill it for the whole place, if we're not careful. It's OK to pay a few racketeers to keep off your back, and I think it's forgivable that the *nomenklatura* stole all they stole. That's just human nature. But we have to make the transition at some point from lawlessness to some sort of business culture and the only way we'll do that is if we start institutions ourselves to support our new way of life.' Borovoi had done his bit, and his exchange had developed into a thriving, mafia-free business. Now he wanted others to follow suit.

'We need businessmen who'll start up finance schools where young people can go and learn about money. It's clear to me that capitalism in Russia had to begin in the shadows of communism. What choice was there? But now we need rules and a business culture and only we—the rich—can create that. We need a Russian Chamber of Commerce in every major city—places where people can go for advice, contacts, contracts. Unless this happens, the mafia will do the job for us. The mafia is thriving because it operates by the old rules—connections, criminality. Nothing has replaced these yet. They are the only things which produce results. So you can say the mafia is the only thing which works properly at the moment. But they want big money fast. It's all short-term investment.'

Hovering on the edge of our conversation was Dmitri Kovalev who'd become a millionaire in the first year of Russian capitalism by buying up prime city real estate in both Moscow and St Petersburg.

'One year ago, you could get rich overnight. If you had connections in the ministries you could steal resources. If you had a bit of money behind you to begin with you could buy property, like I did. I own half of Leninski Prospekt [one of the main boulevards leading into the centre of Moscow on the more affluent side of the city] but those times are over. Now we are moving into a dangerous period. We can allow the mobsters to continue their business, or we can cut them out of business. It's just a question of acting for the country or continuing to act for ourselves as individuals. If we are selfish, we can hire mobsters to put our competitors out of business and those of us who survive will get richer and richer. But there's no challenge in that. The challenge is to do clean business,' said Kovalev.

Indeed it was. It just didn't seem possible in a country where the racketeers were so brazen that honest, small-time traders and shop-keepers were too frightened to advertise what they had to sell. Kovalev promised to introduce me to someone I would remember from the Soviet era who was now involved in clean business. 'Meet me tomorrow at 11 a.m. in the foyer of the Slavyanskaya Hotel,' he said.

Valentin Pavlov's hair was still spiky, just as it had been when he was the Soviet Union's last prime minister, serving the cause of the hardline communists. As I looked at the dashing figure he cut in his new Boss suit, I remembered his last contribution to reform when he told the old Soviet parliament that Mikhail Gorbachev had too much on his plate. Some of the president's powers, he argued, ought to be transferred to him, the prime minister. His plea hadn't been successful, and a month later Pavlov was sitting with the GKChP, his hands trembling with fear and the alcohol poisoning his body. In the year he'd spent in Moscow's Lefortovo Prison before charges of treason against him and his fellow putschists were dropped (as that was easier than mounting prosecutions), he'd had time—lots of it—to rethink!

In the hard currency bar of the Radisson Slavyanskaya Hotel, he was no longer plagued by anti-western thoughts. Nor did command economics hold the key, in his mind, to a new and better future. 'But I'm not a fully fledged capitalist either. I make money and I like making money, but there has to be discipline somewhere in the picture. In the west, there are laws. Here, there's the mafia and unless we're very careful, the mafia will soon be making the laws.

'I'm doing what the old criminals in the Soviet era used to do and for which they were punished. I'm finding supplies and trading links for factories which can't find them on their own. Before the Soviet Union broke up, the Soviet bureaucracy was the problem. It couldn't supply manufacturers with what they needed. Now the problem is that because the country has broken up into fifteen separate countries and all of them are exercising their new-found liberty to trade with whoever they want, they have to find their own supplies and they need someone to help them. Sure, there's the criminals, but I charge less! And I have contacts in government who know which factory produces what. I set up links between producers and they pay me for the service and I pay my government contacts.'

'But aren't you exploiting government connections and corrupting them to make money?' I asked.

'You can look at it that way if you like, but you'd be naive. The fact is that the government doesn't need someone like me to introduce them to the world of dirty business. The link between dirty business and government is well and truly established in this country. I'm not playing that game. I'm playing a different game completely. I don't rely on the security forces to keep me and my business protected. I don't launder state money to make money for myself. I buy information from *apparatchiks* and help factories get started in the process. I'm helping Russia help itself.'

Like others who were well connected, he'd received offers to 'wash down' public money given to business-minded individuals to build badly needed housing or kick-start food producing factories. He could have done what many of his former communist mates did and borrowed ear-marked government grants at exorbitant interest rates to use for private purposes. Dozens of independent banks in Moscow and St Petersburg began life with public funds targeted for projects which were simply put on hold until enough private money had been made. Often the money disappeared and with it the hopes of people on waiting lists for new apartments or child care centres. But not always. If a project came back on course, the private investment component would mean there were more funds which could be used to 'build better houses', and the entrepreneur in whose charge it had been placed would indeed commission bigger, better houses—from which he would snatch a profit. But Pavlov resisted the temptation. Or so he claimed.

Others couldn't. Mostbank's headquarters were unassuming. But behind its drab front Vladimir Gusinsky had made a killing, thanks to his friendship with Moscow's mayor, Yuri Luzhkov, a powerbroker in his own right. Luzhkov gave his old friend the Moscow city government's funds to administer and with them the one-time theatre director created a bank whose profits he ploughed into buying city real estate for himself—an enterprise made easier by his links with top bureaucrats who freed up some of the best buildings for him and cut through the red tape which would have defeated anyone else. Of course his wealth required protection which he bought from the KGB. He hired 3000 security officers, many of them Chechens from southern Russia, led by the former chief of the KGB's political department. Better security was hard to find.

But Mostbank was merely one of thousands of privately owned financial institutions with links to government which privatised parts of the state using the state's funds and created in the process their own little mafias to protect them, ward off competition and collect bad debts.

Russia might have had more banks per square metre than any other country in the world but walk along Moscow's cracked footpaths and you'd be lucky not to trip and break your leg. Try to find a pair of contact lenses in 1993, a cappuccino maker for a cafe, doors and windows for your summer *dacha*, or even a secure privately run warehouse to store what your factory was producing. The belly of the economy was empty, screaming for nourishment. But it would come only slowly for the profits were small and long-term, the overheads high and the game very dangerous to play. But, nonetheless, some tried.

In Norilsk in central Siberia, Volodya, as he was introduced to me, was tired of watching the scams. He'd worked all his adult life at Norilsk Nickel which developed a third of the world's nickel reserves. Its exports had a huge impact upon the supply and demand balances on western markets of not only nickel, the key component of stainless steel, but of platinum and palladium. When the government handed Volodya his 10 000 rouble voucher, he went straight to the Privatisation Office and asked to invest it in the company, hoping that soon Norilsk Nickel would be privatised. But that's not the way it turned out.

Workers' shares in Norilsk Nickel were capped way below 50 per cent while the government kept a controlling block of shares to tender for a loan. In 1993, the government offered its shares in the company to any would-be investor who was prepared to lend the state US$170 million, with what remained of Norilsk Nickel as security. Uneximbank which had organised the loan tender for the government not surprisingly won the deal. But as the term of the loan drew near, the government announced it couldn't pay its debt and the bank was left controlling 38 per cent of a very profitable company. Volodya watched in despair, increasingly despondent about where his country was heading.

'It was a corrupt deal and every worker at the plant knew it. But what could we do? By the time the poorer of us sold our shares to the bank, the workers had less than 15 per cent of Norilsk Nickel. That wasn't even enough to force them to pay us our wages.

'One day I went home and started thinking. It was clear they'd stolen the company from us legally. It was like dancing with the devil. Communism got us one way. Capitalism went about it another. Both ways, we were the losers. So I said to my wife, it's time to start taking risks. Sure I could stay at the plant, working my arse off for no wage while those bastards skimmed cream off the top. But why? Where would I be in twenty years? What would my kids have?

'So I started a business. It was small but it paid the bills and kept us fed and can you believe this—no-one came knocking at the door for a cut! I thought either this is a miracle or my business isn't worth hitting.'

Volodya's business might have looked meagre but it would grow into one of Russia's most successful manufacturers of doors and window frames, distributed from the Volga to the Urals, from Siberia to the Pacific rim. He was even exporting to the Baltic states and won contracts with governments in the central Asian states. By the time the local mafia caught up with him, he was so wealthy he could afford to hire his own security.

'I was low-key. I didn't drive around in a BMW or Audi. I didn't buy my own aircraft to fly me around. And my wife still cooks my meals at night. We're not interested in the high life at all. Probably that's why the mafia missed me.

'I paid all my taxes too. Not once did I cheat which wasn't easy. I was paying 80 per cent of what I was making which meant that growth was very slow. And I legally bought all the steel and aluminium for my plant. I didn't bribe anyone. But the strangest thing was that the people I was dealing with to buy supplies and machinery actually took me seriously. Usually the people with the resources keep it to themselves or they'll only do business with people they know—their own mafia, if you like. But they did business with me. Can you believe that?' he said with one of the heartiest chuckles I'd heard in Russia in a long time.

'You should be very proud of yourself, Volodya,' I said.

'I am. But I'm proudest of the fact that I beat the mob at their own game.' He laughed, bending his left arm and thumping his right fist into the crevice. 'If you'll excuse me, Miss Correspondent, I decided to fuck them over—and it worked.'

Volodya had read an advertisement in a national business newspaper placed by a small company boasting some of the KGB's youngest, strongest defectors. The company had been formed by several ex-KGB officers including my KGB friend Sasha who'd decided to give up his short and unsuccessful career as a mobster. With a couple of his former colleagues, he spent what money he had on creating a new company which hired out its personnel to small entrepreneurs. It was a mafia-like structure with mafia-type responsibilities, but it didn't use mafia tactics. Instead, the mafia was offered the chance to cleanse itself. If it searched the country and found buyers for Volodya's windows and doors, it would get paid commission. The prospect of redemption seemed to work miracles. Volodya's business grew. The mafia made some money and Sasha's company began to get a name for itself.

Not everyone who stood up to the mafia won the day. Ivan Kiveldi paid with his life.

Kiveldi knew the power of Russia's new breed of 'entrepreneur'. Nine of his board colleagues at the Russian Business Roundtable— an association of independent, private businessmen—had been murdered in 1992.

'How could it be,' he asked the business newspaper *Delovye Ludi*, 'that honest businesspeople are being gunned down? There can be only one explanation. Only *they* are benefiting from their activities and this challenges the power of the state.

'The government and the New Russians are in business together. Everyone knows that. Eighty per cent of the Russian economy is privatised but 80 per cent of what's privatised is in the hands of the old *nomenklatura*. The government lets them do what they want. Why not? Officials are getting a good cut of the profit, so in effect not much has changed from the old times. Honest private business is competition. So what do they do? They hit us with extraordinary taxes, forcing us to choose between bankruptcy and felony. That's why Oleg Zverev was killed.'

Zverev ran the InterAtlantic Ocean Fishing Company which largely operated abroad. No Russian government departments or agencies were involved in the licensing of his business activities. And nor was Zverev willing to pay the standover merchants who tried to extort money from him. Repeatedly threatened, Zverev decided to speak out, taking his complaint to the Roundtable and to the newspapers. Within days he was dead.

'If you want to avoid bankruptcy, there is only one choice. You have to join the corrupt officials who run the government, or you have to let organised crime wash your profits, hide your assets and take them abroad for you. Even then you're paying "taxes". It's the way the state settles its accounts with private business,' wrote Alexander Zhilin, the national security editor of *Moscow News* in 1992.

Kiveldi had pledged to organise independent businessmen to campaign against what he called the criminal terrorisation of honest people. 'We will organise against Boris Yeltsin because we know it is Yeltsin who is allowing the gangs to overrun the country, creating chaos while the robber barons swindle the booty,' Kiveldi told *Delovye Ludi*.

Kiveldi also declared his opposition to the Norilsk Nickel–Uneximbank deal. 'Uneximbank is the eighth biggest in Russia. It was built by *nomenklatura* using public funds and all the criminal infrastructure which the party mafia has at its disposal. Now they are organising loans for the government at no interest. Ask yourself why. Because in return they'll get Norilsk Nickel which is worth 150 times more than they've lent the government. That suggests to me that organised crime has managed to seep into the government.'

They were his final words on the matter. Not long after, Kiveldi and his secretary were at work as usual. Both became violently ill and were taken to hospital. Two days later, they died. Traces of a radioactive cadmium-based substance were found in their blood. Boris Yeltsin expressed outrage and promised a thorough investigation to find the murderers. A 21-year-old trainee was put in charge of the case.

CHAPTER 15

LIFE GOES ON

We're very strong on culture, but very weak on civilisation.

VICTOR EROFEYEV, *MOSCOW MAGAZINE*, 1994

Put simply, Russia was in a mess after just two years of freedom. That average people managed to survive at all—live from one day to another—was the most remarkable achievement of the first couple of years after communism's collapse. It was more and more obvious that the Russians were, as Nikolai Gogol put it, more subtle and more cunning than the inhabitants of the rest of the world. How else could they have managed to live, stuck between two systems, one which had smothered them and now threatened to suffocate them beneath its crumbling rubble, the other which forced them to stand alone without the usual protections of a normal civil society. But the Russians straddled both worlds convinced that the future had to be better than the past, even if they had to build it themselves with their sheer desire to live 'normal' lives. It would take time, bitter experience and a moral compass they themselves would have to craft.

At Abortion Clinic Number 14 in central Moscow, the stairway leading to the administration office was filthy. It smelled like dogs and cats had been urinating on it for seventy years. Behind the front desk sat a buxom woman in her fifties. 'You need an abortion?' she asked flatly.

'Actually, no. I'm a journalist from Australia and I've spoken with the director who's going to show me around the clinic.'

'Wait, please,' she replied.

Nadezhda Mikhailovna with her starched white medical hat was full of apologies when she greeted me. The clinic was still stuck in the old days explained the director. I was lucky, she said, that the receptionist bothered to call her at all. 'Why should she? She's only paid twenty dollars a month. But be prepared,' she warned, 'the ways of the old days don't stop here at the front desk.'

In a shabby room at the end of a long barren hallway, a dozen or so young women—some of them no more than fifteen—sat waiting. One or two looked like they were more than three months' pregnant. They stared silent and sullen at the flapping plastic doors to the surgery which were transparent except for the accumulated grime which offered the patients inside the only privacy they would receive during the entire ordeal. There were no psychologists to counsel the women either.

'Psychologists?' said Nadezhda Mikhailovna, astounded at the suggestion.

'We have no sanitary pads to give the girls after surgery. And we don't have strong anaesthetics either. They just have to breathe deeply if they feel pain.' I should have guessed from the screeches of distress which drifted through to the waiting room.

At the foot of the gynaecological bed where the girls were hoisted sat a bucket, emptied only after every three or four procedures. I dry-retched. Nadezhda Mikhailovna apologised again.

'Yes, it's distressing. But imagine what it's like for these girls. We try as often as we can to use the suction method, but it's not always possible. And when it's not, when there are complications, the girl is usually allowed to stay here overnight so that we can monitor her.

That's if we have a bed and someone to stay the night to keep a watch on things. If we don't she goes home and if she has problems she has to go to the hospital.

'The main method of birth control is still abortion,' she said sadly, twiddling her pen as she sat behind her small desk, a huge portrait of Lenin hanging above her. 'We've tried everything to bring the rate down from its current level—5 million a year—but nothing's worked,' she said, her voice weighed down by the facts. It wasn't unusual for a girl to have had three or four abortions by the time she was eighteen. A lot of women in their thirties had gone through six or seven termination procedures.

'The only thing we haven't tried is sex education. But I'm afraid to say no-one in the government can be bothered with the problem. They have other things on their minds.'

Indeed not even Stalin who also had 'other things on his mind' managed to put a dent in the abortion figures when he outlawed the practice in 1934. (He coupled it with a massive propaganda campaign about Heroine Mothers who would produce children to help build the Soviet state.) Soviet factories were set up to produce diaphragms but unfortunately for most the devices came in just two sizes. Birth-control pills were available, but more often than not they were in short supply. As for condoms, well, Soviet condoms were usually referred to as 'galoshes' and were a dead loss because men refused to use them. So by 1955 abortion was legal again, most Russian couples unwilling to have children when they were forced to live with frequent food shortages in cramped apartments with parents or in-laws. As Natasha told me, the only form of contraception which seemed to work in the Soviet Union was the housing shortage!

One-child families were the norm. More than one child made life near impossible. I knew one woman in her forties who'd had six terminations during her marriage.

'I don't even think I bothered to tell my husband when I was pregnant,' she told me. 'I would just take the afternoon off work, go to a clinic and have an abortion. Sometimes at night I'd forget to tell him about it. I told him one time after he screamed at me because I was too washed-out to prepare him something to eat.'

It was as matter-of-fact as that. Nadezhda Mikhailovna said this was a common tale.

'It's hard for westerners to understand this,' she said, 'but abortion is still the only acceptable means of contraception—still, to this day! Sure we can buy the pill now and diaphragms and good condoms, but it's not part of our culture to use them. Whether a woman is married or not makes no difference to the equation. Generally, Russian men don't like the idea of contraception—why should they? They don't have to have the abortion. So, if a woman becomes pregnant and doesn't want to be, she'll have an abortion and the next time it comes to sex she won't think about changing her ways and using a contraceptive. She'll just block out of her mind how uncomfortable and dangerous it was to have an abortion the way we do them.'

I suggested that the abortion rate might begin to slide now that housing wasn't as severe a problem as it had been in the communist years. People were now free to move without permission. Some were making real money and buying bigger apartments. Others who were doing especially well were building their own cottages and *dachas*. Perhaps with room to move people might opt for bigger families, even unplanned bigger families! And surely now that western contraceptives were readily available, they'd become a little more popular.

'Go to a maternity hospital and you'll find the answer,' counselled Nadezhda Mikhailovna. So I did.

It was an experience I could have lived without. In the southern suburbs of Moscow, tucked away behind a psychiatric institution, the only sign that this was where women came to give birth was an old, grimy statue in a garden overgrown with weeds of a woman holding a baby. Inside, it was foul and overcrowded. Women in the early stages of labour shuffled around carefully so as not to trip on the ripped linoleum. The walls looked like they hadn't been painted since the revolution. The nursing staff were cranky. 'I've been on duty fifteen hours already,' one of them snapped at me when I asked for directions to the main office. Doctors came only when they were called and that was generally when the head nurse felt she couldn't cope with the birth at hand.

Masha, who had travelled to the United States to give birth to her children, had warned me before I went that it wouldn't be pleasant: 'The women give birth in the wards. They're not even taken to a private room, and they're expected to produce on call.

'And of course they don't let your husband or partner in with you to share the experience. They think that's degrading for the woman! Not that I think Russian men mind the practice ... but for women it's awful. They're alone with a few nurses who don't give a damn and if they're lucky, a doctor.

'Even if you wanted to have more than one child, why would you in Russia? It's a horrible experience.'

But perhaps times were changing. Perhaps women were bothered, and deeply so, by their treatment. Perhaps that was why in the 1993 parliamentary elections the Women's Party of Russia did remarkably well.

The group hadn't expected to win a single seat. But the reductions in state subsidies to factories and enterprises had hit women the hardest. It was the creches and subsidised food shops which were the first casualties of tighter fiscal policies, along with the more menial jobs which traditionally had been held by women. They were thrown into unemployment, left to search desperately for affordable food, with child care as an added burden. The Women's Party had only to remind women of the appalling lack of health care, the state of maternity hospitals, the fact that most of them could afford only one child. On polling day, the Women's Party polled higher than Russia's Choice, which fielded Boris Yeltsin's candidates. Women wanted to be written into the social equation.

But the finances needed to make life a little easier for women would have to come from the private sector, not the state. Russia's Health Minister was eager to drive home the indisputable fact that the country had seemingly insurmountable problems to resolve. Abortion clinics, maternity wards and sex education would have to wait. 'If women want help,' he was reported as saying, 'they'll have to help themselves.' So they did.

In 1995, two private abortion clinics opened in Moscow and two in St Petersburg. Run by female gynaecologists who urged counselling and support for the young women who came through their doors, they were expensive compared to the alternatives offered by the state. But they were there.

'Sure we have to charge a lot,' said the director of one of them who was too frightened to let me use her name. 'The racketeers might hear about us,' she said.

'We've bought equipment from Europe and we have a lot of staff and our doctors are emigres who've trained in the United States and were willing to come back only for a lot of money. We also emphasise the necessity of cleanliness. But all of this costs a lot in Russia these days. We hope that the time will come when any woman wanting advice on contraception or an abortion if she has no other option will be able to come to us and it will cost her as little as it costs in the state system. That's our aim.'

For Nadezhda Mikhailovna, private abortion clinics were a definite improvement. But it's easy, she reasoned, to attract private investment money to projects which will make money. The key to real change, she argued with Lenin hanging over her head, is sex education in schools.

'Russia, I'm sorry to say, is quite a few years away from having noble people willing to just give their time for free to teach our kids about sex. They get to twenty and after two or more abortions they still don't know how they got pregnant,' she said.

By the end of 1992, seven-year-old pickpockets and twelve-year-old prostitutes were a common sight in Moscow. The railways were full of them. Burglaries and muggings by children as young as six, desperate for money to buy food, were commonplace. Russian newspapers regularly carried stories about racketeering gangs at schools who stood over other kids, forcing them to steal, usually from home, unless they wanted to lose a few teeth. Teenagers who ought to have been at school got jobs with the mafia, stealing and then dismantling cars for spare parts. The drop-out rate was alarming. The Kremlin estimated that 33 per cent of children in Russia earned their own living on the streets selling newspapers or Coca-Cola or weaving through traffic at stop lights offering to wash car windows for a contribution of some sort. School offered them little. Most considered an education superfluous.

I spoke with headmaster Yevgeny Alexandrovich at School Number 18 in a dreary, polluted outer suburb in Moscow's north.

'We've managed to get rid of a few of the more obnoxious aspects of the communist education system. There are no portraits of Lenin in the classrooms anymore. The better schools are no longer strictly reserved for the privileged classes, although the new fee-paying system tends to disadvantage the poor. But now, it's possible in more than just theory for a child whose parents are factory workers to go to the same school as a child whose parents are academics. And of course we try not to teach them the Leninist view of the world and Soviet history, although it's important that they know that a Soviet version of history exists.

'But the problem is that the Education Department just doesn't have the money to print new textbooks or do anything that is new. And because our teachers are very poorly paid, they're often uninterested in taking the initiative themselves and finding books which tell the truth. They're more interested in getting away from school early enough to get to their other jobs. At least they've stayed in the system. We've lost thousands of teachers in the past few years.

Why should they stay with an education system which is confused and can't pay them what they need to live?'

The tragedy was that those who stayed in the system were generally those who couldn't find anything else to do. They weren't equipped for the new Russia and their ideas were old. 'We had one teacher,' said Yevgeny Alexandrovich, 'who refused to say the words "Commonwealth of Independent States" in her classroom. She was teaching her kids that they lived in the Soviet Union! Tell that to a thirteen or fourteen-year-old and they'll pack their books up and never come back. They'll know it's not the truth!'

Distressed and exhausted by the government's constant cry that it had no money to fix the problems, Yevgeny Alexandrovich decided to take matters into his own hands. He'd spend his nights and weekends pulling together material from western texts which he would send to Russian historians for verification, then roneoing them for teachers and students alike. But he was obliged also to send them to the Education Department for approval. Many of the papers were returned to him as 'unsuitable reading material for the young'.

'I decided it didn't really matter what the department said. Half of the *apparatchiks* working there had jobs on the side. They were barely a good example to anyone of dedication to education. I still use my material because it's more truthful than what we have available. If they catch me, they can sack me.'

But other profound problems still lingered from the bad days.

Under communism, children had been taught to blindly accept authority and to be loyal to the collective.

'I'll tell you an interesting story,' said Yevgeny Alexandrovich. 'I read about an experiment which was conducted at an American and a Russian school. The kids were all nine-year-olds. They were told they were on a sinking ship with seven-person lifeboats and they had to group themselves in order to escape. The American kids grouped into lots of seven ready for their escape. It didn't occur to our kids that they must separate. In fact they stayed together. When they were asked what they were doing, several of them said they had to stay together. So they were told again that unless they separated, they would perish. Still they stayed together, refusing to separate.'

For those privileged enough to stay within the safe environment of the school system, the old ways might not do them too much harm. But for those who were forced to earn money on the streets, the old dogmas made the new Russia a very dangerous place.

'There is a mentality in the education system that all children are the same, that they are no more than members of a collective. They're not cultivated as individuals and the official courses don't prepare them for what they're going to find in the real world once they get there. We don't teach economics because there's no money to train the teachers in the principles of market economics. And we don't teach them anything about what it means to be a law-based state because we've never had one. As for moral ethics! It's hard to imagine a teacher brought up in the Soviet Union having the intellectual equipment to teach a child the difference between right and wrong.'

'So where does that leave you?' I asked.

'With near empty classrooms. Why should they stay here when they can make real money robbing apartments and stealing cars?' the headmaster said.

His power was limited but Yevgeny Alexandrovich's hands were anything but tied. On weekends, he and a group of like-minded teachers would take a handful of the children who'd stayed on in the system to their own version of Sunday school. Of course they weren't paid or thanked officially for their effort, but they felt they were investing in the future of Russia and that, they considered, was a good start.

Television was exceedingly dreary in the Soviet Union until Mikhail Gorbachev came along. The communists considered sitcoms and serials to be a western assault on the purity of Leninist thought. But by the late 1980s, it was the ideological intrusion into people's homes of Leninism that had all but disappeared.

Current affairs programs became at the very least lively discussions about the process of change and the impact of seventy years of official lies. The notion of jazzing things up a bit to make information more appealing was still a distant concept, but not many viewers seemed to mind so long as what they were hearing was open, honest discussion.

But open political discussion wasn't the only indication that times had changed. To some what was even more astounding was the advent of soaps on Soviet television. For decades, the western life-style had been labelled bourgeois decadence. But by the late 1980s, people were absorbed in the trials and tribulations of the rich and famous in long-running serials from the United States, Australia and Mexico. By far the most popular of them was the Mexican soap 'The Rich Also Cry'. So absorbing was the drama which screened across the Soviet Union at midday that party bosses in Ukraine demanded it be taken off the air because every day factory workers would down tools to rush home for the next instalment. 'Santa Barbara', 'Dynasty', 'Miami Vice' and even the Australian series 'Chances' made a bit of a splash but nothing to rival 'The Rich Also Cry' whose lead actor was given an official Kremlin welcome by Mikhail Gorbachev when she came to Russia in 1990, causing his enemies to cry that the leader had truly gone mad.

But out of the swamp of commercialism which invaded people's homes each night came a few rays of hope. Russian films and series were being made and shown and although they emphasised all that was wrong about Russian life, they were at least homegrown. There was 'Dom' ('Home') which was set in the sort of prefabricated housing block you could see anywhere in the country. The two families which were its central focus became so entwined in each other's lives that by episode 3 I'd lost track of who was having an affair with whom. But it was distinctly Russian. The kids complained about not having enough money to buy toys they'd seen at stalls on the streets. One of the mothers had caught her boss thieving from the factory and was receiving a bribe in return for her silence. One of the husbands had left his institute for a life of crime. It was the reality of life in the new Russia which had been stripped of its spirit—just like 'Goryachev i Drugie' ('Goryachev and Others') about a vulnerable computer programmer who goes into business with the mafia and by episode 10 is behind bars where he becomes matey with a few gangsters. By episode 15 he's on the streets again, but his old gangster friends have turned on him and kidnapped his child. Sickened by what freedom has delivered them, his wife leaves him and goes to the United States.

'That's our life!' Masha declared. '"Dynasty" without money!'

Last I heard, the Russian soaps were rating poorly against the American soaps. As the director of Russian public television put it: 'Russians get enough reality during the daytime. They need escapism at night! But we'll keep producing it. It's our duty to Russia.'

So too, it seemed, was the production of a Russian Bert and Ernie, better known to their little Russian fans as Vlas and Enik. The Russian 'Sesame Street' has a strong political message. Cookie Monster (renamed Korzhik) and Kermit the Frog (who keeps his name) share the essentials of democracy, confidence, individualism and diversity with their young audience. Korzhik and Kermit like each other a lot and help each other whenever they can, emphasising all along that they're individuals with different needs which need to be negotiated and expressed. Perhaps television would instil in Russia's children those western virtues that, according to Yevgeny Alexandrovich, Russian schools had yet to come to terms with.

Homosexuality had been a major taboo in the Soviet Union. The country was homophobic in the extreme. In fact, the old regime insisted homosexuality didn't exist anywhere other than in the decadent west and 'aberrant' instances of it at home were punished severely. AIDS was seriously said to be American germ warfare.

In the 1990s, things became a little easier. The criminal code making homosexuality a crime was dropped from the statute books. Officially Russia now admits to having more than five AIDS sufferers, which is what was previously claimed. It owns up to 1800 HIV-infected Russians. But the buck stops there. There's no money for HIV education programs, no tolerance for its discussion in the media, and few private entrepreneurs willing to donate some of their millions to establish programs for those who need help. That sort of work is left to activists.

The secrecy surrounding homosexuality began to lift only in 1993 when the first AIDS hotline opened in the basement of a building near the Patriarchs Ponds in Moscow, spurred on by changes in the law and funded by an American computer company. Twenty-seven men, most of them unpaid, manned the phones around the clock, taking calls from people terrified that they'd contracted the virus from toilet seats or from Moscow's giant mosquitoes. The Ministry of Health saluted the efforts of the hotline workers but rejected their safe-sex brochure because it was said to be 'pornographic'. Basically, it outlined the rules for safe sex with a few pictures by way of explanation.

Even so, the hotline workers believed things were slowly improving. In 1994 the Moscow City Council, which was run by liberal-minded democrats, gave a group of gay men seed money to start a newspaper called *Risk*. It was an admission that without sex education in some form, as well as better hygiene practices, an AIDS epidemic is possible in Russia. People were appalled when the authorities tried to cover up the infection with HIV of two hundred babies in a hospital in southern Russia. Each of the babies had received their first inoculations against infant diseases with the same infected syringe.

'Ten years ago, we were considered leaches on society. We were regularly picked up by the police and charged with homosexual offences which could put us in psychiatric institutions for months,' explained phone counsellor Lenaart in between calls at the hotline.

'At least the law has changed. What we need to work on now is the police,' he said.

'Do they still zero in on gays?' I asked.

'Just as before. Only now they can only threaten us, or extort money. It's easy money for them because they know that if they tell our bosses we're gay, that's it. We'd be fired. They don't have the law on their side anymore, but that doesn't stop them from standing over us.'

Mir (World) opened in 1993. It was a gay bar, a seedy sort of place where skimpily dressed male waiters served western beer and Russian vodka in dimly lit surroundings with disco music throbbing in the background. Its owners, introduced as Dima and Mitya, were partners who told me the mafia wasn't their problem.

'Our problem is the police. We pay them a lot of money to stay away but when business is down and we can't pay, they'll burst into the place at midnight and start harassing people. What can we do about it? We can't tell our patrons not to come because we haven't paid the police their regular bribe, can we? If we did, we'd have to close down for good. But it's not pleasant for us to have the police do what they do,' said Mitya.

'We've complained to the local council, even to Moscow City Council and they say they're horrified. But unless the *militsiya* are caught in the act, we have no hope of stopping them. And then you have to ask—who's going to catch them? The special crime units are too busy chasing bandits and thugs. Protecting gays isn't high on their list of priorities. But our clients are used to being picked on. A lot of them have been bashed on the metro while *babushkas* watch, happy to see the "perverts" taught a lesson.

'What will it take to change things? Time and good people. Two things we don't have a lot of at the moment,' said Mitya, pouring another beer from behind the bar.

Having made the decision to tie the knot, Grisha and I went to Wedding Palace Number Four in central Moscow, the only one permitted to join foreigners and Russians in marital bliss. A church wedding, had we wanted one, was out of the question. I wasn't Orthodox.

In the administration office where we had to register our desire to marry, a young official rudely asked us what we wanted, bringing us both back down to earth with a thud.

'We want to get married,' Grisha informed her.

'You and dozens of others!' she barked back.

'Is it possible, do you think? We're hoping we can have the ceremony in about three months time,' he asked politely, ignoring her obvious surliness which showed no sign of waning.

'In three months time, the Palace will be closed for refurbishment and it won't open again for at least a year. I suggest you go to wherever she comes from and they'll do it there,' she answered, nodding towards me as she tidied up a pile of papers and turned towards the door.

'But we'd like to be married in Russia if you don't mind. When's the soonest date available?' persisted Grisha.

'Next Saturday.'

It was rather sooner than we were planning, but we didn't seem to have much say in the matter. I pleaded that my closest friend— Natasha—was in Siberia giving a lecture on the filmmaker Tarkovsky. Would she mind, please, marrying us the week after?

It wouldn't be easy for me to marry in Russia without Natasha. But that's the way it would have to be. Nor was it easy preparing the multitude of documents the Russian authorities required in four days flat. I would have to supply the Russian government with proof that I wasn't married to anyone else. This would have to come from my embassy and be translated into Russian by a special department of the Russian Foreign Ministry. Then I'd have to go to another notary's office—the busiest in Moscow—for a translation into Russian of my passport. I'd also need copies of documents showing that I was a registered correspondent with official permission to live in Russia.

'That's impossible to do in four days!' I protested.

'Then you'll be going to Australia to get married.'

Determined to marry in Russia for the benefit of friends and Grisha's family (and again in Australia for the benefit of mine), we started the dreary march through officialdom to get our 'papers'. The Australian embassy, as always, was happy to help out and armed with a Certificate of No Impediment we made our way to the Foreign Ministry, housed in one of Stalin's gothic Wedding Cakes on Smolyenskaya Square. It took half an hour just to get permission to enter the building, then there were visits to three separate offices in search of the right department to translate my document. Finally, we were directed outside the building, around the corner, towards the back lane where, we were told, we'd find Peter Churbanas who was the only man in the entire 25 000-strong workforce of the Foreign Ministry who was empowered to translate documents relating to any sort of activity of a personal nature between Russians and foreigners.

The *militsiya* guarding Churbanas's door against the hordes who, along with me, needed his services was most unhelpful at first, telling me to come back next week and shoving me back out the door until I was again in the laneway.

'But I'm getting married on Saturday and I need *Gospodin* Churbanas to translate this document. Please!' I begged, hoping to appeal to the Russian love of anything romantic.

A huge smile crept across the officer's face. '*Noo ladno* [Well, OK], just because you're getting married.'

Peter Churbanas didn't bother to look up when I stumbled into his office. He continued writing, his desk piled high with files, and above him the biggest portrait of Lenin I'd ever seen in an office. My immediate thought was that this was either going to take a lot of talking or a lot of money.

He finally looked up, over the rim of his glasses, and in perfect English asked me what I needed.

'Not a problem,' he said when I explained my predicament. 'Come back tomorrow at four and your documents will be ready.'

'Simple as that?' I asked, stunned.

'Were you expecting it to be complicated?' he said.

'Complicated or expensive,' I replied.

'Some of us have to be honest, my dear, otherwise the whole country would go—how do you say it—to the dogs.'

The next day my documents were ready. And Peter Churbanas was justly proud of his bribe-free efforts. But the notary's office was somewhat harder to conquer. The queue ran down the building's old stone stairs, through the snowy courtyard and onto the street. I felt like giving up in despair as soon as I arrived. Time was running out fast. The secretaries were turning people away as they arrived. I'd have to bribe one of them for the right to queue. That in itself wasn't a difficult task. But when I got to him, the notary found all sorts of problems which would need 'overcoming' before he could translate my passport. 'Overcoming' problems was, of course, a euphemism for 'this will cost you a lot of money'.

'It will cost more than the usual twenty dollars,' the notary said, 'more like one hundred and twenty.'

'OK, but please do it fast. I have to get the translation to the Wedding Palace before Friday,' I implored.

'Not a problem, young lady. Come back tomorrow.'

When I returned the next day, the documents were ready. The complex problems had been overcome. Grisha in the meantime had been harassing OVIR—the department which oversaw visas and the registration of foreigners holidaying or living in Russia. It took four days of devoted attention, but we had our documents.

The Wedding Palace was very Soviet, full of doors and corridors. A central staircase led to a foyer where thirty or forty couples waited in an assembly line to be married. We were given a number—34— and paid our 15 roubles (1.5 cents) for the service. To have the 'Wedding March' played by a small group of private musicians hired by the state-run Palace cost an extra 8000 roubles (US$8).

Russian brides in full-length white lace dresses had braved the minus twenty degree temperatures outside to look the part. Bouquets of flowers in one hand and hairbrush in the other, they nervously paced the hallway, ironing out imaginary creases and pasting back rogue pieces of hair with spit delicately placed on a pointed fore-finger. I felt rather conspicuous in my hot pink dress. The grooms, except for mine, looked very worried. They stood in corners smoking furiously until the double doors at the far end of the room opened to release a married couple and it was their turn to face the music.

When our number was called, we handed over our wedding rings which had taken days of searching in shopping malls and tiny shops in back streets to find, and listened to the band strike up Mendels-sohn's 'Wedding March'. The doors were flung open and with Masha walking beside me as my witness—there was no such thing as a bridesmaid in state wedding ceremonies—and Grisha's friend Aliosha next to him, we were led inside to a large, high-ceilinged wedding room, followed by our friends. The very woman who'd suggested we go to Australia to be married was to be the officiant.

'Oh no,' muttered Grisha as we walked down the aisle.

'This is the most important day of your life,' she began in a soft syrupy voice not at all like the gruff tone she'd affected in her office. I didn't listen to much else. I was absorbed by the Soviet hammer and sickle emblem which hung from the wall directly in front of us. I couldn't figure out what it was doing there. Office workers all over Russia were bolstering their meagre wages by ripping them down off their office walls and selling them for as little as US$10 a piece. So absorbed in the decor was

I, the bride, that when I was asked in convoluted high Russian whether I would accept Grigori Sergeyevich as my husband I blissfully ignored the question.

'Yes,' Masha prompted, elbowing me so hard I looked towards her rather than Grisha.

'Yes,' I blurted out. Luckily for me Grisha didn't back down at the last minute either and we were declared married, told to sign a paper or two, ordered to kiss each other and hustled out the door so that couple number 35 could go through the identical seven-minute process.

I'd often seen just-married couples being photographed at the Flame of the Unknown Soldier near the Kremlin, or on Lenin Hills overlooking Moscow on one side and Moscow University on the other. Now it was my turn to go through the ritual, though in minus twenty degrees I was eager that wherever we went, we wouldn't stay too long. Lenin Hills was the collective choice, but apart from almost freezing over, this part of the Russian wedding experience wasn't quite as unusual as the Wedding Palace had been.

The party afterwards was where the real meaning of the occasion was revealed. There, with Grisha's family and all our friends, we could really celebrate. Grisha and his friends got hideously drunk on vodka and sang, largely out of tune, to a scratchy tape of love songs recorded by Zina Pavlova, an emigre singer who lived in Paris, while our guests toasted our marriage with cries of 'Gorko, gorko' which means 'bitter'.

'Ah! The wine is bitter,' say the Russians, 'so kiss to make it sweet.'

It was something I hadn't expected to see in Russia in 1983. On my first day in the Big Potato, a young man befriended me and although he was the son of a member of the old Soviet Politburo, there wasn't much about communism he liked, except its ineptitude. He was amused that a regime built on order and discipline could be so helpless against something—religion—it considered to be subversive of its principal aims.

I remember him telling me as we rode on a rickety old bus towards the snow-covered northern suburbs of Moscow on our way to a 'religious feast' that just about the only one of Lenin's edicts the communists had stuck to was his declaration that the revolutionary proletariat would succeed in making religion a really private affair rather than the opiate of the masses. In this Vladimir Ilych had been right.

Beneath the golden cupola of the Church of St John the Warrior, the church walls, covered in richly coloured icons, shimmered with the glow of candles lit by a venerable throng of *babushkas*. An elderly priest in a gilded robe chanted. The *babushkas*, their heads covered in colourful woollen scarves, milled around in their thick felt boots, crossing themselves repeatedly.

'They'll be here for hours yet,' said Alex, smiling at the look of shock on my face. 'What—you didn't think Russians practised religion?'

'I don't understand. I thought Stalin wiped out religious practice altogether,' I said.

'They even hold services in the church behind KGB headquarters and members of the Politburo attend,' replied Alex.

They had done so even as Stalin viciously suppressed the church. It was only when he needed its assistance to drum up patriotism before the outbreak of World War II that he gave up trying to wipe religion from the Russian slate. It was under Khrushchev, as the party fought furiously to reassert itself, that religious repression began again. Religious activity was punished, its practitioners jailed and even murdered. But by Bolshevik standards of repression, Khrushchev's efforts were paltry, and by the 1970s, Leonid Brezhnev was forced to tolerate the church's activities though he extracted a few favours in return.

Anyone over sixty could practise as often as they liked, so long as they were relatively low-key and the message they received through the church emphasised the importance of their submission to the state and the glories of the Communist Party of the Soviet Union—a message the church carried onto the international stage when it was accepted into the World Council of Churches. It was no less than a propaganda arm of the Communist Party and its prelates (the party's prisoners) and believers (far more than the party could boast) knew this.

Selective prosecutions of churchgoers and clergy managed to keep people wary of religious practice. Any priest who overstepped the party's limits was defrocked. The party's intolerance was also evident in its refusal to allow churches to be built in new towns and cities after 1970. Others were razed to the ground. Before the Bolshevik revolution, there were 70 000 churches. In 1985, there were 6500.

But as with all party measures designed to suppress the free will of the people, they were only partly successful and by the time Mikhail Gorbachev launched *perestroika* and *glasnost*, religion was well and truly out in the open. Churchgoers weren't just the aged who the state deemed to be no longer a potential threat. They were the middle-aged and their offspring whom they'd managed to have baptised despite the state's disapproval.

When I first met Grisha's mother she proudly told me that her son was a very good boy. 'He's even been baptised,' she said.

With a stroke of the pen in 1988, Gorbachev granted freedom of religious worship to everyone, telling people that believers were Soviet working people and patriots who had the right to express their convictions in a fitting manner. The hardliners choked as they repeated the words to each other in discussions about what they were going to do with the rogue party secretary. But in the end, Gorbachev managed to convince them of what I'd heard my father argue over and again: that pure 'communism', untainted by totalitarianism, and 'religion' were not alien concepts.

From the window of my apartment in Krylatskoe, the little church on the hill across the way looked like an ancient ruin. It beckoned me, inviting closer inspection.

The land upon which Peter the Great had built the Church of the Nativity of the Mother of God, as the ruin was called, was once part of the estate of Ivan the Terrible who would rest there on his way back to Moscow after long journeys throughout Russia. The communists closed the church in the 1920s and later used it as the headquarters for the Society of the Blind. When the Olympic Stadium was built nearby in the 1970s, the church was handed over to the Olympic managers so they could store sporting equipment there.

On the other side of the church, over the hills, were row upon row of deadening, soulless prefabricated apartment blocks—among them the one in which I lived. The region had few redeeming characteristics, but for me the fact that at night when people turned on their apartment lights it looked like New York made up for a lot. And sometimes, shadows bouncing off the church's tin cupola added to the magic.

Alexander the Painter, as he was known among the locals in nearby Kuntsevo where he lived, was one of the growing 'party of non-party people', as Yevgeny Yevtushenko called them, who embraced all of the freedoms Gorbachev had granted—including the freedom of religious expression.

With the advent of *glasnost*, Alexander had decided that the Department of Religion deserved to be challenged. Its decision that the church ought to remain devoted to secular pursuits upset him enormously. 'What role does a government department have in these matters?' he asked.

Alexander and a group of local *babushkas* who had been visiting the church regularly despite the fact it was officially closed, inundated the Department of Religion with petitions signed by thousands of people. Prompted by Alexander, the church hierarchy asked the department to allow the church to reopen even though there was no money to pay for its reconstruction.

But a little over a year later, in 1995, the job was almost done, and without state help. The local believers begged on street corners for donations. Baptisms, christenings, weddings and funeral services were all conducted for a small fee. Even the schoolchildren of Krylatskoe chipped in, holding fetes and special sports carnivals to raise money. Some of the more successful businesspeople in the suburb kicked in as well and the church's walls were rebuilt, its windows replaced and the pathway leading up to it from the road repaved. People were helping themselves.

The church hierarchy found some less heartwarming ways to reconstruct other derelict churches. It was bizarre, bordering on the grotesque, to drive through the countryside around Moscow in 1995 and see newly bricked churches with glistening gold domes and glorious stained windows literally perched in the backyards of the two-storey, five-turreted country homes of the super-rich. It was the seedier side of the church's comeback that it so willingly became a haven for tax evaders. The new rich had found a way of avoiding tax which didn't involve sending their enormous wealth abroad. They kept it at home, tucked away in the church's bank accounts which were exempt from the attention of Russia's taxation collectors. In return, the new rich had begun the seemingly endless task of reconstructing village churches. So successful was the scheme that by 1992, the number of churches had risen from 6500 to 16 000.

'God knows the difference between true believers and the rest of them,' Natasha said when I expressed my shock at the fact that the church was also in the business of oil exports and tobacco imports.

Nor did the church hierarchy see much wrong in its support in 1993 of a legislative amendment which required religious parties not based in Russia to apply for formal registration. It was a sign that times had truly changed when the government vetoed the amendment.

My father, a religious man, once asked me whether God had been driven out of Russia by the communists. I could safely answer 'not entirely'.

As capitalism ran wild, I would listen to my friends complain that communism had crippled them, left them unable to go about building a normal country. The state has always thought for us, they'd say. The state told us what we could and couldn't do, what to think and what not to think and that our needs were insignificant against those of the state. So what is the point, I remember Natasha asking, in trying to do things for ourselves? We don't know how to.

But as much as history had conspired against them, it was also working for them. It had taught them how to survive.

CHAPTER 16

SO THIS IS DEMOCRACY?

First they focused on shock therapy. This provoked dissatisfaction from a huge proportion of the population. The next logical step was to start curtailing democracy in order to continue economic reform.

ALEKSEI ARBARTOV, DIRECTOR OF THE INSTITUTE

OF THE UNITED STATES AND CANADA, 1993

As the Russians struggled against inflation and the government's unwillingness and inability to provide the money needed to get the country in shape, the wheels of Soviet-style propaganda were turning, spinning tales of a new and better future. Posters of Boris Yeltsin sporting a bandanna and carrying a tennis racket despite strong rumours of his bad heart and love of the drop hung in the streets where once Lenin and Marx had assaulted the eye. According to the hype, Yeltsin was not only healthy, he was the new Russian tsar, a kind and good democrat who, unlike the party men he had overthrown, wanted to give his people the freedom to make their own choices in life. Like communism it was a perfect theory, but far from the truth. The majority knew they were anything but free. Only the racketeers and bandits, the old party mafia, the new rich and those who'd attached themselves to them were free. The rest of the country was entrapped by poverty.

By 1993, Russians had consumed 200 000 tons of food donated by the United States following the collapse of the Soviet Union. The country was simply unable to produce enough to feed itself. I knew of no-one who bought the American food (sold at rock bottom prices to preserve some semblance of dignity in the purchasers) without feeling humiliated and distressed. Some people told me they would look over their shoulder as they queued for it, watching for familiar faces. If they saw one, they'd quietly leave the queue. 'This is what they meant when they talked of democracy,' Natasha's father said. 'We are meant to feel grateful that the communists can no longer feed us and hold our hands out, without shame, to the United States.

'Imagine how hard it is for us. I cannot remember a time in my life when I thought of the United States as anything but an evil, exploitative empire which wanted to snuff out the most noble theory ever applied to human nature. Now, they've succeeded and they send us what their own people won't eat, expecting us to be happy about it.'

But he, like most, had no choice. Those who continued to work for the state didn't earn enough to buy the imported food which Europe, along with the United States, was dumping on Russia to be sold in kiosks. At least they were paid in money. There were stories about workers on oil rigs in the Arctic Circle being paid in tampons (unavailable to most Russian women). There were factories where workers were paid in donated ironclad roofing for homes they'd never be able to build. Others were paid with what they produced. It wasn't unusual to see workers standing in open markets or at railway stations selling television sets, glass vases or kitchen meat grinders—all manufactured by the factories in which they worked and paid to them in lieu of wages. In these strange times, it was one of the few signs that a market, however primitive, had begun to operate because most would offload their 'wages' to shopkeepers who couldn't obtain the goods through the old, broken distribution channels.

And even though the Central Bank, under the parliament's influence, refused to force the closure of factories which couldn't pay their debts, unemployment kept rising. By the middle of 1993, it had risen by 13 per cent, an enormous jump in a country accustomed to full employment. At the same time, inflation continued to bite, increasing 5 to 7 per cent a month.

The democrats panicked when surveys showed that more and more Russians wanted the strong hand of authoritarianism to seize the country by the throat again and stop the rampaging bull of capitalism. A majority of those polled wanted someone to stop Boris Yeltsin.

Indeed, the president was under siege, locked in a fight with the parliament which he claimed was loaded with recycled communist reactionaries hell-bent on reversing price liberalisation and privatisation. Time and again Yeltsin threatened to dissolve the parliament, declaring that Russia's future prosperity and national security depended on him having free rein to act in the country's interests. But this was pure bluff. Yeltsin had no constitutional power to do what he threatened.

'There's talk of a civil war,' Igor told me as we tried to manoeuvre our way through the thousands of pensioners and housewives crammed onto the footpath outside *Detski Mir* (Children's World) an old Soviet establishment across the road from KGB headquarters. It was March and the cold was lifting. But that didn't seem to make the sellers at this flea market any happier. To bolster their meagre earnings, they were selling their possessions—china, Soviet cosmetics made in the 1950s, food which they'd preserved themselves, empty western beer cans (once popular decorative items) and bits and pieces of clothing. Tired *babushkas* would hold out ugly lurex leggings or packets of chewing gum which they'd mark up 100 or so roubles—not even enough to buy a loaf of bread.

'I can't imagine Russians fighting in a civil war. It would hardly be fair would it?' said Igor. 'The *babushkas* and pensioners would get mowed down by the businessmen and bandits in their Mercedes. They wouldn't need tanks. Anyway, we don't need a civil war in Russia. Yeltsin will determine our fate. Let's see if he's prepared to listen to the parliament,' said Igor, stumbling over a pile of rubbish, a small token of the two tons of trash left behind every day by the army of street sellers.

Civil war was on everyone's mind, though I was hard-pressed to find anyone who really believed that after all they'd been through, the Russians had any desire or energy to fight each other. Not even the nouveaux riches had the energy for another fight and, in any case, for the rich there was an overriding financial consideration. Political uncertainty was profitable. While Yeltsin was concentrating his efforts on winning the war over economic reform with the parliament, on the battlefield huge booties were being stashed away.

The country lost 200 million dollars in just one quarter of 1993 when state credits, mostly loaned to the government by international agencies, were illegally diverted to other purposes—private, of course. Much of the time, when the parliament created a law, Yeltsin would issue a decree contradicting it, no matter its merit, which meant that the new businessmen could do just about anything without breaking the law.

Although he found the chaos depressing, Boris Yeltsin tried to dismiss it as a positive sign that a new political and economic system was evolving. But the parliament—which Yeltsin wanted replaced under a new Russian constitution—would have none of it. Yeltsin was like an angry bull in a china shop. The parliament was challenging his absolute authority. It had not only assumed control of the Central Bank which, under parliament's influence, refused to call in bad debts from factories unable to survive in the world of market economics, but it was claiming the moral high ground in the process.

'Yeltsin would throw workers onto the scrap heap,' bellowed Vice President Alexander Rutskoi from the parliamentary podium. 'He would rather see his own people starve than disobey the orders of the International Monetary Fund to close down the enterprises our fathers and grandfathers spent their lives building for us!'

It was a powerful call to take the fight against inflation, unemployment and unseemly wealth right to Yeltsin's doorstep where it belonged. But the president's men argued that they had no choice in the matter. Russia would collapse without the IMF's help which would be withdrawn if Yeltsin did what the parliament demanded— print money to pump into unprofitable enterprises to keep people from unemployment.

Both sides were right. And for much of 1992 they were locked in an unwinnable battle. The question people hardly dared ask was whether Yeltsin would call on the military to help him achieve ascendancy over the parliament.

The president had the military to call on for help, but the parliament had a private army. Incredibly, the chairman of the parliament, Ruslan Khasbulatov, the main ally of Vice President Rutskoi in the fight against Yeltsin, had created a security force to protect himself and like-minded deputies from the state's security organs.

It was discovered by accident. One evening in October 1992, the police were called to an incident in a Moscow suburb. Someone had pulled a gun on a taxi driver. The man they arrested was a Chechen and, as it turned out, no ordinary hooligan. He had written permission to carry a gun and automatic 24-hour-a-day entry to the parliamentary building, better known as the White House. The story might have ended there except that a few weeks later TASS reported that an officer of the new-look KGB had been gunned down on the steps of the White House. It was a curious incident. Stories about bankers being assassinated, even journalists and politicians, were commonplace. But an officer of the KGB?

Within hours, Ruslan Khasbulatov was implicated. It was his security force—said to be between 1500 and 5000 men strong—which was responsible for the murder. Its huge armoury was stashed in the basement of the White House. But so strange were these times of shadowy connections and gangland skirmishes that within days the story was more or less forgotten by all but Boris Yeltsin and his coterie.

Ruslan Khasbulatov was an aggressive, scheming character with loads of charm and just as much paranoia, and most people didn't think it odd that he had a private army. Most of Moscow's bankers and businessmen did. But what was different about Khasbulatov was that he had political power. He had won the loyalty of the parliament and local councils across Russia who could see that Yeltsin's reforms were hurting people badly. Of course, the political minnows across Russia had other reasons to back Khasbulatov. He was the key to their privileged lives—their cars, apartments in Moscow, offices and staff. If Yeltsin won the brewing battle, the parliament would be disbanded and with it, political privileges.

'If he wins this fight, he could end up president,' one of my colleagues commented as we watched Khasbulatov skilfully control and manipulate the parliament's disparate and disunited factions.

But the truth was there was never any real chance of this. Khasbulatov had been born in Chechnya, a southern province in Russia's rugged mountains, wedged between Azerbaijan and Georgia. And people were terrified of the Chechens. Chechen criminals and thugs were said to be the worst. If you had a problem with the Russian mafia you could pay your way out of it. But a run-in with the Chechen mafia, at least according to modern folklore, always resulted in death. Chechens, Muscovites would say, were responsible for most of the weapons and drug running in the new Russia.

Because he was a Chechen, Khasbulatov was mistrusted. And his private army gave Yeltsin's propagandists a platform from which to spread the rumour that Khasbulatov and the vice president, Alexander Rutskoi, were planning to topple the government. Khasbulatov and Rutskoi, according to the Kremlin, would declare all the president's decrees illegal, then write a constitution which would give extraordinary powers to the parliament. Yeltsin would have his crown, but little else.

The purpose of the rumour was to win sympathy for Yeltsin who was about to face the Russian Congress, which sat only two or three times a year, to ask for an extension of his emergency powers to rule. The Congress turned out to be one of the most riotous sessions I've ever witnessed. Not even the final session of the Soviet parliament was as divided and bitter as this.

For days, deputies accused Boris Yeltsin of being a hopeless drunk and spilled their grievances about his economic reforms, his refusal to listen to their complaints, the poverty and mayhem on the streets of every town and city in Russia. To storms of applause, they'd march out of the meeting hall followed by a clutch of other politicians from the most extraordinary mix of persuasions. Journalists, foreign and Russian, raced up and down corridors trying to corner the more powerful of them to see whether there was any hope the president would get what he wanted—an extension of his power to rule by decree.

In the end, after days of bartering and deal making, Yeltsin's emergency powers were renewed, but only for a few months and he was forced to offer the parliament the right to appoint some of his most important ministers—those who would run the defence, foreign affairs, police and intelligence services porfolios. But power sharing was not in Yeltsin's nature. He wanted a referendum to ask Russians whether they wanted the president or the parliament to run the country. And he wanted them to vote on the basic principles of a new constitution. It was the first move in a high-stakes game of political chess.

It was an interesting question. If Russians wanted Yeltsin to run the country under a constitution he wrote, they'd be asking for more economic reforms and a president with unlimited powers. If they voted to let the parliament run the show, the reforms would be slowed down but power would rest with a body which was essentially conservative and dominated by men who were not convinced of the merits of capitalism.

But nor were the parliamentary deputies confident of being able to win the hearts and minds of the people at a referendum. So they exacerbated the tension by a motion condemning it, while Valeri Zorkin, the Chairman of the Constitutional Court, endeared himself even more to the conservatives by brokering a compromise in which Yeltsin would remain in office, get his referendum but surrender his right to choose a prime minister. Yeltsin would lose Yigor Gaidar, the architect of economic shock therapy, and be presented with a list of candidates approved by the parliament. And so Victor Chernomyrdin, Yeltsin's choice from the list, came to power. Finally, the parliament would have de facto control over the economy.

Yeltsin's authority looked compromised and severely so. Victor Chernomyrdin, from the giant Soviet gas monopoly, was to most of the young liberals in the government an old-style technocrat. And although he would prove to be a powerful ally of the reformers, it looked very much like the era of shock therapy was over. Most I knew were grateful. But Yeltsin fumed and his entourage plotted. In March 1993, Yeltsin declared the introduction of 'Special Rule' by which he wanted people to understand he would rule by presidential decree without reference to the parliament. Chairman Zorkin spluttered that a coup d'etat was under way. And in a sense he was right. The parliament mobilised for an impeachment. But before the vote was taken, Yeltsin's decree was published and it was clear he'd either changed his mind or amended the edict, for 'Special Rule' now meant the parliament would still consider his rulings, but could only reject them if they were deemed unconstitutional. The impeachment failed and the referendum date was set for 25 April.

'So this is freedom!' Igor complained. 'It's just like the old days. The communists held elections too, you know, but it was impossible to vote against them. Now it's impossible to vote against Yeltsin because if we do then he'll think we're voting for the communists and he'll call his friend Grachev [the Defence Minister] and the troops will be on the streets while he sacks the parliament. One man, one idea! Who wants to take the risk?'

Natasha's sister Luda was among the millions who did. She had not long returned to Moscow from Tbilisi, the capital of neighbouring Georgia which was being torn apart by civil wars. The supporters of the ousted Georgian president were fighting those who got rid of him, while separatists in a small corner of the state, Abkhazia, were fighting Georgia for the right to self rule. Luda thought Moscow would be quieter.

She and Natasha sat in my lounge room one evening locked in bitter battle.

'OK, so you vote to let Yeltsin run the country. Who will he be accountable to or is that not important to you?' asked Natasha.

'It's important but it's not the most important issue at the moment. The critical question is one of direction. If you vote to give the parliament real power then we're going to have a rowdy bunch of no-hopers who couldn't get a job in the private world if they prostituted themselves! They want to preserve the old system or at least a part of it. They're saying that all they want is for reforms to slow down, but you're mad if you believe that,' Luda retorted.

'I watch them on TV too. I know they look like a hopeless lot. But they are all we have to stop Yeltsin's quick march to the past,' argued Natasha. 'We have a president who was a communist. You don't really believe he understands how democracy should work, do you? And why should we expect that of him? Just because he overthrew a dictatorial regime? That's not enough. He must understand,

and if he can't then he must be taught to understand that Russians want a strong president and a strong parliament and that we elected the parliament as our voice. That's how it works!'

'You're upset because the reforms are hurting you,' Luda interjected.

'No. I'm upset because Yeltsin hasn't found a way to carry out the reforms which everyone can agree upon. And because he's being challenged, he's acting just like a Bolshevik would. If he has an idea to defend then I would say it's not capitalism. If Yeltsin knows how capitalism in Russia should work so that we all benefit, then let him prove it.'

I was with Natasha when she cast her vote in the referendum. She voted for the reforms.

Given what the Russians were living through it was a shock to many that 54 per cent of those who bothered to vote in the referendum opted for the continuation of economic reforms. Perhaps it had something to do with the saturation media campaign Yeltsin ran which urged people to vote 'Da, da, da, da'. Yes to the president, yes to the reforms, yes to an election for the parliament and yes to an election for the presidency. As Yeltsin pointed out, the Russians had spent decades saying 'nyet'. Even so, only the first two questions passed with a majority. But that was all that mattered for Yeltsin. The people had shown their faith in him. If only they'd known they were about to sustain another blow.

Outside my dining room window, a line of *babushkas* suddenly appeared. There was no bread shop in the building for them to queue at, nor a grocery shop. There was only an old Soviet *Sberkassa*—a savings bank—which because Russians had always tucked their money under their beds was useful only because it accepted payment for electricity, gas and phone bills. Perhaps the government had announced a currency reform designed to make hyper-inflation look like mere inflation, and people were queuing to exchange their old roubles?

It was unfortunately more serious than that. Russians, battered by two years of economic shock therapy and impoverished by galloping inflation, were being told that all banknotes printed before 1993 were worthless. They were given two weeks to change up to 35 000 roubles, though Yeltsin later raised the amount to 100 000 roubles. Still, the government, in effect, was confiscating people's savings.

Down at the *Sberkassa* queue, the only people who weren't in a panic were the kiosk owners. 'I'm sure that the mafia will find a way to change my money into real money,' one of them said to me. 'That's why I pay them every week—to look after me.'

'And what will the mafia do with the old money?' I asked.

'Send it to Chechnya!' he replied.

The move was a huge flop. Yeltsin claimed the government intended an 'exchange' of money, rather than wholesale confiscation. He said the move was aimed at stopping the former republics flooding Russia with roubles printed in the Soviet era while Russia was printing new money. But though he was vague on the question, it was also clear that Moscow wanted to force the former republics to accepting the rouble as their currency. Many had begun printing their own notes and as their money circulated, old roubles were appearing in Russia, sending inflation higher. But the government's tactic failed. It didn't stop the former republics printing their own money. It simply hurt the Russians.

Masha phoned that morning. 'You should come out here to my neighbourhood,' she urged, 'there are people buying out the shops.' To get rid of their money, those who had it were buying anything and everything they could lay their hands on. I saw beat-up old Russian cars tootling down the main boulevards piled to the roof with cartons of cigarettes and Coca-Cola.

That afternoon I went to a media conference called by Ruslan Khasbulatov. He was outraged. Money reform, he said, was a crime, another in a litany committed by a president who didn't care for his people. He'd had no idea money reform was in the offing. 'But watch this space,' he said with a slippery grin, 'the president will say it was my fault.'

It was difficult to judge who was responsible.

'Convince me I was right to say yes to more economic reform,' Natasha asked me a few days after the money fiasco. 'Tell me how it is that a government can make a decision to wipe out the entire savings of its people and claim that it is democratic, for the people? Can you tell me?'

It was a tough call.

The breaking point came in September, after a month of relative peace. It seemed for a while that Russia's politicians were just as tired of the politicking as the people were. As it turned out, everyone was just drawing breath for the next round.

Yeltsin had reappointed Yigor Gaidar—this time as deputy prime minister. The parliament was outraged, believing that Yeltsin's victory in the referendum was not so great that he could assume people would accept more Gaidar-style reforms. But if the referendum result had given Yeltsin confidence, money reform buoyed Khasbulatov. He suggested fresh elections for both the parliament and the president.

'We have to do something,' Khasbulatov told the parliament, 'about this national curse—drunkenness, alcoholism. It is intolerable when officials go out of their way to demonstrate that there's nothing wrong here supposedly. If someone drinks, that means he's our kind of guy! But if he's "our kind of guy" then let him remain as such and let him do peasants' work and not the state's.'

It was a clear reference to Yeltsin. Incensed, the president rejected the offer of elections and presented the parliament with a tough budget knowing it would be turned down. Yeltsin's fiscal blueprint would cut Russia's bloated deficit but cause yet more pain; the parliament wanted more money for enterprises which hadn't yet been privatised. It was the only way, the deputies claimed, to stave off bankruptcies which would close entire towns. Yeltsin could take no more.

For weeks none of the foreign journalists in town had dared to wander too far from home base just in case Yeltsin did what he'd been threatening to do and suspend the only democratic institution Russia had conjured up in two years of freedom. But on the night he made his move, I was watching *Much Ado About Nothing*, the first Western film I had seen on a big screen without subtitles in two years. It was being shown in a central Moscow hotel.

As we left the hotel after the film ended, a Reuters journalist rushed past us. Grisha and I looked at each other in horror. Something had happened.

'What are you doing here?' she asked. 'Doesn't Australia care if Yeltsin's sacked the parliament?'

It was one of the fastest rides back to barracks I'd ever experienced. Wire stories filled the old bathroom where the machines operated day and night. Grisha cut copy as I prepared for a long night's work. By midnight I was in tears. When would the mayhem stop? When would Russia become a normal country?

'You're beginning to sound like Natasha,' said Grisha. 'It's probably time to think about leaving.'

It probably was, but for the moment the drama unfolding at the Russian White House took priority.

The chief judge of the Constitutional Court arrived at the parliament as police and Interior Ministry troops began encircling it. Valeri Zorkin wasted little time in declaring Yeltsin's dissolution of the parliament a violation of the constitution, while in a nearby room those deputies who'd managed to make their way inside the building elected Vice President Rutskoi the acting president. The siege of the White House had begun.

Hundreds of people arrived to camp outside the White House just as they had two years earlier when hardline communists tried the same trick on Mikhail Gorbachev. Those who came claimed they were defending the same democratic principles—chief among them the people's right to choose their future. It was perhaps unfortunate that they were such a motley collection of radicals. Watching groups of young neo-Nazis, bikie gangs brandishing lumps of wood and angry old men carrying the Soviet flag, it was difficult to see the west rallying to their particular defence of democracy as it had in August 1991. But there they gathered, thinking they'd be taken seriously, listening to would-bes if they could-bes—men who had attached themselves to the parliament's cause but were so radical they made the former KGB chief, Vladimir Kruchkov, who was languishing in prison waiting trial for treason, look positively saintly.

The military vowed not to help either side but with both Rutskoi and Khasbulatov holed up inside the White House with a cache of weapons to protect themselves, something had to give. The chief judge wanted to negotiate a compromise but after his judgment on Yeltsin's declaration of special rule, the president wasn't interested in anything he had to say. The truth of the matter was that Yeltsin was cornered, checkmated. An election might have resolved the crisis, but he didn't believe there was any need to submit himself to the judgment of the people. So he upped the ante and ordered those inside the White House to evacuate. And in keeping with contemporary convention, they refused.

In our office, Ira, the manager, tried to reassure me that nothing would happen. 'They're just angry. Anyway, how can they hold out there? Soon their wives and mothers will be more angry than they are and they'll go home.'

Natasha didn't believe either that the siege would end in bloodshed. But my father did.

I had one of the longest conversations with him in months. He was desperately worried that Boris Yeltsin would send in the tanks to end the parliament's life. 'Soviet tanks will obey orders even if they're doing it just to protect what they know really well—a strong hand of authority. It won't matter to them that the parliament is standing up for democracy!'

A day after this conversation I flew home to Sydney. My father died the day thousands of anti-Yeltsin protesters went on a rampage through Moscow, burning cars, smashing shop windows and looting goods, stealing the tyres of parked cars which they burnt in bonfires around the city. He'd always felt, my father, that I'd survived one outburst of Soviet violence but that I wouldn't be so lucky the second time around.

Sheltered by my father's death from the mobs of armed men and young boys who headed towards Lenin's monument on Oktya-brskaya Square, I watched as CNN beamed television pictures around the world of the police and Interior Ministry troops in Moscow simply watching the mayhem unfold. Perhaps they thought that after a week-long stand-off and two days of rampaging, there was little point in trying to bring the protesters under control. But it was odd. Friends in Moscow with whom I spoke on the phone said it felt distinctly as though Yeltsin was allowing the protesters to do what they wanted. Masha and Natasha were genuinely frightened. It didn't feel to them as though the authorities wanted to bring the situation under control. Natasha wondered whether Yeltsin was provoking a civil war. The *Guardian* correspondent, Jonathan Steele, also argued that the protesters were being set up. He witnessed the police retreating without their police cars which they had thoughtfully left behind with the keys in the ignition. But not all the police had retreated. Some had gone over to the parliament's side. The protesters were led to believe they'd won the battle.

Back at the White House, Ruslan Khasbulatov must have been

overpowered by the scent of victory for he sent word to the crowd outside that they should seize the mayor's office next door. Using a small bus to smash their way in, an unruly rabble led by a hardline neo-Stalinist seized the building before setting their sights on the television centre at Ostankino, way over the north side of Moscow.

Whatever was going through Boris Yeltsin's mind at this point it certainly wasn't how he was going to bring the rampaging horde of anti-government protesters to a stop. In fact the president was spending some time with his family at his *dacha*. And rather than barricading the area around Ostankino before the protesters could move in, the authorities left the streets open to all comers as armoured personnel carriers moved into position and hundreds of extra police secured the building's front doors. A friend of mine lived in an apartment with a good view of the television centre and she later told me that she had naively rung the local police to warn them they should shut off the area. They hadn't wanted to know about the problem, and as she hung up she looked outside her window to see a group of men and boys with iron bars and what looked to her like light artillery clambering over hedges to get to the building.

In any event, it was too late to either physically or psychologically restrain their anger. As the parliament's supporters fired a grenade launcher into the building, others of them turned their guns towards anything that moved—including journalists who were trapped between them and the government troops and carriers which had moved in and had started to fire randomly into the crowd. The battle lasted only an hour before the side loyal to Alexander Rutskoi and Ruslan Khasbulatov retreated to the White House. But Yeltsin's forces had not yet won the fight.

I watched the mayhem on television as we prepared to bury my father. The death toll had hit sixty according to western media reports, which referred to 'anti-democratic Stalinists who had tried to topple Boris Yeltsin'. The west had chosen sides already.

'Everyone here is safe,' Masha told me on the phone the day after the Ostankino battle, 'and be grateful you're not here. It's sickening.

I've never seen Rob scared before. But he is now. He's talking of packing up and driving out to the airport to get out of here.

'But it's still too early. I don't know,' she mused, almost as though she were talking to herself, 'I can't see Russians killing Russians, not even for a political idea. This is just a fit of anger. It'll stop soon.' She sounded unconvinced.

'Masha, they're already killing people,' I said.

'I don't blame people for being angry. What is this? Yeltsin sacked the parliament! Now he's trying to tell us this is to preserve democracy. People are saying he set up the protesters for a showdown. If he hadn't ordered them to evacuate the White House, they would have gone home on their own. Rutskoi's wife was probably on the phone to him every five minutes.'

She sounded anxious.

'But will the army move in to get him out of the White House?' Grisha asked her, worried because his parents were in Moscow and the western media were talking of a slide into civil war.

'Who knows,' answered Masha, 'Grachev [the Defence Minister] is probably on Khasbulatov's side.'

And he was. President Yeltsin had tried to persuade him to join Interior Ministry troops in an onslaught on the White House but Pavel Grachev wasn't keen. In the end, Yeltsin jumped into his limousine and drove from the Kremlin to Defence Ministry headquarters to stress the point. Even then, Grachev, Soviet to the end, consulted with his regional commanders but finally did what Yeltsin wanted. The next morning the assault began.

The television pictures looked horrific. Palls of black smoke billowed from every floor of the White House. Armoured assault vehicles shot at the protester's cars and tents. Tanks, their cannon barrels smoking, fired shells into every corner of the building which, two years before, Boris Yeltsin had used to blast the Communist Party to smithereens.

Paratroopers with submachine guns entered the parliament through its side doors, their mission to find Alexander Rutskoi and Ruslan Khasbulatov and arrest them.

For twelve long hours, Yeltsin's tanks fired on the parliament, letting deputies who chose to surrender leave the building as soldiers prepared to take the two ringleaders who had so seriously challenged Boris Yeltsin for authority and power. When Rutskoi and Khasbulatov finally emerged they looked unconditionally defeated. In one day of carnage, Yeltsin's defenders had killed more than 140 people.

'Forgive me,' Boris Yeltsin said to his people, 'for having been so long in dealing with the communist–fascist plot.'

'Democracy is a strange beast,' Alexander Pumpyansky from *New Times* magazine told me when I returned to Moscow. 'And I'm not sure it's suitable for us here in Russia.'

'We supported it because we didn't really understand what it was. We were tired and very confused after all those years of hearing that capitalism was evil, and of course we equated capitalism with democracy. I think many of us thought that democracy meant we'd all be living like they do in "Dallas".

'But we also see collectivism as natural and just, which is why Bolshevism had such an easy time implanting itself here in the first place. And we think autocracy is natural. We like the strong hand of one man to guide us which is why Bolshevism lasted so long.

'Yeltsin has a strong hand, we've seen that many times now. But he doesn't like the idea of collective agreement and he doesn't mind seeing people pursue their own individualism at the expense of the vast majority—and that runs contrary to our core beliefs. Our president stood by and allowed a few people to take most of the wealth.'

A lot had changed since 1917. But could it be that Russians

wanted the sort of collectivism by which wealth was fairly distributed by an autocrat who listened to them?

'Yes,' Alexander Pumpyansky told me, 'and Yeltsin failed them on both counts. He is just an autocrat.'

Moreover, he was an autocrat with the blood of some 140 victims on his hands. I knew few Russians who defended his actions. Most felt utterly betrayed and disgusted.

'Saying you support democracy is one thing,' said Natasha. 'That's what Yeltsin did. But you can only claim to support democracy if you understand what democratic behaviour is. And clearly our president doesn't.'

Olya, one of Natasha's oldest friends, who had become rich since the collapse of the Soviet Union through hard work and imagination, wanted the president she had camped out to support through three rainy nights in 1991 to resign. 'There are no winners in this,' she said. 'If Yeltsin stays, it will be the death of democracy. His policies have suited me and I didn't want the reforms to slow down, not for one minute. But now I can only spit his name. He has killed the only thing we had to believe in after communism.'

Indeed the president's behaviour seemed to betray his tenacious claim to western leaders—who continued to support him—that he was a democrat and understood what was needed to ensure democracy's survival. With his parliamentary foes safely behind bars he called elections for deputies to a new parliament—this one to be named the Duma after the parliament the tsars had presided over. People could elect new deputies who would understand what it was to disagree with the president. Of course they would be free to express themselves. But on the floor of the new Duma, they would be expected to help Tsar Yeltsin, as people began to openly refer to him, mould a new capitalist realism.

And the new reality would be guided by a new post-Soviet constitution. It would be written by the president's inner circle and would give him vast powers, including the power to legally disband the parliament if it disagreed with him again. In a moment Russians had long waited for, Mikhail Gorbachev finally managed to express what most of them felt: 'What happens if Tsar Boris doesn't like the next parliament? Will he blast it away too?'

As we watched the death march of democracy, it became clear that Yeltsin had achieved something remarkable in the past few months. He had managed to convince the west he was a democrat, though it was obvious he didn't quite understand the rules of the game. He was the man the west trusted and wanted to do business with. They believed he had snuffed out communism's last desperate fury. Financial and food aid flowed to Russia as a vote of confidence in him. No-one else could carry the banner of democracy as he could, or lead his people further away from the closed darkness of a bygone era. His image was a powerful one.

But in Russia, people knew the truth. They didn't want to be told that Boris Yeltsin was the only democrat in Russia or that Russia's Choice, the party which would field most government candidates in the election, was their choice. They knew it wasn't.

CHAPTER 17

FASCISM STRIKES

A society in chaos is actually one which is going through
a period of absolute freedom. Any audacious move stands
a chance of success even if it's based on brazen lies.

IGOR ACHILDIYEV, JOURNALIST, 1993

I first came across Vladimir Volfovich Zhirinovsky sometime in 1990 at an anti-Gorbachev protest. He was then a little-known political player without a seat in the parliament—but in possession of a party—the Liberal Democratic Party of Russia (LDPR). And he was more of a sideshow performer, a clown than someone you could take seriously. But he was beginning to earn himself a reputation as a communist hater who could rival Boris Yeltsin for popularity. He would set up on street corners in Moscow and from the back of a truck tell average workers that he was poor too, that he thought like they did and shared their problems—for which Gorbachev and the Communist Party were to blame.

When I first saw him, he was wooing a crowd of workers with a clutch of old, ribald anecdotes about the party and its leaders, describing Russia's problems in language you might have heard if you'd been sitting in a kitchen with the most average of Russians in a small town in Siberia or down on the Volga. But when I asked this man of the people if he'd come down off the truck to give me an interview, he leant over and went to swipe me a punch. I dodged his fist and escaped with just a bruised shoulder, but he made an impression.

'He's a thug but people will listen to him,' Natasha told me when I described my first encounter with Russia's newest nationalist. 'We have a history of loving tyrants—Lenin, Stalin. Maybe that's the way we should be thinking about Zhirinovsky, because he'll try to sell himself as our saviour.'

She wasn't wrong. Zhirinovsky was a brilliant orator and an even better actor, wooing audiences who by 1992 felt hideously cheated by both communism and democracy. Workers cheered as words of hatred tumbled from his mouth, condemning Gorbachev and Yeltsin. His eyes sparkled with excitement at the response. Zhirinovsky promised the return of empire, to be built on the ashes of communism and capitalism, for he professed to hate both. To his listeners all that mattered was the restoration of what was rightly Russia's—Eastern Europe, East Germany and the inner empire.

Fantastical theories weren't in short supply in Russia during the *perestroika* years, but the claim that the KGB had created the Liberal Democratic Party (LDPR) in 1990 to take up where the Communist Party was leaving off was among the most interesting. Not that there wasn't some circumstantial evidence to support the theory. It would seem more than coincidence that the LDPR appeared on the political scene just a few weeks after the Communist Party surrendered its monopoly on power. Just about everyone I knew suspected the communists had agreed to abandon Article Six because they knew they could regain their stranglehold on the country. Zhirinovsky's Liberal Democratic Party certainly shared with the Communist Party a penchant for fascism.

The KGB denied that Zhirinovsky worked for it, but no-one had ever believed the KGB and they weren't about to begin now. The suspicion lingered, especially when it was discovered that just after the LDPR was registered, one of the Communist Party's publishing houses printed tens of thousands of copies of the LDPR's political manifesto. That was not the sort of favour the communists were in the habit of bestowing upon competitors.

Zhirinovsky's rise was inextricably bound to the Soviet Union's decline. Until Yeltsin unleashed economic shock therapy the country's loss of status was the easiest and most obvious source of discontent to target. Even when Mikhail Gorbachev still had some vestige of power, Zhirinovsky travelled the country preaching to people who felt humiliated by the arms concessions the Soviet leader was making to the west. Zhirinovsky would tell workers that life had been better before the mystery which once surrounded the Soviet Union had been dispelled by Gorbachev, revealing a rusted economy and a society riddled with inequity and anger. The Soviet Union had been diminished, in Zhirinovsky's mind, by the truth. It had been a mighty empire. It would be again, but only with Zhirinovsky at the helm. When the Russian presidency was created in 1991, Zhirinovsky ran for the position accusing Yeltsin, too, of being a stooge of the imperialist west.

Zhirinovsky's election antics were memorable. He stood before the nation on television with a pointer in hand furiously jabbing at a map, proclaiming that he would restore Russia's borders to those which existed before 1913. He would retake Poland and Finland. And a lot of people believed him.

Zhirinovsky lost the race for president but he finished in third place, polling 6 million votes—taking 7 per cent of the electorate— not a bad result for someone Yeltsin had thought of as a clown. Barely two months later in August 1991, Zhirinovsky would watch the Communist Party's botched attempt to restore the once powerful Soviet empire. But if his LDPR owed its existence to the Communist Party which the coup leaders killed off, he no longer felt the weight of the debt. Actually he was filled with rage.

It wasn't just the collapse of the Soviet Union, nor the unleashing of economic shock therapy which angered Vladimir Volfovich. Boris Yeltsin was acceding to more and more of the west's foreign policy directives the further in time Russia moved from the tumultuous events of 1991. It all served to drive Zhirinovsky further towards extremism, if that were possible.

I nervously came face to face with him again for an interview in June 1992. He was railing against American food aid despite the fact that I'd come to talk to him about NATO.

'I want to tell the Americans that I will drive them out of Russia back to a United States without Alaska!' he bellowed with a menacing grin I found frightening because there were no television cameras for him to perform for. This was more than mere performance. I asked whether it was wise to threaten the west.

'Do they ever tire of offending us? It was the Americans who conspired to cause the Soviet Union to fall!' he screeched. 'Then they bought Gaidar and Chubais who sent the Russians into poverty. Now they've given us Kozyrev [Yeltsin's Foreign Minister] to force us to our knees before the world. No, no! I will never tire of telling Washington that until 1867 Alaska was ours. The tsars sold it to the United States but they had no right to. I will take it back. Simple! The same with Finland. It's ours too. If Yeltsin and Kozyrev don't give all our nuclear weapons to Washington, then we'll make the point when we are elected to government one day that Russia is a great power, a superpower, an empire which they will be foolish to toy with. Go away and write that for Australia. And tell your leaders not to stick by Washington because one day our soldiers will be sailing in your waters too.' And with that he got up and marched off.

There were dozens of foreign policy issues for Zhirinovsky to manipulate. NATO was a target waiting to be hit.

The collapse of Soviet influence in Eastern Europe had left Russia without a defence bloc. The Warsaw Pact was no more and in its wake NATO was muttering about a 'partnership for peace'. The west wanted to welcome the former Soviet republics into its fold, create a buffer zone around Russia and eventually invite Moscow to join. Zhirinovsky hated the idea. To him, co-operative security, an army under democratic control and defensive rather than offensive policies were just post-Cold War buzz words designed to humiliate Russia.

'I am against, against, against NATO,' he blurted out in heavily accented English on the day Estonia announced it would apply for NATO membership. 'Russia will never allow these imperialists to swim in our backyard. If Estonia or Lithuania think they can join NATO and be protected by the west, they should think again. We will spray them with nuclear waste. The communists were frightened of three weak, dependent Baltic states. I'm not. And I'm not frightened of NATO.'

Zhirinovsky had words of warning for the Japanese too. In late 1992 Tokyo, aware of Russia's dire economic state, offered Boris Yeltsin favourable loans in return for the Kurile Islands, seized by Russia from Japan in 1945. Most Russians found the offer insulting, but Zhirinovsky's reply was hardly diplomatic. 'The Japanese already have the experience of Hiroshima and Nagasaki,' he said. 'But fifty years have passed and perhaps they've forgotten what it means. I'll remind them!'

Zhirinovsky understood that the more radical his rhetoric, the greater his menace would be. But it was no doubt his ability to tap into the Russian psyche, to understand their sense of loss which made him most dangerous. The Russians might have been embarrassed by his antics, they probably wished he wouldn't be elected to any official post, but Zhirinovsky nevertheless filled them with hope, something Yeltsin had failed to do. Yeltsin presided over price increases and *nomenklatura* privatisation. Zhirinovsky told the poverty-stricken workers what they wanted to hear and made them feel someone cared for them.

The way Natasha saw it, support for Zhirinovsky was simply a way to make people feel better. He said the right things, however preposterous—like promising the return of the empire. For most people, democracy had delivered only price rises and more corruption.

'You have to understand how people feel. It's not a good feeling to wake up in the morning in a country which no longer exists, to eat food donated by the west and to feel frightened because you have relatives living in countries which used to be ours but which are tearing themselves apart,' Natasha said.

It was one of the more gruesome features of the second Russian revolution. The world's last empire was exploding into an inferno of war, which swirled around Russia, making the Russians feel even less secure. In Tadjikistan on the Afghan border, civil war had claimed 70 000 lives in just one year. To its west, Armenia and Azerbaijan were blowing up each other's villages in the disputed strip between them called Nagorny Karabakh. Every night, the television news relayed pictures of wailing women mourning their sons and husbands lost in the slaughter. In Moldova, the Russians were being told to go home by an increasingly vocal nationalist army while in the Baltic states the former Soviet invaders were being asked to sit for exam-inations in the local tongue which if they failed would lead to their expulsion from countries in which their children had been born.

Closer to home, Russian generals were manipulating a vicious sep-aratist war with the tiny Georgian province of Abkhazia and the new Georgian leader Eduard Shevardnadze. Tens of thousands of people were being killed. Everywhere you looked, there was fighting. Ugly skirmishes which no-one had any power or ability to put down. Another was brewing just next door in Ukraine, which to most Rus-sians was little more than an extension of Russia. After two years of unsuccessful negotiation with Moscow, the Ukrainian leadership decided to lay claim to the Crimean Peninsula.

The peninsula had been given to Ukraine by Nikita Khrushchev in 1954, though at the time the transfer was meaningless as Russia and Ukraine were part of the same country. On Crimea's pristine shores the former Soviet elite had built their sanatoria and holiday homes as the seven hundred ships of the prized Black Sea fleet moored, for the most part quietly, nearby.

When Boris Yeltsin and Ukraine's Leonid Kravchuk discussed ending the life of the Soviet Union in December 1991, they couldn't resolve the issue of the peninsula's status. Compromise had seemed close on several occasions since then. But each time, both men would back away, terrified of the nationalists at home who were preaching to constituencies which were becoming poorer—and larger—by the day.

Zhirinovsky shamelessly used the Crimean dilemma throughout 1992, spluttering out a declaration on its status whenever a television camera turned his way.

'The Crimean Peninsula is Russian!' he proclaimed. 'It always was and always will be. Now is not the time for bartering land or nuclear warheads. Kiev should think before it talks. Kravchuk should know that those warheads which sit on our ships in the peninsula can easily be turned towards his beautiful city. The peninsula is ours!'

Zhirinovsky took his cry for 'Russia's Crimea' along with his other easy solutions to Russia's worsening economic problems onto the campaign trail for the parliamentary elections Yeltsin had called after he'd blasted away the old legislature. Gorbachev might have lost the outer empire. But Yeltsin would lose the Russians whatever remained, said Zhirinovsky as he waged his campaign for an empire he said Yeltsin would do nothing to restore.

One afternoon in November 1993, I received a call from an acquaintance introduced to me years earlier as the KGB officer who had been charged with guarding Andrei Sakharov when he was returned to Moscow from exile in Gorky.

'I thought it might be interesting for you to see how our young people are reacting to Yeltsin's democracy,' he said. 'Perhaps you'd like to see a youth forum discuss where Russia is heading and talk to some of them?'

In a redbrick warehouse on the northern edges of the capital, we were waved through a heavy metal gate behind which sat three men brandishing rifles. Inside some boys were setting out copies of a political manifesto for Pamyat—an anti-Semitic, right-wing paramilitary organisation of out-of-work thugs, bursting with hatred.

'Leave your microphone and recorder here please,' came the first order. 'Now step over here so we can frisk you.'

'You've been invited here to observe and correctly report our activities. We don't have many friends but we don't need them,' said Anatoly Barkashov, the group's leader. 'We have tens of thousands of members and people calling us day and night to join. If you sign this document pledging yourself to accurate non-biased reporting we will allow you to record our proceedings.'

I signed and recorded an extraordinary event.

'Volchek, take your turn at the podium!' shouted Barkashov.

'Thank you sir!' said Volchek moving confidently towards centre stage, his adolescent arms so tattooed barely a centimetre of skin was untainted.

'We are here to affirm our belief that the country is being taken into a dead end. Our television screens are inundated with non-Russians [a euphemism for Jews] and the leadership has sold our soul to the west. We are faced with a crisis and we see no choice but to begin a heavy recruitment drive so as to stop our youth falling into the hands of no-gooders. Many in this district have chosen to join Zhirinovsky even though he himself is a Jew. But we have decided that we must unite against the one real enemy—Yeltsin.

'Pamyat is joining the Liberal Democratic Party, the Russian National Congress, the Russian Republican Party and Russian National Unity. Together we will urge people to vote for the nationalists in the parliamentary election. Those who choose not to will pay the price!'

Three generations of Russian men rose to their feet to applaud young Volchek, while above the noise Barkashov asked whether I'd like to record an interview with the youngest in the room. He was fourteen.

'Why am I here? Because I am only very young and already I have no future. The democrats tell me I have no past. It was a huge lie. Now they are robbing me of my potential. What chance do I have of being able to pay for an education, or of finding work?

'I believe that the Jews are responsible for our problems at the moment. They are the rich businessmen who've stolen our property. And there are too many Jews in the government,' he said.

'And when you say that those who vote against the nationalists will pay the price, what do you mean?' I asked.

'We mean that they will be responsible for losing Russia. Russians must stand up and be counted because unless we act we will lose more than just land. We will be raped by scavengers.'

Perhaps he'd been ordered not to be explicit. Perhaps he was too young to have understood what the group was preaching but the message was clear nonetheless. An assorted bunch of the unemployed, the downtrodden, under-paid factory workers and grandfathers with chests heavily laden with war medals believed that Zhirinovsky was the new messiah. That he happened to be of a race they despised had to be put to one side for Russia's sake. After all, Zhirinovsky, despite his origins, hated the Jews as much as they did and he shared their ideals—the resurrection of a great and mighty Russia with its neighbours under Moscow's control and a nuclear arsenal capable of reducing the rest of the world to a quivering, compliant mess. Beyond this, it was all a bit academic.

Zhirinovsky sat with his legs thrust wide, staring not at the television interviewer but straight down the camera lens. It would be one of the most important performances of his campaign in the December 1993 parliamentary elections. But as we watched, Grisha noted that Zhirinovsky was using a different tactic. Gone was the promise of a renewed empire. Now he was offering what Russians wanted even more after two years of economic hardship.

It was an astounding grab bag of lies. Workers' wages would be increased. Price liberalisation would be reversed. Russia's alcoholics would get free vodka. Young women would get husbands and free bras. Privatised enterprises would be returned to the workers. People would be free to lynch bandits on street corners or wherever they happened to catch them. Anyone who'd lost their savings in the recent money reform fiasco would have them returned and the process of privatisation would be stopped immediately. The strangest thing about the interview was that despite the incredulity of the host and the obviousness of the lies, it was all utterly believable.

'You've got to admit the promise of free vodka and subsidised prices is pretty appealing,' said Masha, responding to my outrage at Zhirinovsky's latest ploy. 'It's a great strategy,' she said. 'Isn't that what you do in the west?'

It was as though Zhirinovsky had tapped into the minds of those struggling to survive under capitalism. 'He's what we need,' I heard older people saying on the streets. 'He'll bring back some order.'

The money to pay for all he promised would be easy to find. Russia would rev up its military–industrial complex and begin producing weapons to sell to America's enemies, including Saddam Hussein. Russia would take whatever resources it needed to regain its rightful place in the world from its now independent neighbours who, in return, would be forced to pay world market prices for any resources they required from Russia. And if they refused to pay, they would be starved or nuked. It was crazy stuff. But to a nation searching for a new nirvana, a new saviour, whatever Zhirinovsky promised was music to their ears, even if people didn't really believe he was capable of delivering. That didn't matter. The communists promised nirvana and failed to deliver. The democrats promised freedom and failed.

One night in the final stages of the parliamentary election campaign, I threw a *tusovka* (get together) and with friends sat around discussing what we'd been hearing on the streets about the poll.

Sasha Lubimov, a television journalist who'd turned his hand to the new ways and become a very successful media entrepreneur, said he knew people who believed that Zhirinovsky would deliver them to a new and fair nirvana.

'They think he's offering them a paradise on earth. It's as intoxicating as communism! He has no scruples. He just makes promises he can't keep—just like the communists did.'

Olya piped up. 'At least his aim is clear. He says to Russians: "Vote for me, I'm a dictator." And they know the benefits of dictatorship. All Yeltsin can say is to vote for the democrats because they're democrats.'

'I think it's deeper than that. He's riding the sentiment of the nation,' said Natasha. 'People feel robbed and they want their empire back. Zhirinovsky is just saying, "OK. Have it back. It's your fate, your destiny."'

'That's true,' said Sasha, 'but our people are naive. Most people don't see that it's a political trick. And there's no reason for people not to believe him. He's never been in power and he's never made promises that he's broken. Even I see the merit in voting for someone who can say, "I have never been a communist".'

'Here we go again. Let's hang all the communists because only they break their promises,' said Natasha. 'The democrats are so moral, aren't they Sasha?'

'Moral they might not be but they're not promising to restore the empire when there is no empire to bring back!'

Television advertising is an expensive business in Russia. Western-based multinationals exposing their products to arguably the biggest untapped open market in the world would pay up to US$35 000 for a minute of air time in 1993. For Russia's Choice, led by Yigor Gaidar, air time was free during the 1993 parliamentary election campaign.

Night after night, saturation political propaganda told Russians they could make only one choice when they cast their vote—Russia's Choice. Unless the democrats took a majority of seats in the new Duma, the chaos would continue, according to the advertisements. Russia needed stability. It needed a parliament with which the democratically elected president could work. Times had been tough, Russia's Choice admitted, but life would soon get better. People needed only to trust Yeltsin—the man who had delivered them from the evil clutches of communism.

'They probably think that if they ignore Zhirinovsky he'll go away,' said my husband Grisha. But just because the communists are gone doesn't mean we've miraculously acquired the ability to recognise lies when they're told. Surely the democrats don't think that people understand that the rubbish coming out of Zhirinovsky's mouth is all lies?'

Not even when Zhirinovsky revealed his vision of Russians as the 'master race' did the democrats consider that they ought to warn the electorate about the dangers they would face if they voted for Zhirinovsky.

In pamphlets and videos distributed free to anyone who'd take them, Zhirinovsky, over pictures of young men and women with black caps and green military uniforms marching in unison and singing patriotic songs, vowed to restore order. He would nuke any country, even former republics, if a single Russian was harmed by them. And inter-ethnic marriage was unacceptable, he declared. 'When you mate a collie with a German shepherd what do you get? Breeding is the most valuable thing in the world. Breeding means quality,' he'd told *Moscow Magazine* in 1990.

It was perfect campaign ammunition for the democrats. But Russia's Choice ignored it. The Russians, they said, would see Zhirinovsky for what he was, a fascist. The LDPR, they thought, would not notch up enough votes to pass the 6 per cent barrier to take up seats in their own right within the new parliament. As Russia's Choice put to air long-winded justifications (spoken by Yigor Gaidar, the man most Russians loved to hate because of his economic shock therapy) for the two years of horror Russians had endured, Zhirinovsky spoke to the voters in a language they understood, without reference to a market economy or inflation. Life, he told them, would simply be better under him.

By the time Russia's Choice realised that Zhirinovsky had millions of followers, it was too late. Far too late.

On 12 December 1993 as we watched the poll results trickle through on computers donated to Russian television by the European Union, the news for Russia's Choice was all bad. The LDPR snatched 23 per cent of the vote, beating Russia's Choice hands down. The reborn Russian Communist Party came off second best with 12 per cent of the available seats in the new parliament which would operate under Yeltsin's new constitution which voters had also approved and which gave the president virtually unlimited new powers.

More than a handful of people I knew thought about leaving Russia. I too felt like packing my bags and heading home.

Grisha didn't seem at all upset when I told him I'd been offered the chance to present a radio current affairs program at home. It was November and already freezing cold. But that was just about all that was remotely like the Russia he'd been born to.

Russia was rather like the wild west for him now. Of course there were lots of opportunities for a Russian with fluent English to hop on the business bandwagon, but there was little for Grisha to do in the new Russia which didn't entail some degree of criminality. He seemed happy enough to give Australia a try. I was just tired. Exhausted. After nearly four years of constant revolution, every time anything resembling a story began to break I was overcome with black depression. And it was becoming painful to watch people being thrown from pillar to post as the political intrigues forced the lofty notion of democracy further and further into the distance. It hurt to watch people being cheated. I needed quiet and Sydney certainly had that to offer even though with sickness in the family being home would be anything but peaceful. It was a painful decision to make, leaving Russia. But in the end a combination of exhaustion and a draining emotional insecurity resulting from my father's death and my brother-in-law Paul being struck down with cancer shook the ground beneath me. I needed to go home.

We tried desperately to put a positive spin on the decision but our friends didn't bite the bait. Natasha was dubious we'd ever return. 'But at least you're taking a little bit of Russia with you and maybe that will bring you back. We'll see,' she said when I told her our news.

Masha thought the decision brave. 'We should start thinking about leaving too, but I'm not sure how to live without this place!'

Nor were we.

As we sifted through years of accumulated newspapers and notes, old clothes and pots and pans, preparing to pack up, Russia slid deeper and deeper into winter and economic depression. The prime minister, Victor Chernomyrdin, tried to fix the problems. And for a month or two inflation began to fall slightly from an annual high of 2000 per cent. Boris Yeltsin gave Chernomyrdin his full backing and even the reformers who remained in cabinet believed Chernomyrdin would haul Russia out of the abyss. But the malaise was too deep. The old *nomenklatura* continued to corrupt bureaucrats in order to grab what they could. The rich refused to invest in Russia, sending their millions overseas. Factories struggled and state subsidies became scarcer and smaller. The rouble continued to nosedive as the mafia became stronger. Little changed.

The Duma which Yeltsin had hoped would be more helpful than the last parliament disintegrated into high farce. Zhirinovsky turned it into a hell-on-earth for the democratic deputies, screaming at Foreign Minister Andrei Kozyrev and Privatisation Minister Anatoly Chubais, the only two reformers who weren't purged from the government after the poll, that they were both 'candidates for a mental asylum' (a reference to the Communist Party practice of throwing its more vocal opponents into psychiatric institutions). He physically assaulted others who challenged him, including a female deputy from the Women's Party of Russia. But Zhirinovsky saw nothing unseemly in his behaviour. To him, the reformers were enemies.

As the packers moved into our apartment to begin loading boxes of our possessions for the trek home, I felt like a bloated capitalist tucking away the loot from years of plundering—the busts of Lenin, the ten-volume tomes of his works in Russian, the *perestroika* art and Soviet kitsch. It all made me feel guilty, as though I was stealing a part of a system which, for all its faults, hadn't left people hungry and unemployed.

'So you're a correspondent,' remarked one of the packers.

'Yes, a correspondent going home,' I answered.

'Why do you want to take this shit with you? I took all my busts of Lenin and Stalin down to the garbage the day they brought Gorbachev back from Foros. And you know it felt good. But you foreigners, you're quite mad you know. Are you sentimental about the Soviet Union? Sad that we're free or something?'

I could barely contain my embarrassment, blurting out that I was delighted the Russians were now free. Only I wished it were a different sort of freedom.

'Ah! Don't be silly,' said the packer, 'freedom is freedom.'

'But what about inflation? And that madman Zhirinovsky? Don't you wonder about where you're headed when there's armed conflict right here in the middle of Moscow? Doesn't that make you think about the sort of democracy you've got?' I asked.

'No. Not at all. I voted for Zhirinovsky in December. You know why? I thought he'll keep them on their toes in the Duma, keep their minds on the threat of fascism while we get on with our lives. Political intrigue means real freedom. You've probably been sitting around Moscow for four years trying to make some western sense out of our politics, sending yourself crazy. You'd have been better off thinking like a Russian.'

CHAPTER 18

FROM THE ASHES

Russia is a kingdom almost unknown in Europe during the last centuries ... This vast empire embraces all variety of climate and comprehends every species of resource ... solitary resistance is vain against an empire which can produce soldiers like grains of sand.

GUSTAVUS III OF SWEDEN

'They'll never kill the KGB,' friends would tell me after the collapse of the Soviet Union. 'It's too big, too strong,' they'd say. 'The Communist Party is only the flesh of evil. The KGB is the soul.'

The Communist Party might have been back in business but it was struggling for air beneath the rubble Solzhenitsyn predicted would suffocate his blessed Russia. Not so the party's guardian, the KGB. Everyone knew it had been spared destruction and was watching the chaos from its yellow stone headquarters not far from the Kremlin.

Still operating with a workforce of almost half a million, the KGB was given a new name, the Federal Security Service (FSB), a new boss and new orders from the new regime, but at the Ministry of Love—as George Orwell had dubbed its parody—even though life was outwardly different, things were really still the same.

The KGB had transformed every Soviet citizen into a victim of the political system it sustained using a very simple philosophy.

Anyone with a political view opposed in any way to the one touted by the regime was a traitor. All others—millions of them—were potential informers.

Now, as the empire slowly sank, at the Lubyanka (KGB head-quarters in Moscow) those who didn't want to enter the world of capitalism bunkered down for the storm, certain that with their expe-rience and deadly armoury they would outlast whatever punishment democracy threw their way. More so because the agency established by Lenin to protect the revolution was not being forced to open its records to the public.

Others, too, were not unhappy that the records would remain closed. 'That's not such a bad thing,' Marina Sokolova told me at a 1992 candlelight memorial service outside Lubyanka held to com-memorate KGB victims, among them her parents. Both were minor functionaries in the Leningrad administration but had disappeared in the dead of night in 1939.

Marina was fifteen then. The NKVD (as the KGB was known at the time), informed her by letter in two short sentences that her parents had been sent to prison for anti-Soviet agitation of an unspe-cified nature. Marina waited for them to be released. But they never were.

'I spent fifty years becoming bitter, trying to remember their faces. The men who took my father, then my mother two nights later. I thought that I might see them some day on the street and I could ask them why. What had my parents done? Even now I sometimes think I would like to find those men. But what would I achieve? What would any of us here achieve if we knew who killed our fam-ilies and our friends?

'We might end up hating more than just the party. Who amongst us hasn't been an informer for the KGB, or hasn't known that someone in their family has been compromised? If it wasn't one person, then it was another.' She paused, distressed.

'And if they open the files, then what happens? We queue outside Lubyanka for the moment of truth and we discover that the man or woman who lived next door to us for thirty years was telling the KGB who came to visit us and what we said to each other; that they were listening through the walls. I don't want to know. In thirty years I never spoke with my neighbours or my friends without a fear I cannot describe to you—you see, we were all victims, both sides. I was too frightened to share my fear with my own child in case he innocently repeated at school that his mother thought somebody or other was KGB!'

But the KGB had not only infiltrated every crevice of every mind across the Soviet Union, it had a stake in every corner of the empire.

In December 1991 a Russian newspaper published for the first time details of the KGB's various directorates and their functions. It was mind-boggling. The KGB controlled the Soviet Union's borders ensuring they were never breached. It guarded nuclear installations and operated anti-terrorist units which specialised in assassination, and units within those parts of the military which controlled the Soviet Union's nuclear weapons. There wasn't an institution or factory across the old Soviet Union where a KGB cell wasn't searching for dissenters, vetting workers for any hint of anti-Leninism. It controlled all communications. The KGB was literally everywhere in the old Soviet Union. It would have been impossible to destroy. If its men accepted its destruction, the borders and strategic installations would be left without central control. If they didn't, they had a huge arsenal to turn against the new regime. The best Boris Yeltsin could do was break it up into fifteen smaller organisations—one for each of the former republics.

The new Federal Security Service (FSB) was meant to be a professional intelligence agency, respecting the rights of individuals and the rights of its sovereign neighbours. But if Boris Yeltsin thought giving the KGB on Russian territory a new name would automatically tame it, he was sorely mistaken. It kept in close contact with its sibling security organs across the former Soviet Union, one of which—in Belorussia—didn't even bother to pay lip service to reform by dropping the KGB title.

The KGB's all-Union empire might have disappeared, but if its soldiers had learnt a lesson from the decades of terror and bloodshed they and their predecessors had inflicted, it was how to protect themselves, how to be loyal. Democracy wouldn't tear them apart. For most of the new KGB chiefs in the outlying republics, there was, by 1992, a new common enemy—Yeltsin, who was trying to tear the organisation apart, and his economic reforms whose tremors were being felt from Siberia to Tadjikistan. That the KGB might strike back must have been among Boris Yeltsin's greatest fears as the break-up of the Soviet Union created near to 300 million paupers, and as Russians living in the 'near abroad' (the former Soviet republics) began to feel the anti-Russian wrath of newly independent governments which treated the KGB as vermin.

Gorbachev's reforms had restrained the KGB, but not crippled it. They certainly hadn't delivered Boris Yeltsin an organisation which was prepared to answer for its actions and exercise loyalty towards the elected government. Indeed, it bitterly resented Yeltsin's role in the break-up of the Union. And without a loyal FSB, Yeltsin was undoubtedly vulnerable.

General Dmitri Belyaev was a grey man who wore a grey suit which looked like it had seen better days and grey plastic shoes which zipped up the side. When the KGB became the FSB it decided to establish a public relations office and Belyaev was one of its officers. He tried terribly hard to be open, helpful and hardworking, like he thought a western PR man would be. But it didn't come easy, that much was obvious. To begin with, the general was in the Soviet habit of 'popping out' for hours at a time, or disappearing for days. After literally dozens of phone calls, the upshot was that I'd have to wait my turn for a tour of Lubyanka and a friendly chat with people who worked there.

My friends were genuinely baffled. Why would I want to smell the blood of their history? Wasn't it enough, Masha asked, that I was watching as the Russians made their way towards real freedom? Why did I need to look back to a time they wanted to forget?

'You'll learn nothing by going there,' declared Natasha, 'except perhaps that they're just like us. But with blood instead of dirt under their nails.'

Belyaev was standing on the street outside the main door of the Lubyanka to greet me. I felt a tinge of pity for him. He looked a sad figure, dwarfed by the enormity of the yellow stone house of horror across the road from which, on a grassy square, the mighty statue of Felix Dzerzhinsky (the founding father of the CheKa, the security police established by Vladimir Lenin) had once stood. Now both Lenin and Dzerzhinsky were gone and the general looked alone, as much a victim as everyone else.

He was a slight man. He barely looked strong enough to push open the huge wooden doors to the foyer. As he did, I heard the creak of mechanical springs. I looked towards the ceiling and no fewer than fifteen camera lenses were turning their gaze towards us.

'How do you say? Snapshots! For the family album,' laughed the general.

The building was enormous, fearsome, austere. Narrow corridors, every third light bulb burnt out, gave way to hundreds of offices in a maze which left me confused about which side of Moscow they looked out upon. Perhaps that's why the Russians said that every office in the building had a view of Siberia. Nor did there seem to be many people around the stuffy, dank second and third floors to which the general had confined my tour. Perhaps the FSB warriors were buried in the basement, among the bones of their victims, combing through files. The air was stale. I wondered whether it might have smelled different when the place bustled with people who were being threatened and tortured, when people like Belyaev extracted confessions from the innocent for no reason other than a paranoic bloodlust. I asked the general who I would be meeting.

'Me!' he said.

'Just you?' I asked.

'Just me!'

Standing in the belly of the most dreaded building in Russia, I feigned contentment and pulled out my tape-recorder as the general directed me to a chair in his office, calling in his secretary to order the mandatory cup of black tea, the favoured potion of every Soviet official I'd ever visited. He was obviously a fastidious man, his desk was clean and tidy with neatly piled documents in one corner.

'For most of our men, the break-up of the Soviet Union is inconvenient,' he started, even before I managed to ask my first question. Even so, he continued, his colleagues supported President Yeltsin. But people had to understand that the secret police had been as much the victims of economic reform as everyone else.

'Our new chief [Nikolai Golushko] is a good leader. Yes, he is from Ukraine. But that's what we need at the moment. Someone who understands the tendency in our countries to be together—for our general economic benefit,' said General Belyaev, assuming that I would agree with him that the Soviet Union was the only legitimate form in which the members of the new CIS could live and prosper.

It had been a high-risk strategy for Boris Yeltsin to appoint Golushko, who had been the KGB chief in Ukraine. Yeltsin had tried to humiliate the FSB by placing it under the control of the Police Minister, a move which the highly trained security police resented. But that edict had been rescinded by the Constitutional Court which reasoned that the creation of a super-ministry of Russia's security organs was dangerous given the country's history. Now Yeltsin was wooing the organisation by letting it believe he too wanted the reintegration of a union of sorts. Given the political tension between the government and the parliament the strategy could easily have backfired. The parliament also considered reintegration a sensible option and there was a chance that it would attempt to use the FSB to achieve its aim. It was not clear where Golushko's allegiances would fall.

'I think the director of the FSB would like to see a sane outcome to this dispute. We are all one people, you know. The people of the former Soviet Union have blood ties which can't be easily torn apart. If there are reforms in Russia, they are felt in Uzbekhistan. We have lived together for far too long,' said the general, offering another cup of tea.

'Where will the FSB stand,' I asked, 'if there's a showdown between President Yeltsin and the parliament?'

'Well, I'm not sure I can answer that question, he said, 'I'm just a cog in the wheel. Perhaps you'd like to put it in writing and I'll ask Director Golushko.'

'Did you support the putsch against Gorbachev in 1991?' I asked.

'I had no choice. I follow orders,' he replied.

When the president turned his tanks on the White House in October 1993, Nikolai Golushko stood by the parliament and was duly sacked early in 1994. In his autobiography, Yeltsin claims Golushko was sacked after a disagreement over the terms of the amnesty granted by the parliament to Rutskoi and Khasbulatov who had led the October uprising. Whatever the real reason, Golushko's sacking left Yeltsin with an angry, vengeful security apparatus he couldn't control and which seemed to back his opponents. And the man who succeeded Golushko was a Union man. Sergei Stepashin wasn't boss for long, but long enough to establish a permanent KGB secretariat with head-quarters in Moscow to co-ordinate what remained of an army with extraordinary capabilities, an underground empire.

As Natasha put it, 'People don't like the KGB but it's thinking the same way most of them do. They think the only hope for us now is to create another Union.'

The push for reintegration hadn't escaped Yeltsin's political anten-nae either. If he wasn't listening to the FSB, he had surely heard the piercing cry of the Russians who voted for Vladimir Zhirinovsky in the 1993 parliamentary election. People wanted the reforms to slow down. The old Union, evil though it might have been, was beginning to take on a rosy glow, the sort that only comes with a profound sense of loss. The era of 'multicentrism' was about to come to an end. There could be only one centre—Moscow. Politically Boris Yeltsin had no choice.

Russian foreign policy did an about-turn, becoming more assertive, even chauvinistic. Suddenly the very liberal Foreign Minister, Andrei Kozyrev, was mouthing the words, ever so reluctantly, of the nationalists. Russia was a great power. Backed by an empire, who needed NATO? A Russian empire with a mighty military and a strong KGB could protect itself and its neighbours. Russia's natural role in the region was to dominate. For a year after Zhirinovsky's parliamentary win, the Kremlin moved steadily away from reform.

By the end of 1994, after three years of virtual war with the FSB the Kremlin officially proclaimed its objective to be the reintegration of the Union. And what better way to improve relations with the former Soviet states than by using the only organisation which remained whole, strong and capable—the empire's secret police.

The FSB Chief Sergei Stepashin, like the chief of the president's guard (a KGB colonel, Alexander Korzhakov) believed fervently that the Union had served Russia well. Over and over, they whispered in Boris Yeltsin's ear that a new Union purged of communism could harmonise the economies of the old republics, while making them subservient to Russia which, after all, had borne the financial burden of spiriting them into the modern world. The timing was perfect, with most of the old republics on their knees. Russia could use Ukraine's pipelines and coal, Azerbaijan's oil, Uzbekhistan's cotton, Kazakhstan's wheat, uranium, gold, silver and platinum, Tadjikistan's aluminium, gravel and sand, and Georgia's zinc. The store of wealth was unfathomable. All Russia needed was a new Union with capitalism rather than communism as the guiding light.

As 1994 drew to a close, speculation about Boris Yeltsin's health reached a frenzied peak. That he drank was obvious. The Moscow-based media was accustomed to the maverick's more colourful characteristics—his paranoia, his drinking. But no-one knew whether to believe the rumours when they started circulating as early as 1989 that the president of Russia was ill with a chronic heart condition.

It was like a game of cat and mouse trying to pin down the nature of the president's condition, even after 1992 when he was running Russia alone and his health had a bearing on things. No-one in his press service or his office seemed to know exactly what was wrong with him. And if they did, they weren't going to let on. Who could blame them? The health of leaders in the lost era had been a closely guarded secret. Anyone who suggested that Leonid Brezhnev, Yuri Andropov or Konstantin Chernenko were dead, for all intents and purposes, long before their hearts stopped beating was demoted with enormous loss of privilege. No-one was ever allowed to think that the 'leader' was incapable of leading.

When, in 1992, Boris Nikolaevich first disappeared from public view for a longer than usual period, people assumed he was drinking. He loved a drop or two. This had been public knowledge since his infamous trip to the United States in 1988 when he stepped down from an Aeroflot jet and, according to Russian journalists travelling with him, promptly turned towards the nearest wheel upon which he urinated. Most Russians I knew laughed off the incident. They didn't mind the fact that he was a bit of a larrikin who liked his vodka. So did they. Boris Yeltsin was a Russian *muzhik*—a real man. And in Russia, real men drink a lot. Drinking didn't matter so long as he could still govern Russia.

When he appeared in the congress in 1993, at the height of his battle with the parliament, his hair flopping over his puffed eyes, his speech slurred, the typical reaction on the street was: 'Well, he's a man under enormous pressure. He has to release it somehow.' Even his enemies forgave him when they discovered his mother had just died. In every way, Yeltsin was the public embodiment of the average Russian male.

Any circumstance—or lack of it—could provoke the call for a quick, clean shot of glistening vodka, chased down by a pickled cucumber wet with brine and a corner of brown bread. It was the Russian cure-all. I stopped being shocked by the level of vodka consumption about one month after I arrived in Moscow on my ABC posting. I could only guess what things might have been like in the 1970s before vodka rationing. In 1990, there were as many drunks as *babushkas*. It wasn't uncommon to walk through a park and stumble over them, curled up sleeping in long uncut grass, or to see them snoozing on ice-packed footpaths in the middle of winter. Nor was it exceptional to see a drunk stagger up to a perfect stranger, then another, and offer to share a bottle or two. It was called *'na troikh'* (by three)—the idea being that a bottle of Stolichnaya could adequately satisfy the alcohol craving of three people. I lost count of the number of times Russian friends would pass out after a couple of bottles of Stolichnaya, only to wake up the next morning and reach for more. In Russia everyone liked drinking. But by 1994, drunks had almost disappeared from the streets even though the ritual of vodka drinking lived on in people's homes. For most people, drinking had become confined to real occasions. For most, except the president.

He continued to drink regardless of its appropriateness. In April 1992 he forgot to turn up at a meeting with the American Treasury Secretary, Nicholas Brady. No-one seemed too bothered by this— standing up an American Treasury official was putting him in his place. But by 1994, Yeltsin's drinking began to cause the Russians enormous embarrassment, especially when he insisted on drinking on visits abroad. In Germany to mark the 1994 departure of Russian troops, Yeltsin seized a band conductor's baton, taking charge of the music and dancing as he waved the baton at the bemused musicians, and in Russia people cringed. It didn't help when two months later he couldn't get off a plane during a stopover at Shannon Airport in

Ireland where the Irish prime minister was waiting on the tarmac to greet him.

But it wasn't the drinking which worried his Kremlin keepers. It was his heart. By 1993 it was clear that the bouts of angina were in fact attacks of myocardial ischaemia which restricts blood flow to the heart, and that they were becoming more frequent. At least twice they led to an actual heart attack. Each time Yeltsin was hospitalised his aides would insist he was still in control, with the nuclear button by his side along with piles of paperwork and documents which he was signing. But he was spending more time in hospitals, sanatoria and on holidays than in the Kremlin which he left in the hands of the so-called 'Party of War'—the first deputy prime minister, the chief of the Kremlin Guard and the director of the FSB. Keeping tabs on the three was Yeltsin's prime minister, Victor Chernomyrdin, whose loyalty was assumed despite his presidential ambitions.

But the president's condition gave rise to more than ambition. Inevitably, there was frenzied speculation that the Russian leader was far sicker than the Kremlin was conceding and that perhaps he wasn't doing much leading at all.

Each time Yeltsin was rushed to hospital, the US dollar rose sharply on foreign exchange markets. And Russians began asking who was in charge. Who was running the mighty battleship Russia? Yeltsin or the Party of War?

Had the president's aides been more open about the nature of his condition, the speculation might have stopped. It wasn't enough that when he was feeling up to it the Kremlin would film the president playing tennis with his cabinet colleagues. Indeed, it merely compounded the fear that Yeltsin, like the geriatrics who'd ruled before him, was largely incapacitated and, like Brezhnev, plugged into an energizer for the occasional public appearance. There was a growing feeling among Russians that they were being lied to about the leader's state of health, much as they'd been lied to about Brezhnev, Andropov and Chernenko.

With elections to the nationalist-dominated parliament due at the end of 1995, it was doing the president's cause no good at all to be cast in the same light as the old men whose era he had swept away.

Nadya Chertkova had believed the geriatrics of the Communist Party when they promised nirvana. But *perestroika* had exposed their promises as empty. She was among the tens of thousands whose anger Gorbachev had unleashed in the late 1980s. She had gone sleepless for three nights in August 1991 to prove she would not submit to an idea and a system which had long ago failed. And she had every reason to despise the communists. Her grandfather died in Stalin's camps. Her father was hounded out of work because several times he had mildly criticised the regime before his bosses. And yet she had followed the party men. Nadya wanted more now. She wanted a normal life. Stability. Peace.

I met her in January 1995, a few weeks after Grisha and I returned to Moscow for a short visit. She was a friend of friends. A few weeks earlier Russian troops had surrounded Grozny, the capital of the Russian province of Chechnya which, three years earlier in the aftermath of the 1991 coup attempt, had unilaterally declared its independence from Russia. Chechnya could be crushed in a few hours, the Defence Minister, Pavel Grachev, told Boris Yeltsin who was yet again out of public sight, and unable to answer the crucial question: Why had the Kremlin decided to mount a military campaign to bring Chechnya to heel some three years after it had declared independence?

As she'd boarded a train bound for the rugged southern Caucasus, Nadya wondered whether her life could withstand this final assault. Her son was one of the Russian conscripts sent to fight the Chechen rebels. She was going to search for him.

'It was horribly cruel for them to send him to war without training. He was inducted only in November, one month before they declared war on Chechnya. My God! I cannot even think about how he lived.

'How is it that an army as mighty as ours was, with generals not only schooled in war but born with it in their blood can think they can win one against Chechnya with young boys?

'I went to Grozny and I found Ilya. He was in shock. He was weeping as our aircraft dropped bombs on the city and then he saw that it was not just the Chechens we were killing. We were killing Russians too. And for what?'

Nadya talked her son into deserting. It wasn't easy, she told me. He feared punishment.

'I told him that the only person he had to fear was God and God alone. This is a barbaric, loathsome war, I said to him. He still wasn't sure what to do. I begged him to ask his commanders who they were fighting for. Why had they been sent to Chechnya three years after it had broken with Russia?'

Ilya returned to Moscow with his mother. But she was among the lucky ones. Other mothers also went to Grozny to find their boys, but most returned home alone.

Boris Yeltsin sold the war in Chechnya to a deeply shocked western world by claiming that Russia was merely protecting its sovereignty. It was a matter of keeping Russia whole, together, for the sake of long-term stability and peace. But this was only part of the story.

Chechnya produces oil. Not much of it but enough to make it an object of Moscow's desire. More importantly, the area is home to a huge and sophisticated refinery able to process the oil under the control of the Russian new rich and send it to foreign countries via the Caspian Sea. But Chechnya, since it declared independence, had stopped co-operating with Moscow. The war, if it could be won, would deliver Russia not only the Chechen rigs but another means of processing oil for export which, with closer economic integration, would reap Russia's privileged, as well as the government, a veritable fortune. All that stood in Russia's way was the rebel Chechen government. If the Party of War could shut the southern republic down, kill the talk of independence, and with it Chechnya's burning hatred of Moscow, it would make the handful of businessmen and mafia bosses close to it richer than they might ever have dreamt of becoming. If Chechnya could be crushed in just a couple of hours, the risks involved in waging a war on Russian territory would be worth it—or so thought the Party of War.

By 1994 the Kremlin could officially report that the illegal export of resources and capital had slowed down. The KGB seemed to have regained control of most of the old Soviet borders, with the glaring exception of that between Tadjikistan and Afghanistan and those around Chechnya. Nonetheless, if the Kremlin's claim was exaggerated, it was clear, when Grisha and I returned in 1994/95, that some things had changed.

Fewer people were complaining about the racketeers. More of the old state shops were in private hands. Armies of young people ran the hundreds of small kiosks into which the grand old marble-floored Soviet shops had been divided. Often one kiosk would have three or even four attendants on hand, all of them well-dressed and happy to sell a remarkable range of expensive imported electronics and clothing. And although most people browsed out of curiosity, a lot also bought.

'They work for banks or importers,' explained one of the kiosk workers when I asked him who bought his top-of-the-range, latest-model mobile telephones and cameras.

There were signs of a middle class in the making, squeezing into overcrowded, dirty trains nudging aside poverty-stricken *babushkas* who no longer even bothered to whine about the snazzy new clothes of the young. Just a year before, the old women would have snickered and lectured young women in their brightly coloured mini-skirts or young men in their well-cut suits with briefcases in hand. Now they were a more common and acceptable sight. The well-heeled and securely employed no longer looked sideways to see whether anyone was watching as they stepped over old men and women lying in the metro subways, begging for money to buy food.

Somehow, alongside the desperate, gruelling, heart-wrenching poverty, an economic miracle was unfolding in Moscow. A little over 80 per cent of the old state shops had been privatised, along with nearly 20 000 small and medium-sized factories and enterprises. The new private sector had begun soaking up refugees from the state sector. And with their earnings the new middle class wanted to buy, buy, buy!

Those who inherited the small country plots given to their parents by the communist system wanted to build houses on them. Others wanted washing machines, dishwashers, dryers, television sets, furniture, clothes, food which wasn't imported, and airlines prepared to fly not just in and out of Moscow and St Petersburg but to remote corners of the country.

'It's simple to understand,' our friend Aliosha explained. 'You get a middle class when people begin to find work outside the state sector, in private business. Then everyone gets paid and when they get paid they want to buy. But what can they buy here? The state produces nothing. They can buy refrigerators imported from Sweden. Good for the super rich but no-one else.

'The *nomenklatura* have always been able to recognise an opportunity when they see one. And they've seen that there's more money, both in the short and long term, to be made doing legitimate business—like making things people can use. Even the racketeers are doing legitimate business. They can see that racketeering is a limited money machine. If people don't go into business because they're frightened of the racketeers, then who will the mafia hit? It's better off producing things.'

Most people believed that the barons of Russian industry, the mafia clan leaders and the government had done a deal. The government would make life more profitable for the rich by turning a blind eye to their failure to pay taxes and by giving the extremely rich a stake in what remained of the giant Soviet monopolies. In return, the rich would agree to begin investing their wealth at home by producing what Russia needed. It was a smart ploy. If only they could find a way of neutralising the impact of Chechnya's economic might on their future prospects.

It wasn't just the mafia, the government and the Party of War which wanted the economic might of the Chechen mob destroyed. Everybody did. I was surprised to hear western news reports in December 1994, when the Chechen war began, claiming the Russian people held no particular animosity towards the Chechens and that they opposed the assault on Grozny. Even when I lived in Moscow, Russians had spoken with utter contempt of their southern brothers and sisters whom they considered to be criminals living in an illegal state run by thugs making their money by drug-running, stealing weapons from Soviet military bases and from a refinery built by the Russians. As the mafia phenomenon hit Russia, it was the Chechens who were the most visible, with the best weapons and the highest number of assassinations. The Russians I knew wanted to drive the Chechens back home, force the rebel Chechen government into submission and impose 'order'.

It was only towards the end of 1995, a year into the Chechen imbroglio, that attitudes began to change. The war was becoming unpopular, if only because the military had botched the job. The Chechens were not crushed in three hours as the Defence Minister had promised. Tens of thousands of people were dying. And most were young Russian soldiers. The Chechens, armed to the teeth, simply wouldn't give up.

And the Red Army was no longer what it had been. It was a

pathetic, demoralised force with an ever dwindling budget. Not only
were military defections at an all-time high, fewer and fewer boys
of conscription age were answering the call to duty. With 'mini-wars'
raging around Russia's borders, they didn't want to play lambs to the
slaughter. Draft dodging had reached mammoth proportions. In
1994 it stood at 60 000 lost recruits and was growing. Nor did the
military have the manpower or money to chase draft dodgers. Those
the hierarchy managed to drag into service were generally regarded
by their superiors as unfit for duty. Generals bemoaned the fact that
the best sergeants had left the military for jobs in the private sector
which paid them a wage. What they were left with were untalented
boys and corrupt no-hopers who, due to the scarcity of funds, were
also poorly trained.

Field exercises were suspended in 1993, rendering tank and infantry divisions unfit for combat. Fifty-one of eighty-one divisions of
the Russian ground forces were non-operational. Because the military—industrial complex had been forced to its knees, the production
of equipment was in near terminal decline. Russia was spending less
than 10 per cent of America's defence budget on its armed forces.
It's true that the military had been dramatically reduced in size—
from 4 million down to just over 1 million personnel. Even so, there
were dozens of reports of soldiers dying of starvation and cold.
Mothers were protesting and snatching their sons back. And just as
tens of thousands of ordinary workers went unpaid, so too did the
defence forces. To make ends meet they sold tanks, weapons, anything under their command. And when there was no more to sell,
they moonlighted while living in barracks. The military had also lost
control over nuclear weapon fuel, creating a black market for
weapons grade plutonium and enriched uranium. The Red Army was
in dire straits.

The boys who were sent to Grozny in the opening stages of the
war were doomed from the start. When the initial assault failed to
cower the Chechens in two or three days, the Interior Ministry
weighed in, then the FSB. Somehow the Party of War produced

soldiers—thousands of them—to fight the Chechens.

When we arrived in Moscow in December 1994, Grisha, my husband, found he'd received a letter from his former divisional headquarters asking him to 'please call in relation to MB', which we correctly assumed meant mobilisation. In the old days, Grisha explained, not only would the army have sent a letter. They would have sent around the police to bash down the front door if necessary to find their victim. He didn't expect this to happen in 1994, but at passport control at Sheremetyevo Airport as we left the country a month later we were petrified. Still travelling on a Russian passport, we could only pray that the antiquated and inefficient cross-checking system the Russians had inherited from the Soviet Union hadn't been updated and that Grisha wouldn't be stopped from leaving Russia. I had visions of sitting depressed and defeated on the same train which had carried Nadya Chertkova to Grozny to find her son. But the system didn't work and the military hadn't alerted the border guards to stop Russians under the age of forty from leaving the country. Others, however, must have answered the curt letters they received, or been tracked down, for when Russia needed them they were there—cannon fodder for the Chechen debacle.

No-one was sure why Boris Yeltsin stuck by his henchmen in the Party of War. Perhaps it was simply that he was rarely well enough to make decisions of major note. Perhaps he believed the Defence Minister, the FSB chief and the head of the Kremlin Guard when they told him the war could be won. No-one else did. Average Russians saw a deepening conflict which was so protracted, so humiliating, it compounded their already wounded national pride. But the president was too isolated to see Russia was losing the war.

He would become angry when asked why it was that in the rubble of Grozny, the Chechen capital, only the oil refinery hadn't been bombed. He refused to answer allegations about his good friend

General Korzhakov who was not only among those directing the war against the Chechens but becoming a billionaire through alliances with a handful of Russia's biggest oil barons. Nor did Yeltsin see anything wrong with the harassment of the media proprietor Vladimir Gusinsky whose television network reported the haphazard, mostly incompetent bombing of Chechnya. Korzhakov used the Presidential Guard to surround the headquarters of Gusinsky's Mostbank which he'd built on funds diverted from the Moscow City Council. The banker and media boss fled Russia. He found the courage to return only when his network's coverage of the war had been tamed.

Throughout it all, Yeltsin was being told by reformers who he had dumped that the Party of War was wrong about Chechnya. The Chechens would never surrender. The war could not be won. Russians and Chechens were dying. The continued bombardment of Chechnya—for an oil refinery and a route to the Caspian Sea—was madness. Inhumane, barbarous madness. Like Gorbachev before him, Yeltsin was blind and blinkered.

Perhaps he reasoned that to withdraw the Russian troops would be another blow to national pride, worse than watching the military's bungling. Maybe the workers would blame economic reforms for having sapped the country of any ability to maintain an army.

Whatever his reason, Yeltsin had handed the nationalists and the communists a political gift as they geared up for the 1995 parliamentary election. Now his opposition had a cause—the revival of the military.

'How do you make a rational choice between generals, fascists and communists? That's what I'm being asked to do.'

Natasha was tired of the political prattle which bellowed out of her television every night as Russians again prepared to choose who to put into the Duma.

'What about the democrats,' I asked her, 'would you think of voting for them?'

'Why? We know what they stand for. They've made it clear— frozen food and war. If that's all the democrats stand for then why shouldn't we consider giving the communists another chance?' she said.

Despite the small mercies reform was finally bestowing and the fact that more than just a handful of the well connected were living better than they had since 1993, the polls were looking dangerously hopeful for the Russian Communist Party. It hardly seemed possible that the Russians felt it was time to take the first step back towards communism. But many people, especially the old, were tired of being poor and that was as compelling a reason as any other to vote for the communists. For the elderly, the communists were the only way forward, even if they were walking backwards.

Natasha told me how the residents in Belye Stolby would cheer when they heard Communist leader Gennady Zyganov talk of wanting to end the economic reforms and confiscate property 'illegally acquired' from the state.

'He tells people there are 40 million Russians living below the poverty line and that Yeltsin's constitution gives him more power than the last Russian tsar and the last General Secretary of the Com- munist Party combined. I heard him at a rally in Moscow telling people that no-one could handle that much power even if they were in perfect health and sober! And people applauded.'

But it wasn't just the elderly who were turning to Zyganov. For others, some only just in their thirties and prepared to suffer poor state wages for the sake of democracy, it was the fact that the promise of democracy and reform had faded into a dull, aching memory that drove them to communism. Many who had embraced Boris Yeltsin in August 1991 as he stood up to the Soviet Communist Party now found themselves with nothing to believe in. The presi- dent had promised them democracy, but the Party of War was calling the shots. The war in Chechnya, a class of filthy rich, unemployment and inflation, which though edging downward was still crippling for most, made the dreary, brown-suited Communist Party leader Gennady Zyganov look like an angel in pink.

The president's men saw hope in the embryonic middle class. Perhaps the young who were beginning to make money in the private sector would see the merit of voting for one of the handful of democratically inclined groups which would be forced to support the government's economic policies on the floor of the parliament even if they opposed the war. But were there enough of them?

I knew a young woman, an economist, who at twenty-five was making good money working for a Norwegian fish exporter. Marina didn't want to vote for the communists, nor for Zhirinovsky, but she simply couldn't bring herself to vote for the democrats.

'It would be a wasted vote. If I vote for the democrats, they'll support Yeltsin and his government and the war. I'd like a middle road but there isn't one. It's just like the old days—only rather than the old Soviet apparatus, we have clans tripping over each other for the president's ear and a seat in the government. First there was the *nomenklatura* clan which stripped us of our assets. Now the most powerful clan is the Party of War, so I don't trust the democrats when they say they're opposed to the war in Chechnya. They don't have the strength to topple the president's men.'

Marina said that few of her friends were prepared to vote for the democratic parties. Most just wanted to get out of Russia. Marina said when they talked about what had changed in Russia since the last time they'd voted, they could point only to the massive steel fence which had been erected around the parliamentary building bombed two years earlier, and the number of buildings which had tumbled down but not been rebuilt in towns and cities across the country. The majority of people were still poor, the authorities were still corrupt. The only difference now, Marina said, was that the bribes were much bigger. And Yeltsin, even for the young, had become a drunken Soviet-era boss with diminishing control over the organs of power, especially the military and the FSB. Few of them believed he was healthy enough to rule.

Some would have preferred to give Zhirinovsky's Liberal Democratic Party another chance, even if only to avoid giving the communists their vote. But Zhirinovsky alienated many people with his call for Chechen rebel bases to be napalmed. Nor were they impressed when he threatened World War III if any of the former Soviet satellites in Eastern Europe joined NATO. With Zhirinovsky's credibility diminishing, many of Russia's young decided to place their trust in Gennady Zyganov. They thought the communists must surely have reformed.

Natasha thought Marina's friends naive in the extreme. They don't remember their grandparents, she said, that's the problem. And they weren't of her generation which had watched its idealism shattered by a ruthless party which was beyond reform.

'Even though we knew the party was corrupt and immoral, we believed in the idea of utopia. So we joined the communists, hoping that our presence in the party would be a good influence. Now these young people are going to make the same mistake. We were all young Gorbachevs, believing we could purge the party of its reactionaries. We learned the truth through bitter disappointment,' she explained.

Natasha was three-quarters of the way to completing the circle she'd begun as an eighteen-year-old in Tatarstan. She had wanted a perfect and just society and hoped that the Communist Party would deliver it. But it hadn't. She had joined its ranks to push for change but been crushed in the process. Still she held on tightly to utopia. Throughout the Gorbachev era she argued relentlessly with me. Communism was the only way forward, she would say. When communism collapsed, she felt cheated. When democracy died, she felt vindicated. Now, two years on, she had reason to rethink. Nothing was as it seemed.

'When I was at school, I listened to Khrushchev's promises that the current young generation of Soviet people would experience communism. I was so happy. I counted how old I would be when communism arrived in twenty years. I thought, I'll be thirty. Not bad. I'll be able to live in a perfect society. There'll be total order, the roads will be repaired, there'll be no beggars, no-one will be thrown onto the streets like a wild dog without worth. Everything will be bright, clean—in the towns and villages as well as the big cities. We will all have the chance to fulfil our potential, the potential of our talents and dreams.

'But then Brezhnev came along and it became clear to me that not everyone who called themselves a communist was a communist. A lot of people used their status and I was shocked. The party was full of careerists who didn't care about communism at all.

'At film school we were all fond of Lenin and Trotsky. I knew of dissidents and I knew the works they were publishing underground which criticised the reality of our life and our leaders. I myself was feeling more unhappy every day with the same reality. But there were noble people too. True believers, you would call them. And they needed allies.

'The last straw for me came at an Art Council meeting at *Mosfilm* [the Moscow state film studio] at which a screenplay written by Vasily Shukshin [a well-liked film director and author] was under discussion. The council members were criticising the film and demanding changes because it reflected the reality of our lives too closely. Shukshin tried to defend himself but the council's ears were closed. Then suddenly the Communist Party's appointment to the Art Council stood up and defended Shukshin and the rest of them nodded in agreement with her—after they'd condemned him!

'Being a member of the party gave you power, it seemed to me, to help in the fair struggle for a better life. So I joined. And I was very active. With my degree in film, my task was to give political lectures on the problems of mass culture and I tried to do it honestly. People came to my lectures and some of them listened. But then I realised that most of them came because if they didn't, they would have problems at work. My lectures became an absolute nonsense because nothing I said made any difference to our life, it couldn't be applied to life. I could lecture endlessly, but no-one had the ability to try to make life better. They couldn't. It conflicted with the way we were allowed to live. The party had left us no room to move, to live.

'Maybe I was just too late. This idealistic theory to create harmony in an ordered system had already turned into a dictatorship and we lived in terror of it. The laws of equality and fairness had become laws on the limitation of personal freedom and potential.

'The theory is tempting, but it might just be that life needs more freedom than communism can afford to give people because it needs order. And it needs to purge humanity of individualism, egoism I call it. When you force this on people and give them power to create order, you get dictatorship.

'I never thought I'd be able to tell you this after all these years of arguing with you about how good communism is. But I now think it should always be in opposition. Power is the single factor which turns the ideal into dictatorship.

'We need an ideal, utopian goal. But we can't achieve utopia with guns and blood. Only by sending up balloons and calling out pipers for people to follow can we get there.

'But there's a lesson here for the capitalists as well. Yes, capitalism has managed to give people the means by which they can realise their own potential and it has an inherent order which makes sense and is logical. But not everyone is capable. Some people need help or else they are crushed in the stampede of the able and the wealthy. Capitalists must share their wealth!'

On the day of the parliamentary poll, the communists were the victors. They took 22 per cent of the Duma's seats, followed closely by Zhirinovsky's fascists. Together they controlled fourteen of the Duma's twenty-eight all important committees, among them the most influential—defence, security and economic policy. And the communists were strong enough to snatch the Chairmanship of the Duma which had the power to coerce and manipulate deputies in order to oppose government policy.

But Gennady Zyganov's mind was not on power bartering, nor on the Duma. It was on the Kremlin, the top job.

As the reconstruction of the Cathedral of Christ the Saviour began in Moscow, the communists must have been cursing the democrats. The Moscow City Council had convinced the city's capitalists to contribute generously towards the project. It would be a gesture of capitalistic goodwill, testimony to the strength of democracy. It would be a dramatic show of faith in Russia and God and a reminder of the atheism and cruelty of the Communist Party which six decades earlier had ordered the destruction of the original cathedral.

It had taken forty-three years to build the cathedral in honour of Russia's victory over Napoleon. Demolition crews started hacking away at it in 1931. But it was too big a job for mere mortals. A year later, the OGPU (one of the KGB's predecessors) was called in to finish off the job with dynamite.

Stalin had ordered the cathedral's destruction in order to make way for the Palace of Soviets which, had it been built, would have overwhelmed Moscow. It would have stood more than 300 metres tall with an ornate Stalinesque facade. It was to feature a 100-metre tall aluminium statue of Lenin with eyes which would beam bright red lights across Moscow. But it was not to be. Construction was interrupted by the war. At war's end the Kremlin ordered a massive, outdoor, heated swimming pool to be built on the site instead—and there it stood until the Moscow Mayor, Yuri Luzhkov, consolidated his popularity by ripping it out to begin the reconstruction of the cathedral.

By June 1996, when I returned to Moscow for the presidential election in which Boris Yeltsin would square off against the communist leader Gennady Zyganov, the cathedral was well on its way to completion. Two thousand kilograms of gold leaf had been spread onto its dome and Patriarch Alexsei II had consecrated it during a nationally televised ceremony attended by every democratically inclined political leader in Russia. Boris Yeltsin basked in its glory.

So too did most people I knew in Moscow. Visits to their apartments would invariably open with a peek outside one window or another from which some part of the cathedral could be seen. Their pride in it was overwhelming.

'Now, when you leave here,' said a friend, Lena, 'as you drive down Michurinsky Prospekt, you'll see the cathedral in full view. You can probably get a good picture of it from there if you can stop. It is beautiful, isn't it?'

Indeed the cathedral could be seen from almost all corners of Moscow—much as most people could catch at least one of the spires on one of Stalin's Wedding Cakes from their homes and workplaces.

Larissa had worked for eight years at *Gosfilmofond*, the State Film Archives, where Natasha, her sister, still toiled for a little less than 500 000 roubles (just under US$100) a month.

For eight years, Larissa bit her tongue as the *babushkas* who were also employed at the archives heckled her about the amount of money she received each month. They thought it unfair that she was paid slightly more than them, even though she did more and held a degree.

'I was a university graduate, yet these old Bolshevik women who were employed just because they lived in Belye Stolby [where the archives were located] thought they should receive the same money I did.

'Every month, they'd come to me and peer over my shoulder as I was paid, whining about the fact that they got so little. I couldn't stand it,' she told me.

But it was the fact that after eight years Larissa had to struggle to remember the occasions when her work was used by any of her colleagues which finally broke her. She wrote critique after critique of Soviet films, analysis of film techniques and biographies of film-makers. But her efforts lay in folders collecting dust.

'It was deeply unsatisfying. No-one needed me. No-one needed anyone really. The system was so decrepit. We worked just to collect a wage and fill in the hours of the day.'

In 1996, Larissa jumped off the state gravy train to 'tick off numbers' for Schweppes Drinks which had opened in Moscow two years earlier. There, the second eldest of the Yakovlev sisters, Luda, had already found her dream job, travelling the Russian countryside selling the western drink, now manufactured in Russia, to small kiosks and shops.

Larissa was over-qualified for the work she was doing, but she didn't mind checking figures if it was important to the enterprise. And it was.

'They pay me little but probably three times what I earned at the archives. I can afford to buy myself some nice clothes to wear at least every two months. I go to work and people are pleasant. There are no angry *babushkas* and sullen faces.

'You know, Monica,' she said excitedly, 'if the lift door opens in the morning and there are too many people already inside, people at Schweppes don't all squash in, feeling like if they miss out this time they've been robbed of something. They wait for the next lift.' For Larissa, the mean-spiritedness of the Soviet era had given way to a generosity she could still scarcely believe, even if she suspected it was a chimera.

'And a few months ago, I had 7000 roubles stolen from my bag. Do you know, everyone in my office contributed money so that I wouldn't be out of pocket! Can you believe that? At *Gosfilmofond*, the mother of one of our colleagues died and she couldn't afford the funeral, so I went around to everyone and asked for money to help her. If they gave, they did so reluctantly. The *babushkas* just snarled at me.'

There was nothing about the new Russia Larissa didn't like. As for the poverty which had struck her own parents, her thoughts were simple. It was up to her and her sisters to pull them through the bad times. In return, her parents should vote for Boris Nikolaevich Yeltsin in the looming showdown with the communist leader, so that their children would have a chance to enjoy life.

In the year and a half since I'd last been in Moscow, the city centre had changed dramatically. The cynical might say that the president and his rich backers were sprucing up the capital to make people think capitalism actually worked.

Building cranes blocked out the summer sky. Old pre-revolution-ary buildings were getting a much needed facelift, while western-style skyscrapers with dark glass and shiny steel lifts were making an appearance for the first time. There were even petrol stations complete with numerous pumps, attendants, and flower boxes. The days of the old midnight queue which I had sat in regularly during 1990 and 1991 were gone. Corners of the city were looking decid-edly Parisian. The Zamoskvareche district, across the Moscow River near the Kremlin, had given its medieval churches a new coat of paint and replaced the brass locks on the front gates which had disappeared in the Soviet era. The mansions of the merchants who'd lived there before the revolution had been refurbished and bought by Russian businesses which hung their brass nameplates on the front doors. The cracked footpaths had been repaved and blended with

the streets to form pedestrian thoroughfares. Even the wooden construction walls protecting passers-by from the heavy machinery used
to construct new buildings were turned over to civic use. The children of the area were given materials by the local council to paint
graffiti.

'Is this area off limits to the racketeers?' I asked our friend Kolya
who had lived in the Zamoskvareche district all his life.

'I think the news is even better than that. They're a little more
civilised now. They still demand a cut but not as much of a cut as
before. It's an improvement. In this district there are more grocery
shops than almost anywhere else in Moscow.

'Actually, the racketeers are becoming respectable businessmen.
They need governments, at all levels, to do their job—collect taxes,
make better roads and get the heating systems working properly
again. And they need the police to catch the robbers who break into
their offices and homes. I think it's as simple as that. So long as
everyone does what they're supposed to do, the businesspeople can
do business and the state can collect taxes from them so that the
police will be better paid. Everyone is beginning to understand how
this capitalist game works.'

Not even the *babushkas* who sat chatting on park benches whined
as loudly as they had a year and a half earlier. Not in the city centre
at least. Pensions had increased slightly and though people were still
struggling, prices had dropped in the free markets as the government
wrestled inflation from its 1992 high of 2000 per cent a year down
to 25 per cent in 1996. Even some of the more able beggars had
decided to help themselves and had taken out franchises on street
newspaper selling, while in the huge farmers' markets stall holders
had begun to understand the basic principle of the free market—
unless their prices were competitive, no-one would buy what they
were selling.

Moscow was an oasis of prosperity where young women and men
dressed well, ate out in new restaurants designed for the middle class
(like the American Diner which was a castle of American kitsch),

and lived in newly painted apartments which they furnished with cheap Russian-made furniture. They could ring for a taxi, have it pick them up at their front door and travel to work with a meter ticking over, counting the kilometres and calculating the fare. It was even possible to order a pizza by phone and use credit cards to get cash advances at Automatic Teller Machines. In the old days, I'd have to drive across Moscow to get to one of the hard currency shops for food not readily available on the streets. Now there were two well-stocked grocery shops, crammed with western imports and which gladly accepted roubles, within walking distance of my old apartment.

But the news wasn't at all hopeful outside the city centre. Even just fifteen minutes away from the Kremlin, poverty struck the eye with as much force as it had when I was last in Moscow. The grey outer suburbs were as depressed as they had been when the communists were in power. The kiosks which crowded the pavements around metro stations looked sad and depleted. No point buying products to sell, one of the owners told me, when no-one has any money to buy them. Outside the Maladoshnaya metro station, not far from where I had lived, a long line of *babushkas* from the villages surrounding Moscow sold potatoes at a quarter of the price they went for at the markets. Others came bearing a few sprigs of herbs grown on their balconies during the brief summer.

'Come here, young lady,' one of them called to me, 'buy some of my parsley. It's fresh and tasty!'

'I don't need any at the moment,' I answered, 'but I'll buy some tomorrow.'

'Ah, you foreigners, you're all the same. Your pockets are bursting with money but you're too mean to help out!' she said, turning her back on me to complain to her neighbour.

So much yet so little had changed. Those who couldn't help themselves were wallowing in uncertainty and poverty, being teased from both sides by democrats promising freedom and a better life and communists offering nostalgic memories of a time when no-one had to beg. Towering over the squalor of the Maladoshnaya metro station were two huge billboards, one bearing the beaming smile of Boris Yeltsin with the slogan, 'We're not building illusions', and another which advertised American jeeps with the English words, 'accessories', 'service' and 'sales' in Russian Cyrillic script. For those who could afford to buy an American jeep, it mattered more that they were 'buying foreign' than to understand what was on offer.

Along the road to the *dachas* of the rich and famous, cute wooden cottages, dilapidated and without amenities, were robbed of sunlight by enormous multi-storeyed mansions, some with as many as five turrets. But the chauffeur-driven Mercedes Benzs and BMWs which sped by, carrying their owners to certain luxury, didn't bother to stop to buy the flowers, vegetables and fruit which the village dwellers sat by the road trying to sell.

'They prefer to buy in Moscow one of the sellers told me when I stopped for flowers. 'Not even my neighbours buy from me,' she said, pointing towards the brand new brick home with leadlight windows built right to her land border.

'Life is still hard for you?' I asked.

'At times unbearably. And for what? To watch them in the expensive cars taking their pretty young wives to their big houses. Ah! It'll all end badly for us,' she said.

'So who will you vote for?' I asked.

'Zyganov of course!' she answered.

The president's election arsenal was full to bursting. He travelled widely, doling out money the country didn't have to woo workers who hadn't received a wage in months. He visited war-torn Grozny, the capital of Chechnya, and signed a peace agreement with the Chechen leader declaring with the usual Kremlin pomposity that the war which had claimed 80 000 lives was over. But the fighting continued. Every cultural figure of note, along with well-known business figures, came to his aid, believing that Boris Yeltsin had almost no chance of winning the presidency for a second term.

The media too, especially television, was unashamedly on the president's team. They feared that despite the attempts of Gennady Zyganov and his Communist Party to portray themselves as benign, market-friendly social democrats, they still considered individualism, freedom of thought and speech, and the pursuit of wealth to be 'bourgeois'.

In the end, for people like Nikita Mikhailkov, the Russian film director whose film *Burnt by the Sun* won an Oscar in 1995, it boiled down to a simple question of choosing between two systems— communism and capitalism. As the president's powers were virtually unlimited, whoever held the position would determine the future— whatever the Duma may argue.

Mikhailkov, whose film portrayed the tragedy of a system which crushed the loyal as viciously as the dissenters, appeared regularly on television. His films were shown almost on rotation. He was interviewed on current affairs programs nightly, peddling the message that the importance of the election was not just in changing the portrait of the boss on office walls.

'It's about changing the social system and that's why we are at a dangerous point. We haven't yet forgotten what it was like before. But although it has been destroyed, we haven't yet built anything to replace it. We are in the process of making something new.

'Today, everything depends on people and that's scary because we are used to living with collective lack of responsibility. Of course, for a lot of people, it's easier to live in a goose line—like in the army. And some people are angry. Some are lost. The problem is that you hear most from people who are angry. The others just go on living and working.

'We have to make sure that we don't go racing around another circle to nowhere. We lived for seventy years in a particular setting and people knew what was going on. They told jokes about Brezhnev in their kitchens and laughed! Now the fear is gone. The Soviet system of power was based only on fear, nothing else. A lot of people, especially those who are not making money, want to hold onto that fear because it propped up the system which enabled them to get by,' he said.

The Kremlin's propaganda team came up with some devastatingly powerful slogans including *'Ne Dhai Bogh!'* ['God forbid, the communists!'], and a poster, pasted in shop windows throughout the major cities, which reminisced about the 'good old days' of food shortages, queues and bleak city streets, and compared them with the new Russia of shop shelves overflowing with Russian food— which had not been seen for so long people had forgotten it existed at all.

Boris Yeltsin was forced into a second round of voting. In the first, he led the communists by a mere two and a half million votes. The communist campaign had been schizophrenic but it seemed to have worked. To those who hated privatisation, Zyganov promised to revise decisions already taken to make sure the privatisation laws hadn't been violated. To those who complained of having to pay high prices for food and services, he promised the re-establishment of price controls and state monopolies. Russia would again become a mighty superpower. There would be no compromise with the Japanese over the Kurile Islands. The war in Chechnya would be won. It was music to the ears of those for whom democracy and capitalism had come to represent nothing more than their humiliation and abject impoverishment.

To make the run-off easier, Boris Nikolaevich took on board a popular general whose race for the presidency had been more successful than expected. Alexander Lebed had come in third in the first round of voting. He was a big man with a gruff, gravelly voice who promised Russians that he would stop corruption, restore the honour of the military and purge Russia of foreign influence, among which he counted the propagators of the Mormon religion and western businessmen.

It was a dangerous tactic, but Yeltsin was adept at high-risk strategies. By aligning himself with an extreme but popular conservative who stood outside the communist–fascist camp, he might absorb some of his support. But perhaps Russians had learnt the tricks of political campaigning. Perhaps they would understand that Lebed had been bought and they'd switch their allegiance to the communists.

That Boris Yeltsin disappeared from public view soon after he sacked a member of the Party of War—Alexander Korzhakov, now being called the new Rasputin, who led the Kremlin Guard—didn't help him much. Aborting a campaign visit to the Volga city of Samara and cancelling an address to more than three thousand farmers who'd come to Moscow to be convinced of the merits of private farming, speculation was rife that Boris Yeltsin's health had failed again.

'He is too ill to rule. Again, Russia will have an ailing leader at the helm, kept alive by machines!' roared Zyganov. People listened. They didn't want another Brezhnev or Andropov in the Kremlin.

The Kremlin, of course, tried desperately to pretend that all was normal. The president, it claimed, had lost his voice because of the number of public engagements he'd attended throughout the campaign. He had not had a heart attack, insisted the president's aides. But not even those who supported him believed the Kremlin. Businessmen who had contributed heavily to Yeltsin's campaign were lining up for visas to Europe.

Yeltsin remained out of public view until the night before the second vote. Out in Belye Stolby, where I had joined Natasha to watch the poll, the Kremlin had managed to fool no-one.

'Did you see him last night?' a woman in her eighties asked me when I approached her to ask where her vote would be going.

'He's had another heart attack. I know that look. My husband died of heart failure. The Kremlin is lying,' she said.

'But would you have voted for him had he not taken ill?' I asked.

'No! Now don't you go down there [to the polling booth] and tell them that, will you? Promise me, you won't. I don't like people knowing who I vote for. My children have begged me to vote for Yeltsin. But I won't. Not for anything. He's a scoundrel and a liar. And he's a thief, giving all our property to the *nomenklatura*. I would rather have the old *nomenklatura* back, without property! And I want Russia without you westerners thinking you've won the war.

'I don't mean to offend you personally, my dear. But I don't want to see your discos and drugs corrupting my grandchildren, and your western clothes making my daughter feel like a second-class citizen. You understand me, don't you, dear? It's not you personally. It's what your country stands for,' she said as she headed towards the town's community centre where local officials were ticking off names and handing out voting sheets.

As she hobbled up the stairs, a young man in bright blue track-suit pants and a grubby white singlet snickered to his pals.

'*Vot ani priydut!* ['Here they come!'] They've managed to stay alive long enough to waste their vote on the communists,' he said.

After she cast her vote, Natasha asked the election officials if they would go to her parents' home to take their vote. They were too frail to walk to the community hall.

'Oy! Natasha!' said the official, beaming with pride. 'How times have changed. Remember the old days? Remember how we would cast a vote for every member of our family living and dead?'

'Yes,' laughed Natasha, 'this is now the pre-democratic phase of our illustrious development. In another twenty years we'll reach democracy!' she said, mocking the constant cry of the communists that nirvana was close.

In Moscow, Grisha had been urged by his mother not to forget to vote.

'It's important, son,' Julia told him, 'you might want to come back and live here one day. Remember that!'

Julia had been begging everyone she knew, regardless of their political disposition, to remember to vote—for Yeltsin.

Yeltsin won by a 15 per cent margin. It was respectable enough a victory for Zyganov to accept the verdict with grace. And it was a remarkable comeback for a man who led a deeply unpopular government which had failed to fill the ideological vacuum created by communism's downfall. But even the president's men knew this was an election the communists had lost rather than one the president had won.

Zyganov had frightened many more people than he managed to win to his cause. His shadow cabinet included men who had been on the State Emergency Committee which had tried to overthrow Mikhail Gorbachev in 1991. There had been disconcerting echoes of Vladimir Zhirinovsky in his election promises. And the old generational problems which had so haunted Gorbachev had come full circle. The elderly might have wanted to vote for the communists but their children stood over them, begging them not to.

Democracy had produced a very strange beast. It was embryonic but unformed. Capitalism had emerged from behind the mirror. But communism had risen from the grave.

CHAPTER 19

OUT OF THE SHADOWS

To read only children's books, treasure
Only children's thoughts, throw
Grown up things away
And rise from deep sorrows ...

OSIP MANDELSTAM, FROM 'STONE' IN *SELECTED POEMS*, 1989

Two months after the presidential election, the new FSB chief demanded sweeping new powers, including control of the 'armed units' of which the FSB had been stripped after the 1991 coup attempt against Mikhail Gorbachev. 'There is nothing to be afraid of,' declared the FSB—it was a new security organisation in a new country in which democracy was now five years old!

Three months after the poll, Kremlin doctors finally admitted that Boris Yeltsin had indeed suffered a heart attack before the second round of voting. His aides had lied to the Russians for the sake of victory.

As they prepared for a commemorative rally to mark the third anniversary of the failure of the armed uprising against the president in October 1993, the president's new confidantes considered banning the meetings of those they believed to be enemies.

General Alexander Lebed, whom Boris Yeltsin had appointed secretary of the powerful Security Council in order to win over the 13 million people who had voted for him in the first round of the election, beamed with pride as he declared his first task in government complete and a success. 'The war in Chechnya is over,' he told a Russia which was mesmerised by him, besotted by his gruff, down-to-earth formulas for a new Russian paradise.

As Russian troops began withdrawing from Grozny, they fired on Chechen rebels while Lebed, whose declared ambition was to become president of Russia, promised that if crime and corruption could not be tamed by reason and persuasion, his forces would shoot people. 'But reasonably, with minimal losses for the law enforcement bodies, and only those people who refuse to be persuaded.'

The general who led Russia's disastrous campaign in Chechnya was promoted. As Interior Minister Anatoly Kulikov vied for authority with Lebed whom he accused of preparing to take Moscow by force—the mutiny to be spearheaded by a 50 000 strong Russian legion—Lebed threatened to sue Kulikov. 'I'll sue for one rouble. I don't need his money which comes from bribes,' he declared.

A day later Lebed was sacked. An ashen-faced Boris Yeltsin appeared on national television, staring into the wrong camera as he dismissed the general whose 13 million votes he'd bought to save his presidency.

'The Russian state is not a country,' declared Lebed, 'it is a circus.'

The men who had bankrolled the president's election campaign were duly rewarded for their efforts. A western consortium preparing to bid for Russia's telecommunication sector was unceremoniously told not to bother. The billion dollar shareholding was simply divided between two private Russian banks—one of which, Mostbank, was owned by Vladimir Gusinsky whose sanitised coverage of the war in Chechnya had won him more than a few brownie points in the Kremlin.

State workers, in the meantime, were left unpaid. The Kremlin owed its workers 80 million dollars. Adding insult to injury, the minimum price for vodka was increased to raise revenues. As well as consumers, the producers and importers were hurt. They were char- ities—the National Sports Foundation, the Russian Fund for Invalids of the Afghan War and the All Russian Society for the Deaf. They had enjoyed tax breaks but now their privileges were abolished to save the government asking its friends in big business to pay their tax bills. In the meantime, the average life expectancy of the Russian male had dropped to 56 years.

In neighbouring Belorussia, which had never been happy about the break-up of the Soviet Union, the Belorus president demanded and won sweeping new powers which made him virtually a dictator. He promptly sacked the parliament which had opposed the refer- endum he'd called to ratify his new powers. A year later, Russia and Belorussia announced a new union which they hoped other CIS countries would join.

Pravda closed. In the glory days its circulation had been one million copies daily. At the time of its death it was down to 170 000 copies and it carried advertisements. It had survived Yeltsin's ban on its publication in the aftermath of the 1991 coup attempt and a takeover bid by a Greek businessman.

But Lenin's mausoleum remained. Vladimir Ilych was taken away for a makeover just before the presidential election and returned to his tomb. Yeltsin had not yet found the political strength to bury him alongside his mother in St Petersburg. Perhaps the Russian pres- ident figured he may yet need him.

Despite the mafia's new-found occupation with legitimate busi- ness, crime continued unabated and unchecked. A few months after the election, gunmen opened fire on the apartment of the chairman of the Russian Central Bank. It was a warning against his attempts to force commercial banks into fiscal conformity.

Yevgeny Primakov, who replaced Andrei Kozyrev as Foreign Min- ister when he was sacked, declared that Russia had gone too far in befriending the west. Primakov was the stuff of which good com- munists were made. He'd worked for *Pravda* abroad and was assumed to be a KGB operative. He'd also been a member of the Soviet Presidential Council where he sat not entirely uncomfortably along-side Gorbachev's cabinet of deceivers.

In a 1997 cabinet shake-out, Yeltsin reappointed Anatoly Chubais, the man who engineered *nomenklatura* privatisation, as deputy prime minister and endorsed Boris Nemstov as his successor. Nemstov had been the Governor of Nizhni Novgorod where he had experimented successfully with capitalism on a small scale.

As Boris Yeltsin rested in Moscow's Central Clinical Hospital waiting for a heart bypass operation, Sonia and her mother were staying with us in Sydney. They'd come from Moscow to visit relatives.

Sonia was eight. Bright as a button, artistic and energetic, she sat on her bed playing with a matrioshka doll—one in which Yeltsin revealed Gorbachev, then Chernenko, Andropov and so on.

'Open this doll for me,' Sonia beckoned. 'I want to see what's inside.'

'OK. Who's this?' I asked her as Boris Nikolaevich gave way to Gorbachev.

'Oh! That's easy. That's Mikhail Sergeyevich.'

'And this?' I asked, peeling Gorbachev away to reveal Konstantin Chernenko.

'I don't know. But he's very old!' said Sonia.

'And this?'

'How funny he looks,' she giggled, 'who can he be?'

'He's Yuri Andropov,' I told her. 'And this. Do you know him?'

'No. But he thinks he's some sort of hero with all those medals, doesn't he?'

'That's Leonid Brezhnev. Have you ever heard of him?'

'Never. Who's next?'

'Do you know this man?' I asked.

'No. But he's very fat. Was he stupid?'

'Some think so. He's Nikita Khrushchev. And this man, do you know this man?' I asked, showing her Joseph Stalin.

'Never seen him before in my life. Is he still alive?' she asked.

'No, he died a long time ago.'

'And did people cry?' she asked.

'Yes, they did.'

'Mama too?'

'She wasn't even born then Sonia.'

'So who's next?'

'You tell me,' I said, showing her Vladimir Ilych Lenin.

'Ah, I know him!' she said, jumping up and down with excitement. 'He's Lenin!'

'And what did Lenin do?' I asked.

'That's a hard one,' she said, pausing for a moment. 'I know he did something really big. But I'm not sure what!'

NOTES ON SOURCES

CHAPTER ONE: An Empire Crumbling

Many have written about the Soviet Communist Party, describing it, analysing it, and ultimately judging it. Among the best descriptions are those of Jonathan Steele in his book *Eternal Russia*, Geoffrey Hosking in *A History of the Soviet Union* and Alexander Yakovlev, known to those of us privileged to watch the final chapter of Soviet history in the making as Mr Glasnost. His book *The Fate of Marxism in Russia* is a powerful indictment of his own belief system. I have drawn on these works in my analysis of the party, which is by no means exhaustive.

Descriptions of *Homo Sovieticus* are numerous and I am indebted to many authors and academics who chronicled the Soviet period— among them Jonathan Steele. As well, Mikhail Gorbachev, throughout 1989 and 1990 when it became clear that his reforms were troubled, repeatedly blamed the Soviet desire for an 'equality of poverty', the indifference of Soviet workers and their learned dependency on the state for his personal and policy inadequacies.

Much of the rest of this chapter is personal experience and that of friends. Svetlana exists though I have changed her name at her request. Some of the chapter is the experience of others—amongst them the poet Vladimir Mayakovsky whose tale of the Poets Cafe is told in the book *I Love: The Story of Vladimir Mayakovsky and Lili Brik*, by Ann and Samuel Charters. Mikhail Zhvanetsky, the Russian satirist much loved for the honesty and affection with which he portrays Soviet life contributed insights which were recorded on cassette at a private party attended by a friend of a friend. Masha and Natasha, as always, provided the human dimensions of a system which few have described as well as Hedrick Smith in his 1970s blockbuster *The Russians*. To him, I am indebted for descriptions of the Soviet production and retailing systems, in particular the Five Year Plan and its inefficiencies. Igor, as a worker, understood how confusing the whole system could be for a non-Russian looking in and took pity. Vera exists. She is the mother of a friend, Max.

Geoffrey Hosking's *A History of the Soviet Union* gave insight into the roots of Russia's military-mindedness and the origins of the defence mentality.

CHAPTER TWO: Kingdom of Connections

Hedrick Smith's *The Russians* is indispensable reading for anyone trying to understand the nature of Soviet life. I owe much also to Geoffrey Hosking's *A History of the Soviet Union* for its description of the *nomenklatura* and the privileges they enjoyed.

The experiences of my husband Grigori (better known as Grisha), who was born into Krushchev's brief moment of thaw, but grew up in Brezhnev's era of stagnation, also helped me understand and trace the growth of *blat*.

Other sources were friends—Natasha, Masha and Aliosha, who deserves special thanks for his frank account of his own life as 'blatnoi'.

Stalin's pronouncement concerning equality came from the Seventeenth Party Congress in 1934 and is quoted in R.V. Daniels (ed.) *A Documentary History of Communism in Russia: From Lenin to Gorbachev*.

The statistics on the usefulness of blat in Soviet life came from *Soviet Grassroots* by Jeffrey W. Hahn.

The Yakovlev quote on the bacchanalia of Soviet communism

came from his book *The Fate of Marxism in Russia*.

I visited the Fraternal Grave (or the House on the Embankment) in 1990 and compiled a report for ABC radio. I spoke with Tamara Ter-Egiazaryan and Victoria Volina. A story by Andrew Meier entitled 'The House That Joe Built', published in *Moscow Magazine* in September 1991, was also helpful.

The notion that the communists maintained the command system because it kept them in the good life and the masses suppressed is not new. I have read it in several accounts of the Soviet Communist Party including Alexander Yakovlev's book, *The Fate of Marxism in Russia*.

Mikhail Zhvanetsky's quote is taken from a tape recording of a performance he gave at a private dinner party in Moscow.

The story of the couple from Rostov who married Muscovites only in order to divorce them and continue living in Moscow was told to me by Masha. As usual, Natasha's insights were invaluable.

CHAPTER THREE: A Question of Trust

I'd watched Yelena Georgiovna Bonner on television and seen her speak at countless pro-democracy rallies. But meeting her and speaking quietly in the comfort of her Moscow apartment made sense of *Homo Sovieticus*—Soviet man. She explained a life she both loved and hated which I recorded for a story for ABC radio. The quoted comment of her husband, Andrei Sakharov, was made to a Swedish journalist, Olle Stenholm, in 1973 (*The Russians* by Hedrick Smith, p.538).

In this chapter I am also indebted to Alexander Yakovlev for his analysis of Bolshevism's legacy.

Natasha's experiences of Soviet life in the 1960s and 1970s and how they affected her in the 1980s and even the 1990s made all the difference. So too did the stories told to me by Maria Sergeyevna, an old woman whose life had twice been reduced to rubble by the system—the first time by Stalin who stole her parents and the second time by Gorbachev who robbed her of stability.

Some statistics on landmarks and monuments in Moscow have been taken from Dan Richardson's *Moscow: The Rough Guide*. Those on Lenin's embalmed body came from Dmitri Volkogonov's tome on Lenin entitled *Lenin: Life and Legacy*.

Vera, Max's mother, also contributed to this chapter through our numerous long conversations over glasses of black tea in the kitchen of her apartment in Kuntsevo.

The statistics on Moscow's burgeoning crime problem were provided by *Moscow Magazine*, 1992.

CHAPTER FOUR: And Then There was Lenin

Much of this chapter is drawn from the work of Dmitri Volkogonov, the Soviet military historian who died in 1995, not five years after he came to grips with the enormity of the lies he had believed. His book *Lenin: Life and Legacy* was written just as the Lenin myth was exploding. His archival discoveries have thrown a whole new light on the Soviet revolutionary guru, dispelling to some extent the Lenin myth passed down through the generations by means of adulatory anecdotes. I found Churchill's comment on the Russians in Volkogonov's *Lenin: Life and Legacy*.

Other sources for this chapter include the Soviet publications *The Central Lenin Museum* and Vladimir Chernov's *Moscow*, both published by Progress Press, Moscow, as well as *I Love: The Story of Vladimir Mayakovsky and Lili Brik* by Ann and Samuel Charters.

The account of Volkogonov's journey from Stalinism to reformism is drawn both from his book on Lenin and from David Remnick's *Lenin's Tomb* from which I have drawn direct quotes. Included also are quotes from Khrushchev's speech to the Twentieth Party Congress in 1956 which are taken from Volkogonov's *Lenin: Life and Legacy*.

Otherwise, I drew from friends and people I sought out for interview—among them Tatyana Taptapova whose parents perished in the Stalinist purges and Natalia Khrenova who shared her thoughts on Stalin and Bolshevism with me in 1996. Galina Arsenievna of the Central Lenin Museum in Moscow, whose dedication to the Lenin myth knew no boundaries, also contributed in an interview recorded for the ABC. Yelena Fedorovna of the bread shop in Krylatskoe was living testimony to the success of the Lenin myth, and countless others helped me to form an understanding of why the party was so strong.

CHAPTER FIVE: Generation vs Generation

Why Soviet people didn't rise up and overwhelm the party was difficult for me to understand. I was lucky to have friends willing and able to explain the politics of dissent.

Yevgeny Yevtushenko, the poet, receives special acknowledgment for having exploded for me the myth that he was a great dissenter and a man of bravery. At best he was a secret dissenter. His views on Andrei Sakharov's attempt to force the regime to repeal the death penalty came from his book *Fatal Half Measures*.

Many have written about the *shestidesyatniki* including Geoffrey Hosking, Boris Kagarlitsky and Angus Roxburgh. I have drawn from them all.

Georgi Shakhnazarov met with me three times for interviews which were broadcast on ABC radio. Each time he made the awesome task of questioning him much easier by mapping out the areas of Gorbachev's inconsistencies.

But I spent far more time with Nikolai Shishlin who would always greet my requests for meetings with: 'You bring the little red Lada to the big brown doors of the CPSU and we'll go look for coffee.' He was tolerant of my inability to understand what a reconstructed communist would be like. But then he himself gave up on the idea.

Vitaly Korotich also gave me interviews which were broadcast on ABC Radio.

My friend Igor never missed a protest, which was lucky for me because many of the important ones had been staged by the time I arrived in Moscow on my posting, particularly the protests against Article Six. Zhenya who is quoted here and elsewhere throughout this book was a highly sensitive and talented young man. He died in September 1996.

My information about the move to abandon Article Six comes largely from secondary sources, among them David Remnick, Jonathan Steele, Angus Roxburgh and various editions of the journal *New Times* (English editions) and the newspaper *Komsomolskaya Pravda* throughout 1989.

And though Artyom Troitsky says he's not much of a protester, he was in his own way. It would probably be hard to find anyone else of his cultural disposition who did more to undermine the party than Artyom. His books *Tusovka* and *Back in the USSR* are true insights into Soviet rock culture and a generation gap which no-one in the west would envy. His account of the generational differences between himself and his father came both from a conversation with me and from an article he wrote for *Moscow Magazine*, August/September 1991, in which he also detailed how his family voted in the 1991 referendum on the future of the Soviet Union.

Boris Yeltsin's book *The View from the Kremlin* is an authoritative account in the form of political biography, though naturally skewed to his own agenda. But it stands as testimony to the dilemmas one faces when taking on the might of the biggest mafia in the world. The account of his rise and rise within the party and his falling out with it comes largely from his own account, with contributions from both Angus Roxburgh and Jonathan Steele who in his book *Eternal Russia* expounds the theory that Yeltsin's character was divided between the anti-communist and the careerist.

Moscow Magazine published Artyom's story about not wanting to save the USSR in April 1991. The quote from Alexander Yakovlev comes from his book *The Fate of Marxism in Russia*.

Natasha, as usual, provided the midnight lessons in all things Soviet at the kitchen table while Masha put meat on the bones. Their colourful and honest descriptions are everywhere in this chapter. Zhenya's experiences as a 'child of *glasnost*', confused and embittered by all he'd lost, are also in this chapter.

PART TWO: CHANGE

CHAPTER SIX: An Uneasy Death

I wasn't in Moscow for the May Day Parade of 1990 so the account I have given of it is second-hand. But the sources are impeccable. Igor thankfully never missed the chance to watch people express themselves on the streets, whether in official parades or protest marches. 'It's better than television,' he would say. And so his account of the 1990 May Day march and that of Natasha are presented here. Various western correspondents were also there, among them David Remnick whose account I have drawn upon. I have also used accounts which appeared in the English edition of *New Times*, a Moscow publication, and used descriptions given to me by Alexander Pumpyansky, the editor of *New Times*.

Co-operatives were well and truly entrenched as part of Gorbachev's economic revolution before I was posted to Moscow in October 1990, and their difficult birth was well documented by Geoffrey Hosking and various correspondents in their daily or weekly news reports. The co-operatives have also been the subject of numerous feature articles in the western media. Information about their economic impact and the state of the economy in 1990 came largely from Angus Roxburgh's *The Second Russian Revolution*. The stories of how the co-ops were destroyed came directly from people I knew, among them Mikhail Borisovich and Galina Vladimirovna, the latter with whom I shared a special friendship. Vladimir Tikhonov of the United Co-operative Alliance gave me personal interviews. And *Moscow Magazine*, September 1990, carried a useful article written by Tikhonov which detailed the measures being taken by the government against the co-ops.

Millions of words have been written about Alexander Solzhenitsyn and I have drawn on various western and Russian media accounts of his life and work including those of Hedrick Smith. The essay to which I refer in this chapter was published in *Komsomolskaya Pravda* in September 1990. Igor Malashenko's comments came from interviews he granted me which were broadcast on ABC Radio, while reactions from ordinary young and middle-aged people were gleaned from those I knew in Moscow and St Petersburg. The story about Stalin is one often quoted by Russians.

The 7 November parade is a personal account and I am indebted to David Remnick for having opened my eyes to the power of the KGB chief Vladimir Kruchkov.

My account of the Baltic crisis owes much to the work of Jonathan Steele in *Eternal Russia* which deals extensively with the issue of Baltic nationalism, and also to Geoffrey Hosking's *The Awakening of the Soviet Union*. I am grateful also to Angus Roxburgh. Yevtushenko's line about the 'party of non-party people' comes from his book *Fatal Half Measures*. Yevgeny Kisilev who is now a major media player, the presenter of a critical current affairs program called 'Itogi' ('Results'), also contributed insights during conversation.

I was in the parliament when Eduard Shevardnadze resigned from his post as Foreign Minister of the Soviet Union. My account of the influence of the National Salvation Front came largely from Victor Alksnis, the 'Black Colonel', with whom I met on many occasions for interviews, all of which were broadcast on ABC Radio.

I was also in Lithuania in the days after the Soviet invasion. Interviews with members of *Sajudis* and defenders of the Lithuanian parliament were mostly broadcast on ABC Radio.

CHAPTER SEVEN: Blinkered and Blind

I attended Gorbachev's post-Vilnius press conference in Moscow. I was also present at several of the rallies at which Nikolai Travkin and Sasha Lubimov were speakers which took place in Moscow in the weeks following the Soviet attempt to suppress *Sajudis*. I watched and read the television and press coverage of the Lithuanian incident to which I refer.

Some of the views on Mikhail Gorbachev's 'popularity' in the Soviet Union are my own, others are those of my friends. Present in this analysis also are the views of Stanislav Shatalin, an economist who tried to convince Gorbachev of the merits of change, and Jonathan Steele whose account of Gorbachev's failings seems to me to be without flaw. I have also included comments made to me in interview by Georgi Shakhnazarov and Nikolai Shishlin, both of whom worked with Gorbachev throughout the *perestroika* years and beyond.

Boris Kagarlitsky was inspirational not only because of the raw energy he exuded but because of his fine political analysis. He sacrificed many hours of his time to walk the streets of Moscow with me, explaining his theories and his concerns about where Russia was heading as it prepared to elect Boris Yeltsin as its first president in 1991. Many of these conversations were broadcast on ABC Radio.

I was in Russia during the first presidential election and much of what I have written reflects the views of my friends. I was also present at Boris Yeltsin's inauguration.

The negotiations between Mikhail Gorbachev and the presidents of the republics on a Union treaty seemed interminable. But they weren't. There were literally dozens of press conferences granted by all players—among them Gorbachev himself. Many of them I attended. I have included remarks made to me in interviews and doorstops by Ivan Polozkov, the First Secretary of the Central Committee and Victor Alksnis of *Soyuz* in the chapter.

The account of Yeltsin's final treaty meeting with Gorbachev comes from his book, *The View from the Kremlin*.

CHAPTER EIGHT: Summer Heat

Details of the holidaying habits of the Soviet elite are drawn from Hedrick Smith's *The Russians* and from my own observation.

Throughout the months leading up to the attempted coup against Mikhail Gorbachev I kept clear and copious records of events. As I wrote them, I thought to myself I would never need them as I would remember always the tension and fear of those times. This chapter combines both notes and memory.

But it also draws on Russian newspaper reports contained in *Isvestia, Nevavisimaya Gazeta, Komsomolskaya Pravda, Argumenti e Fakti,* and from the Russian wire service TASS. Western press reports were also invaluable—*Time*, the *Guardian* and Reuters.

In the aftermath of the coup attempt, Russian television meticulously pieced together the warning signs which Gorbachev ignored.

Victor Alksnis continued to speak to anyone who would listen, even as he and the KGB chief pulled together the emergency committee to overthrow Gorbachev.

Oleg Kalugin was not only a near neighbour in Moscow but a reliable contact who freely gave interviews. He supplied much of the information contained in this chapter about his career, and other details came from *The KGB: The Inside Story* written by Christopher Andrew and Oleg Gordievsky. Many interviews I recorded with Kalugin were broadcast on ABC Radio, including the one quoted in this chapter recorded just before the coup.

But I am most indebted to my KGB friend, Sasha, who risked personal security to give me insights and information which kept me in Moscow during August 1991 when most foreign correspondents and indeed, Mikhail Gorbachev himself, fled the capital for the holiday season.

CHAPTER NINE: Cold Revenge

The three days in which Soviet tanks occupied Moscow are days I am sure I'll never forget. Much of this chapter is based on my observation and experience. And yet when one is on the ground and in the midst of the mayhem, it is often difficult to piece together exactly what is happening. And so for the sequential detail of the first two days of this coup gone wrong, I am grateful to Boris Yeltsin who in his book *The View from the Kremlin* relives the period. Russian television also meticulously documented the three days of the coup in a program which was broadcast two weeks after the coup's collapse. It revealed exactly what the coup plotters were doing throughout the ordeal.

But the most gripping account of how the President of the Soviet Union was isolated, threatened, what he felt, how he reacted, came from Mikhail Sergeyevich himself. When he returned from Foros to Moscow on 20 August 1991, he gave a long media conference, the first about which those of us lucky enough to be present did not complain. He had committed every detail to memory during what must have been the longest two and a half days in his life. I sat in the front row.

His wife, Raisa Maximovna also recounted the ordeal in her own way in her book *I Hope*.

Gennady Yanaev gave me a personal interview while he was waiting to be tried for treason. This was broadcast on ABC Radio and appears in this chapter.

The account of Ilya Krichevsky's fatal foray into the world of Soviet revenge is based largely on a story which appeared in *Moscow Magazine* in December 1991. Other details of the event which claimed three lives during the coup come from my own experience.

CHAPTER TEN: The Fallen

Much of this chapter is based on my own observations and experience, but special insights came from David Marr who wondered whether the coup leaders were capable of Stalinist cruelty. David's contribution as an 'outsider', someone who wasn't as tired or as involved as I was, was invaluable during the hours of conversation which took place as the coup was collapsing.

Igor Malashenko provided me with one of the best scoops I'd ever known as a journalist. It was my misfortune that there were no phones in downtown Moscow in 1991 capable of relaying the story of the coup plotters' flight to Foros at the moment I was given it. Why Gorbachev refused to go the Russian parliament in the aftermath of the coup is documented by Jonathan Steele in his book *Eternal Russia*.

Mikhail Sergeyevich's post-Foros press conference and wire stories from TASS and Reuters have contributed to this chapter as well. Gorbachev's appearance before the Russian parliament was broadcast live on television.

All accounts of people's anger during and following the coup attempt are based on my personal observation.

CHAPTER ELEVEN: Talking Freedom

Boris Yeltsin's account in *The View from the Kremlin* was indispensable to this chapter. The president was in the box seat when he and the other two Slav leaders were ending the Soviet Union's existence. But the account of the secret meeting near Brest given by Jonathan Steele helped me enormously.

Zhenya and his father's sentiments about the USSR's collapse, as well as those of Natasha, came from conversations I had with them.

George Blake's comments were given to me in personal interviews which were not recorded at his request. During the interviews he seemed to be doing little more than rattling off what he'd already written in his autobiography *No Other Choice*. The copy he loaned me is still in my possession despite my best efforts at finding him to return it.

I visited Ukraine in the lead-up to its 1 December 1991 referendum in which people voted overwhelmingly for independence. This, the account of the day the Soviet Union ceased to exist, and of New Year's Eve when the Soviet flag was lowered for the last time are personal observation.

PART THREE: RUSSIA

CHAPTER TWELVE: Hope Fades

To be on the streets of Moscow during the first six months of 1992, Russia's first year of real independence, was to be exposed to an abundance of source material. Russians had long since lost their fear of complaining and price liberalisation gave them a lot to complain about. I spent many days talking with *babushkas*, young people and friends to find out how they were coping with the reforms and what they thought of them. Natasha's parents and Grisha's mother were also happy to speak freely about the reform process despite the fact that in the case of Natasha's parents they were battling their own ideological baggage to do so. Oleg Borisovich, the military officer whom I befriended on Red Square, was extraordinarily open and emotional and eventually I recorded an interview with him, part of which was broadcast on ABC Radio. Russian newspapers carried several dozen reports of surveys on reactions to impending capitalism and few seemed to show overwhelming support for it. I found conversations with people like Alexander Pumpyansky of *New Times* extremely helpful in coming to grips with the Russian culture of absolutes. The concept of *poryadok* (order) is a central one in Russia and one can hear the word on any street corner at any time of the year, muttered by people of all ages. Order is critical to Russians, as I have tried to point out. Many people helped me understand how critical order is to the Russian psyche, among them Grisha and Natasha.

My conversation with Igor was not recorded or broadcast. However the survey which purported to prove that young Russian girls were deciding in their droves to become prostitutes was published in several Russian newspapers, among them *Nevavisimaya Gazeta*.

Details of Yigor Gaidar's family history come from various sources including *Moscow Magazine* and Bruce Clark. The outline of the program of economic shock therapy devised by Yigor Gaidar came from reports to the Russian parliament, media conferences, *New Times* (the English translation) and Jonathan Steele's *Eternal Russia*.

Details on prices in the 1970s came from friends and from Julia, my mother-in-law.

Jean-Paul Foglizzo of the International Monetary Fund gave me several interviews, all of which were broadcast on ABC Radio. And Yeltsin's admission about shock therapy was made nearly two years after it hit in his autobiography *The View from the Kremlin*.

CHAPTER THIRTEEN: But Not for All

Moscow Times, an English language newspaper in Moscow, reported instances of elderly Muscovites being robbed and murdered.

The voucher system was the backbone of the privatisation process which was a central plank in Yigor Gaidar's economic shock therapy. I attended many voucher auctions but the one about which I have written in this chapter took place at Sokol in central Moscow in April 1992. It was by then already clear to most that the process of privatisation was being corrupted. Boris Kagarlitsky's comment was made during an interview for ABC Radio. And the scams of the old *nomenklatura* were regularly and clearly detailed in the Russian newspapers disposed to revealing them. Since then, they have been written about and commented on extensively. The quote from Grigori Yavlinsky was made during an interview with me in his Moscow office in July 1992.

The details concerning the Constitutional Court's hearing of the case concerning Boris Yeltsin's banning of the Communist Party come both from first-hand observation, as I attended many days of the hearing, and from documents tendered to the court but shown to the western media at open press conferences by lawyers for the Russian government. I was present at the opening of the hearing when protesters unfurled their anger.

Izvestiya's story about Gorbachev's alleged Florida acquisition was published in May 1992. Gorbachev's comment about the Constitutional Court hearing was widely published.

I was in court on judgment day and spoke with Vladimir Ivashko.

CHAPTER FOURTEEN: God Instructs Us to Share

This was one of the hardest chapters in the book to write, largely because the Russian mafia is such a diffuse entity. The works which helped clarify the issues were: *Russia 2010 and What it Means for the World*, by Daniel Yergin and Thane Gustafson, 'Mafiosi and Matrioshki (Organised Crime and Russian Reform)' by Jim Leitzel, Clifford Gaddy and Mikhail Alexeev in *The Brookings Review*, vol. 13, no. 1, Winter

1995, pp. 26–9; and the internet pieces 'Russian Organised Crime: A Growth Industry' by Alexander Zhilin (national securities issues editor for *Moskovskie Novosti*) <http://CITM1.met.fsu.edu>; 'The Sexy Russian Mafia' by Lydia S. Rosner <http://www.alternative.com.crime>; 'Mafia Capitalism in Moscow' by Adrian Kreye, 1994 <http://www.users.interport.net.>; and 'Primakoff and the Ambitions of a Great Power' by Vladimir Zviglyanich, January 1996, *A Bi-weekly on Soviet Affairs* (the Jamestown Foundation website).

Also present in this chapter is the analogy drawn by Masha and Natasha, and also by Leitzel, Gaddy and Alexeev between the old communist party and the new Russian business world.

Anatoly Chubais' comment was made to a media conference at the Foreign Ministry press centre in December 1992.

Details on the real estate buying habits of the New Russians came from *The Economist*, 28 October 1995, while crime figures are drawn from the works of Alexander Zhilin. Other sources include the 1994 internet piece 'Mafia Capitalism in Moscow' by Adrian Kreye.

I interviewed Boris Kagarlitsky and Konstantin Borovoi and, at the other end of the spectrum, Sergei, the clan thug who claimed a state enterprise.

The Moscow Police Chief made his comment at a Moscow press conference in December 1992. Victor Yerin, the Interior Minister, passed his comment to *Nevavisimaya Gazeta* in January 1993. Boris Yeltsin's comment on business and crime was made at the All Russia Conference on Measures to Combat Crime and Corruption in 1993.

The comments included in this chapter from Ivan Kiveldi were drawn from *Delovye Ludi* over several months. I am also indebted to Alexander Zhilin's work on the Roundtable for information contained in this chapter.

CHAPTER FIFTEEN: Life Goes On

This chapter consists of several short essays on aspects of Soviet life. In the opening section there is a quote from Nikolai Gogol's *Dead Souls*.

The first essay concerns abortion. Much of the information came from my own research into abortion clinics in Russia and interviews I conducted and has been used in reports for the ABC. The information concerning the Women's Party of Russia came from my own relationship with the party stemming from stories I'd worked on for the ABC. Some historical facts are drawn from Hedrick Smith's *The Russians*.

The essay on children and education also came from first-hand observation and interviews conducted at Children's School Number 18 in Moscow.

The essay on television was drawn largely from hours of watching Russian television, and contacts with the Russian television industry, including my husband Grisha who worked in the field. The Director of Russian Television was quoted in the *Moscow Times* in February 1995.

The essay on homosexuality was based on interviews conducted with a number of homosexuals in Moscow, including Lenaart (not his real name) who wishes to remain anonymous. Lenaart was active at the AIDS Hotline as well as in the political sphere. Dima and Mitya who opened and ran the gay bar 'Mir' were generous with their time and were happy to share their experiences. Some factual detail came from *Moscow Magazine* and the *Moscow Times*.

The essay on my own wedding comes completely from first-hand participation!

The essay on religion came from a number of sources, among them a friend who took me to the Church of St John the Warrior in 1983. The history of the Russian Orthodox Church came largely from Geoffrey Hosking's *A History of the Soviet Union*. Gorbachev's comments about religious patriots were quoted in *Pravda*, 30 April 1988, and requoted in Hosking's book which also made the connection between the ills Gorbachev was trying to cure in Russia and religious morality. Some historical facts came from Hedrick Smith's *The Russians* and from Bruce Clark's *An Empire's New Clothes*.

The Church of the Nativity of the Mother of God was just across the hill from where I lived the entire time I was posted to Moscow and I spent many hours talking to the locals who worked desperately hard to resurrect it. Alexander the Painter gave me interviews for ABC Radio. Also helpful was an article in *Moscow Magazine*, September 1990.

CHAPTER SIXTEEN: So this is Democracy?

Statistics on food aid consumption in Russia in the first few months of reform came from *Moscow Magazine*, March 1993.

I am indebted to Natasha and her father for their insights into the humiliation of economic reform. Unemployment statistics came from Theodore W. Karasik (ed.), *Russia and Eurasia: Facts and Figures Annual*, 1993.

The survey by the Institute for Social Research in early 1993 was published by Reuters and TASS wire services.

Statistics on how much capital left Russia during the months of political turmoil were published by Alexander Zhilin of *Moskovskie Novosti*. Boris Yeltsin's comments on the chaos are from his auto-biography, *The View from the Kremlin*. Alexander Rutskoi's comments were recorded in the parliament and widely reported.

As a reporter, I witnessed much of the battle between Boris Yeltsin and the parliament. But where memory has failed me and where my notes are less than adequate I have relied on the works of Jonathan Steele and Bruce Clark. I have also cross-checked with John B. Dun-lop's 'Russia: in Search of an Identity?' in Ian Bremmar & Ray Tarras (eds), *New States, New Politics: Building the Post Soviet Nations*.

Yeltsin's comment about Russians having spent their lives saying 'nyet' comes from his autobiography, while the details of the gov-ernment's money reform were personal observation. I was also present at the media conference called by Ruslan Khasbulatov to condemn the move.

Khasbulatov's comment about Yeltsin's drinking habits was widely reported and is referred to by Yeltsin in *The View from the Kremlin*.

As I was not in Moscow for the violence which followed Yeltsin's disbanding of the parliament, I have relied on the television accounts of the CNN network and of ABC TV's Moscow correspondent, Deborah Snow, who witnessed much of the uprising. I have also relied on the accounts of my friends, all of whom were in Moscow. I have used Jonathan Steele's assertion that the protesters were provoked into battle. Boris Yeltsin's comment about bringing the communist–fascist plot under control was made as troops entered the area around the White House and was broadcast on national television as well as internationally.

As always, Alexander Pumpyansky was indispensable in putting the human side of the story and when I returned to Moscow he spent time with me explaining what it was about democracy that made people feel uncomfortable. I am also grateful to Yuri Schekochikhin of *Literaturnaya Gazeta* who wrote in 1995 that the biggest problem the democrats faced was the fact they had no ideology.

CHAPTER SEVENTEEN: Fascism Strikes

Correspondents became aware of Vladimir Volfovich Zhirinovsky around 1988. He was a highly visible phenomenon, albeit one taken less than seriously. But his persistence at street rallies throughout 1989 and 1990 as the Soviet Union began to unravel made us believe we would be ill-advised to ignore him completely.

The book by Elena Klepikova and Vladimir Solovyov, *Zhirinovsky: the Paradoxes of Russian Fascism*, is quoted in this chapter and I have also used other aspects of their research, in particular Zhirinovsky's comments on issues such as the Kurile Islands. Other comments by Zhirinovsky are taken from personal interviews given in 1992 and 1993.

The link between the KGB and the LDPR was frequently referred to in the Russian press in 1990 and 1991.

Zhirinovsky's reaction to the suggestion of NATO movements towards Russia and other countries of the CIS are taken from a 'doorstop' he gave at the Hotel Moscow at which I was present.

The dispute between Russia and Ukraine over the Crimean Peninsula was the subject of much Russian and foreign reportage in 1992 and 1993 and Zhirinovsky skilfully exploited it in both his campaign rallies and propaganda during the 1993 parliamentary election campaign.

Zhirinovsky's election promises are contained in LDPR propaganda, including 'Pravda Zhirinovskova' and 'Zhirinovsky's Falcon' which were widely and freely distributed in Moscow and St Petersburg. They are also detailed in Klepikova & Solovyov's book *Zhironovsky: The Paradoxes of Russian Facism*. I have reported in this chapter a television interview Zhirinovsky gave to Russian Television's Boris Notkin in the lead-up to the 1993 parliamentary election. The LDPR's Youth League videos and pamphlets were distributed throughout the campaign.

Zhirinovsky's comment to Anatoly Chubais was recorded and reported by Russian Television news. Other assaults on deputies were widely reported and recorded by Russian Television.

CHAPTER EIGHTEEN: From the Ashes

The KGB was an organisation which held enormous and endless fascination for foreign correspondents in Moscow—particularly during the Soviet era. But it was no less powerful nor fascinating during the early Yeltsin years. Much of my knowledge of it came from published reports in the Russian media and from friends and acquaintances within the KGB. Works which were enormously helpful include *The KGB: The Inside Story* by Christopher Andrew and Oleg Gordievsky, *An Empire's New Clothes* by Bruce Clark, Amy Knight's *Spies without Cloaks: The KGB's Successors*, excerpts of which were published in the *Washington Post* in May/June 1996 and Vitaly Shentalinsky's *The KGB's Literary Archive*.

Marina Sokolova related the tragedy of her life to me at a memorial service in Moscow in 1992. Similar stories were told to me by many others whose families had suffered a similar fate.

My tour of Lubyanka was the subject of a story for ABC Radio.

I reported on the recurrence of monocentrism in Russian foreign policy in 1994 and 1995. Supplementary notes came from Vladimir Zviglyanich's 'Primakoff and the Ambitions of a Great Power', published on the internet in January 1996 in *A Bi-weekly on Soviet Affairs* (the Jamestown Foundation website).

The changes in Russian foreign policy were articulated by the former Russian Foreign Minister, Andrei Kozyrev, to the Conference on Security and Co-Operation in Europe on 14 December 1992 in Stockholm and were widely reported in the Russian and foreign press.

The influence of Mikhail Barsukov and Alexander Korzhakov on Boris Yeltsin and their desire for a renewed Union were documented regularly in the Russian press.

Nadya Chertkova who found her son in Grozny in the weeks after the start of war in Chechnya was introduced to me by a friend in Moscow during a trip my husband and I made there in December 1994–January 1995.

The account of the reasons for the Chechnya war was drawn largely from the work of Bruce Clark in *An Empire's New Clothes*, and from rogue press reports in Moscow in publications such as *New Times* (English translation) and *Nevavisimaya Gazeta*.

The comments about the hopeful economic signs in Moscow in 1995 came from a friend, Aliosha, an economist, and personal observation.

The negative views expressed in this chapter on the Chechens were drawn largely from conversations which took place among my friends, but they are commonly heard throughout Russia.

Information on the disarray in the Russian military has been drawn from a number of sources including *Time* magazine August 1996, September 1996 and October 1996 and *US News and World Report*, October 1996. Reports to the parliament's Defence Committee in 1996 and 1997 were also helpful.

The problems faced by the businessman Vladimir Gusinsky have been well documented in both the Russian and English press.

Natasha's account of her hopes and aspirations as a young communist and her subsequent disappointment was written by her especially for this book.

The historical notes on the Cathedral of Christ the Saviour are taken from *Moscow: The Rough Guide* by Dan Richardson.

Larissa is Natasha's sister and the conversation recorded here took place during our return visit to Russia for the 1996 presidential campaign.

Comments about the new Moscow of 1996 come largely from observations I made during my 1996 visit there. The comments by Nikita Mikhailkov were made during an interview with Eilleen O'Connor of CNN in July 1996.

I was in Belye Stolby, outside Moscow, for the second round of voting for the Russian president.

CHAPTER NINETEEN: Out of the Shadows

The demands of the FSB chief were reported by Reuters in August 1996.

The Kremlin's admission on the real state of Boris Yeltsin's health was probably unavoidable but was inadvertently blurted out by a Kremlin doctor in an interview with CNN in September 1996.

Alexander Lebed's comments about taming crime and corruption were reported by *Moscow Times* in July 1996, as was his public falling out with Anatoly Kulikov and subsequent comments. His observation that the Russian state is a circus was reported by *Time* magazine in October 1996.

Pravda's closure was internationally reported. So too the assassination attempt on the Chairman of the Russian Central Bank.

In late 1997, Anatoly Chubais was still in the ministry, alongside Boris Nemstov, a reformer from the Volga city of Nizhni Novgorod (formerly Gorky). Boris Yeltsin has recently annointed Nemstov as a possible presidential successor.

Sonia is real. She lives in Moscow with her mother.

BIBLIOGRAPHY

Aganbegyan, Abel 1989, *Moving the Mountain*, Bantam, London.

Akhmatova, Anna, 1921, from 'The Seventh Book', in Lydia Chukovskaya, *The Akmatova Journals*, Harvill, London.

Alliluyeva, Svetlana 1968, *Twenty Letters to a Friend*, World Books, London.

Andrew, Christopher & Gordievsky, Oleg 1990, *The KGB: The Inside Story*, Hodder & Stoughton, London.

Barnett, Anthony 1988, *Soviet Freedom*, Picador, London.

Bialer, Seweryn 1986, *The Soviet Paradox*, Knopf, New York.

Blake, George 1990, *No Other Choice*, Jonathan Cape, London.

Borovik, Artyom 1991, *The Hidden War*, Faber & Faber, London.

Borovik, Genrikh 1994, *The Philby Files*, Warner, London.

Charters, Ann and Samuel, 1979, *I Love: The Story of Vladimir Mayakovsky and Lili Brik*, Farrar Straus Giroux, New York.

Chernov, Vladimir 1979, *Moscow*, Progress, Moscow.

Chukovskaya, Lydia 1994, *The Akhmatova Journals*, Harvill, London.

Clark, Bruce 1995, *An Empire's New Clothes*, Vintage, London.

Conquest, Robert 1989, *Stalin and the Kirov Murders*, Century Hutchinson, London.

Daniels, Robert V., ed., 1993, *A Documentary History of Communism in Russia: From Lenin to Gorbachev*, University Press of New England, London.

Daniloff, Nicholas 1988, *Two Lives, One Russia*, Bodley Head, London.

Derzhavina, Martha 1986, *The Central Lenin Museum*, Raduga, Moscow.

Deutscher, Isaac 1966, *Stalin: A Political Biography*, Oxford University Press, New York.

Dmytryshyn, Basil, ed., 1967, *Imperial Russia: A Source Book*, Holt, Rinehart & Winston, New York.

Du Plessix Gray, Francine 1989, *Soviet Women: Walking the Tightrope*, Virago, London.

Dunlop, John B. 1997, 'Russia: In Search of an Identity?' in Ian Bremmer, Ray Taras, eds, *New States, New Politics: Building the Post Soviet Nations*, Cambridge University Press, Cambridge.

Ebon, Martin 1994, *KGB: Death and Rebirth*, Praeger, Westport.

Garrard, John and Carol, 1990, *Inside the Soviet Writers' Union*, I. B. Taurus, London.

Gogol, Nikolai 1915, *Dead Souls*, 4th edn, T. Fisher Unwin, London.

—— 1948, *The Inspector* (Russian version), Ministry of Education, Moscow.

Gorbachev, Mikhail 1987, *Perestroika*, William Collins, London.

—— 1991, *Dekabr–'91, Moya Pozitsiya (December '91, My Position)*, Novosti, Moscow.

—— 1994, *The August Coup*, HarperCollins, New York.

—— 1996, *Memoirs*, Doubleday, New York.

Gorbachev, Raisa 1991, *I Hope*, HarperCollins, New York.

Hahn, Jeffrey W. 1988, *Soviet Grassroots*, I. B. Taurus, London.

Hope, Christopher 1990, *Moscow, Moscow*, William Heinemann, London.

Hosking, Geoffrey 1985, *A History of the Soviet Union*, Fontana, London.

—— 1990, *The Awakening of the Soviet Union*, Mandarin, London.

Ikkonikov, Andrei 1988, *Russian Architecture of the Soviet Period*, Raduga, Moscow.

Kagarlitsky, Boris 1988, *The Thinking Reed*, Verso, London.

—— 1990, *Farewell Perestroika*, Verso, London.

Kaplan, Karel 1991, *Report on the Murder of the General Secretary*, I. B. Taurus, London.

Kapuscinski, R. 1994, *Imperium*, Granta Books, London.

Karasik, Theodore W., ed., 1993, *Russia and Eurasia: Facts and Figures Annual*, Academic International Press, USA.

Khruschev, Nikita 1990, *Khruschev Remembers: The Glasnost Tapes*, Little, Brown, Boston.

Klepikova, Elena and Solovyov, Vladimir 1995, *Zhirinovsky: The Paradoxes of Russian Fascism*, Viking, London.

Knight, Amy 1996, *Spies without Cloaks: The KGB's Successors*, Princeton University Press, Princeton, New Jersey.

Leitzel, J., Gaddy, C. and Alexeev, M. 1995, 'Mafiosi and Matrioshki (Organised Crime and Russian Reform) in *Brookings Review*, vol. 13, no. 1, Winter.

Lenin, Vladimir 1965, *Lenin on Religion*, Progress, Moscow.

—— 1975, *Selected Works*, Vol. 2, Progress, Moscow.

—— 1978, *The State and Revolution*, Foreign Languages Press, Peking.

Mandelstam, Osip 1989, *Selected Poems* (translated by James Greene), Penguin, London.

Marshall, Herbert 1965, *Mayakovsky*, Dobson Books, London.

Marx, K., Engels F. and Lenin, V. 1978, *On Communist Society*, Progress, Moscow.

Marx, Karl 1970, *Critique of Hegel's Philosophy of Right*, Cambridge University Press, Cambridge.

Medvedev, Zhores 1986, *Gorbachev*, Basil Blackwell, Oxford.

Mstislavskii, Sergei 1988, *Five Days which Transformed Russia*, Century Hutchinson, London.

Neville, Peter 1990, *A Traveller's History of Russia*, Windrush Press, Morton-in-Marsh.

O'Clery, Conor 1991, *Melting Snow: An Irishman in Moscow*, Appletree, Belfast.

Page, Bruce, Leitch, David and Knightley, Philip 1977, *Philby: The Spy who Betrayed a Nation*, Sphere, London.

Pipes, Richard 1974, *Russia Under the Old Regime*, Penguin, London.

Remnick, David 1993, *Lenin's Tomb*, Random House, New York.

Richardson, Dan 1995, *Moscow: The Rough Guide*, Penguin, London.

Rosenstone, Robert 1981, *Romantic Revolutionary*, Vintage, New York.

Roxburgh, Angus 1991, *The Second Russian Revolution*, BBC Books, London.

Sakharov, Andrei 1990, *Memoirs*, Knopf, New York.

Schapiro, Leonard 1963, *The Communist Party of the Soviet Union*, Methuen, London.

Shentalinsky, Vitaly 1995, *The KGB's Literary Archive*, Harvill, London.

Smith, Hedrick 1976, *The Russians*, Sphere, London.

Solzhenitsyn, Alexander 1990, 'How Can We Revitalise Russia?', *Komsomolskaya Pravda*, 18 September.

Steele, Jonathan 1994, *Eternal Russia*, Faber & Faber, London.

Subtelny, Orest 1988, *Ukraine—A History*, University of Toronto Press, Toronto.

Throssell, Ric 1990, *My Father's Son*, Mandarin, Melbourne.

Troitsky, Artyom 1987, *Back in the USSR*, Omnibus, London.

—— 1990, *Tusovka: Who's Who in the New Soviet Rock Culture*, Omnibus, London.

Tsvetaeva, Marina 1983, *A Captive Spirit: Selected Prose*, Virago, London.

Vernadsky, George 1964, *A History of Russia*, Yale University Press, New Haven.

Volkogonov, Dmitri 1994, *Lenin: Life and Legacy*, HarperCollins, New York.

—— 1996, *Trotsky: The Eternal Revolutionary*, The Free Press, New York.

Wettlin, Margaret 1992, *Fifty Russian Winters*, John Wiley, Toronto.

Wolfe, Bertram D. 1984, *Three Who Made a Revolution*, Penguin, London.

Yakovlev, Alexander 1993, *The Fate of Marxism in Russia*, Yale University Press, New Haven.

Yeltsin, Boris 1990, *Against the Grain*, Summit, New York.

—— 1994, *The View from the Kremlin*, HarperCollins, New York.

Yergin, Daniel and Gustafson, Thane 1995, *Russia 2010 and What it Means for the World*, Vintage, New York.

Yevtushenko, Yevgeny 1991, *Fatal Half Measures: The Culture of Democracy in the Soviet Union*, Little, Brown, Toronto.

Zinoviev, Aleksandr 1994, *Kommunizm Kak Realnost*, Tsentrpoligraf, Moscow.

INDEX